The Inaugural Addresses
of Twentieth-Century
American Presidents

THE INAUGURAL ADDRESSES OF TWENTIETH-CENTURY AMERICAN PRESIDENTS

Edited by
Halford Ryan

Praeger Series in Political Communication

Westport, Connecticut
London

Library of Congress Cataloging-in-Publication Data

The Inaugural addresses of twentieth-century American presidents /
    edited by Halford Ryan.
        p.   cm.—(Praeger series in political communication, ISSN
    1062–5623)
    Includes bibliographical references and index.
    ISBN 0–275–94039–X (alk. paper)
    1. Presidents—United States—Inaugural addresses—History—20th
century.   2. United States—Politics and government—20th century.
I. Ryan, Halford Ross.   II. Series.
J81.C93   1993
353.03′54′0904—dc20   92–34950

British Library Cataloguing in Publication Data is available.

Library of Congress Catalog Card Number: 92–34950
ISBN: 0–275–94039–X
ISSN: 1062–5623

First published in 1993

Praeger Publishers, 88 Post Road West, Westport, CT 06881
An imprint of Greenwood Publishing Group, Inc.

Printed in the United States of America

The paper used in this book complies with the
Permanent Paper Standard issued by the National
Information Standards Organization (Z39.48–1984).

10 9 8 7 6 5 4 3

Contents

Series Foreword

Those of us from the discipline of communication studies have long believed that communication is prior to all other fields of inquiry. In several other forums I have argued that the essence of politics is "talk" or human interaction.[1] Such interaction may be formal or informal, verbal or nonverbal, public or private, but it is always persuasive, forcing us consciously or subconsciously to interpret, to evaluate, and to act. Communication is the vehicle for human action.

From this perspective, it is not surprising that Aristotle recognized the natural kinship of politics and communication in his writings *Politics* and *Rhetoric*. In the former, he establishes that humans are "political beings [who] alone of the animals [are] furnished with the faculty of language."[2] And in the latter, he begins his systematic analysis of discourse by proclaiming that "rhetorical study, in its strict sense, is concerned with the modes of persuasion."[3] Thus, it was recognized over twenty-three hundred years ago that politics and communication go hand in hand because they are essential parts of human nature.

Back in 1981, Dan Nimmo and Keith Sanders proclaimed that political communication was an emerging field.[4] Although its origin, as noted, dates back centuries, a "self-consciously cross-disciplinary" focus began in the late 1950s. Thousands of books and articles later, colleges and universities offer a variety of graduate and undergraduate coursework in the area in such diverse departments as communication, mass communication, journalism, political science, and sociology.[5] In Nimmo and Sanders' early assessment, the "key areas of inquiry" included rhetorical analysis, propaganda analysis, attitude change studies, voting studies, government and the news media, functional and systems analyses, technological changes, media technologies, campaign techniques, and research techniques.[6] In a survey of the state of the field in 1983, the same authors and Lynda Kaid found additional, more specific areas of concerns such as the presidency, political polls, public opinion, debates, and advertising, to name a few.[7] Since the first study, they also noted a shift away from the rather strict behavioral approach.

A decade later, Dan Nimmo and David Swanson argued that "political communication has developed some identity as a more or less distinct domain of scholarly work."[8] The scope and concerns of the area have further expanded to include critical theories and cultural studies. While there is no precise definition, method, or disciplinary home of the area of inquiry, its primary domain is the role, processes, and effects of communication within the context of politics broadly defined.

In 1985, the editors of *Political Communication Yearbook: 1984* noted that "more things are happening in the study, teaching, and practice of political communication than can be captured within the space limitations of the relatively few publications available."[9] In addition, they argued that the backgrounds of "those involved in the field [are] so varied and pluralist in outlook and approach, . . . it [is] a mistake to adhere slavishly to any set format in shaping the content."[10] And more recently, Swanson and Nimmo called for "ways of overcoming the unhappy consequences of fragmentation within a framework that respects, encourages, and benefits from diverse scholarly commitments, agendas, and approaches."[11]

In agreement with these assessments of the area and with gentle encouragement, Praeger Publishers established in 1988 the series entitled "Praeger Studies in Political Communication." The series is open to all qualitative and quantitative methodologies as well as contemporary and historical studies. The key to characterizing the studies in the series is the focus on communication variables or activities within a political context or dimension. As of this writing, over thirty volumes have been published and there are numerous impressive works forthcoming. Scholars from the disciplines of communication, history, journalism, political science, and sociology have participated in the series.

"Every four years," James David Barber observes, "a gong goes off and a new presidential campaign surges into the national consciousness: new candidates, new issues, a new season of surprises. But underlying the syncopations of change there is a steady, recurrent rhythm from election to election, a pulse of politics, that brings up the same basic themes in order, over and over again."[12] After the battle of the campaign, a "new" president emerges to address the nation. On each Inauguration

Day history is made and another chapter of American history is carefully recorded during the next four years.

Early in American history, presidential inaugurals served as opportunities for the winners to revel in their victory and to proclaim the significance of the election to the people. Contemporary presidents, however, use them as opportunities to unite, to inspire, and to offer visions of the future.[13] In the words of Theodore Sorensen, who worked on John F. Kennedy's inaugural, the speech is designed "to address the American people of our time but have meaning for all people for all time. For they embody the best of our heritage from the past and the best of our hopes for the future."[14]

This volume on presidential inaugural addresses of the twentieth century brings together the thoughts and ideas of nineteen outstanding scholars of political communication and rhetorical studies. Each critic discusses the political context surrounding the inaugural, persuasive strengths and weaknesses, and social impact. In addition, many of the scholars conducted original research at presidential libraries discovering the evolution of the final speech through various drafts and contributions from staff members. The result is a collection of one of the most comprehensive and systematic analyses of presidential inaugurals to date.

This book makes several important contributions to the study of political discourse. First and most obvious, we gain insight into the development and execution of twenty-four presidential inaugural addresses since 1905. Second, we gain insight into inaugural addresses as unique rhetorical events in American history. Finally, the essays contribute to the development and assessment of critical theories and methods by challenging the assumptions and applications of genre theory and criticism.

I am, without shame or modesty, a fan of the series. The joy of serving as its editor is in participating in the dialogue of the field of political communication and in reading the contributors' works. I invite you to join me.

Robert E. Denton, Jr.

NOTES

1. See Robert E. Denton, Jr., *The Symbolic Dimensions of the American Presidency* (Prospect Heights, Ill.: Waveland Press, 1982); Robert E. Denton, Jr. and Gary Woodward, *Political Communication in America*, 2d ed. (New York: Praeger, 1990); Robert E. Denton, Jr., and Dan Hahn, *Presidential Communication* (New York: Praeger, 1986); and Robert E. Denton, Jr., *The Primetime Presidency of Ronald Reagan* (New York: Praeger, 1988).

2. Aristotle, *The Politics of Aristotle*, trans. Ernest Barker (New York: Oxford University Press, 1970), 5.

3. Aristotle, *Rhetoric*, trans. Rhys Roberts (New York: The Modern Library, 1954), 22.

4. Dan Nimmo and Keith Sanders, "Introduction: The Emergence of Political Communication as a Field," in *Handbook of Political Communication*, ed. Dan Nimmo and Keith Sanders (Beverly Hills, Calif.: Sage, 1981), 11–36.

5. Ibid., 15.

6. Ibid., 17–27.

7. Keith Sanders, Lynda Kaid, and Dan Nimmo, eds. *Political Communication Yearbook: 1984* (Carbondale: Southern Illinois University, 1985), 283–308.

8. Dan Nimmo and David Swanson, "The Field of Political Communication: Beyond the Voter Persuasion Paradigm," in *New Directions in Political Communication*, ed. David Swanson and Dan Nimmo (Beverly Hills, Calif.: Sage, 1990), 8.

9. Sander, Kaid, and Nimmo, *Political Communication Yearbook*, xiv.

10. Ibid., xiv.

11. Nimmo and Swanson, "The Field of Political Communication," 11.

12. James David Barber, *The Pulse of Politics* (New York: W. W. Norton, 1980), 3.

13. Barbara Hinckley, *The Symbolic Presidency* (New York: Routledge, 1990), 9.

14. Theodore Sorensen, *Kennedy* (New York: Harper & Row, 1965).

Acknowledgments

Without the thorough research and critical acumen of the chapter authors, this book would not exist, for the task of treating in the requisite depth and scope twenty-four inaugural addresses is too herculean a task for even the most redoubtable rhetorical critic.

I thank professors Dale Leathers, first vice-president of the Speech Communication Association (SCA); Robert E. Frank, Leathers's administrative assistant; and David Henry, chair of SCA's public address division, for assigning an excellent meeting room at the 1991 SCA convention in Atlanta for a two-day seminar on presidential inaugural addresses by the contributors to this book.

The Maurice L. Mednick Fund and the Washington and Lee University Glenn Grant funded my research in the Harry S. Truman Library, and the Eleanor Roosevelt Institute funded earlier research in the Franklin D. Roosevelt Library.

Professor Martin Medhurst's research in the Dwight D. Eisenhower Library was funded by The Center for Presidential Studies at Texas A&M University and by the Texas A&M Minigrant Program.

Professor Gary Woodward acknowledges suggestions by Harold Hogstrom and research support from the Trenton State College Faculty and Institutional Research Committee.

Introduction

This book studies the inaugural addresses of twentieth-century U.S. chief executives in the context of the rhetorical presidency that arose in this century.[1] This construct holds that the president delivers persuasive speeches to move the Congress and the people and to move the people to stir the Congress if it is intransigent. Hence, even on Inauguration Day, a largely ceremonial occasion, a presidential persuader still seeks acquiescence and action from the Congress and the people in his first rhetorical deed as the nation's new chief executive. The book commences with Theodore Roosevelt's inaugural address and treats all subsequent presidential inaugurals. Gerald Ford's address, delivered to the Congress upon his assumption of the presidency on August 12, 1974, although perhaps in a technical sense not an inaugural, is included on the grounds that Ford's speech functioned for him and for the nation as an inaugural address. Accordingly, this book offers twenty-four chapters that correspond to presidential inaugural addresses since 1905.

In composing their chapters, the authors were asked to consider several rhetorical topics. Each author discusses the political situation surrounding the inaugural with regard to rhetorical purpose. Each also gives special attention to campaign rhetoric that may have been carried forth into the address. This possibility has been overlooked by critics who erroneously assume that all presidents necessarily make a clean break with their rhetorical past. For instance, in terms of the issues addressed, Woodrow Wilson's First Inaugural, Warren Harding's, Calvin Coolidge's, Herbert Hoover's, and Ronald Reagan's First Inaugural can all be conceived as their last campaign speeches.

To fulfill their missions, the contributors to this book conducted original research in the presidential libraries or with other appropriate archival materials. They explicate the evolution of the speech's preparation, with special attention given to the president's themes and emendations versus the speech staff's contributions. They consider the style of the language and the organizational strategy in relationship to persuasive purpose. Utilizing the available resources, they also criticize, to the extent possible, the speech's delivery.

Every chapter evaluates the persuasive strengths and weaknesses of the address by accounting for its reception by the media and public. Many of the authors examined the reaction files in the presidential libraries or archival collections in order to determine how contemporary Americans received the inaugural, as such information is usually lacking in other works that examine these addresses. Each contributor has also determined the extent to which every inaugural address conforms to generic prescriptions.

The inaugural addresses of U.S. presidents, genre critics would have us believe, are a discrete kind or type of oratory. "Conventional wisdom," hold Karyln Campbell and Kathleen Jamieson, "and ordinary language treat inaugural addresses as a class. Critics have intuitively taken them to belong to a distinct rhetorical type, but generalizing about them has been difficult."[2] Despite the difficulty, Campbell and Jamieson determined that presidential inaugurals are a genre distinct from other forms of presidential discourse, that inaugurals are an instance of epideictic or ceremonial rhetoric, and that all inaugurals contains four generic elements, which are oriented toward contemplation rather than action:

The presidential inaugural (1) unifies the audience by reconstituting its members as "the people" who can witness and ratify the ceremony; (2) rehearses communal values drawn from the past; (3) sets forth the political principles that will govern the new administration; and (4) demonstrates that the President appreciates the requirements and limitations of the executive function. Each of these ends must be achieved through means appropriate to epideictic address, i.e., while urging contemplation not action.[3]

Such a claim assumes that diverse presidents, from different partisan perspectives, facing disparate factional exigencies, grounded in a distinctive political milieu, on Inaugural Day respond with recurring generic rhetoric. Such a claim is startling. Indeed, Kenneth Thompson observed the ever-changing nexus between a president, an inaugural text, and a historical context:

It would be false . . . to suggest that the role of inaugural addresses by Presidents is everywhere the same. The context of such addresses is the spirit of the times. While the President imposes himself upon the form of the address, it is the times in part that shape the President's outlook, and what he feels called on to say. Moreover, each historical era brings with it social and intellectual tendencies that influence contemporary thought.[4]

With regard to a generic theory of inaugural addresses, this book advances several propositions.

At least in the case of inaugural addresses, genre theory hinders more than it helps. It invites the critic to confirm, which is usually the case, or to confute, which is rarely the case, certain generic tenets at the expense of examining the inaugural speech *in situ*. It entices the commentator to make *a priori* assumptions about an inaugural before beginning to analyze it; therefore, one may miss other significant rhetorical features of the inaugural under investigation. A better analytical approach to inaugural addresses is the *tabula rasa*. The critic should utilize the methodology of the case study to treat a president's responses to political exigencies at a juncture in U.S. history.

All twentieth-century inaugural addresses do not contain all generic elements. Richard Joslyn weighed whether "all inaugurals contain all four of the specified elements,"and he hinted that they do not.[5] Moreover, Martha Solomon questioned the validity of conceiving the inaugural as a type of oratory when she opined: "One is left to ponder the value of a generic framework when studying inaugural addresses."[6] Although the individual chapter authors indicate what elements are missing in their respective inaugurals, and a number of inaugurals do have all four elements, the generic element of powers and limitations of the executive function is significantly absent in the following presidential inaugurals: Harding's, Wilson's Second, FDR's Second and Fourth, Harry Truman's, Dwight Eisenhower's First, Lyndon Johnson's, and Richard Nixon's First. The want of a generic element in these inaugural addresses, delivered by Republican and Democrat presidents throughout the twentieth century, casts doubts on the validity and reliability of a generic theory.

The inaugural address is not an instance of Aristotelian epideictic rhetoric. According to Aristotle, epideictic or ceremonial oratory "either praises or censures somebody . . . is, properly speaking, concerned with the present . . . [and] proves honour or the reverse."[7] A plain reading of Aristotle's *Rhetoric* reveals that his characterization does not describe a presidential inaugural address. An epideictic speech praised or blamed a person. Such a speech, according to W. Rhys Roberts, was one of " 'display,' 'show,' 'declamation,' and the result is a 'set speech' or 'harangue.' "[8]

No twentieth-century inaugural has functioned as an Aristotelian epideictic speech. A case could be made that some of them did, but this reasoning has not been made hitherto. For instance, implicit in Woodrow Wilson's First is a repudiation of Republicanism, if not William Howard Taft and Theodore Roosevelt by name. One always discerns hapless Herbert Hoover behind every verbal parry in FDR's First. In his Second, Richard Nixon repudiated, in language that was not carefully veiled, the Democratic socialism of the Kennedy–Johnson administrations. Ronald Reagan coyly invited comparisons of himself with Jimmy Carter and Democrats who ruined the government that Reagan planned to resurrect. And even George Bush gently distanced himself from his former boss by calling for a kinder nation that was not devoted as much to materialism. Yet these forays into blaming the defeated candidate and, as appropriate, the other political party, have not been portrayed elsewhere as Aristotelian epideictic rhetoric. The reason is straightforward: Aristotelian epideictic rhetoric is incompatible with the generic element of reconstitution and unification of the people, for how could a president hope to unify the whole electorate while concomitantly castigating the losing candidate and party, which were supported by upwards of 40 percent of the voting population?

Although a seemingly harmless gambit to conceive the inaugural as Aristotelian epideictic rhetoric, the move has troublesome consequences. To assert that inaugurals aim toward contemplation tortures Aristotle's *Rhetoric*. For instance, when Campbell and Jamieson argued that Abraham Lincoln's First Inaugural contained some "deliberative means" but concluded that "Lincoln's speech displays epideictic contemplation as a precursor to deliberative decision,"[9] Dan Hahn implored:

Why not just admit that Lincoln presents deliberative argumentation? Indeed, why not conclude that inaugurals may be some kind of hybrid between epideictic and deliberative? Were the authors to do so they would not have to gloss over the deliberative features of inaugurals and could say that inaugural addresses vary substantively because presidents present deliberative argumentation grounded in their own ideologies.[10]

For instance, anyone conversant with a number of inaugurals, such as Taft's, Harding's, Coolidge's, Hoover's, FDR's First, Truman's, Eisenhower's First and Second, Kennedy's, Nixon's Second, and Reagan's First and Second, would acknowledge that their addresses have substantial deliberative elements in them and that these persuaders sought action and acquiescence from the American people and Congress.

But to quibble over the mix of contemplation and deliberation is to miss an inaugural's persuasive function as an instance of presidential rhetoric. If one must use the Aristotelian system, and I would rather not, then the argument is that inaugurals are instances of deliberative rhetoric wherein action, not contemplation, is the persuasive goal. Joslyn rightfully questioned whether "epideictic rhetoric in general and presidential inaugurals in particular are unconcerned with 'action as a goal.' If one understands obedience, compliance, and quiescence as political action, then clearly most of the rhetoric studied here, no matter how 'contemplative,' has action as a pervasive, enduring, and consequential goal."[11]

Halford Ryan

NOTES

1. James W. Ceaser, Glen E. Thurow, Jeffrey Tulis, and Joseph Bessette, "The Rise of the Rhetorical Presidency," *Presidential Studies Quarterly* 11 (1981): 351–57; Jeffrey K. Tulis, *The Rhetorical Presidency* (Princeton, N.J.: Princeton University Press, 1987), 47–51.

2. Karlyn Kohrs Campbell and Kathleen Hall Jamieson, "Inaugurating the Presidency," in *Form, Genre, and the Study of Political Discourse*, ed. Herbert W. Simons and Aram A. Aghazarian (Columbia: University of South Carolina Press, 1986), 203. Their essay was originally published in *Presidential Studies Quarterly* 15 (1985): 394–441.

3. Ibid., 205.

4. Kenneth W. Thompson, Preface to Dante Germino, *The Inaugural Addresses of American Presidents* (Lanham, Md.: University Press of America, 1984), x.

5. Richard A. Joslyn, "Keeping Politics in the Study of Political Discourse," in *Form, Genre, and the Study of Political Discourse*, 303.

6. Martha Solomon, review of *Form, Genre, and the Study of Political Discourse*, in *Quarterly Journal of Speech* 74 (1988): 109.

7. Aristotle, *Rhetoric*, trans. W. Rhys Roberts (New York: Modern Library, 1954), 1358b6–59a5.

8. Ibid., 32.

9. Karlyn Kohrs Campbell and Kathleen Hall Jamieson, *Deeds Done in Words: Presidential Rhetoric and the Genres of Governance* (Chicago: University of Chicago Press, 1990), 29.

10. Dan Hahn, review of ibid., *Southern Communication Journal* 56 (1991): 318.

11. Joslyn, "Keeping Politics in the Study of Political Discourse," 335–36.

The Inaugural Addresses of Twentieth-Century American Presidents

Chapter One

President Theodore Roosevelt's Inaugural Address, 1905

Robert Friedenberg

On January 2, 1899, the most famous man in America of his time delivered his inaugural address as governor of New York.[1] "We must realize on the one hand, that we can do little if we do not set ourselves a high ideal," claimed Theodore Roosevelt, "and on the other that we will fail in accomplishing even this little if we do not work through practical methods and with a readiness to face life as it is, and not as we think it ought to be."[2] In this characteristically balanced sentence, Roosevelt foreshadowed the essence of each of the inaugural addresses he delivered between January 2, 1899, and March 4, 1905.[3]

It is unlikely that any other president has delivered as many inaugural addresses as Theodore Roosevelt did in as short a period of time. An examination of two of those addresses, one as governor of New York and the other as vice president of the United States, suggest Roosevelt's basic beliefs and approach to this form of address.[4] For Theodore Roosevelt, the presidential inaugural address of March 4, 1905, was the third such address he had given in the preceding six years.

ROOSEVELT'S PRIOR INAUGURAL ADDRESSES

Roosevelt had at least three beliefs about inaugural addresses. Perhaps the most striking characteristic is their brevity. Each address, only one and one-half pages long, was delivered in about five minutes.[5]

The fact that these addresses are so brief suggests Roosevelt's first attitude toward inaugural addresses: that they were of some consequence but not enough to call forth a major effort. That Roosevelt likely did not consider such speeches of major importance is also suggested

by the fact that scant evidence of early drafts or other advance preparation exists for either speech in any of the Roosevelt papers, in contrast
to his speech preparation for important addresses. Said Oscar Strauss,
who served in Roosevelt's cabinet: "I have had hundreds of opportunities to observe his methods. When he accepted an invitation to deliver
an address or write an article he would prepare it immediately even if
the occasion were two, three, or six months off. He revised considerably,
showed his work freely to friends and associates for criticism, but completed it at the earliest opportunity."[6]

Certainly, the absence of draft manuscripts for these addresses is not
a telling argument, although drafts for many of his major addresses can
be found. Nor is the absence of any indication that Roosevelt discussed
these speeches or sought the advice of others on them a telling argument.
Yet it is suggestive in the light of his practice to circulate drafts and
discuss major speeches. Hence, the evidence indicates that Roosevelt
did not deem inaugural addresses worthy of the extensive drafting and
consultation that he engaged in as he prepared many of his other addresses. Finally, although Roosevelt treated a variety of his speeches in
his autobiography, he never mentioned any of his inaugural addresses.
Written four years after he left office, his autobiography also suggests
that he did not deem these speeches of major consequence.[7]

The brevity of these addresses and the likely lack of preparation for
them suggests a second possible belief that Roosevelt may have had:
that inaugural addresses were a time to use well-tested and frequently
spoken themes, particularly the importance of character in the conduct
of national affairs, rather than to develop and present new ideas. Such
a belief would be consistent with the brevity of the addresses, for Roosevelt presented nothing of note that warranted extensive elaboration,
and it would be consistent with the evident lack of normal preparation,
for Roosevelt offered little that required such preparation. Finally, such
a belief would be consistent with Roosevelt's failure to mention them
in his autobiography, for since they merely presented well-worn themes,
they would not warrant special mention.

Elsewhere, Roosevelt's speaking has been characterized as "the rhetoric of militant decency" and has been shown to center around five basic
themes, or *topoi*.[8] Perhaps paramount among those themes was Roosevelt's belief in the vital importance of character. "Alike for the nation
and the individual," he claimed, "the one indispensable requisite is
character—character that is active in the performance of virtue no less
than firm in the refusal to do aught that is vicious or degraded." Virtually
all Rooseveltian scholars concur in claiming that if Roosevelt had one
supreme belief, it was in character.[9] His early inaugural addresses suggest that the third attitude he had about inaugural addresses is that they

presented an excellent opportunity to preach on the importance of character.

In his Albany inaugural of 1899, Roosevelt observed that "there is much less need of genius or of any special brilliancy in the administration of our government than there is need of such homely virtues and qualities as common sense, honesty, and courage," the very characteristics he elsewhere used to define character.[10] He observed that he would strive to embody these qualities of character as he administered his office. In his vice presidential inaugural, Roosevelt spoke to the importance of legislative bodies, such as the Senate over which he was about to become the presiding officer. He focused on three of the common themes of his rhetoric of militant decency: character, power, and work. In this address, he stressed the importance of legislative work, particularly in the principal legislative body of "one of those world powers to whose hands, in the course of the ages, is intrusted a leading part in shaping the destinies of mankind." Implicit in his discussion was his desire to preside over a body that acted with character "at the outset of the twentieth century."

Third, Roosevelt evidently felt that inaugural ceremonies were an appropriate time to preach. Both addresses are homiletic in nature. Both open with an introduction that Roosevelt then amplified in the body. Roosevelt opened his inaugural address as governor by observing, "A very heavy responsibility rests upon the governor of New York State, a State of 7,000,000 inhabitants, of great wealth, of widely varied industries and with a population singularly diversified, not merely in occupation, but in race origin, in habits of life, and in ways of thought." He began his inaugural address as vice president by observing that "the history of free government is in large part the history of those representative legislative bodies in which from the earliest times, free government has found its loftiest expression." In both addresses, he amplified this opening text and then returned to it in his conclusion.

THE ELECTION OF 1904

Theodore Roosevelt is often thought of as a sickly youth who grew up to become a cowboy and Rough Rider. Time and time again he is pictured as a naturalist and explorer, whose trips to Africa and the Amazon wilderness, on behalf of organizations such as the Smithsonian Institution, contributed much to our knowledge of those areas. He is frequently acknowledged to be among the first national leaders who had an international outlook, which contributed to his concern over the establishment of a canal in Panama and his receipt of the Nobel Peace Prize for his work in negotiating an end to the Russo–Japanese War.

Roosevelt is fondly recalled by scholars as a president of the American Historical Association, whose histories of the Naval War of 1812 and the winning of the American West, as well as his biographies of Thomas Hart Benton and Gouverneur Morris, are still used today. Yet all of these facts obscure the central fact of Theodore Roosevelt's life: that he "was a professional Republican politician from New York. He made a career of seeking and holding public office. His professional concern was with politics and government, with parties, elections, legislation and rule. These simple, central facts in Roosevelt's life have been ignored, almost forgotten."[11] And in forgetting these facts, we also forget that he was a consummate and often ruthless politician who dominated his age.

In 1904, however, those facts were not forgotten. Roosevelt had been running for president almost from the moment he succeeded McKinley in 1901. During the three years after McKinley's assassination, Roosevelt had dramatically enhanced his own already high public standing by battling the trusts, intervening in the coal strike, securing veterans' legislation, and acquiring the Panama Canal Zone. Moreover, with little public awareness, he had vigorously manipulated the patronage system to take control of the Republican party from McKinley's most logical heir, Ohio senator Marcus Hanna. By January 1904, Roosevelt could confidently write:

that outside all the Southern States I am now as certain as I well can be that if Hanna made the fight and with all the money of Wall Street behind him, he would get the majority of the delegation from no State excepting Ohio; and from the South I should have from a third to a half of the delegates and most of the remainder would have been pledged to me. . . . I believe that the best advisers among my opponents themselves see this and have very nearly made up their minds to give up the contest.[12]

Hanna's unexpected death signaled the collapse of any remaining opposition to Roosevelt.[13] Thus, at the outset of the 1904 campaign, the personally popular Roosevelt led a highly unified, well-financed party that governed a prosperous nation at peace.

The Democratic party, in contrast, was in chaos. After the election of 1900, conservative elements of the party attempted to take control from the liberal elements that had nominated William Jennings Bryan in both 1896 and 1900. Having twice lost the presidency, Bryan was no longer a viable candidate for a third race, though he still harbored aspirations and maintained a following, primarily in the western states. Yet the party had few viable alternatives. The most respected national figure in the party, former president Grover Cleveland, was too old to be a serious candidate. The man who was perhaps the wealthiest person in the party, newspaperman William Randolph Hearst, who was also interested in the nomination, had little experience in public life and suffered from a highly unconventional private life that would be a major liability in a national campaign. Almost by default, the party eventually turned to Judge Alton B. Parker of New York. Parker's chief qualification, it seemed, was that as a judge he had remained above the party quarrels and public issues of the day.[14]

Amazingly, for a campaign in which Theodore Roosevelt was the central figure, the election of 1904 can best be characterized as colorless and dull. Roosevelt stuck loyally to the unwritten guideline of the day that incumbent presidents do not take to the stump. Parker also refrained from campaigning.

It was not until October 1, scarcely a month prior to the election, that the *New York World* stirred up the only excitement in the campaign. The *World* alleged that George B. Cortelyou, Roosevelt's secretary of commerce who also served as national chairman of the Republican party, had solicited major campaign contributions from the very corporations that his department was supposed to regulate. Although he was slow to follow up on the *World*'s allegations, by late October Parker and other Democratic speakers had made "Cortelyouism" the only point of controversy in an otherwise lifeless campaign. Roosevelt remained largely silent until the closing days of the campaign when Parker used the *World*'s charges to claim that Roosevelt and his administration had "blackmailed" American corporations. That language was too much for the Rough Rider to ignore:

Mr. Parker's accusations against Mr. Cortelyou and me are monstrous. If true they would brand both of us forever with infamy; and inasmuch as they are false, heavy must be the condemnation of the man making them. . . . The assertion that there has been any blackmail, direct or indirect by Mr. Cortelyou or by me is a falsehood. The assertion that there has been made any pledge or promise or that there has been any understanding as to future immunities or benefits in recognition of any contribution from any source is a wicked falsehood.[15]

On November 8, 1904, the nation gave Roosevelt the greatest popular majority a presidential candidate had ever received, more than 2,540,000 votes, and an electoral majority of 336 to 140 for Parker, who carried virtually no state outside the Democratic South. In addition, Roosevelt proved to have long coattails: Republicans rolled to an almost one-hundred-seat majority in the House. The *New York Sun*, a paper not always friendly to Roosevelt, acknowledged that the voters had given him "one of the most illustrious personal triumphs in all political history."[16]

THEODORE ROOSEVELT'S PRESIDENTIAL
INAUGURAL ADDRESS

Preparation

The inaugural address that Roosevelt delivered on March 4, 1905, was among the shortest such addresses in American history. Although not as short as the 136 words address George Washington delivered on the occasion of his second inaugural, it is rivaled in brevity only by the Second Inaugurals of Abraham Lincoln and Andrew Jackson and the Fourth Inaugural of Franklin Roosevelt. Theodore Roosevelt's address is approximately 900 words long. The brevity, consistent with that of other inaugural addresses Roosevelt had delivered, again suggests that he did not consider it of paramount importance, in part perhaps because it did not require the development of new and novel ideas. Moreover, Roosevelt apparently did not prepare extensively for this address. Certainly he did not follow his usual practice with major addresses of preparing a first draft months in advance. Rather, the first draft was prepared on February 5, twenty-six days prior to delivery.[17]

Additionally, there is little evidence that Roosevelt considered this address important enough to circulate widely, as was his custom for a major address. His personal correspondence indicates that he shared it in advance only with his long time political associate and close personal friend, Henry Cabot Lodge. Lodge praised the address: "I read and re-read it over again with perfect satisfaction, content and admiration. It is fine." He was sensitive to the speech's succinctness, observing, "You are most wise to be brief. It will add to the effectiveness greatly."[18] Although the absence of other correspondence concerning this address does not prove that Roosevelt did not seek the advice of others, it is highly suggestive that he did not circulate this address widely.

Evidently this address was not the subject of repeated drafts. The first draft was edited only once, with only minor stylistic changes made.[19] The vast majority of changes took one of two forms. First were changes in word choice or small additions that added a more formal tone to the address. For example, the original draft read, "To us as a people it has been given." Roosevelt subsequently changed the last word to *granted*. "And this can be said in a spirit not of boastfulness" was subsequently changed to read, "and this is said reverently, in no spirit of boastfulness."

The second group of changes were additions, primarily of phrases, to give greater emphasis. For example, the emphasized phrase in the following is an addition to the original draft: "We have duties to others and duties to ourselves; *and we can shirk neither*. We have become a great nation." The most extensive change between the first draft and the final speech is the insertion of two sentences, which are emphasized here:

The conditions which have told for our marvelous material well-being, which have developed to a very high degree our energy, self-reliance, and individual initiative, have also brought the care and anxiety inseparable from the accumulation of great wealth and industrial centers. *Upon the success of our experiment much depends, not only as regards our own welfare, but as regards the welfare of mankind. If we fail, the cause of free self-government throughout the world will rock to its foundations, and therefore our responsibility is heavy, to ourselves, to the world as it is today and to the generations yet unborn.* There is no good reason why we should fear the future, but there is every reason why we should face it seriously, neither hiding from ourselves the gravity of the problems before us nor fearing to approach these problems with the unbending, unflinching purpose to solve them aright.

The limited nature of the changes, nevertheless, is not necessarily indicative that Roosevelt did not consider this a major speech. He was a talented writer and rarely made large changes in his first drafts. Nevertheless, the cumulative effect of all of the available evidence—the brevity of the address, the fact that the address was drafted relatively late for a major address, the limited nature of the changes, and Roosevelt's subsequent neglect to mention it in his autobiography—suggests that he did not consider this address worthy of extensive effort. The ceremonial nature of the inaugural address seems to have motivated Roosevelt to rely on well-tested themes that may have warranted little need for preparation. Such a conclusion is consistent with Roosevelt's treatment of his prior inaugural addresses.

Also consistent with Roosevelt's approach is the homiletic nature of this address. He opened by observing that "no people on earth have more cause to be thankful than ours," and remarked that "this is said reverently, in no spirit of boastfulness in our own strength, but with gratitude to the Giver of Good who has blessed us with the conditions which have enabled us to achieve so large a measure of well-being and happiness."[20] He presented his text at the conclusion of his first paragraph, observing that his generation had inherited a strong and powerful nation that had not suffered from the disabilities that afflicted much of the rest of the world:

Under such conditions it would be our own fault if we failed; and the success which we have had in the past, the success which we confidently believe the future will bring, should cause in us no feelings of vainglory, but rather a deep and abiding realization of all which life has offered us; a full acknowledgement of the responsibility which is ours; and a fixed determination to show that under

a free government a mighty people can thrive best, alike as regard the things
of the body and the things of the soul.

The balance of this address amplified the text. First, Roosevelt claimed
that U.S. conduct of foreign policy must reflect its social responsibility
as a world power and its determination to thrive as a free government.
Second, he claimed that "our relations among ourselves" must also
reflect the nation's social responsibilities and determination to thrive as
a free government. To do so, Roosevelt characteristically concluded, will
require of Americans the highest standards of character. "We must
show," he concluded,

not merely in great crises, but in the everyday affairs of life, the qualities of
practical intelligence, of courage, of hardihood, and endurance, and above all
the power of devotion to a lofty ideal, which made great the men who founded
this Republic in the days of Washington, which made great the men who preserved this Republic in the days of Abraham Lincoln.

As with his prior inaugural addresses, Roosevelt evidently looked at
this occasion as one that provided him with yet another opportunity to
preach on the importance of character.

Themes

The body of his four-paragraph address treats two issues: foreign
policy and domestic affairs. In each instance, Roosevelt observed that
the specific problems faced by his generation differed from those of the
past. Internationally, America had matured as a nation and now was
"forced by the fact of its greatness, into relations with the other nations
of the earth." Although he noted the importance of treating other nations
with justice and generosity, simultaneously he stressed the need to
speak and act from a position of power: "No weak nation that acts
manfully and justly should ever have cause to fear us, and no strong
power should ever be able to single us out as a subject for insolent
aggression." Roosevelt's remarks stressing the need for strong nations
to behave in a socially responsible fashion toward weak nations and
implying that the availability and threat of power were excellent deter-
rents to the use of it are a microcosm of his speaking on foreign policy.[21]
Foreign policy issues were not the only concerns that the nation and
its chief executive confronted, he claimed, warning:

We now face other perils, the very existence of which it was impossible that
they [our forefathers] should foresee. Modern life is both complex and intense,
and the tremendous changes wrought by the extraordinary industrial devel-

opment of the last half-century are felt in every fibre of our social and political being.

Roosevelt offered no specific solution to the nation's domestic problems. Rather, he found that the nation had to act "responsibly" and with "unbending, unflinching purpose to solve them aright."

Roosevelt concluded by claiming that "after all, though the problems are new, though the tasks set before us differ from the tasks set before our fathers who founded and preserved this Republic, the spirit in which these tasks must be undertaken and these problems faced, if our duty is to be well done, remains essentially unchanged." Drawing together all the challenges, both foreign and domestic, that confronted him as the nation's leader, he preached a characteristic solution:

We know that self government is difficult. We know that no people needs such high traits of character as that people which seeks to govern its affairs aright through the freely expressed will of the freemen who compose it. But we have faith that we shall not prove false to the memories of the men of the mighty past.

Although Roosevelt touched on several of his most common themes in this speech, he inevitably returned to the central importance of character. Acting with "the qualities of practical intelligence, of courage, of hardihood, and endurance, and above all the power of devotion to a lofty ideal," traits that he often utilized to define character, the nation under Roosevelt's leadership would resolve its problems in the spirit of the great men "who founded this Republic in the days of Washington" and "preserved this Republic in the days of Abraham Lincoln."

His inaugural address was vintage Theodore Roosevelt. The bully pulpiteer knew he had a national audience. His response was predictable: He preached the simple truths that he had been preaching throughout his career, for he stressed the importance of character in the conduct of both individual and national affairs.

CONCLUSIONS

When discussing outstanding inaugural addresses, rhetorical critics and historians rarely include Roosevelt's inaugural address. Rather, as Waldo Braden wrote, they typically depict it "as adequate for the occasion but not one of his better addresses."[22] Although it was undistinguished in form, and some might argue in substance as well, such judgments may be overly harsh. As William Harbaugh has observed, one should consider the address's "relevance as a testament of Roosevelt's faith and intent."[23] Theodore Roosevelt's inaugural address is clearly a reflection of the man. In this fact is its ultimate value.

The inaugural largely satisfies the elements that Campbell and Jamieson posit as constituting the essential presidential inaugural:[24]

1. It unifies the audience. Roosevelt referred repeatedly in the opening paragraph to "us as a people" and throughout the speech referred to Americans as "a people," "a republic," a democratic republic. He constantly used collective nouns as a means of implying unity both among the diverse elements of the nation and among those elements and himself.

2. It speaks to communal values that Roosevelt drew from the past. He repeatedly referred to "our forefathers," "our fathers, and "the men of the mighty past," in general, and to the principles of Washington and Lincoln specifically.

3. It speaks to the political principles that will govern his administration though only in the most general terms. Indeed, virtually the only political principle he spoke of is "self government." Rather he spoke of principles of character.

4. He demonstrated that he appreciated the "requirements and limitations of the executive functions," as Campbell and Jamieson suggest most presidents do. He established a tone of humility and reverence toward both the people and a higher authority.

Finally, Roosevelt's inaugural address, as Campbell and Jamieson suggest, is contemplative rather than action-oriented. Campbell and Jamieson claim that inaugural addresses take place in "the eternal present." It should have a timelessness that "affirms and ensures the continuity of the constitutional system and the immortality of the presidency as an institution, and timelessness is reflected in its contemplative tone and by the absence of calls to specific and immediate action."[25] Theodore Roosevelt's inaugural address spoke to the timeless virtue of character; it called for no specific action. The fact that it can be read, understood, and appreciated today and that an incoming president could deliver this speech as an inaugural today with very few changes speaks to Roosevelt's ability to capture "the eternal present."

Although Roosevelt's inaugural address does not fully reflect all the elements Campbell and Jamieson perceive as essential in a presidential inaugural, and indeed Roosevelt's failure to deal with some of those elements as extensively as he might have, may well contribute to the fact that this address is not normally considered among the first rank of presidential inaugurals, nevertheless, it has considerable merit. It reflected his values and beliefs, forecast his approach to the issues of his time, and gave listeners a sense of the personality of the speaker.

NOTES

1. Edmund Morris uses this phrase to describe Roosevelt upon his return from the Spanish-American War. See his *The Rise of Theodore Roosevelt* (New

York: Coward, McCann & Geoghegan, 1979), chap. 26. Morris bases this claim on the contemporary observations of the *New York World*. See note 10, p. 852.

2. Theodore Roosevelt, "Inaugural Address as Governor of New York," in Theodore Roosevelt, *The Works of Theodore Roosevelt: National Edition* (New York: Charles Scribner's Sons, 1926), 4.

3. In the wake of his popularity as the hero of San Juan Hill and the Spanish-American War, Roosevelt was elected governor of New York in 1898 and delivered his inaugural address as governor on January 2, 1899. In 1900, running with William McKinley, he was elected vice president and delivered a vice presidential inaugural in the U.S. Senate Chamber on March 4, 1901. Assuming the presidency upon the September 1901 assassination of President William McKinley, Roosevelt did not deliver an inaugural speech but sent his first annual message to Congress on December 3. Karlyn Kohrs Campbell and Kathleen Hall Jamieson, "Special Inaugurals: Speeches of Ascendant Vice Presidents," in *Deeds Done in Words: Presidential Rhetoric and the Genres of Governance* (Chicago: University of Chicago Press, 1990), claim that this written message served as Roosevelt's inaugural address for the last three and one-half years of McKinley's term, which Roosevelt served as president. Finally winning election in 1904, Roosevelt delivered a more traditional presidential inaugural address on March 4, 1905.

4. Roosevelt's first annual message to Congress may well be characterized as a "special inaugural address." Campbell and Jamieson use this characterization in *Deeds Done in Words*, 44–45. However, three principal considerations distinguish this "special inaugural" from Roosevelt's other inaugural addresses, making it of little value in helping to determine how he perceived inaugural addresses. First, he assumed office upon the assassination of McKinley rather than upon his own election. Second, because of the manner in which he assumed office, he felt compelled to eulogize his predecessor and discuss anarchists. Third, he used a fifty-seven-page written message rather than a relatively brief oral presentation.

5. All references to Theodore Roosevelt's inaugural address as governor of New York are to the text as found in *Works*, 15: 3–4. All references to Roosevelt's inaugural address as vice president are to the text as found in ibid., 15: 77–78.

6. Oscar Straus, *Under Four Administrations: From Cleveland to Taft* (Boston: Houghton Mifflin, 1922), 208. Roosevelt rarely, if ever, used ghostwriters. Repeatedly his associates commented on his ability to dictate excellent first drafts from which he revised. Frequently, as Straus, Gifford Pinchot, and many other Roosevelt associates testify, he sought the impressions of others as he worked through major manuscripts. On occasion he sent drafts of major manuscripts to others for their comments.

7. Theodore Roosevelt, *Theodore Roosevelt: An Autobiography*, in *Works*, vol. 19.

8. See Robert V. Friedenberg, *Theodore Roosevelt and the Rhetoric of Militant Decency* (Westport, Conn.: Greenwood Press, 1990), esp. 15–36.

9. Theodore Roosevelt, "Character and Success," in *Works*, 13: 386. On the primacy of Roosevelt's belief in character, see John Morton Blum, *The Republican Roosevelt* (Cambridge, Mass.: Harvard University Press, 1954), 33; David H. Burton *Theodore Roosevelt* (Boston: Twayne Publishers, 1972), 45–46; Carl A. Dal-

linger, "Theodore Roosevelt: The Preacher Militant," in *American Public Address: Studies in Honor of Albert Craig Baird*, ed. Loren Reid (Columbia: University of Missouri Press, 1961), 135; Harold Zyskind, "A Case Study in Philosophical Rhetoric: Theodore Roosevelt," *Philosophy and Rhetoric* (Summer 1968): 228–30.

10. Theodore Roosevelt, *The New Nationalism*, (New York: Outlook Company, 1910), 194–95. Also see Theodore Roosevelt, "Character and Success," in *Works*, 13: 384–85.

11. Blum, *Republican Roosevelt*, 7.

12. Quoted in ibid., 54.

13. See ibid., 37–54; William Harbaugh, *Power and Responsibility: The Life and Times of Theodore Roosevelt* (New York: Farrar Straus and Cudahy, 1961), 149–212; and George Mowry, *The Era of Theodore Roosevelt and the Birth of Modern America: 1900–1912* (New York: Harper & Row, 1958), 106–23, for clear discussions of Roosevelt's first years in office, which focus on his efforts to secure his nomination and election in 1904.

14. For a sound discussion of Democratic party politics prior to the election of 1903, see Mowry, *Era of Theodore Roosevelt*, 176–77.

15. For a good account of the campaign that includes liberal excerpts from the *World*'s article, and Roosevelt's response, see Henry F. Pringle, *Theodore Roosevelt: A Biography* (New York: Harcourt Brace Jovanovich, 1956), 248–51. Similar accounts of the campaign, stressing its dullness, can be found in Paul F. Boller, Jr., *Presidential Campaigns* (New York: Oxford University Press, 1985), 183–86, and Mowry, *Era of Theodore Roosevelt*, pp. 177–79.

16. For an excellent examination of the election results, which includes the *New York Sun* quotation, see Harbaugh, *Power and Responsibility*, 230–31. Also see Mowry, *Era of Theodore Roosevelt*, 179–80 and Boller, *Presidential Campaigns*, 184–85.

17. The clearly labeled and dated first draft of Roosevelt's inaugural is in the Library of Congress's Theodore Roosevelt Papers. All subsequent references to changes to the first draft are to the changes in Roosevelt's hand made to this typescript draft. The Theodore Roosevelt Papers have been microfilmed, and the draft inaugural is most widely available on reel 419, Series 5A, Speeches and Executive Orders, August 1904–February 1907, Theodore Roosevelt Papers.

18. Henry Cabot Lodge to Theodore Roosevelt, February 18, 1905, in *Selections from the Correspondence of Theodore Roosevelt and Henry Cabot Lodge*, ed. Henry Cabot Lodge, (New York: Charles Scribner and Sons, 1925), 2: 114–15.

19. See the draft manuscript in the Roosevelt Papers. Roosevelt did not alter 90 percent of the original draft.

20. This and all subsequent quotations and references to Roosevelt's inaugural are to the text found in Roosevelt, *Works*, 15: 267–69.

21. See Friedenberg, *Theodore Roosevelt and the Rhetoric of Militant Decency*, chap. 2.

22. Waldo W. Braden, "Theodore Roosevelt," in *American Orators of the Twentieth Century* ed. Bernard Duffy and Halford Ryan (Westport, Conn.: Greenwood Press, 1987), 356.

23. Harbaugh, *Power and Responsibility*, 213.

24. Campbell and Jamieson, *Deeds Done in Words*, 15.

25. Ibid., 27.

Chapter Two

President William Howard Taft's Inaugural Address, 1909

Craig R. Smith

A surprise ice storm raged along the Potomac the day President Taft was inaugurated. For the first time in seventy-six years, a president was forced to deliver his address inside the Capitol.[1] Over breakfast Taft told Theodore Roosevelt, "I knew it would be a cold day when I was made President of the United States," to which Roosevelt replied, "I knew there would be a blizzard clear up to the moment I went out of office."[2] The two arrived at 10:30 A.M. through swirling snow. When the assemblage was seated in the Senate Chamber at 11:45 A.M., the doorkeeper announced the arrival of the president and the president-elect, who strode down the center aisle to much cheering. Mrs. Taft believed that moving the ceremony into the Senate Chamber improved it, since inaugurals outside were hard to hear and marred by restless crowds.[3] In the presence of the Supreme Court, the diplomatic corps, the heads of the armed forces, and other dignitaries, Vice President Charles Fairbanks opened the ceremony by declaring the Sixtieth Congress at a close. Vice President James Sherman was then sworn in; he called the pro forma session of the Sixty-first Congress to order, delivered a short address, and swore in several senators who had been recently elected. This played into the passage in Taft's inaugural in which he called Congress back into "special session."

Chief Justice Melville Fuller administered the oath of office to Taft, who smiled at his wife and his children in the gallery. He then kissed the Bible to great applause and read his inaugural address from typed sheets.[4] From the first reference to Roosevelt through many succeeding points, the address was interrupted by enthusiastic applause from the gallery and House members and more dignified clapping from the senators.[5] Wrote the reporter for the *Los Angeles Times*, "No inaugural address of recent years has won such great success, measured by its effect upon its immediate hearers."[6]

TAFT'S PRIOR REPUTATION

This effect was more a function of Taft's stature than his style or delivery. The fifty-one-year-old president won a credible victory over several prominent but leftist opponents. With 7,678,908 popular votes, Taft received 321 electoral votes to 162 for William Jennings Bryan, whose popular vote was 6,409,104. Eugene Debs received almost half a million votes as a Socialist, and Prohibitionist Eugene Chaffin won a quarter million.

Taft came from Mark Hanna's Ohio stable with a stellar education that included an undergraduate degree from Yale, where he had delivered the senior oration. After graduating from Cincinnati Law School, he had been appointed assistant prosecuting attorney for Hamilton County in January 1881, and he had been named collector of internal revenue in January 1882 for the First District of Ohio by President Chester Arthur. He resigned that position in March 1883 for a stint in private practice but returned to public service as an assistant county solicitor in 1885 and then as judge of the Superior Court of Ohio in 1887. He was elected to the Ohio Supreme Court in April 1888.[7] President Benjamin Harrison appointed him U.S. solicitor-general in 1890 and a circuit judge for the Sixth Circuit in 1892. In that capacity, Taft wrote several decisions damaging to unions, which explained their opposition to his candidacy in 1908, but he also handed down a decision on February 8, 1898, in which he opposed businesses unfairly restraining interstate commerce.

McKinley appointed Taft to the Commission of the Philippines in 1900 at the request of Secretary of War Elihu Root. On July 4, 1901, he became its civil governor, which brought him to the attention of Theodore Roosevelt, who admired the way Taft had brought home rule to the islands and had reformed various abuses. Next, Roosevelt offered Taft a Supreme Court appointment in 1902, but Taft turned it down; instead, he replaced Root as secretary of war, in 1904. In September 1906, he became the provisional governor of Cuba and a few months later indicated to Roosevelt that he would like to be his replacement.

Certainly Taft was qualified to run for president, but campaigning was not his cup of tea. He traveled no farther west than Omaha—Bryan's stomping ground—to campaign for the nomination. When he won it on June 18, 1908, he resigned from the cabinet and waited for the Democrats to nominate Bryan for the third time. During the ensuing campaign, Taft was criticized for his Unitarianism and his refusal to take a stand on the question of Prohibition.[8] Although he refused to take campaign contributions from trusts, he did receive $20,000 from Andrew Carnegie. The electoral victory, nevertheless, was easy and expected.

THE POLITICAL MILIEU

Sitting in the warm, packed Senate Chamber listening to his hand-picked successor deliver his lengthy inaugural address, Roosevelt could not have known that less than four years later a bitter struggle between them would result in the election of Woodrow Wilson. Rumors of a rift between the two began in the campaign when Roosevelt seemed condescending to Taft; the rumors grew more intense when Taft chose his own cabinet.[9] In an early draft of the inaugural, Taft had written that there would not only be "a change of person but of policy" in the new administration.[10] Taft acknowledged the tension in a note to Roosevelt accepting his invitation to an inaugural eve dinner: "People have attempted to represent that you and I were in some way at odds during the last three months, whereas you and I know that there has not been the slightest difference between us."[11] Despite a nervous White House staff, the occasion went off "without a hitch."[12] The internecine fighting between Roosevelt and Taft did not begin in earnest until 1910; this animosity between the conservatives and moderates in the Republican party would be revived by Taft's son Robert, who in 1952 was frustrated by the moderate Dwight Eisenhower, and it lasts to this day.

Taft's inaugural did not encourage this enmity, however. Rather, it reflected the platform of the 1908 convention, which promised a lower tariff, federal incorporation of interstate companies, income tax reform, regulation of railroad stocks and bonds, further antitrust legislation, and the continuance of Roosevelt's national defense and conservation programs.[13] Following his nomination of the first ballot, Taft, on the advice of Roosevelt, had taken these themes into his campaign. By October he had narrowed his focus to the tariff, foreign policy, particularly with regard to the Philippines and Panama, Republican prosperity, defending his record with labor, and attacks on Bryan's socialist tendencies.

Immediately after the election, Taft was inundated by suggestions regarding these issues during his vacation in Hot Springs, Virginia. Congressman Joseph Gaines came to talk about the tariff; Theodore Burton of Ohio and Vice President–elect Sherman soon followed.[14] When Taft interrupted his vacation to meet with Roosevelt for discussion of his final State of the Union address, he received more advice. He returned to Hot Springs, where he met with House Speaker Joe Cannon and Senate Majority Leader Nelson Aldrich to discuss tariff reform and the new cabinet. After visiting Roosevelt once more, Taft continued his vacation in Augusta, Georgia, where he received more visitors, including Senator Henry Cabot Lodge. The locale may have influenced that section of the inaugural devoted to the South, as Taft's trip to Panama in late January may have inspired the section on the canal.

Perhaps the most important meeting on the inaugural took place in late February, when Taft and Roosevelt discussed a draft. Roosevelt wrote to Taft on February 26, 1909: "I cannot imagine a better inaugural, and it marks just exactly what your administration will be."[15]

THE INAUGURAL ADDRESS

Taft opened his inaugural address by echoing the pledge of his acceptance of the nomination:

I have had the honor to be one of the advisers of my distinguished predecessor, and, as such, to hold up his hands in the reforms he has initiated. I should be untrue to myself, to my promises, and to the declarations of the party platform upon which I was elected to office, if I did not make the maintenance and enforcement of those reforms a most important feature of my administration.[16]

True to his pledge, Taft would break up more trusts in his administration than Roosevelt had in his. Furthermore, Taft called Congress into special session to lower the Dingley tariff.[17] He called for a graduated inheritance tax, more land for national parks, preserving forests, and a strong national defense. Thus, this inaugural was action oriented in a deliberative sense.

His pledge played to the international arena, where Roosevelt had enjoyed stunning diplomatic successes. It recalled the voyage of the twenty-eight-ship flotilla, known as the Great White Fleet, which began on December 19, 1907, and concluded only a week before Taft's inaugural. In the context of international order, Taft specifically mentioned and presciently foreshadowed the Boxer Rebellion of 1910 when he referred to "controversies that are likely to arise in the Orient growing out of the question of the open door."[18]

The observation provided a rough segue into immigration policy. The year 1907 was the peak for immigration; 1.3 million had entered the country while it was suffering a short depression. European immigrants flowed into the United States through Ellis Island, and Japanese and Chinese were arriving in Seattle and San Francisco, which led to strident protest from the far western states in 1908.

Americans abroad had been harassed due to race and religion, and Taft began to address this problem by defending the rights of Americans to travel abroad. Reflecting the common racism of the day, he touched on the national anxiety over immigration: "The admission of Asiatic immigrants who cannot be amalgamated with our population has been made the subject either of prohibitory clauses in our treaties and states

or of strict administrative regulation secured by diplomatic negotiation."
He covered himself when he said we must "punish outbursts of race
feeling" and protect legal aliens from assault and injury.

Although the panic of 1907 was undoubtedly on the minds of his
listeners, Taft paid little attention to it other than to hold it responsible
for the projected deficit. He hoped to solve this problem with a com-
bination of revenue measures, especially tariff reform and new taxes.
The troubled U.S. currency, the need to subsidize steamship service,
and progress on the Panama Canal were addressed by Taft. As with the
immigration problem, successful completion of the needed tasks would
not occur until the Wilson administration. Taft would have more success
with his call for a postal savings bank system, which was passed into
law in 1910.

Next, Taft addressed the issue of governance of "Porto Rico and the
Philippines." Since Albert Beveridge's "March of the Flag," this issue
of American imperialism had been the province of the Republican party.
Taft brought particular credibility to the debate since he had been com-
missioner and governor of the Philippine Islands. He noted that business
conditions were troubled there but that tariff and electoral reform should
solve the problem.

Again without transition, Taft moved to a new subject: the South's
relations with "other sections of the country." The region was of special
concern to Taft, who had urged southerners to vote their consciences
instead of their traditions in the 1908 campaign. Although his plea fell
on deaf ears, he was determined to bring the South into the Republican
party.[19] In a series of speeches between the election and the inaugural,
he had called on southerners to support his administration.[20] In the
inaugural, he said, "My chief purpose is not to effect a change in the
electoral vote of the Southern States. That is a secondary consideration."
Nonetheless, he promised not to appoint blacks to posts in geographic
areas experiencing racial strife.

Taft knew that bitterness lingered from the Civil War, and anxiety
was increasing over the rapid rise of the Ku Klux Klan and the Knights
of the White Magnolia. On September 22, 1906, antiblack riots had
rocked Atlanta, resulting in twenty-one deaths (three white and eighteen
black). In the strongest language of the address, Taft called for "the
tolerance of political views of all kinds" in the South. While he acknowledged that the Thirteenth (emancipation) and Fourteenth (due process,
equal protection) amendments had been enforced, the Fifteenth (black
suffrage) had been circumvented.[21] Taft called for reform, echoing his
friend Booker T. Washington in the midst of this passage: "The colored
men must base their hope on the results of their own industry, self-
restraint, thrift, and business success, as well as upon the aid and comfort and sympathy which they may receive from their white neighbors

of the South."[22] Taft could also reflect the thinking of his abolitionist father: "The negroes are now Americans. Their ancestors came here years ago against their will, and this is their only country and their only flag. They have shown themselves anxious to live for it and to die for it."

Since Taft believed that his party had an obligation to Lincoln, the discussion of race was the longest and most heartfelt section of the address. A review of the drafts reveals that Taft struggled with it the most. For example, he changed "but it is perfectly clear that it is within the power of the people of the Southern States to prevent so-called negro discrimination" to "but it ought to be, and the tendency of Southern legislation today is toward the enactment of electoral qualifications which shall square with the fifteenth amendment."[23] In each new draft, Taft rewrote the strongest lines in this section; in the final draft, they read: "This is a great protection to the negro. It will never be repealed, and it never ought to be repealed."

Taft next turned to the complaints of unions. He endorsed the recently passed child labor law for the District of Columbia and pledged to seek more of such legislation. He indicated he would follow the example of his "distinguished predecessor" but revealed his conservative bias when he argued that the courts must keep their injunctive powers to prevent "lawless" union members from having their way.[24] Hitting directly on one of the most controversial issues of the day, Taft said: "The secondary boycott is an instrument of tyranny, and ought not to be made legitimate."

Two paragraphs later, Taft concluded his address. It had reflected the major issues of the day, the presence of his predecessor, and his legislative agenda, but it ignored certain issues that would grow in importance during the next decade. The deterioration of relations in Europe and the latent threat of anarchy were not mentioned, despite the fact that in 1901 an assassin's bullet had felled President William McKinley. Taft gave only one sentence to the danger of European nations arming for war: It warned against becoming "foolish idealists."

Although certain values were addressed, this inaugural is much more a deliberative effort than an epideictic one. For example, paragraph 6 read, "I hope to be able to submit at the first regular session of the incoming Congress . . . definite suggestions in respect to the needed amendments to the antitrust and the interstate commerce law and the changes required in the executive departments concerned with their enforcement." In fact, passages in the sections on civil rights and labor are forensic in that they concern legal action and guilt and innocence.

THE INAUGURAL'S STYLE

The speech is clearly deliberative in its thrust from the beginning, "a summary outline of the main policies of the new administration." That fact may have justified a less elegant style than an epideictic address might.[25] As he had with others, Taft wrote this address himself. The first draft is in longhand. The second was typed and then edited by Taft, as is the third, which, when revised, became the final version.[26] Taft was a lawyer and a judge, so it is not surprising that legal phrasing dominates.[27] As the *Independent* wrote, "Mr. Taft's tone is that of the bench, not that of the platform or pulpit."[28] His language is clear, matter of fact, and legalistic, but not artistic.

A few stylistic flourishes stand out but only because they are so sparse. For example, of the very few tropes and figures that Taft uses, alliteration is one of his favorites. The third paragraph of the speech begins: "To render the reforms lasting, however, and to secure at the same time freedom from alarm on the part of those pursuing proper and progressive business methods, further legislative and executive action are needed. Relief of the railroads from certain restrictions. . . ." His metaphors were common: "party platform," "steps," "heavy weight of responsibility," and "the scope . . . has been widened." No wonder the *Outlook* commented that Taft's address "contains no striking phrases or startling ultimatums. . . . [His style is] plain and simple."[29]

Worse, the speech lacks coherence. The preview of ideas is perfunctory and incredibly brief, a problem that carries over into transitions, which are stilted when they occur. More often than not, Taft moved from one topic to another without informing his listeners, as this example from the seventh to eighth paragraphs demonstrates:

I believe that the amendments to be proposed are just as necessary in the protection of legitimate business as in the clinching of the reforms which properly bear the name of my predecessor.
A matter of most pressing importance is the revision of the tariff.

The problem with transitions is compounded by the use of long, complicated sentences with phrases or clauses that seem out of place and certainly interrupt the flow of thought. For example, late in the speech, Taft said:

We should have an army so organized and so officered as to be capable in time of emergency, in cooperation with the national militia and under the provisions of a proper national volunteer law, rapidly to expand into a force sufficient to resist all probable invasion from abroad and to furnish a respectable expeditionary force if necessary in the maintenance of our traditional American policy which bears the name of President Monroe.

There are a surprising number of redundancies. Taft even repeated the metaphor about "holding up the hands" of our leaders, a reference to Moses during the battle with Amalek. The *Nation* claimed: "President Taft could not write in the 'Ercles vein if he would, and he has chosen to give his Inaugural address an agreeably quiet tone."[30] This strategy may have been induced by the fact that Taft's predecessor was one of the most effective phrasemakers to occupy the White House.

REACTION TO TAFT'S INAUGURAL

Newspapers and magazines praised the speech in general, paraphrased its substantive recommendations, and often quoted specific passages, most notably on the tariff, treatment of aliens, and racial equality in the South.[31] The *Boston Herald* called it the "best inaugural" in recent times. The *Detroit Press* said that "The bent of the constructive mind is seen throughout the address." The *New York Times* wrote of the address that "there is not a word in it to disturb the peace of mind of any honest man, either through fear that he himself may be wrongfully persecuted, or that his interests may suffer through the persecution or the prosecution of men not so honest." The *New York Evening Post* was equally effusive: "The day of [people] being arbitrarily harried is past." The *New York Sun*, the *Philadelphia Public Ledger*, and the *Chicago Tribune* followed suit.[32]

But while these and other papers praised the speech overall, their reactions to various parts were different. For example, the *New York Times* praised the president's position on the tariff while the *New York Evening Post* lamented it. *The Independent*, a weekly magazine, said it "was like a Democratic heresy." Many papers reflected congressional and European feeling that the United States had armed itself sufficiently during Roosevelt's reign. The *Independent* claimed the navy was strong enough but did repeat Taft's warning about the growing strength of Japan and Germany. But the *North American Review* agreed with Taft that coastal fortifications and naval strength were insufficient.[33]

As the address was reported across the country, the sections on race relations drew the most praise. The *Independent* and the *North American Review* commended the call for protection of aliens by federal courts. But more papers, including the *Independent*, commented on the president's lecture on racial equality. Since it took up one-fifth of the address and demonstrated more passion than other parts of the speech, it caught the attention of reporters, editorialists, and other opinion leaders. The day after the inaugural, the Reverend William Lawrence, bishop of Massachusetts, said in his sermon that "Mr. Taft's manner of meeting the race question should give us the greatest assurance." However, the *Nation* was more ambivalent because his promise not to appoint "negroes" to local office in areas of prejudice "will undoubtedly be hailed by negro-haters in the South," but his desire to see that the "war amendments" are prosecuted "will certainly do as much for the negro as his predecessor did." *Current Literature* also focused on the president's desire not to inflame the situation in the South with appointments of blacks in areas caught up in racial strife: "This part of the address . . . received more applause than anything else in the speech. . . . It came from both Northern and Southern men." Not surprisingly, the *Atlanta Journal* wrote: "This is indeed a new doctrine for the Republican party, and one which will do much to entrench Mr. Taft in the affections of the people of the South." The *Columbia State*, the *Fort Worth Record*, and the *Richmond Times* expressed similar sentiments.[34]

Remarkably, many newspapers in abolitionist New England also praised Taft's balanced approach. The *Springfield Republican* claimed that there was no evidence that blacks' rights would be trampled; the *Boston Herald* asserted that "in all he says [the new president] speaks with greater wisdom, more patient understanding, than any other President since Lincoln."[35] Certainly such commentary would help unite the country behind its new president.

On other issues, there was less unanimity. A month after the inaugural, *Current Literature* reported that no other presidential inaugural in memory had evoked so much interest from foreign diplomats. The British complained that Taft's call for more armaments would make "angels weep." The *Richmond Times* condemned the president's nationalist tendencies and his immigration policy. The *New York American*, run by William Randolph Hearst, who supported Bryan, called the speech a "monumental instance of the radicalism of some time ago becoming the conservatism of today."[36]

CONCLUSION

When Taft finished, Roosevelt leaped up and threw an arm around his huge successor and told him his speech was a "great document." Receiving an ovation equal to that of Taft, Roosevelt departed from the inaugural ceremony.[37] Because he did not like the tradition of riding back to the White House with a successor, Roosevelt ended it, which gave Mrs. Taft a chance to start a new tradition. As the sun emerged, the First Lady rode in the carriage with her husband along the parade route, delighted to be "doing something which no woman had ever done before."[38] While Roosevelt made his way to nearby Union Station to catch the train for New York, Taft and Vice President Sherman sat through the three-hour parade, protected against the cold by huge overcoats. The inaugural ball was held in the warm but cavernous Pension Building, while fireworks exploded over the Mall. Taft rested contentedly that evening knowing he had embarked on a mildly different course from his predecessor. The inaugural, which could easily pass for a State of the Union address, is clearly deliberative; focusing on generic, epideictic components would do it a great injustice.

NOTES

1. President Jackson was forced into the Capitol in 1833; President Reagan was forced into the Rotunda in 1981.

2. "Blizzard Changes Inaugural Plans," *Los Angeles Times*, March 5, 1909, 4. See also Mrs. William Howard Taft, *Recollections of Full Years* (New York: Dodd, Mead, 1944), 328.

3. Taft, *Recollections*, 331. See also William Manners, *TR and Will: A Friendship That Split the Republican Party* (New York: Harcourt, Brace & World, 1969), 71.

4. "Blizzard," 4.

5. "The frankness, the directness, the practical good sense, the fairness to all sections and interests expressed in this declaration of policy and purpose roused round after round of applause from the leading men of the nation, who constituted the major part of the assemblage." Walter Wellman, "Historic Scene Meets with Approbation," *Los Angeles Times*, March 5, 1909, 1.

6. Ibid.

7. During his tenure, Taft wrote a majority opinion opposing secondary boycotts. This position surfaces in his inaugural.

8. According to Taft's *War Secretary Diaries* (Cleveland: World Publishing Co., 1937), 3796, Carry Nation, who met with Taft on September 17, 1908, called him an infidel when he refused to assure her of his position on Prohibition.

9. When he was nominated, Taft had assured Roosevelt that he would retain the Roosevelt cabinet. Taft changed his mind after his election. See Henry F. Pringle, *The Life and Times of William Howard Taft* (Hamden, Conn.: Archon, 1964), 1: 384.

10. Taft Papers, Series 9C, Library of Congress, March 4, 1909–June 8, 1911.

11. As printed in Judith Anderson, *William Howard Taft, An Intimate History* (New York: W. W. Norton, 1981), 119.

12. Ibid.

13. Taft had added with his own hand the line, "The incoming Congress should promptly fulfill the promise of the Republican platform" and the next several lines following. Taft Papers, Series 9C, March 4, 1909–June 8, 1911.

14. Manners, *TR and Will*, 64.

15. Ibid., 67.

16. Unless indicated otherwise, all excerpts are taken from *Inaugural Addresses of the Presidents of the United States* (Washington, D.C.: U.S. Government Printing Office, 1974), 187–98.

17. On August 5, 1909, Taft signed the Payne-Aldrich Tariff Act. A month later he was hooted down when he labeled it the best "Republican" tariff bill ever. See "Taft on the Tariff," *Nation*, September 23, 1909, 271–72.

18. Wellman reports in "Historic Scene," "[Taft's] clear, strong outline of our foreign policy particularly as to oriental difficulties, so much interested the diplomatic corps that Ambassador Takohira from Japan leaned so far forward in his absorption that he almost fell out of his chair" (12).

19. See, for example, his speeches in Chattanooga, October 16, 1908, and Richmond, October 17, 1908. Taft Papers, Series 9C, August 19, 1907–March 1, 1901. Taft lost every southern state from Virginia to Texas in the election. Bryan carried only five states outside the South.

20. See, for example, his speech of December 7, 1908, to the North Carolina Society meeting in New York City and his speeches in Atlanta on January 15, 1909, Birmingham, Alabama, on February 13, 1909, Hattiesburg, Mississippi, and Meridian, Mississippi on February 14, 1909. Taft Papers, Series 9C, August 19, 1907–March 1, 1901.

21. He had tested this line on December 7, 1908, before the North Carolina Society.

22. Taft had agreed to consult with Washington regarding the appointment of blacks in the new administration. See Washington to Taft, December 1, 1908, Taft Papers, Series 3. See also Archie Butt, *Taft and Roosevelt: The Intimate Letters of Archie Butt*, (Garden City, N.Y.: Doubleday, Doran & Co., 1930), 457. The notion of self-help and education was rehearsed during the campaign at several stops. See Taft Papers, Series 9C, August 19, 1907–March 1, 1909.

23. The line received one more minor change in the final draft. Taft Papers, Series 9C, March 4, 1909–June 8, 1911.

24. Taft was directly responsible for the passage of the Mann-Elkins Act on June 18, 1910, which protected railroad employees.

25. The *Independent*, a weekly magazine published in New York, noted this characteristic (March 11, 1909, 541). The *Washington Post* called the speech "plain . . . simple hearted." See Anderson, *William Howard Taft*, 120.

26. See Taft Papers, Series 9C, March 4, 1909–June 8, 1911.

27. A review of Taft's campaign speeches reinforces this point.

28. *Independent*, March 11, 1909, 542.

29. "Mr. Taft's Inaugural," *Outlook*, March 13, 1909, 576.

30. "The Inaugural," *Nation*, March 11, 1909, 240.

31. See, for example, *North American Review*, 89 (March 1909): 635–38.

32. These opinions were reprinted in *Current Literature* 46 (April 1909): 349–58.

33. See *Independent*, March 11, 1909, 541; *North American Review*, March 1909, 636.

34. See "Lawrence Praises Taft," *New York Times*, March 5, 1909, 5. See *Nation*, March 11, 1909, 240; *Current Literature*, 355.

35. As reprinted in *Current Literature*, April 1909, 356.

36. See "Taft In, Roosevelt Out," *Current Literature* 46 (April 1909): 349, 350, 357.

37. "Blizzard," 4.

38. Taft, *Recollections*, 332.

Chapter Three

President Woodrow Wilson's First Inaugural Address, 1913

James R. Andrews

"There has been a change in government," the twenty-eighth president of the United States solemnly announced after taking office. There had, indeed, been a change, and Washington was well aware of it. Following sixteen years of Republican control of the White House, jubilant Democrats swept into the nation's capital. The stalwarts of Tammany Hall were delighted, after twenty years, to take part in the inauguration of a president of their own party. Over fifteen hundred strong, wearing white beaver hats and carrying red, white, and blue umbrellas, they marched in the great parade; Sheriff Harburger, on their behalf, pronounced the day "superb, marvelous, unprecedented." Even the weather, often blustery and unpleasant in early March, was fine: "a delightful day, warm, but not too warm, with a pleasant little breeze blowing. All things considered," the *New York Times* opined, "nobody ever took the oath under better omens." The crowds that gathered to hear and see the new president inducted into office were, by all accounts, massive. Most believed it to be the largest inaugural audience ever assembled. The president-elect arrived for the ceremonies at the Capitol Building and immediately sent word to the troops cordoning off a large area not to hold the crowd back. Surging forward with a "whoop," something close to a hundred thousand people packed the space stretching from in front of the platform to cover over two acres. Chief Justice Edward White administered the oath; the new president answered with a firm "I do," and kissed the Bible—the same Bible upon which he had sworn the oath upon assuming the governorship of New Jersey—opened to the 119th Pslam, "And take not the word of truth utterly out of my mouth."[1]

The address that President Wilson then delivered was the culminating statement of the 1912 campaign, a sweeping overview of the principles he had enunciated in hundreds of campaign speeches, explicit as to the philosophy and values that would drive his new administration but less so as to the specific programs that would implement these principles. The address was also a clear reflection of Wilson's own character and vision; the idealistic tone evidences the intellectual reformer at work. It is buttressed by the ethos of a progressive governor with strong moral convictions who had faced down the political bosses and established a reputation as the champion of good government in triumphing over political corruption.

THE STRUCTURE OF THE ADDRESS

The speech began with the simple declaration that there "has been a change of government" and asked, "What does the change mean?"[2] The opening paragraphs explained that the Democratic party would serve as the instrument to bring about the changes needed, asserting that as America had achieved greatness, it had "not stopped to conserve the exceeding bounty of nature" and had "not hitherto stopped thoughtfully enough to count the human cost." For Wilson, his election signified that "we have come now to the sober second thought." Changes are possible now that the "scales of heedlessness have fallen from our eyes."

The changes Wilson enumerated in the seventh and eighth paragraphs of his speech are a virtual litany of the Democratic program. The address set six basic aims for the government.

1. *Revision of the tariff.* The tariff hampered the country's ability to participate in the commerce of the world, made for unjust taxation, and rendered government the tool of private interests.
2. *Reform of the banking system.* The system was too likely to concentrate cash resources in the hands of a few and restrict credit.
3. *Alteration of the industrial system.* The system restricted capital as well as the liberties and opportunities of labor, and it wasted natural resources.
4. *Redirection of agricultural activities.* Agriculture was not afforded the opportunities of big business because the credit system was not adapted to its needs and scientific advancements were not directly applied to farming.
5. *Conservation of natural resources.* Resources were not developed properly, and reclamation and preservation had been neglected.
6. *Conservation of human resources.* No thought had been given to protecting the health of the people. Men, women, and children needed to be shielded from the effects of social and industrial processes that were beyond their control. Sanitary laws, pure food laws, and laws determining the condition of labor were needed.

This blueprint for change, "some of the things we ought to do," was immediately followed by the admonition not to leave undone "the old-fashioned, never-to-be-neglected, fundamental safeguarding of property and individual right." Careful to distinguish change from radical experimentation, Wilson assured the nation that "we shall deal with our economic system as it is and as it may be modified, not as it might be if we had a clean sheet of paper to write upon."

The president concluded with the assertion that the "nation has been deeply stirred" by the realization that government had "too often been debauched and made an instrument of evil." He pledged that efforts to restore justice would not be a "mere task of politics" and brought the speech to a close by declaring, "This is not a day of triumph; it is a day of dedication," in which were mustered "not the forces of party, but the forces of humanity." He called upon all "honest . . . patriotic . . . forward-looking men" to "counsel and sustain" him.

The structure of the speech, thus, set up the failings of a profligate system, delineated specific changes to be made, reinforced the commitment to stability and traditional values, and issued a call for nonpartisan support for the worthy goals of the new administration.

At first glance, the address might be said to exhibit characteristics called for by the ceremonial nature of the occasion. It took a high moral ground, enunciated principles by which the new administration would be governed, recognized established principles, and asked for the support of all citizens regardless of party. Such judgments, however, mask the unique qualities of this speech and its direct relation to the context out of which it emerged. Perhaps if President Taft had been reelected, his inaugural would have exhibited the same features, but it would not have been the same speech. Obviously, there is a certain restraint imposed on inaugural addresses; allowing, however, for the obvious convention that one does not directly attack the opposition parties or candidates, Wilson's speech was the speech of the successful Democratic candidate who urged that party's prescription for change throughout the campaign of 1912.

ECHOES OF THE CAMPAIGN

Consider the areas of change Wilson specified in the address: the tariff, banking and currency, the industrial system, agriculture, and conservation of natural and human resources. All of these matters were treated by Wilson in campaign speeches he had given day after day across the country. Throughout the canvass, Governor Wilson had hammered away at the need for tariff reform.[3] In his speech accepting the nomination on August 7, he lashed out at the tariffs as "a method of fostering special privilege" and insisted that "the economic freedom of our people, our property in trade, our untrammeled energy in manufacture depend on their reconstruction from top to bottom in an entirely different spirit." In his Labor Day speech, delivered in Buffalo on September 2, Wilson pledged that "if the Democrats should be successful," they "will alter the tariff duties, will lower them, will put a great many articles on the free list, will set the process going which will destroy the special privileges being enjoyed by many classes of employers in this country." In an interview with *Harper's Weekly*, the candidate pointed out that "we all of us agree that the central issue in the present campaign is . . . the question of the tariff," and he acknowledged in a message to the American people on October 19 that "in practically every speech that I make, I put at the front of what I have to say the question of the tariff."

Although the tariff issue was central to the campaign, each of the "things that ought to be altered," as Wilson put it in the inaugural address, received attention in the campaign. From the steps of Princeton's Second Presbyterian Church on September 24, he had charged that "the banking and currency system of this country isn't ready for the expansion of business, and if the business begins to expand rapidly we may find ourselves in the grip of one of the most tremendous crises we have ever had, unless in the meantime we correct our currency system." The industrial system was taken to task again and again. Taking away special privileges, Wilson said in an address on October 12, "will set the government free from the influences which now constantly control it and would set industry free." He went on:

The enterprize and initiative of all Americans would be substituted for the enterprize and initiative of a small group of them. Economic democracy would take the place of monopoly and selfish management. American industry would have a new buoyancy of hope, a new energy, a new variety. With the restoration of freedom would come the restoration of opportunity.

"What is the use of having industry," Wilson asked a crowd gathered on September 18 at the Minneapolis parade grounds, "if we die in producing it?"

To the farmers, Wilson reiterated his pledge that the fruits of science and knowledge should be put to their practical use. In Washington Grove, New Jersey, on August 15 he described the mass of information "that would be extremely useful to the farmer, if only the farmer could get to it." It was government's responsibility, Wilson argued, to get such information to the farmer. "It is our business," the governor told the rural crowd gathered for a picnic, "to see that all the investigation that has been going on in the world of science for a generation and more," information on such matters as the chemistry of soils and rotation of crops, "be carried to the farms."

In accepting the nomination, Governor Wilson professed that "I do not know any greater question than that of conservation. We have been a spendthrift nation, and now we must husband what we have left." Writing on the eve of the election for the *Woman's Home Companion* on "The New Meaning of Government," Wilson called for preservation and renewal of forests, prevention of the waste of mineral resources, and the renewal of water resources. "The government," he asserted, "must administer our resources as a good trustee would administer a great estate for the support of the living and the benefit of those yet unborn."[4]

On the matter of conserving human resources, Wilson's campaign speeches show a consistent and persistent concern for those whom he identified in the inaugural as "the men and women and children upon whom the dead weight and burden has fallen pitilessly the years through." At a rally in Madison Square Garden on October 31, for example, Wilson said that "there is no cause half so sacred as the cause of the people." He continued:

There is no idea so uplifting as the idea of the service of humanity. There is nothing that touches the springs of conscience like the cause of the oppressed, the cause of those who suffer, and we give not only our sympathy but our justice, our righteous action, our action for them as well as for ourselves.

In the candidate's last major speech before the election, at a Democratic rally on November 2, Woodrow Wilson summed up the campaign, rehearsing the issues and themes that would inform his inaugural address:

The next four years will determine how we are to solve the question of the tariff, the question of trusts, the question of the reformation of our whole banking and currency systems, the conservation of our natural resources and of the health and vigor of our people . . . the right application of our scientific knowledge to work a healthy prosperity of our whole population, whether in the fields or in the factories or in the mines.

He further called for "the extension of the uses of government to . . . programs of uplift and betterment."

As well as illustrating the use of the specific issues Wilson noted in the inaugural, the campaign speeches demonstrate the philosophic underpinnings of Wilson's program as it emerged on March 5, 1912. Wilson asserted in the inaugural that "the success of a party means little except when the Nation is using that party for a large and definite purpose." In the Madison Square Garden speech, he had stated his conviction that "government is an enterprize of mankind, not an enterprize of party. The parties are but the poor servants of the cause of mankind" and he reminded those at the last rally of the campaign that triumph at the polls would be no "triumph of party or factions, but the triumph of a people.

The Democratic party will be, not the selfish victor, but the trusted instrument."

In the inaugural, Wilson recognized that while the nation's achievements had been prodigious, "evil has come with the good . . . inexcusable waste has occurred." Not only the "bounty of Nature" had been squandered, but there had been a "human cost," a "fearful physical and spiritual cost"—a theme he had expressed when he began the campaign and reiterated throughout it. On accepting the nomination, he recognized that the "nation has grown immensely rich. She is justly proud of her industries and of the genius of her men of affairs. But what of the other side of the picture?" The government had responsibility to cope with the bad that came with the good: "No law that safeguards their [working people's] life, that makes their hours of labor rational and tolerable, that gives them freedom to act in their own interest, and that protects them when they cannot protect themselves, can properly be regarded . . . as anything but a measure taken in the interest of the whole people."

In the inaugural address, Wilson made clear that although change was the order of the day, it was not to be a radical change. He had often spoken of change during the campaign, asserting to a crowd in Sioux City, Iowa, on September 17, for example, that "the great difference between the Republican Party and the Democratic Party is that the Republican Party doesn't propose to change any of the essential conditions that make our present difficulties." He told the Woodrow Wilson Working Men's League on September 4 that it amazed him that "any political party should propose to fix the present condition of things upon the people and to let things stand where they are." He blasted Roosevelt's proposal to set up a regulatory commission as no remedy at all: "To remedy an evil by making it permanent is something that I cannot understand. . . . To say to the people, we cannot change what has taken place . . . is to proclaim a helplessness . . . [that is] the very opposite of the whole process of civilization." Wilson's prescription for change, however, was not a radical one. Although the differences between the Progressive and Democratic platforms were not as clear and dramatic as the candidates asserted in the heat of the campaign, there was one radical candidate whom the major contenders generally ignored: Eugene Debs, who carried the Socialist banner into the election fray with the demand for sweeping alterations in the social and economic systems. Furthermore, Republican regulars liked to portray a Democratic victory as the prelude to business collapse and economic chaos. Wilson pointed out from time to time during the campaign his aversion to class division and class warfare and reassured the electorate that he was no wild social experimenter. He was motivated to be "a Progressive," he said in a September 25 speech in Hartford, Connecticut, "because we have not kept up with changed conditions." In that speech he lay down his prescription for progressive change:

We ought to go very slowly and very carefully about the task of altering the institutions we have been a long time in building up. I believe that the ancient traditions of a people are its ballast. You must knit the new into the old. If I did not believe that to be progressive is to preserve the essential of our institutions, I, for one, could not be a Progressive.

His inaugural promises for change were clearly consistent with this perspective: "We shall restore, not destroy. We shall deal with our economic system as it is and as it may be modified . . . and step by step we shall make it what it should be." Wilson decidedly did not advocate "the excitement of excursions" that led "whither they can not tell."

In the issues and principles that informed Wilson's inaugural, there were few surprises for those who had followed the campaign closely. This inaugural exemplified not a beginning, not a statement of new directions, but a transition between the rhetoric of presidential politics and the rhetorical construction of the goals of the new administration. Although it may be nonpartisan in profession and tone, it suggested a coming together on Wilson's terms, grounded firmly in and growing naturally from the Democratic candidate's campaign rhetoric. In short, the inaugural address contained, in the words of a *Washington Post* editorial of March 6, "nothing that Woodrow Wilson has not consistently and untiringly set forth as his political creed."[5]

INTERPRETING THE OCCASION: WILSON AND THE MEANING OF CHANGE

Wilson's inaugural sought to explain the meaning of the political change that had occurred. On his interpretation of the powers and limitations of the presidency, Wilson was silent. He did not address the role of executive powers in effecting change; rather, he chose to emphasize the idealism inherent in the rhetoric that typified his quest for the nation's highest office. "Sometimes people call me an idealist," he once observed. "Well, that's the only way I know I am an American. America is the only idealistic nation in the world."[6]

Wilson's political career could be cast as the idealist reformer versus the cynical political bosses, and Wilson often made much of his political independence as governor of New Jersey. Recalling the skepticism of New Jersey voters in his bid for the governorship, Wilson described their surprise when, after he had assumed office, "it began to dawn on them . . . that perhaps if he were given a chance he had just so little experience in politics that he would actually undertake to do what he said he would undertake to do." On another occasion he quipped: "When I became Governor of New Jersey I hadn't been in politics long enough to promise things I did not intend to carry out." In responding to a charge by Senator Albert Beveridge that Wilson would be controlled by bosses if elected, the Democratic presidential candidate observed that he "didn't know Senator Beveridge was a humorist" and asked, "When did he ever hear that I had changed all my political habits? The way you can tell whether a man is going to be controlled by bosses or not is to judge whether he is being reached by a boss or not." Untarred by the brushes that blackened some of the local and state leaders of his own party, Wilson's integrity remained unchallenged, despite sporadic attacks. The idealist in politics had fought and won a national campaign and now approached the inaugural podium to instruct the nation on how those ideals were to inform his new administration.[7]

In the address, Wilson made use of a stylistic feature that afforded him the opportunity to match his ideals with his practices. Antithesis formed the building blocks of Wilson's eloquence, as both a rhetorical device and as rhetorical form. Antithesis is a particularly effective way to contrast what should be with what is, to counter the failings of the present with the promise of what can be, to project in vivid images common values alongside common practices.

This antithetical mode was one that Wilson had often put to use to compare ideals and action. "Men are bad, not societies," he told the Princeton baccalaureate audience in 1908. "We shall find our reforms, not in law, but in conscience." To the American Bankers Association he said, "It is the duty and opportunity of those who control wealth to pay less attention to the business of making particular individuals rich and more attention to the business of making the country rich."[8]

Throughout the inaugural address, Wilson painted a vivid picture of contrasts: What we have become and what we accept is exposed as antithetical to what we believe we should be. He began with the recognition that much in American life was great: "its material aspects . . . its body of wealth . . . energy . . . the industries that have been conceived and built." The nation was great, too, in "its moral force . . . [its] system of government." Against this backdrop, however, is the antithesis: The "evil has come with the good." Riches are obtained through "inexcusable waste," "industrial achievements" gained without regard to human cost, "great government" used for "private and selfish purposes."

The meaning of the change in government that the country was now experiencing was that "we see the bad with the good, the debased and decadent with the sound and vital." The exploitation of the people by the rising industrial greatness is captured by Wilson's mechanistic metaphor. Guided by the thought, " 'Let every man look out for himself, let every generation look out for itself,' " Americans had created "giant machinery, which made it impossible that any but those who stood at the levers of control should have a chance to look out for themselves." In contrast, the American people, through the change that brought about the new government, had "made up our minds to square every process of our national life again with the standards of justice and fair play we so proudly set up at the beginning and have always carried in our hearts." This antithetical form led Wilson to the point wherein he could call for positive change while insisting on the conservative nature of that change: "Our work is a work of restoration."

At this juncture, Wilson moved to catalog the evils to which he had pointed throughout the campaign and to which he directly alluded now: "We have itemized with some degree of particularity the things that ought to be altered and here are some of the chief items." This section served the antithetical form of the address, it stood in direct counterpoint to the notion introduced early in the address that "we see that in many things life is great." The needed alterations are stated in negative terms, accentuating the contrast between the realities of life and the achievement of greatness. Tariffs had "cut us off" from world commerce; the industrial system "restricts the liberties and limits the opportunities of labor"; watercourses were "undeveloped," forests "untended," waste heaps "unregarded" at the mines. The contrast is emphasized with the concluding antithesis: "We have studied perhaps as no other nation has the most effective means of production, but we have not studied cost or economy as we should either as organizers of industry, as statesmen, or as individuals."

Wilson went on to project his vision of the true role of government, which was in stark contrast to a government that served "those who stood at the levers of control." For him, government must be "put at the service of humanity." The metaphoric machine that enabled the most powerful to destroy the humblest must be controlled: "Men, women and children" must be "shielded in their lives, their very vitality, from the consequences of great industrial and social processes which they can not alter, control, or singly cope with." The machine should not destroy itself: "Society must see to it that it does not crush or weaken or damage its own constituent parts."

Change, however, was balanced with continuity. Antithetical to the evil present was both the past and the future. While change led Wilson to urge the nation to undertake in the future "the things we ought to do," continuity led him to assert that we could not leave "others undone, the old-fashioned, never-to-be-neglected, fundamental safeguarding of property and individual right." Wilson might have been idealistic, and his program of social reform might call for new directions, but he was not Eugene Debs. He did not call for the obliteration of the economic system; rather, he "will deal with" it "as it is and as it may be modified."

The nation's passions "have been stirred by the knowledge of wrong, of ideals lost, of government too often debauched and made an instrument of evil." In contrast with the present evils, consistent with past ideals, Wilson called for a future that would be "a new age of right and opportunity."

He concluded the address with a final set of antitheses: "This is not a day of triumph; it is a day of dedication." The celebration of the victory of his party in the present is dwarfed by the solemn obligations of the future: "Here muster, not the forces of party, but the forces of humanity."

The new president had infused his conception of change into the meaning of the occasion. Evil practices of the present, antithetical to the new spirit that infused the nation, would be countered by the humane actions of his administration. Serving humanity, however, would not be equated with the destruction of old values and ideals, since the heedless, selfish actions of the present were also antithetical to American ideals of greatness. The "new freedom" would be predicated on old principles, newly interpreted and fairly applied: "justice, and only justice, shall always be our motto."

RESPONDING TO THE OCCASION: THE NATION VIEWS THE CHANGE

For most Americans the words of the inaugural, along with interpretations of their meaning, impact, and quality, came from the press. Very few actually heard the address spoken; it was not audible far from the platform, and most of the thousands gathered knew the ceremony was over only when the carriages arrived to take away the assembled dignitaries.

For the most part, editorial writers commended the president for his efforts. The Philadelphia *Public Ledger* placed the address among "the best of State papers"; the Cleveland *Plain Dealer* believed that for "vigor, dignity, earnestness and lucidity it stands nearly on a par with Lincoln's speech at Gettysburg"; Wilson's "voice," proclaimed the *Globe* of Boston, was "the voice of a prophet and a leader"; Wilson's words "should thrill the heart, not alone of every true Democrat, but of every true American," Louisville's *Courier Democrat* observed. The new president's personal integrity, his grandness of vision, and his dedication were universally acknowledged. Wilson was seen as "a very practical idealist," by the New Orleans *Times-Democrat*, an idealist who could, according to the Charleston *News and Courier*, "divine the needs of the masses of his fellow-citizens and . . . constitute their spokesman and their champion." The inaugural was "spoken courageously and sincerely," a message, as described by the editorial writer for the *Denver Republican*, that was "broad, sincere, and coming from the heart of the man."[9]

Wilson's theme of change—his vision of a government acting with justice to serve all its citizens—and the orderly nature of change was clearly perceived as he set it forth. The Springfield, Massachusetts *Republican* voiced typical reactions in reassuring "conservative people" that they "have no cause for alarm if this inaugural reveals the high mission of President Wilson as he himself interprets it. He stands firmly on the fundamental principles of the older Democracy, which recognized the rights of property and the safeguarding of the individual's freedom." That said, the editorial went on to recognize Wilson's fundamental message: "But he does and will make valiant war upon the abuses of the time; the while seeking in every possible way to put the Government at the larger service of humanity."[10]

True it is that the taste of grapes gone sour was in the mouth of a few editors. The *Los Angeles Times* hoped that Democrats would "content themselves with the offices and keep their experimental and ravaging hands off the throat of the industries and prosperity of the country," and the Memphis *Commercial Appeal* expressed its concern for this "year of experimenting," clearly dubious about those who "feel that in legislation there are remedies for every ill." This Memphis editorial writer scornfully dismissed "men who think that a system of government can be devised that will reduce the necessity of man's toiling and will guarantee and provide for all food and drink 365 days in the year." The *Kansas City Star* acknowledged the worth of the spirit that demanded "fuller control of the Government by the people" and the cause of "social and industrial justice," but it was at pains to assert that that spirit was "the heritage that Woodrow Wilson receives from Roosevelt and the Progressives."[11]

It is also true that there were some allusions to the vagueness of the message—not in tone and direction but in specific programs. "All in all," the *New York Times* observed, "the message does not reveal very clearly what the outworking of the Wilson Administration will be," and the *Chicago Tribune* pointed out that "it presents no definite recommendations for action." The *Inter-Ocean* (Chicago) commented that "many will regard Mr. Wilson's ideas as quite vague, and so academically expressed as to inspire doubts whether the speaker has been able to reach any clearly framed intentions or has thought out any definite method of doing what he believes ought to be done." But there can be no doubt that few escaped the tone and meaning of the inaugural. The Atlanta *Constitution* summed up prevailing editorial readings of the speech:

Unquestionably the inaugural address foreshadows a gradual but thoroughgoing readjustment of Governmental methods and standards. Government is going to be brought more closely to the people, in a helpful sense. It is to be humanized, equalized. It is to be made to take cognizance, sanely and not hysterically, of that "brotherhood of man" theory which is becoming the dominant thought even of politics.[12]

CONCLUSION

Wilson's inaugural address explicated for his audience the meaning of the change in government that he proclaimed. The change was firmly based on the principles enunciated in the campaign; it was to return the government to the service of the people from whence it had strayed in the heedless national rush to greatness. That this meaning was especially clear to those who believed with Wilson that the rights of the people had been neglected by a government dedicated to serving the powerful few is epitomized in a letter to the new president from labor leader Frank Morrison.

In a few words in your inaugural address you indicated in the most certain terms the reforms needed to turn the tide of discontent among our people to something akin to the feeling that the human equation will soon be solved, and when solved, the answer will be the equal protection and opportunity for each citizen.

When Congress enacts legislation in harmony with your inaugural address, it will kindle afresh in many, and for the first time in the hearts of millions of our citizens the hope that enactment of wise legislation will gradually eliminate from our present civilization the many inequalities and injustices which bear heavily upon many of our people.

You said to Mr. Gompers and myself that you thought we would be satisfied with your address. I am satisfied, and will do what I can to have Congress enact the legislation necessary to secure the splendid reforms which you have clearly outlined in your address.[13]

Soon after inauguration day, on April 8, President Wilson broke with long-standing precedent, appearing in person before Congress to recommend tariff reform legislation. The change in government advocated in the 1912 presidential campaign and firmly asserted in Wilson's inaugural address had begun in earnest.

NOTES

1. "Wilson Sworn in as President," *New York Times*, March 5, 1913; "The Ceremonies in Washington," *New York Times*, March 5, 1913, 16; "New York's Share in Capital Pageant," *New York Times*, March 5, 1913, 4; *Chicago Tribune*, March 5, 1912, 1.

2. All quotations from the address are from Woodrow Wilson, "First Inaugural Address," in *Inaugural Address of the Presidents of the United States from*

George Washington 1789 to George Bush 1989 (Washington, D.C.: U.S. Government Printing Office, 1989), 227–231.

3. All campaign speeches are identified by date and place in the text. They are taken from *Presidential Papers Microfilm: Woodrow Wilson Papers*, Series 7A: 1912 September 27–1916 October 28, Reel 477, Library of Congress.

4. Woodrow Wilson, "The New Meaning of Government," *Woman's Home Companion* (November 1912): 4.

5. Cited by *New York Times*, March 5, 1913, 4.

6. Raymond F. Pinsey, ed., *Woodrow Wilson: Idealism and Reality* (Verona, Va.: McClure Press, 1977), 3.

7. *New York Times*, August 20, 21, September 17, 1912.

8. "Baccalaureate Sermon," June 7, 1908, in *The Papers of Woodrow Wilson*, ed. Arthur S. Link et al. (Princeton, N.J.: Princeton University Press, 1966–   ), 332 (cited hereafter as *PWW*; "The Banker and the Nation," September 30, 1908, *PWW*, 18: 433.

9. *New York Times*, March 5, 1913, 4. Editorial opinion is sampled extensively in this edition; citations of press reaction are from this source.

10. Ibid.

11. Ibid.

12. Ibid.

13. Frank Morrison to Wilson, Washington, D.C., March 7, 1913, in *PWW*, 27: 159–60.

Chapter Four

President Woodrow Wilson's Second Inaugural Address, 1917

Gary C. Woodward

We are provincials no longer. The tragical events of the thirty months of vital turmoil through which we have just passed have made us citizens of the world. There can be no turning back. Our own fortunes as a nation are involved, whether we would have it so or not.[1]

Woodrow Wilson's Second Inaugural was a last call for peace in the final weeks before the United States entered World War I. We learn something essential about Wilson at the time by reviewing the notes of a friend who was summoned to the White House for a late evening meeting. Journalist Frank Cobb reached the president's study at 1 o'clock in the morning and was greeted by a tired and troubled leader. The President wanted to talk, apparently unable to sleep after months of watching official American neutrality eroded by British threats and German submarine attacks. Cobb sensed the president needed reassurance that he had not missed an opportunity to stay out of the war. Just three weeks had passed since the inaugural, and now Wilson was on the eve of his agonizing appearance before Congress to declare war against Germany. The journalist recalled that the president had an "uncanny" understanding of his dilemma that evening. "He had the whole panorama in his mind." Wilson lamented that "he had considered every loophole of escape" to avoid going to war, "and as fast as they were discovered Germany deliberately blocked them with some new outrage."[2]

Events were quickly overtaking the president's ability to manage them. Newspaper headlines already told of the bloody and futile battles between the Allies and Germans near the French village of Verdun and throughout the Somme River Valley to the north. Weapons of efficient destruction had claimed nearly 2 million soldiers in just those stalemates.[3] Most Americans were outraged at Germany's efforts to solidify its position in what had already become a drawn-out and protracted war. Many recalled the bizarre appearance a few months earlier of a German U-boat in the harbor at Newport, Rhode Island. Taking advantage of U.S. official neutrality, its crew assembled a package of American newspapers that detailed the sailing times of ships on the eastern seaboard. Within twenty-four hours the same submarine cruiser had sunk nine of the listed vessels.[4] There was also the famous Zimmermann Telegram, a cable intercepted by British intelligence and made public by Wilson, revealing that Germany would exploit American tensions with Mexico by inviting the Mexican government to join the Central Powers. Germany's promise to support Mexico in reconquering portions of the American Southwest was the ostensible inducement.

In his March 5 inaugural, Wilson still held out some hope that a policy of armed neutrality would be sufficient to avoid U.S. involvement in what many Americans believed should remain Europe's own bloodbath. But the address was essentially a prelude to war, one of many attempts by Wilson in early 1917 to employ again the rhetoric of moral authority in an effort to gain some time and distance from the tribal warfare that consumed an entire continent. The late-night meeting with Cobb revealed Wilson's increasingly precarious position. For his sometimes bitter foe, Theodore Roosevelt, the prospect of war in Europe was more of an opportunity than a time for political agonizing. For a man who sought to embody the idea of orderly and humane statecraft, however, war was failure, the antithesis of his political and rhetorical instincts. Others might see bloodshed as an instrument that could further national goals, but the former president of Princeton regarded political acts as redeemable only in the currency of high-principled rhetorical defenses. This war, he correctly judged, offered little chance for a successful and stable outcome. In his extremely close election battle with former Supreme Court justice Charles Evans Hughes, Wilson profited from the campaign slogan, "He kept us out of war."[5] But the nation began the campaign of 1916 as ill prepared militarily as Wilson was psychologically for the increasing certainty that the United States would be joining the military alliance of France, England, and Russia. "If there is any alternative," he told Cobb, "for God's sake, let's take it."[6]

For Woodrow Wilson, politics was a rhetorical process as much as anything else. Oratory was an essential vehicle for defining the broadest principles of American political culture. As president, he lived out his childhood fantasy of becoming a statesman, leading citizens by declaring high principles and encouraging others to act on them. A president's task was to persuade citizens to be "right-thinking men," a basic first principle that matched Wilson's admission that he possessed "an unmistakable oratorical temperament."[7] He was perhaps among the last chief executives to view seriously the political opportunities of the presidency in terms of the rhetoric of moral leadership. Communicating the principles and morality of policy was often more important to him than were the details of the policies themselves.

By the spring of 1917, the kind of presidency that Wilson wanted for himself and the nation was undone by an unraveling of the political fabric of Europe that he could not prevent. Wilson knew that he could no longer lead a nation that focused on an agenda of domestic reform, but rather that he would lead one that would have to spend its treasure, energies, and goodwill in ways that would end its generous impulses. Once Americans are led into war, he told Cobb,

They'll forget there ever was such a thing as tolerance. To fight you must be brutal and ruthless, and the spirit of ruthless brutality will enter into the very fibre of our national life, infecting Congress, the courts, the policeman on the beat, the man on the street.[8]

Wilson doubted that the Constitution could survive a major war, and he worried as much about the destruction of the American psyche as its men and materiél. War, he noted, turns bystanders into haters and casts off the chances for peace by replacing the values of peacetime civilizations with those of angry villains and victims. His anguish was prescient. In general terms, he predicted for Cobb what would actually come to pass: The conflict would lead to a defeat for Germany, a failed treaty of peace, and the kind of humiliation that would set the stage for a distant second war. A declaration of war, the president told Cobb, "would mean that Germany would be beaten and so badly beaten that there would be a dictated peace, a victorious peace." Wilson clearly understood that this outcome would result in only temporary stability rather than permanent peace. "It means an attempt to reconstruct a peace-time civilization with war standards, and at the end of the war there will be no bystanders with sufficient power to influence the terms. There won't be any peace standards left to work with."[9]

THE RHETORICAL SETTING

Some inaugurals serve as benchmarks that signal new styles of leadership and different political agendas. The first words uttered by President John F. Kennedy, for example, were clearly intended to demonstrate a contrast with the outgoing Eisenhower administration and display the intentions of JFK's new administration: "We observe today not a victory of party but a celebration of freedom—symbolizing an end as well as a beginning—signifying renewal as well as change." But second inaugurals cannot easily serve this benchmark function, and in Wilson's case the occasion was reduced in its impact further by a series of public events that eclipsed the inaugural's rhetorical effect. Most directly, three well-covered speeches by Wilson to Congress on January 22, February 3, and February 26, 1917, had already defined the dominant political circumstances. The prominence of these addresses, combined with a last-minute fight with a handful of senators over whether to allow the arming of merchant ships, had the effect of making the inaugural a relatively unimportant speech in a very important time.

In the first of these addresses, Wilson spoke to the Senate on possible peace terms in Europe and outlined his continued hope for a brokered "peace without victory."[10] As Edward House, his aide and alter-ego later noted, the inaugural was essentially "a replica" of this address, offering in less detail the same goals and basic principles that were explained to the Senate.[11] The last two speeches dealt with the immediate crisis caused by the German decision to target American merchant shipping. On February 3 Wilson notified the Congress that he had suspended diplomatic relations with the German government because of its refusal to honor naval rules of notification with regard to the attack of nonarmed vessels. Facing stark evidence that American neutrality would be sabotaged by more submarine attacks on merchant ships, he sought to invoke international law as a protection for the movement of American goods in European waters.[12] Combined with newspaper stories about war preparations, these addresses to an increasingly restless Congress made conflict seem to be only a matter of time.

But it was actually the third speech, on February 26, that had the effect of making the inaugural only a short pause in what was now a steady march toward a declaration of war. In response to Germany's decision to define all shipping as fair game for its highly effective submarine fleet, Wilson proposed legislation to arm merchant vessels. The armed shipping bill, he explained, would equip these vessels with "defensive" artillery and some naval crews: "No one doubts what it is our duty to do. We must defend our commerce and the lives of our people in the midst of the present trying circumstances."[13] The House quickly agreed. But a vocal minority in the Senate (Robert La Follette, William Borah, and others) filibustered against the legislation. Although seventy-five members supported the bill, twelve isolationists—aided by generous Senate rules for stopping legislative action—were enough to prevent final approval. Thus, just one day before his inauguration, Wilson faced a legislative crisis that presaged his effort to win Senate approval for the League of Nations. When the Senate adjourned without acting on the armed shipping bill, it was a moment of high political drama, intensified by an uncharacteristically angry statement issued by the White House:

In the immediate presence of a crisis fraught with more subtle and far-reaching possibilities of national danger than any other the government has known within the whole history of its international relations, the Congress has been unable to act either to safeguard the country or to vindicate the elementary rights of its citizens. . . .

A little group of willful men, representing no opinion but their own, have rendered the great government of the United States helpless and contemptible.[14]

The beginning of Wilson's second term occurred in the shadow of these fast-moving events. The American public was all too aware of the coming war with Germany and the strains it would place on their daily lives. Contemporary accounts of the inaugural were colored by the gloomy anticipation of an impending disaster. In the words of one newspaper account, Wilson's inauguration was "not a festival; it was a momentary interlude in a grave business":

Doubtless there will be accounts written of this inauguration in which well-meaning writers will use, from the best of motives, the old phrases about the enthusiasm of this crowd, about great demonstrations. . . . But there is no reason of patriotism for suppressing the truth, since the truth is one to do credit and not discredit to the patriotism of the people, and the truth is that there were no demonstrations, no torrents of applause, no happy, irresponsible enthusiasm. The crowd's mood reflected the feeling of the Government, and the Government is in no holiday mood.[15]

Extant copies of the address indicate that Wilson followed his usual practice in preparing this message. He wrote an early first draft in shorthand, neatly double-spaced on the wide lines of a writing tablet. He then edited his ideas and prepared a final printed reading copy. He also continued his habit of reading the message to a trusted friend or political leader. In this case, two days before the inauguration, Edward House listened to the president read through the message.[16] If there was any change from past practice, it is perhaps found in the extent to which Wilson went back to recent congressional messages for his general ideas and themes. The prospect of war apparently encouraged him to view the message as a recapitulation of the political conditions that he believed could still prevent U.S. participation in the war. Rather than a celebration, therefore, it was a grim summary of "the things we shall stand for, whether in war or in peace."

Wilson spoke near the east front of the Capitol building in the early afternoon of a cold and windy day. Newspapers estimated the crowd at nearly fifty thousand. Most had come to witness what was actually the second swearing-in ceremony, duplicating what had already taken place inside the Capitol. Few of those attending would actually hear the address. As the *New York Times* recorded, many began to leave "as soon as the President began his inaudible speech."[17] Public address systems and reliable radio broadcasts were still several years in the future. Some newspapers reprinted the whole twenty-minute address, while others included extensive extracts.

THE INVESTITURE SPEECH

Wilson began his address by noting that the occasion demanded that "this is not that time for retrospect."[18] The domestic reforms of his first administration "to correct the grosser errors and abuses of our industrial life, liberate and quicken the processes of our national genius and energy" would not be reviewed in this speech.[19] Now "other matters have more and more forced themselves upon our attention" even "despite our wish to keep free of them." Threats of economic sanctions by the British and attacks on merchant vessels by Germany now made the European war a reality even for official neutrals:

The war inevitably set its mark from the first alike upon our minds, our industries, our commerce, our politics, and our social action. To be indifferent to it or independent of it was out of the question. And yet, all the while we have been conscious that we were not part of it. In that consciousness, despite many divisions, we have drawn closer together.

Part of the unitary theme of a common closeness binding Americans together built on the increasing sense of national outrage at German attacks on American neutrality. Wilson echoed this anger but tempered it with a call for reasoned action rather than a military response:

We have been deeply wronged upon the sea, but we have not wished to wrong or injure in return; have retained throughout the consciousness of standing in some sort apart, intent upon an interest that transcended the immediate issues of the war itself. As some of the injuries done us have become intolerable we have still been clear that we wished nothing for ourselves that we were not ready to demand for all mankind—fair dealing, justice, the freedom to live and be at ease against organized wrong.

Wilson went on to remind Americans that "we stand firm in armed neutrality" while seeking a way to "vindicate and fortify peace." But at the same time he alluded to the increasingly clear prospect of American involvement in the war, a reality that would become official in less than a month's time:

We have been obliged to arm ourselves to make good our claim to a certain minimum of right and of freedom of action. . . . We may even be drawn on, by circumstances, not by our own purpose or desire, to a more active assertion of our rights as we see them and a more immediate association with the great struggle itself.

Shaking off the long period of isolationism that became discredited with each new attack on American shipping, Wilson predicted the coming American century: "We are provincials no longer. The tragical events of the thirty months of vital turmoil through which we have just passed have made us citizens of the world."

As in earlier addresses throughout and after the campaign, Wilson attempted to give an idealized American perspective to a war that, like most others, had its origins in far more obscure factional differences. He used the remainder of his remarks to restate what he had described in more detail in a recent Senate speech: to assure listeners that American participation would be governed by an "unselfish purpose" and certain high "principles in which we have been bred." Although they had been ignored by the belligerents for years, he enumerated the political principles that he hoped would guide diplomacy and the search for peace in 1917:

That all nations are equally interested in the peace of the world and the political stability of free peoples, and equally responsible for their maintenance;

That the essential principle of peace is the equality of nations in all matters of right or privilege;

That peace cannot securely or justly rest upon an armed balance of power;

That governments derive all their just powers from the consent of the governed and that no other powers should be supported by the common thought, purpose, or power of the family of nations;

That the seas should be equally free and safe for the use of all peoples, under rules set up by common agreement and consent . . . ;

That national armaments should be limited to the necessities of national order and domestic safety;

That the community of interest . . . imposes upon each nation the duty of seeing to it that all influences proceeding from its own citizens meant to encourage or assist revolution in other States should be sternly and effectually suppressed and prevented.

Wilson ended by asking for the prayers and support of the nation. This ritual expression of humility predictably linked him to the American public and the deity: "I pray God I may be given the wisdom and the prudence to do my duty in the true spirit of this great people. I am their servant and can succeed only as they sustain and guide me by their confidence and counsel." But it was also a political necessity in a nation that had both a long tradition of isolationism and a history that meant that many of its citizens would retain allegiances to their European roots:

We are being forced into a new unity amidst the fires that now blaze throughout the world. In their ardent heat we shall, in God's providence, let us hope, be purged of faction and division, purified of the errant humours of party and private interest, and shall stand forth in the days to come with a new dignity of national pride and spirit.

"For myself," he closed, "I beg your tolerance, your countenance, and your united aid. The shadows that now lie dark upon our path will soon be dispelled and we shall walk with the light all about us."

THE RHETORICAL SIGNATURE OF A DYING CIVIC CULTURE

Reflecting what social theorist Richard Sennett describes as a distinctly eighteenth-century conception of the obligations of a public figure, Wilson presented himself to the American public as a national visionary, while at the same time excluding the public as much as possible from the private world of his family and his feelings.[20] He was careful to keep his emotions inside or to use them sparingly as instruments in service to his political agenda. The jocularity that presidents today cultivate with members of the press or other political colleagues would have been utterly alien to Wilson, not because he was a humorless man but because he believed that the presidency carried a special kind of moral authority. The remnants of this view are still part of the legacy and tradition of the office, but they are far less central to the modern occupants, who are generally more comfortable with the pluralism of contemporary political life. Even in 1917, events conspired to challenge Wilson's faith in knowledge and reason—what he often called "the right"—as the basis for political consensus.

Scholars such as Elmer Cornwell and Jeffrey Tulis have credited Wilson with giving the modern presidency a number of rhetorical and public relations innovations.[21] They are partially right. But the Second Inaugural also illustrates the passing of an older and ultimately doomed portrayal of American civic culture. Wilson's later addresses—including the inaugural and those thoughtful speeches delivered in the course of his fateful attempt to win U.S. participation in the League of Nations— represent more of an idealized set of beliefs about the American community than presidents in touch with the realpolitik of modern life would want to profess. Ironically, most inaugurals to this day still retain the rhetorical style of this older culture, represented frequently in the spacious public rhetoric that evolved between the Civil War and World War I.[22] In these addresses we often find ritual expressions of singular purpose, unchallengeable principle, and the enactment of natural destiny. We also expect them to embrace the idea of an American community that shares a common faith about what will serve the public good.[23] The difference with Wilson was that he not only used the outlines of this celebratory rhetoric, but he firmly acted on them as well. He continued to employ images of a nation linked by a culture of deeply shared experiences and values.

Given these natural political and rhetorical instincts, the period of the Second Inaugural caught Wilson in a bind that a more eclectic leader might have been able to ignore. The war outstripped his ability to invent new rhetorical initiatives or to educate the public about issues of his own choice. In this setting at this critical time, it was not possible to use the presidency as Wilson wished it to be: an instrument for carrying the nation in the direction reason and principle dictate that it must go. The Calvinist certainty about the "spirit" and "high purpose of the nation" that had served Wilson well through much of his political life had no easy outlet on the eve of a declaration of war.

As the well-known author of *Congressional Government* and other books on American political life, Wilson was a shrewd observer of the structural and cultural roots of American pluralism. He understood how the separation of powers between the chief executive, the legislature, and the courts would create different political constituencies and represent various kinds of factions. And this practiced debate coach was hardly naive about the difficulties of reaching consensus on issues of great complexity.[24] But his rhetoric was continually premised on a set of political values that he took to be more or less universal and unchallengeable in American life. Part of this belief has its roots in a kind of religious certainty that makes public life a calling to serve the right that already exists in the American spirit. "There is," Wilson once wrote, "a very holy and very terrible isolation for the conscience of every man who seeks to read the destiny in affairs for others as well as himself, for nation as well as for individuals. . . . That lonely search for the spirit of the right perhaps no man can assist."[25] For a president, the nation's voices must "unite in his understanding in a single meaning and reveal to him a single vision, so that he can speak what no man else knows, the common meaning of the common voice."[26]

In the years that followed Wilson's presidency, political philosophers such as John Dewey and Walter Lippmann conceded the existence of a banal kind of political uniformity, but they also expressed doubts about the older civic discourse of national purpose that presumed the existence of a public living in what Dewey described as a singular "Great Community."[27] In 1955 Lippmann expressed what is now the modern non-Wilsonian view of American civil life, even as he decried it:

In the prevailing popular culture all philosophies are the instruments of some man's purpose, all truths are self-centered and self-regarding, and all principles are the rationalizations of some special interest. There is no public criterion of the true and the false, of the right and the wrong, beyond that which the preponderant mass of voters, consumers, readers, and listeners happen to be supposed to want.[28]

Evidence of Wilson's deep faith in the civic culture of the great community is revealed in the Second Inaugural. The requirements of the setting are such that even the most cynical victor would be impelled to find a true public philosophy to articulate.[29] But what suggests that Wilson's inaugural style is genuinely more reflective of his deepest convictions is that there are similar appeals to principle in virtually all of Wilson's public rhetoric. "From his youth," biographer John Morton Blum noted, "he had determined to find principles by which men might justly order their affairs; he had wished to articulate in poetic periods his noble ideals, to identify himself with them, and govern for them."[30] In a pattern that is evident in many of Wilson's addresses, administrative policy flows from principled starting points—"the things we shall stand for"—in an unambiguous progression. "We shall be the more American if we but remain true to the principles in which we have been bred," among them, as they are listed in this address and others throughout the war period: freedom of the seas, nonintervention in the affairs of other nations, a deep antimilitarism, and faith in democratically elected governments. Thus the unitary pronoun *we* appears over thirty times in the Second Inaugural, often paired with descriptions (six times) of particular "principles" and "purposes" (seven times). Wilson talked of the "principle of peace" as a self-evident given and one of "the principles of a liberated mankind." "I need not argue these principles to you . . . ," he noted, "they are your own, part and parcel of your own thinking and your own motive in affairs. They spring up native amongst us."

This is not to suggest that Wilson's standards for action were necessarily higher than his predecessors' or that he had a vision of the nation that was superior to those of the pragmatists who have since inherited the office. What made Wilson one of the last carriers of this style was his deep belief that the politics of a national and international community—what we might today call the politics of inclusion—had a desirable and certain inevitability. Forceful and eloquent presidential leadership, he assumed, would eventually allow reason to prevail.

In some cases, his faith was clearly misplaced and idealized, particularly before and after the war. Not only did he misjudge the need to compromise with the Senate over the League of Nations treaty, but he also seemed to underestimate the value of conflict for states competing for dominance on the same continent. Even Wilson's most sympathetic biographer, Ray Stannard Baker, concedes that he missed the difference between the ostensible ideals of an individual state and its sometimes less honorable practical interests:

Wilson continually made the mistake of assuming that the chief end the belligerents sought was a just and durable peace. He himself took the better world order, which he was now passionately advocating, to be the highest goal. The Allies did not. The Central Powers did not. They only sought military victory: they had far-reaching material purposes, some of them outspoken, others still concealed by undeclared secret treaties.[31]

It is Wilson's failure to recognize the limitations imposed upon him by these disparate interests that turned the Second Inaugural into the first act of an unfolding tragedy. The better impulses of a leader who envisioned peace without an "armed balance of power" were fated to be swept aside by nationalist dogmas he could understand but not accept.

NOTES

1. Woodrow Wilson, Second Inaugural Address, March 5, 1917, in *The Papers of Woodrow Wilson*, ed. Arthur S. Link (Princeton, N.J.: Princeton University Press, 1983), 14: 334.

2. Ray Stannard Baker, *Woodrow Wilson: Life and Letters* (Westport, Conn.: Greenwood Press, 1968), 6: 505–506.

3. J. M. Winter, *The Experience of World War I* (New York: Oxford University Press, 1989), 140.

4. Baker, *Woodrow Wilson*, 329–30.

5. For analyses of this campaign, see S. D. Lovell, *The Presidential Election of 1916* (Carbondale: Southern Illinois University Press, 1980), and Arthur S. Link and William M. Leary Jr., "Election of 1916," in *The Coming to Power: Critical Presidential Elections in American History*, ed. Arthur M. Schlesinger Jr. (New York: Chelsea House, 1971), 296–321.

6. Baker, *Woodrow Wilson*, 507.

7. Wilson quoted in Erwin C. Hargrove, *Presidential Leadership: Personality and Political Life* (New York: Macmillan, 1966), 34.

8. Baker, *Woodrow Wilson*, 506–7.

9. Ibid., 490.

10. Woodrow Wilson, Address to the Senate, January 22, 1917, in *Papers*, 40: 533–39.

11. Edward House, From the Diary of Colonel House, March 3, 1917, in *Papers*, 41: 317.

12. Woodrow Wilson, An Address to a Joint Session of Congress, February 3, 1917, in *Papers*, 41: 108–12.

13. Woodrow Wilson, An Address to a Joint Session of Congress, February 26, 1917, in *Papers*, 41: 283–87.

14. Woodrow Wilson, A Statement, March 4, 1917, in *Papers*, 41: 318–20.

15. "50,000 See Wilson Inaugurated Again," *New York Times*, March 6, 1917, 3.

16. See Dayton McKean, "Woodrow Wilson," in *A History and Criticism of American Public Addresses*, ed. William Norwood Brigance (New York: Russell and Russell, 1960), 981–82; Woodrow Wilson, Inaugural Address, in *Papers*, 41: 336; Edward House, Diary, in *Papers*, 41: 317.

17. "50,000 See Wilson Inaugurated Again," 3.

18. Woodrow Wilson, Second Inaugural Address, in *Papers*, 41: 332–35. All subsequent references are from this source, which is reproduced from a printed reading copy located in the Wilson Papers, Library of Congress.

19. The president demonstrated some modesty here. His domestic accomplishments in his first term were considerable, including the modernization of the banking system and the adoption of tough antitrust laws. Wilson also won support for much of the progressive agenda involving a broad range of social and economic reforms with the support of a wide coalition of party regulars and activists. See, for example, John Morton Blum, *Woodrow Wilson and the Politics of Morality* (Boston: Little, Brown, 1956), 69–83.

20. Richard Sennett, *The Fall of a Public Man* (New York: Vintage, 1978), 259–87.

21. See Elmer E. Cornwell, Jr., *Presidential Leadership of Public Opinion* (Bloomington: Indiana University Press, 1965), 31–60, and Jeffrey K. Tulis, *The Rhetorical Presidency* (Princeton, N.J.: Princeton University Press, 1987), 117–36.

22. In *The Ethics of Rhetoric* (Chicago: Henry Regnery, 1953), Richard Weaver discusses a "spaciousness of old rhetoric"—largely political rhetoric from the 1800s—that matches many of the traits found in Wilson's public comments. "The orator then enjoyed a privilege which can be compared to the lawyer's 'right of assumption.' This is the right to assume that precedents are valid, that form will persist, and that in general one may build today on what was created yesterday. What mankind has sanctified with usage has a presumption in its favor. Such presumption, it was felt, instead of being an obstacle to progress, furnishes the ground of progress. . . . Accordingly, consider the American orator in the intellectual climate of this time. He was comfortably circumstanced with reference to things he could 'know' and presume everyone else to know in the same way" (169).

23. A related but different kind of transcendent public philosophy is described by Dante Germino in *The Inaugural Addresses of American Presidents* (Lanham, Md.: University Press of America, 1984), 1–14. By reference to the "older civic culture" I mean a rhetorical style predicated on an epistemic certainty and on a faith in reason and ultimate agreement about many events and principles.

24. Hardin Craig, "Woodrow Wilson as an Orator," *Quarterly Journal of Speech* 38 (April 1952): 145–46.

25. Wilson quoted in Arthur Beron Tourtellot, *The Presidents on the Presidency* (Garden City, N.Y.: Doubleday, 1964), 365.

26. Wilson quoted in Tulis, *Rhetorical Presidency*, 135.

27. John Dewey, *The Public and Its Problems* (Chicago: Swallow Press, 1954), 142.

28. Walter Lippmann, *The Public Philosophy* (Boston: Little, Brown, 1955), 114.

29. An exception may be Ronald Reagan's 1980 inaugural address, which

partly excludes a positive role for government. "In the present [economic] crisis," he noted, "government is not the solution to our problem; government *is* the problem." See Paul D. Erickson, *Reagan Speaks: The Making of an American Myth* (New York: New York University Press, 1985), 140.

30. Blum, *Woodrow Wilson*, 4.

31. Baker, *Woodrow Wilson*, 357.

Chapter Five

President Warren G. Harding's Inaugural Address, 1921

John T. Morello

After almost eight years of Woodrow Wilson's administration, a nation that stood ready to forget the horrors of war and that was tired of idealistic crusades to make the world safe for democracy, heard a candidate for the presidency proclaim that America's greatest need was "not nostrums, but normalcy."[1] Many Americans in 1920 found comfort in the pleas for a return to normal life. "And when the Republicans managed to simultaneously convert . . . 'normalcy' into a synonym for prosperity and an antonym for Wilsonism, they became invincible."[2] Riding a near tidal wave of support, Warren G. Harding claimed victory with the largest percentage of the popular vote of any previous presidential election.

It was perhaps fitting that the appeal for "normalcy" came from a man whose oratorical style epitomized nineteenth-century eloquence. Harding's oral language suited his frequent stump speeches in small-town Ohio locations, his lectures under the billowing Chautauqua tent, and his ceremonial addresses on public holidays.[3] While immensely successful with these audiences, Harding's rhetoric often struck more urbane critics as overcooked.[4] William G. McAdoo derided Harding's "big bow wow style of oratory," full of "rolling words which had no application to the topic at hand. . . . His speeches left the impression of an army of pompous phrases moving over the landscape in search of an idea."[5] Contemporary pundit-at-large and tireless Harding-basher H. L. Mencken was much irritated by the vapidness of the style he labeled "Gamaliese."[6] Harding, on the other hand, boasted of his ability to "bloviate."[7]

As critics saw it, the inaugural address of the twenty-ninth president was full of bloviation. Official newspaper reaction was positive if restrained. The *New York Times* while admitting that the address did not fall below expectations, rated it only average.[8] Later critics have been less supportive, calling the language of the speech "archaic,"[9] "solemn and ponderous,"[10] "banal,"[11] and "vague."[12] And yet the public liked the speech: "Harding made in general a favorable impression. . . . There were frequent nods of approval and now and then a burst of instant applause or an emphatic 'that's good.' "[13] The speech captured the average citizen's mood and easily attracted support[14] because it was "a fit vehicle for sentiment of the kind dear to a million American firesides."[15] To a nation ready for soothing platitudes,[16] Harding's inaugural succeeded by enabling men and women to hear in the expressions of the president some of their own ideas.[17]

Attention to the language expressing these comforting ideas has focused almost exclusively on the inaugural's uniquely polysyllabic style, on its repetition of platitudes, and on its several grammatical errors. Despite the validity of these criticisms, exclusive attention to its lack of clarity and accuracy overlooks significant features of this speech as revealed through its language. Close examination of the wording of the address, and especially to changes Harding made, affords an interesting glimpse into the state of his thinking on two issues. First, the development of the address shows Harding's unmistakable movement away from his professed goal of encouraging American participation in an international organization for peace. Second, Harding's conception of the role of the president reflects not the nineteenth-century view expected of the man who called William McKinley one of his heroes but the emerging doctrine of the rhetorical presidency. While Theodore Roosevelt and Wilson have been credited with elevating mass appeal, or popular rhetoric, to a position of prominence in the presidential arsenal of instruments for governing, Harding's contribution to the philosophy of leadership by popular will has been overlooked.

THE PRODUCTION OF THE SPEECH

No detailed accounts of the speech's composition exist, and the few isolated references to its development cloak the question of authorship in some confusion.[18] Harding employed speech writers, but he frequently, including on important occasions, did much of the writing himself.[19] Charles E. Hard, assistant secretary to Harding during his presidency, described Harding's approach to composing his speeches in some detail. Although his comments do not imply that the president worked in the same fashion on the inaugural address, the significance of the occasion leads one to conclude that he might have. Generally, for "important speeches," Harding wrote initial longhand drafts (usually in pencil) on "a big pad." After these drafts were typed, he reviewed them and wrote corrections on the typed pages. When he finished the editing, the last draft was sent to a public printer, and copies were made for distribution on the day of the speech. He typically labored well into the night while writing his speeches.[20] Regardless of the amount of personal energy Harding devoted to the scripting of his speeches, the fact remains that many of the ideas contained in them resulted from consultation, collaboration, and compromise with advisers and other trusted confidants. But, even if Harding absorbed from others some of the thoughts contained in his speeches, he expressed them in a style that was unmistakably his own.[21]

An examination of the various inaugural manuscripts in the Harding Papers sheds some light on the manner in which Harding put the stamp of his mind on the address. Four versions of the address exist: three are typescripts with handwritten notations and changes, and the fourth is a fine-printed copy marked, "Released Friday, March 4th, at noon, Eastern Standard Time, unless hereafter notification of a change is given." On two of the drafts, notations appear in Harding's handwriting.[22] A third typescript is marked as "possibly a preliminary draft of [the] inaugural address." The fine-printed copy of the speech includes no notations other than numbers from 1 to 19 at various places in the gutter to the left of the blocks of type.[23]

The typescript marked as a possible preliminary draft is obviously the earliest version, and I refer to it here as "first draft." This embryonic eight-page text includes several paragraphs that survive to the final copy, though in much-revised form. Its style is plain and devoid of many of the figures of speech found in the subsequent versions, thus raising the possibility that Harding did not write this draft. Nevertheless, the circumstantial evidence of textual emendations supports the view than this unadorned first draft was probably Harding's work, and its style merely reflects the early state of his thinking. On the last page of the speech appears a note "for Senator Harding" reminding him of the source and complete line of the "all's right with the world" quotation included in the conclusion of this and all other versions of the inaugural text. Also, squiggly lines are located in the lefthand margin next to portions of two paragraphs. The portions of the text so marked are deleted from the next draft. In the subsequent drafts that bear Harding's handwriting, identical markings occur.

The second draft is a typed copy titled "Inaugural Address." It contains extensive revisions in Harding's hand, and all of these changes are incorporated into type on the next version, the third draft, also titled "Inaugural Address." On the third draft appear additional, but fewer, corrections in Harding's writing. These few corrections are included in the fine-printed version that was the final text. Although many of the speeches attributed to Harding are of "uncertain origin,"[24] the inaugural address expressed Harding's thoughts, even if it cannot be proved he developed those ideas entirely without help.

HARDING'S DWINDLING COMMITMENT TO AN INTERNATIONAL ORGANIZATION

Wilson had declared the election of 1920 a great and solemn referendum on the League of Nations. Democratic candidate James Cox endorsed American entry into the League without reservation. Republican candidate Harding waffled; he condemned "the Wilson League of Nations" and simultaneously supported a "world court"[25] or "an association with the other nations of the world under which each may be free to express and maintain its own nationalism,"[26] adding the cautionary note, "I shall not risk embarrassing the final solution of a problem so momentous by undertaking to lay down advance specific details or plans."[27] The solemn referendum thus appeared to involve a choice between *the* League and *a* league.

Harding's straddling of the issue earned him some retrospective praise for a shrewd political maneuver. The Republican party was badly split on the League issue, with opinions running the gamut from pro-Leaguers through reservationists to irreconcilable opponents. Somehow the presidential candidate had to fashion a durable if fragile harmony out of this discordant chorus. Despite the ambiguity of Harding's position, his strategy unified the factions of the party and kept the campaign intact.[28]

Harding believed in the consistency of his campaign position and failed to understand the public turmoil over it.[29] But was he serious about establishing an international association of nations after he took office? Studies of the Harding presidency have not determined whether his advocacy of an international league was a sincere policy objective or just an expedient campaign pledge.[30] The development of the inaugural address sheds some interesting light on that subject. As his ideas progress from the first to final draft, Harding's opposition to the League gains more forceful expression, while his advocacy of an alternative international organization becomes increasingly ambiguous.

Diction Changes

In the first draft, Harding clearly had Wilson's League in mind as he wrote, "This country cannot depart from its traditional policy of non-involvement in European affairs except as its conscience and judgment in each instance may determine" (1213). In the second draft, Harding's opposition was strengthened: "The recorded progress of our republic in itself, materially and spiritually, proves the wisdom of the inherited policy of non-involvement in European affairs" (1187). *Inherited* attributes a more forceful historical warrant to the policy of noninvolvement than the adjective *traditional* does. With this change, Harding simultaneously evoked the memory of past presidents and suggested that his expression of opposition to the League had been literally handed down and must not be disavowed, in much the same way that one would be expected to honor the bequest of a friend or relative.

On the second draft, Harding replaced *European* with *old world*. This change appears in type on the third draft (1198) and in print on the final version (1221). *Old world* attaches a more negative connotation to the business of the League than *European* does, especially given Harding's references to America as "new world" and his frequent use of *progress* and *genius* when describing the United States. Harding gradually excised all references to Europe so that the only nation-state named in the final address is America—a fact that ultimately did not impress many European observers.[31]

Another important diction change occurred in the section of the speech where Harding justified his position against involvement in the League. In the first draft, the sentence immediately after the declaration of non-involvement read this way: "It [this country] can be a party to no military alliance, it can enter into no political commitment, it can assume no economic obligation that will subject the nation's choice and will as to vital interests or constitutional prerogatives to the decision of any other than its own authority" (1213). By the second draft, this sentence had been greatly changed and occurred later in the speech: "But America, our America, the America built on the foundation laid by the inspired fathers, can be a party to no military alliance. It can enter into no political commitments, it can assume no economic obligations which will subject our decisions to any other than our own authority" (1187). The addition of the phrase "foundation laid by the inspired fathers" was particularly noteworthy. Here Harding reminded his audience of the founding fathers' last will and testament by recalling the words of George Washington's Farewell Address. This *argumentum ad verecundiam* appropriated a sentiment often invoked at family funerals—show praise for the dead by acting as they would like us to act—to justify noninvolvement in the League.

The only other reference to the League in the first draft comes two paragraphs after the statement about noninvolvement, following an intervening paragraph in which Harding pledges his support for an international association of nations. The paragraph begins: "It is in this way [an association of nations] that we are likely best to serve the cause of world peace." The text continues: "With no interest or design in European affairs other than the common advantage which comes from international relation, the United States desires to remain a great moral force cherishing ideals of justice and peace and encouraging the nations of the world to agree when differences threaten" (1214). This paragraph underwent radical surgery on the second draft. The claim that an association of nations best serves the cause of world peace is cut out altogether. The promise to remain a "moral force cherishing the ideals of justice and peace and encouraging the nations of the world to agree" becomes just an aspiration to "a high place in the moral leadership of civilization." The sentence occurs later in the speech, apart from any discussion of international organization. This shift in the location of the pledge served to mute further the commitment to an international organization. The originally straightforward pledge of disinterest in European affairs became, in the second draft, an appeal for disengagement that was the first applause-line of the speech: "We do not mean to be entangled" (1187).[32] Only minor changes are made from the wording of this portion of the speech in subsequent revisions.

Harding's increasingly hard anti-League line was joined by a corresponding softening of the support for some other sort of international organization. The only reference to Harding's view of an international association in the first draft occurs early in the speech, and its objectives were remarkably clear given that they emanated from a man who had earlier avowed that he did not wish to be specific about his plan:

We stand ready to encourage, if need be to initiate, an association of nations for the codification of international law, for the consideration of a world court to decide international questions of a justiciable character, for the appointment of commissions to investigate questions that threaten war to the end of enlightening public opinion as to the issues involved and for the examination of any other measures that may be agreed upon by the nations to lessen the probability of war. (1213)

By the second draft, Harding's vision of his association of nations had clouded:

We are ready to associate ourselves with the nations of the world, great and small, for conference, for counsel; to seek the expressed views of world opinion; to recommend a way to approximate disarmament and relieve the crushing burdens of military and naval establishments. We choose to join in suggesting plans for mediation, conciliation, and arbitration, and would gladly join in that expressed conscience of progress, which seeks to clarify and write the laws of international relationship and establish a world court for the disposition of such justiciable questions as nations are agreed to submit thereto. (1187–88)

The pledge to encourage, "if need be initiate," an association of nations became mere readiness to associate. And the tasks appropriate for such organization have dwindled: International law will not be "codified," it will be clarified and written; justiciable questions may now only be submitted to the world court when nations agree to do so; and the promise to establish commissions to investigate the conditions that threaten war has vanished. In its place are vague invitations for conference, counsel, mediation, arbitration, and conciliation with no mention of the issues suitable for such action. Instead of seeking to avert war, Harding hopes only to "approximate" disarmament. The third draft finishes the weakening of Harding's pledge as he changes "choose to join in" to "elect to participate in."

Wording changes in the inaugural thus clearly show Harding moving toward stronger condemnation of the League and away from enthusiastic endorsement of an alternative association of nations—attitudes reinforced by alterations in the organization of the address.

Dispositional Changes

Revisions of the speech reveal an organizational strategy that further muffled Harding's call for American participation in a league of nations. Although the general disposition of this speech is best characterized as elusive, the section dealing with international organization has an apparent method. Harding sandwiched claims of support for international association between reminders of the importance of American national sovereignty. The organizational approach, not present in the first draft, takes shape in the second draft and remains in all subsequent versions of the speech.

In the first draft, Harding offered his statement of the traditional policy of noninvolvement (paragraph 3 of the text) followed by the paragraph outlining the broad goals of his conception of an international association and another paragraph articulating for the United States a desire to encourage the nations of the world to agree on actions to avert hostilities when war threatened. Next, Harding advanced his international perspective by talking about South America. "In seeking accord among nations," he said, "our first concern must be to strengthen good will in the Western Continent." In two paragraphs, Harding mentioned the importance of strong ties between the United States and South American nations, ending with a call to "send the best we have in men and resources" and asking "of them . . . only that stability and security upon which close intercourse depend" (1215). After this statement, the original draft shifted attention to domestic affairs. Discussion of involvement in international affairs thus ends positively.

In the second draft, the development of the section of the speech concerning international relations changed. Pledges of involvement in international association were surrounded by reminders that the United

States must not relinquish the right to determine its own destiny in foreign affairs. Thus, in paragraph 3 of the second draft, Harding identified the "inherited policy of non-involvement." In the next paragraph, he noted "the new order of the world, the closer contacts which progress has wrought" (1187). But then he quickly added the reminder that the United States can enter into no agreements subjecting decisions to any other authority than its own.

Following his paean to national sovereignty, Harding again expressed interest in making nations that would resort to "national warfare prove the righteousness of their cause or stand as outlaws before the bar of civilization" (1187). This hope, offered in the fifth paragraph of the second draft, is followed by the paragraph in which Harding stated readiness to associate with the other nations of the world for conference, counsel, and conciliation. But that announcement was followed by the reminder that "every commitment must be made in the exercise of our national sovereignty" (1188). After all, Harding concluded, the exercise of sovereignty was "patriotic confidence in the things which made us what we are" (1188).

In the next paragraph of the second draft, Harding stated that his emphasis on the importance of national sovereignty did not mean the United States would ignore "the aspirations of human kind" (1188). He next noted that the recent election expressed what Americans intended should be the result "of a suggested change in national policy, where internationality was to supersede nationality" (1188). Still not done, in the ninth paragraph, Harding stated again readiness to participate in "any seemly program likely to lessen the probability of war" (1189). But then he concluded that "a maintained America . . . [is] not only an inspiration and example, but the highest agency of strengthening goodwill and promoting accord on both continents" (1189).

In the new organizational structure of the second draft, each mention of American involvement in an international association of nations occurs between statements of the importance of national sovereignty or testaments to the significance of the American example. These dispositional features remain in each subsequent version of the text, and only minor changes in wording occur. While still expressing support for international association, Harding repeatedly emphasized the primacy of American objectives.

Immediate reaction to the inaugural's passages on international association interpreted his remarks as either the final nail on the coffin for U.S. participation in the League or an interest in seeking some other international association.[33] One later comment on the differences between Wilson and Harding's rhetoric on the question of international organization suggested that a "careful study might show that the difference between Wilson's insistence upon the United States joining the world and Harding's invitation for the world to join the United States were variations on a theme rather than opposing positions."[34] The preceding examination of the development of Harding's inaugural reveals not only considerable variation from Wilson's approach but movement away from strong support for American involvement in an association of nations.

As Wilson had realized, the success of an international organization rested on the degree to which nations could willingly transcend national interest. Without that commitment, any league of nations was little more than a house of cards. The international moral consciousness necessary for such an association, which was yet to be created, would be endangered by rhetoric emphasizing a willingness to participate only on terms that did not jeopardize American sovereignty.[35] Thus, the arguments Harding emphasized when pronouncing his interest in developing an international association were grounded on a premise (national sovereignty) that ran contrary to internationalism. Four times in the inaugural, Harding referred to the importance of the United States controlling its national interest in international affairs; on nine occasions, he offered the United States as an example that the rest of the world ought to emulate. Could there be any viable international association if other countries, following our "example," agreed to join only if they controlled their sovereignty as well? Harding's inaugural rhetoric not only departed from Wilson's, but it also emphasized the very appeal Wilson thought would undermine the prospect for creating a league of nations.[36]

Harding said his inaugural would be brief and would only outline ideas he planned to develop more thoroughly in his addresses to Congress.[37] Even if much of his address recited adherence to abstract goals few people would find objectionable, on the matter of international association, his rhetoric clearly moved in a direction against the League and toward less definite support for an alternative association. In declaring his objectives with respect to international organization, Harding behaved not merely as a ceremonial orator expressing ideas for audience contemplation but as a leader enunciating a position as a prelude to action.

HARDING'S INAUGURAL AND THE
RHETORICAL PRESIDENCY

"Since the presidencies of Theodore Roosevelt and Woodrow Wilson," wrote James Ceaser and his colleagues, "popular or mass rhetoric has become the principal tool of presidential governance."[38] Indeed, Wilson "gave the Inaugural Address (and presidential speech generally) a new theme. Instead of showing how the policies of the incoming administration reflected the principles of our form of government, Wilson sought to articulate the unspoken desires of the people by holding out a vision of their fulfillment."[39] In the twentieth century, the inaugural address was no longer an occasion for a discussion of the meaning of the Constitution. Only half of the inaugurals delivered in this century even mention the word, and none of them contains an extended analysis of the meaning of the Constitution.[40]

Theodore Roosevelt often referred to the presidency as his "bully pulpit," and Wilson saw the president as the chief interpreter of the desires of the hearts of the masses. Thus, leadership in mobilizing the will of the public was central to the rhetorical doctrine envisioned by these two presidents. Through popular appeal, the president could move an intransigent Congress by going to the people.

While Harding campaigned for a return to "normalcy," his inaugural is not typical of nineteenth-century addresses but instead fits the emerging mode of popular rhetoric. Constitutional discussion was absent. In the final version of the address, the Constitution is mentioned only twice: once as "organic law" and once in a reference to "constitutional freedom" (1221). In neither case, nor elsewhere in the speech, did Harding discuss the meaning of the Constitution or express how his administration would interpret the constitutional authority of the presidency. Rather, he focused squarely on what he perceived to be the will of the people as expressed in his election to office.

But unlike his predecessors, the popular appeal of Harding's rhetoric was grounded not in a desire to mold public opinion but in his commitment to lead by giving voice to the will of the public. Harding, in fact, minimized the significance of the presidency while emphasizing the power and force of popular opinion as the engine of government action. Harding mentioned the office of president only once (as "the Executive") and only at the very end of the speech. It is again only at the end (when he at last mentions the oath of office) that he acclaims himself installed as leader of the people. The great majority of the pronoun references in the speech underscore the importance of the people and that Harding is but one of them.[41] One hundred thirty-three times in the speech, Harding unified himself with the people by mentioning what they hold in common: calls to "we," "our," and "us" emphasized this unity. Only twenty-two times did Harding refer to himself in the first person, and on most of these occasions he asked his audience for permission to carry out their will. He said, among other self-references, that "I would like to" and "I would rejoice" and "I earnestly hope." Harding intended to lead popular will by reflecting it. Government's authority—and Harding was quite clear about this—derived from popular sentiment. He pledged "an administration wherein all the agencies of Government are called to serve, and ever promote an understanding of government purely as an expression of popular will" (1221).

His position on involvement in international organizations affords the clearest enunciation of popular will as the grounds for government action:

> The success of our popular government rests wholly upon the correct interpretation of the deliberate, intelligent, dependable popular will of America. In a deliberate questioning of a suggested change of national policy, where internationality was to supersede nationality, we turned to a referendum, to the American people. There was ample discussion, and there is a public mandate in manifest understanding. (1221)

The statement appeared for the first time in the second draft of the speech, and only a few changes occurred in subsequent versions. *Our* was added to the first sentence in the third draft, underscoring the "jointness" of the idea expressed. The more definitive *questioning* replaces *contemplation*. The second draft had originally ended this way: "There was ample discussion, and there is manifest understanding. Misinterpretation does not seem possible" (1189). The substitution of *public mandate* for the final sentence better emphasizes the definitiveness of the referendum's outcome.

Later in the speech, Harding repeated the importance of "the people" to his presidency:

> If I felt that there is to be sole responsibility in the Executive for the America of tomorrow I should shrink from the burden. But here are a hundred millions, with common concern, answerable to God and country. The republic summons them to their duty, and I invite co-operation. (1221)

In one of several appeals to cooperation in the speech, Harding ended with a promise to accept his part "with single-mindedness of purpose and humility of spirit" (1221). He vowed to lead by expressing the will of the people that had already been made clear.

While appeals to public will permeate both Wilson's and Harding's inaugural rhetoric, Harding's desire to express rather than to formulate popular opinion resonated well with a public grown tired of eight years of "presidential leadership." Wilson dominated government, especially "in his personal conduct of foreign affairs in disregard of the popular judgment which he had himself asked."[42] The election was more a referendum on Wilson and his assertive management of governmental affairs than it was a simple repudiation of the League.[43] Harding's inaugural communicated that adherence to his vision of what public opinion was, not declarations of what that vision ought to be, would inspire his presidency.

If rhetorical presidents seek to accomplish actions through popular appeal, it follows that the inaugural address of a rhetorical president might identify the desired policy objectives of such rhetoric. This assumption contrasts with that of Karlyn Campbell and Kathleen Jamieson, who have contended that inaugural addresses are examples of ceremonial discourse that have as their purpose contemplation, not action. These addresses, they contend, possess four qualities differentiating them from other forms of epideictic rhetoric.[44] Harding's address fits uncomfortably the inaugural genre as Campbell and Jamieson define it since the elements they describe are not present in Harding's speech. Expression of appreciation of the requirements and limitations of the office, for example, did not occur. Harding referred directly to the office only once and then only at the very end of the speech. Other elements of the rhetorical genre, while present, served different purposes.

Harding's statements about the League were precursors of calls to action he would later deliver to Congress. Campbell and Jamieson argue that the mention of policies in inaugurals serves an expository function designed to illustrate the political philosophy of the new president. While this is perhaps the case in some inaugurals, Harding's speech reveals that declarations of policies may sometimes serve only to elucidate governing principles while at other times grounding a call to action. When Harding lists several domestic reforms that he "stands for," such as lightened tax burdens and a halt to government's experiment in business, his suggestions identify him as a mainstream Republican. But when he referred to the League and international association, his rhetoric committed the nation to a foreign policy doctrine predicated on the wisdom of the nation's founders.

While portions of Harding's inaugural were undoubtedly meant for contemplation only, his expressions on the League signaled action authorized by his perception of popular will. Campbell and Jamieson argue that presidents use the inaugural to reconstitute the people as witnesses and ratifiers of the ceremony. Harding reconstituted the presidency as the lead agent of popular will and pledged himself to carry out the desires expressed on election day. His rhetoric previewed abandonment of the League and delay in the quest to formulate an alternative.

As Harding pledged quiescence to American traditions in international affairs, his conservative rhetoric had action as its goal if "one understands obedience, compliance, and quiescence as political action."[45] Here the new president indeed rehearsed traditional values, but he used these values as grounds for his argument against the League, which was, if not dead on Inauguration Day, dying. In his first formal speech to Congress, on April 12, 1921, Harding pronounced the League dead and offered even less explicit assurances of support for American involvement in another such international body or "world court" than in the inaugural. Not until February 1923 did Harding announce and push forward a proposal for entry into the World Court at the Hague, and this initiative met with quick defeat.

FINAL ASSESSMENT

Presidential oratory that decreases the distance between the president and the people, presents an alternative to the imperial presidency, and expresses empathy for and appreciation of the values of the public "is apt to be very eloquent speech."[46] Judged by that narrow criterion, Harding may have produced a memorable inaugural. He reassured American voters that they had, in fact, replaced Wilson with a very different man.

But it is hard to forgive many of the flaws in this address. Harding's irritating habit of omitting objects for transitive verbs contributed to much of the vagueness of the speech. It is difficult to label as eloquent an inaugural in which the speaker says, "I would like government to do all that it can to mitigate: then . . . our tasks will be solved" and, "Since freedom impelled, and independence inspired, and nationally exalted, a world super-government is contrary to everything we cherish" (1221).

The address also suffers from logical deficiencies too glaring to slough off. It asserted that "our freedom has never sought territorial aggrandizement through force," that "no one may justly deny the equality of opportunity which made us what we are," and that "minorities are sacredly protected" (1221). Belief in these claims requires severe stretching, or ignorance, of the facts. Furthermore, Harding's positions frequently contradict. Aside from his waffling about international organizations, Harding simultaneously endorsed expanded trade and higher tariffs. And he pledged to decrease taxes in the same speech in which he endorsed a series of social measures (freedom from poverty, guarding against the perils of unemployment, and assurances of access to education) that sounded very much like something one would find in New Deal oratory. Perhaps these apparently incompatible goals could have been achieved simultaneously, but that is a question not pursued in the address.

Ultimately justifying his position on the League of Nations as both consistent with the will of the nation's founders and a reflection of the public's wishes, Harding's inaugural illustrated the work of a rhetorical president grounding his appeal on words, not political power. The architects of the rhetorical approach to presidential governance attempted to move the public by setting before them grand and ennobling ideas. These early practitioners appealed for support for new ideas and bold visions that changed traditional ways of thinking. But rhetoric can appeal for action or reaction; Richard Nixon has been mentioned as a president whose rhetorical counteroffensive challenged the liberal expressions of those preceding him.[47] Previously overlooked when the roster of rhetorical presidents is announced, Harding was an early proponent of the popular appeal, which, by expressing adherence to long-standing foreign policy principles, moved the nation to do more than contemplate his position on the League of Nations. The development of his thinking on that issue as he prepared the inaugural address moved him and the nation to a point where only one action was possible.

NOTES

1. Warren G. Harding, speech to Home Market Club, Boston, May 14, 1920, Warren G. Harding Papers, Ohio Historical Society, Columbus, Ohio (microfilm edition, roll 238, frame 1293). Subsequent references to the papers are noted as "HP" followed by roll and frame information.

2. Robert K. Murray, *The Politics of Normalcy: Government Thinking and Practice in the Harding-Coolidge Era* (New York: W. W. Norton, 1973), 15.

3. Robert K. Murray, *The Harding Era* (Minneapolis: University of Minnesota Press, 1969), 122. See also Francis Russell, *The Shadow of Blooming Grove: Warren G. Harding in His Times* (New York: McGraw-Hill, 1968), 160.

4. Harold F. Alderfer, "The Personality and Politics of Warren G. Harding" (Ph.D. diss., Syracuse University, 1928), 175.

5. Quoted in Hope R. Miller, *Scandals in the Highest Office* (New York: Random House, 1976), 201.

6. H. L. Mencken, "Gamalielese," in *A Carnival of Buncombe*, ed. Malcolm Moos (New York: W. W. Norton, 1973), 39.

7. To "bloviate" meant to go on (literally) for hours speaking about safe subjects while lacing the address with frequent patriotic and familiar clichés. The term originally meant, in rural Ohio parlance, to "loaf around and chat." See Rexford G. Tugwell, *How They Became President* (New York: Simon and Schuster, 1968), 357–58; Geoffrey Perrett, *America in the Twenties* (New York: Simon and Schuster, 1982), 112; Paul F. Boller, *Presidential Anecdotes* (New York: Oxford University Press, 1981), 229.

8. "The Inaugural Address," *New York Times*, March 5, 1921, 12.

9. Eugene P. Trani and David L. Wilson, *The Presidency of Warren G. Harding* (Lawrence, Kans.: Regents Press, 1977), 54.

10. Andrew Sinclair, *The Available Man* (New York: Macmillan, 1965), 198.

11. H. L. Mencken, "A Short View of Gamaliese," *Nation*, April 27, 1921, 622.

12. Samuel H. Adams, *Incredible Era: The Life and Times of Warren G. Harding* (Boston: Houghton Mifflin, 1939), 222.

13. Elbert F. Baldwin, "Exit Wilson: Enter Harding," *Outlook*, March 16, 1921, 415.

14. Murray, *Harding Era*, 15. Harding's speech earned contemporary praise for its delivery, in spite of his mechanical, declamation-style gestures. See "Crowds Stand in the Cold," *New York Times*, March 5, 1921, 2, and "Turns Senate Clock," 2.

15. "A Good Official Style," *New York Times*, April 24, 1921, 2: 2.

16. John F. Wilson, "Harding's Rhetoric of Normalcy, 1920–23," *Quarterly Journal of Speech* 48 (1962): 406.

17. "A Good Official Style."

18. Moos, *A Carnival of Buncombe*, 3, holds flatly that Harding did not write the speech, that it was produced by an unnamed professor of political economy at Johns Hopkins University. In contrast, Trani and Wilson, *Presidency*, p. 53, write that Harding, proud of his reputation as an orator, "worked hard on his address." Long-time Marion, Ohio, resident and friend, George Christian, Sr., wrote in an unpublished biography that the inaugural was "prepared by him [Harding] to the last crossing of a 't' and dotting of an 'i.' " "Biography of Warren G. Harding," George B. Christian, Sr., Papers, HP, roll 249, frame 0217. The distinctive, if somewhat outdated, phrasing of the speech moved others to conclude the inaugural was Harding's own. Adams, *Incredible Era*, 173. See also Harry M. Daugherty to Cyril Clemens, October 15, 1938, Cyril Clemens Collection, HP, roll 254, frame 0190. One biographer, Randolph C. Downes, *The Rise of Warren Gamaliel Harding, 1865–1920* (Columbus: Ohio State University Press, 1970), mentions nothing about the inaugural's preparation. Neither does an exhaustive treatment of Harding as a speaker in Dale Cottrill's *The Conciliator* (Philadelphia: Dorrance and Co., 1969).

19. Wilson, "Harding's Rhetoric," 409. See also Daugherty to Clemens, October 25, 1938, Cyril Clemens Collection, HP, roll 254, frame 0190. Harding was the first president to put a full-time speech writer on his executive staff. See Michael Medved, *The Shadow Presidents* (New York: New York Times, 1979), 169.

20. Charles E. Hard to Clemens, November 23, 1939, Cyril Clemens Collection, HP, roll 254, frame 0439–40.

21. Murray, *Harding Era*, 123.

22. All texts are in the Speeches of Warren G. Harding, HP, roll 239. Quotations will be cited by frame numbers inserted parenthetically at the end of each quotation in the text. Included in the collection are typed, printed, and handwritten scripts. Hard provided two useful documents in his collection, which helped to identify the writing on the inaugural texts. One is a "copy of the original manuscript" of a speech that Harding gave to the Associated Press in New York (Charles E. Hard Papers, HP, roll 256, frame 0497–0532). The writing on it matches that on the inaugural texts. Hard also saved a typed copy of that speech to show how Harding hand-corrected speech texts before they were printed (HP, roll 256, frame 0533). The writing of the corrections also matches that found on the inaugural scripts. Only important emendations relevant to the League issue and Harding's view of the role of popular opinion are examined.

23. Harding often delivered speeches from "clean" fine-printed versions cut and placed on sheets small enough to fit in the hollow of his left hand. Hand-written numbers on the fine-printed inaugural text evidently mark where this large sheet would have been cut apart for the reading text. Harding did deliver the inaugural from a fine-printed text cut apart. See "Turns Senate Clock '15-Minutes' Just before Noon," *Richmond Times Dispatch*, March 5, 1921, 2.

24. Wilson, "Harding's Rhetoric," 409.

25. Speech to Indiana delegation, August 28, 1920, HP, roll 239, frame 0198–0200.

26. Speech in Louisville, Kentucky, October 15, 1920, HP, roll 239, frame 0895.

27. Speech in Des Moines, Iowa, October 7, 1920, HP, roll 239, frame 0810.

28. Murray, *Harding Era*, 61.

29. Ibid., pp. 60–61.

30. David Jennings, "President Harding and International Organization," *Ohio History* 75 (1966): 149–65, finds Harding a strong advocate of a world court at the time of his death. The strength of his commitment at the time of the inaugural is not discussed. Deena Fleming, *The United States and the League of Nations, 1918–1920* (New York: Putnams, 1932), 471, thought that "habit and the vague belief he may have developed let Harding go on after the election promising an association, which he admitted he did not know how to bring about."

31. "Harding's Address Disappoints Paris," *New York Times*, March 6, 1921, 3.

32. "Senators Commend New Foreign Policy," *New York Times*, March 5, 1921, 3.

33. "Mr. Harding's Attitude toward Europe," *Literary Digest*, March 19, 1921, 14–15.

34. Dante Germino, *The Inaugural Addresses of American Presidents: The Public Philosophy and Rhetoric* (Lanham, Md.: University Press of America, 1984), 10.

35. Jeffrey Tulis, *The Rhetorical Presidency* (Princeton: Princeton University Press, 1987), 147–61.

36. Ibid., 158–61.

37. "Inaugural Speech Will Be a Short One," *Evening Star*, March 1, 1921, 1.

38. Tulis, *Rhetorical Presidency*, 4.

39. James W. Ceaser, Glen E. Thurow, Jeffrey Tulis, and Joseph M. Bessette, "The Rise of the Rhetorical Presidency," in *Rethinking the Presidency*, ed. Thomas Cronin (Boston: Little, Brown, 1982), 239.

40. Tulis, *Rhetorical Presidency*, 51.

41. Bruce Gronbeck, "Ronald Reagan's Enactment of the Presidency in His 1981 Inaugural Address," in *Form, Genre, and the Study of Political Discourse*, ed. Herbert Simons and Aram Aghazarian (Columbia: University of South Carolina Press, 1986), 233, argues that examination of small details such as these yields meaningful insight into a speaker's rhetoric.

42. "The Election of Mr. Harding," *Outlook*, November 10, 1920, 454.

43. "March of Events," *World's Work* 41 (December 1920): 108 and Baldwin, "Exist Wilson," 414.

44. Karlyn Kohrs Campbell and Kathleen Hall Jamieson, "Inaugurating the Presidency," in *Form, Genre, and the Study of Political Discourse*, 211.

45. Richard Joslyn, "Keeping Politics in the Study of Political Discourse," in *Form, Genre, and the Study of Political Discourse*, 336.

46. Ibid., 321.

47. Ceaser, Thurow, Tulis, and Bessette, "Rise of the Rhetorical Presidency," 235.

Chapter Six

President Calvin Coolidge's Inaugural Address, 1925

Warren Decker

The 1924 presidential campaign, by most standards, was fairly uneventful. Coolidge was, according to Donald McCoy, the "beneficiary of rising agricultural purchasing power" and "was fortunate that no crises either at home or abroad occurred during the campaign. Everything seemed to be well handled and he did nothing to contradict that impression."[1] Overall, Coolidge had decided not to participate beyond a few ceremonial, quasi-political speeches. The *Washington Post* observed in mid-October that "Coolidge will make a few addresses over the radio, but they will be semipolitical."[2]

Circumstances partially explained his general lack of participation. Perhaps foremost was the loss of his son, Calvin. Sixteen-year-old Calvin Coolidge, Jr., died on July 7, 1924, from an infection that developed as a result of a blister he got while playing tennis. President Coolidge took the loss very hard, and as a result further reduced his involvement in the campaign. But Coolidge had another reason for his lack of participation: "I don't recall any candidate for President that ever injured himself very much by not talking."[3]

Coolidge, like most other incumbents, enjoyed the advantages associated with his office and of being a front-runner. The *Washington Post* explained his aloofness in this way: "President Coolidge will make no speeches of a purely political nature before election day. . . . The situation has improved so materially from a Republican viewpoint in the last month that neither the President nor any of his close advisers thinks it necessary for him to take any active part in the campaign."[4] Coolidge's desire to maintain a low profile was made easier because of a lack of issues that attracted the interest of large numbers of voters. Occasionally, it even appeared as if both the Democrats and the third-party Progressives had to create issues in order to attack Coolidge, and those issues failed to attract widespread attention. For example, the opposition accused Coolidge of being soft on the Ku Klux Klan because he failed to take a public stand against it.[5] They attempted to make an issue out of Coolidge's receipt of $250 for a speech he gave as vice president to a veterans' group. Claude Fuess noted in his biography of Coolidge: "It was obvious from the opening of the campaign that [John] Davis [his Democratic opponent] would find it difficult to make an issue out of what Calvin Coolidge had done or not done since August 3, 1923."[7] These issues failed to mobilize significant support for either the Democrats or the Progressives.

A COOLIDGE VICTORY

The campaign of 1924 culminated with the landslide election of the Coolidge-Dawes ticket. Their rather convincing win was explained in a variety of ways. Donald McCoy thought that "while his opponents were promising better things to the country, he seemed to be delivering them. There were no crises facing the nation, farm prices were rising, business was getting better, and labor conditions seemed to be improving. The campaign slogan of 'Keep Cool with Coolidge' summed up the President's view that one should not tamper with a good situation. Coolidge had guessed correctly: the old shouts and cries, whatever their source, would make no impact. What the majority wanted was to be left alone and Coolidge did that masterfully."[8] Supreme Court Justice Oliver Wendell Holmes characterized the spirit of the situation: "While I don't expect anything very astonishing from Coolidge I don't want anything very astonishing."[9] Most critics concluded, as did McCoy, that Coolidge won because "it was a case of Davis putting the voters to sleep, [Robert] La Follette [the Progressive candidate]] not being able to arouse many of them, and Coolidge not even trying."[10] The issues that Coolidge did address, as one might expect, were generally good for Coolidge.

THE CAMPAIGN ISSUES

In a radio broadcast dedicating the new home of the U.S. Chamber of Commerce ten days before the election, Coolidge finally spoke to the primary issues of the campaign, one of them the League of Nations: "We have abstained from joining the League of Nations mainly for the purpose of avoiding political entanglements and committing ourselves to the assumption of the obligations of others, which have been created without our authority and in which we have no direct interest." He indicated his direct opposition to the call for a referendum on joining the League by suggesting that it would be "costly, futile, and uncon-stitutional"; however, he did urge "membership in the Permanent Court of International Justice, under desired conditions or limitations." He advocated pursuing additional reductions in armaments through the hosting of international conferences and attempts to "devise consulta-tional covenants which will look to the outlawing of aggressive war."[11]

Regarding domestic issues, he declared that he was opposed to gov-ernment ownership of railroads and to "the heavy tax upon railroads, corporations and all great incomes which are eventually paid through higher prices." He promised further tax reductions made possible by "drastic economy" in government and urged the continuance of the protective tariffs of the time: "American industry cannot exist, American wages cannot be paid, American standard of living cannot be maintained without a protective tariff." He declared his opposition to the "proposal advanced by the Third Party to nullify Supreme Court decisions in Con-gress." "If this system should be adopted and put into effect," Coolidge concluded, "the historian would close a chapter with the comment that the people had shown they were incapable of self-government and the American Republic had proved a failure."[12]

Additionally, Coolidge addressed the maintenance of a strong mili-tary, the necessity to decrease sectionalism in the country, and agricul-tural problems, and he urged private funding for the restoration of Europe.

INAUGURAL ISSUES

The inaugural address that Coolidge delivered on March 4, 1925, in many respects continued his campaign themes. Coolidge reiterated his views on membership in the League of Nations: He desired neither the "isolation [nor] entanglement of pacifists and militarists," nor could the United States "barter away our independence or our sovereignty," for "we are determined not to become implicated in the political contro-versies of the Old World." His policy was to avoid the League of Nations, because the United States should be aloof: "We can contribute most to these important objects by maintaining our position of political detach-ment and independence."[13]

Although Coolidge rejected membership in the League, he favored the establishment and support of the Permanent Court of International Justice:

In conformity with the principle that a display of reason rather than a threat of force should be the determining factor in the intercourse among nations, we have long advocated the peaceful settlement of disputes by methods of arbitra-tion and have negotiated many treaties to secure that result. The same considerations should lead to our adherence to the Permanent Court of International Justice.

He summarized his position relative to the court by saying, "The weight of our enormous influence must be cast upon the side of a reign not of force but of law and trial, not by battle but by reason." As in his campaign, he continued his push for membership in the World Court.

Having rejected the League, Coolidge cannily yet paradoxically favored using international conferences as a mechanism to solve problems:

If we are to judge by past experience, there is much to hope for in international relations from frequent conferences and consultations. We have before us the beneficial results of the Washington conference and the various consultations recently held upon European affairs, some of which were in response to our suggestions and in some of which we were active participants. Even the failures can not not be accounted useful and an immeasurable advance over threatened or actual warfare. I am strongly in favor of continuation of this policy, whenever conditions are such that there is even a promise that practical and favorable results might be secured.

His inaugural stand was in line with his campaign rhetoric wherein he was "committed to the policy of international conferences."[14]

As in the campaign, Coolidge addressed the concept of outlawing war in his inaugural. On October 24, he had stated: "Personally, I view with favor the attempt to devise constitutional covenants which would look to the outlawing of aggressive war."[15] His inaugural rhetoric is quite similar: "Much may be hoped for from the earnest studies of those who advocate the outlawing of aggressive war."

Coolidge next turned his attention to a number of domestic issues. He indicated that the Progressives, who advocated public ownership of railroads and certain electric utilities, had met with "unmistakable defeat." The Progressives also advocated congressional override of Supreme Court decisions, an issue to which Coolidge had dedicated significant time in the chamber of commerce speech. This theme too appeared in the inaugural:

The expression of the popular will in favor of maintaining our constitutional guarantees was overwhelming and decisive. There was a manifestation of such faith in the integrity of the courts that we can consider that issue rejected for some time to come. The people declared that they wanted their rights to have not a political but a judicial determination.

Issues of economy in government and tax reduction, which were prominent in the campaign, surfaced in the inaugural. Coolidge argued:

The policy that stands out with the greatest clearness is that of economy in public expenditure with reduction and reform of taxation. The principle involved in this effort is that of conservation. . . . No matter what others may want, these people want a drastic economy. They are opposed to waste. They know that extravagance lengthens the hours and diminishes the rewards of their labor. I favor the policy of economy, not because I wish to save money, but because I wish to save people.

He finished his inaugural analysis of this issue by assuring Americans that "the time is arriving when we can have further tax reduction, when, unless we wish to hamper the people in their right to earn a living, we must have tax reform. The method of raising revenue ought not to impede the transaction of business; it ought to encourage it. I am opposed to extremely high rates, because they produce little or no revenue, because they are bad for the country, and, finally, because they are wrong." As he had outlined his position in the campaign, Coolidge continued his advocacy of economy in government and tax reductions.

Coolidge briefly mentioned the tariff issue in his inaugural: "Under the helpful influences of restrictive immigration and a protective tariff, employment is plentiful, the rate of pay is high, and wage earners are in a state of contentment seldom before seen." The fact that the tariff was virtually passed over is in contrast to the substantial amount of time dedicated to it in the chamber of commerce speech. Perhaps because it was an existing policy, Coolidge decided to spend his more limited inaugural time on policies requiring action.

The remaining issues—the maintenance of a strong military, the attempt to decrease sectionalism in the country, agricultural problems, and private funding for the restoration of Europe—were also addressed in the inaugural. Coolidge revealed his conceptualization of a military force: "It ought to be a balanced force, intensely modern, capable of defense by sea and land, beneath the surface and in the air." But lest he be perceived too bellicose, he quickly added that it should be used only as an "instrument of security and peace."

Coolidge made two fairly distinct remarks regarding sectionalism, the first embedded in a historical reference to the Revolutionary period:

The old sentiment of detached and dependent colonies disappeared in the new sentiment of a united and independent Nation. Men began to discard the narrow confines of a local charter for the broader opportunities of a national constitution. Under the eternal urge of freedom we became an independent nation. . . . The narrow fringe of States along the Atlantic seaboard advanced its frontiers across the hills and plains of an intervening continent until it passed down the golden slope to the Pacific. Throughout all these experiences we have enlarged our freedom, we have strengthened our independence. We have been, and propose to be, more and more American.

Late in the speech, he returned to the theme: "It is true that we could, with profit, be less sectional and more national in our thought." These remarks reflected the concerns he related prior to the election when he stated that America "cannot thrive upon sectionalism or privilege, but must take into consideration all quarters of the land."[16] Coolidge clearly urged an antisectionalist position.

Agricultural problems, such as the tariff, warranted only passing comment. He noted that "agriculture has been very slow in reviving, but the price of cereals at last indicates that the day of its deliverance is at hand." The chamber of commerce speech had devoted a great deal more time to the agricultural problem.[17] This difference is probably accounted for by the fact that agriculture prices had recovered in the intervening months. Finally, Coolidge referred to the private financing of loans to help restore Germany in both his campaign and in the inaugural.[18]

THE INAUGURAL AS COOLIDGE'S LAST CAMPAIGN ADDRESS

The similarity between the issues addressed in the campaign and the issues addressed in the inaugural is substantial: of the approximately fifteen issues addressed in the inaugural, twelve of them appeared at some length in his final major campaign speech to the chamber of commerce. The two issues that appeared in the inaugural but not in the final campaign speech were references to the need for law and order and a commentary about the role of the political party in the American political process. The absence of these two issues can be explained rhetorically. The issue of political parties was situationally oriented and was appropriate only for the inaugural address because of the seating of a new Congress. The law and order comments, which were a veiled anti-Klan comment, Coolidge studiously avoided mentioning during the campaign for obvious political reasons. The inaugural reflected virtually all of the issues in the campaign, and Coolidge urged fairly specific action on several of these issues.

One issue was conspicuous by its absence, however. Coolidge chose not to respond to the opposition's charges of Republican corruption. Both of his opponents, John Davis and Robert La Follette, the Progressive candidate, attempted to garner support by continuing to condemn the corruption of the Harding-Coolidge administration. Coolidge ignored it, hoping silence would be a more effective strategy than response. During much of the campaign, Coolidge was successful in projecting the attitude that he did not care "to prostitute his high office in order to gain votes," an attitude that gave him significant flexibility in his responses.[19]

THE COOLIDGE INAUGURAL AS EPIDEICTIC SPEAKING

Did Coolidge's inaugural exhibit the characteristics usually associated with epideictic speaking? The *New York Times* set the tone for this discussion:

It is customary for Presidents to include generalities in the speeches which they make on inauguration. There are historical references. There is a survey of the state of the country. There is a restatement of the aspirations of the American people. Such things cannot be omitted, as they were not omitted in President Coolidge's Inaugural Address yesterday, but the attentive reader will pass them over quickly in order to get at the ideas, the policies, the immediate program which the Chief Executive has closest at heart.[20]

Indeed the *New York Times* perceived both epideictic (general) and deliberative (specific) proposals in Coolidge's address. This distinction seems appropriate when viewing the Coolidge inaugural.

Coolidge included a number of generalities in his inaugural. For instance, he commented on how well the country was doing, how hard working the American people were, and how citizens should learn from the past. One can argue, however, that some of these generalities served specific persuasive purposes. Coolidge's commending the American public on its hard work is an obvious form of praise, which might endear him to his audience and thereby provide a friendlier reception for later ideas.

A few of these generalities also fulfilled some of the basic inaugural elements that Campbell and Jamieson have identified. They selected Coolidge's phrase—"we cannot continue these brilliant successes in the future, unless we continue to learn from the past"—to serve as an example of how Coolidge rehearsed traditional values.[21] But it is unclear whether Coolidge was urging action or placing these ideas in the speech only for his audience to contemplate.

Coolidge also communicated political principles. "We must frequently take our bearings from these fixed stars of our political firmament if we expect to hold a true course," he observed, and then he connected this reasoning with the issue of creating a more "national" character. Doubtless, he was reacting to the problem of sectionalism, and his goal was to make the entire country more "American." The West and Midwest were distrustful of the East, and, given that the Progressive party had attempted to exploit that division, Coolidge had reason to be concerned. In addition, the solid South still existed; it was a definite force with which to be reckoned, for the fear of a sectionalized America was still quite real.

Indeed, Coolidge's call to pay close attention to the past was interpreted by some of his contemporaries as a direct call for action. The

Washington Post perceived Coolidge's call in this way: "If this suggestion by Mr. Coolidge should bear fruit in an earnest study of American political history by the citizens of this country, this inaugural address will have proved one of the most important and useful deliverances of American statesmanship. When Americans have gone wrong it has been invariably due to ignorance of the country's institutions or neglect of the plain warnings of experience."[22] The phrase Campbell and Jamieson referred to can be said to be rehearsing communal values; however, with Coolidge's rather clear demands for action, the fit into the epideictic genre is a bit cloudy. To contend that the passage has no immediate policy implications is to mask its primary significance. Coolidge was genuinely concerned about the sectionalization of the country. The argument could be made that at this point in American history the communal values that Coolidge advocated were still in their formative stages. Coolidge's inaugural assisted in the formation of those values, and therefore the speech did more than merely rehearse those values.

Coolidge seemed to have veiled appeals to action concerning other generic elements. When he made reference to "becoming more and more American," he appeared to fulfill the generic element of "unifying the audience by reconstituting the members as 'the people' who can witness and ratify the ceremony."[23] However, he then stated, "We believe that we can best serve our country and most successfully discharge our obligation to humanity by continuing to be openly and candidly, intensely and scrupulously, American." This passage immediately followed a paragraph dedicated to promoting the concept of one people, his answer to sectionalism. Coolidge may well have had a specific action in mind as he delivered these remarks. A reasonable case can be made that these phrases served multiple purposes.

Coolidge's two paragraphs describing the role of political parties in American politics did not seem to be and were not received as attempts to reconstitute the people. Rather, they were generally taken as a promise that the disloyal members of the party would be driven from the ranks. Indeed, the *Washington Post* wrote, "His words are not merely a castigation of the renegades who have recently been punished for their mutiny, but are a solemn warning to the Republican majority in the new Congress."[24]

Coolidge made several references to the Constitution, but none appears to conform ideally to the generic element of indicating an appreciation for the requirements and limitations of the executive functions. In the 1924 campaign, the Progressives advocated a policy that would allow Congress to override decisions of the Supreme Court. Coolidge saw this as a direct attack on the Constitution, and in this context he mentioned the Court in his inaugural: "Our system of government made up of three separate and independent departments, our divided sovereignty composed of Nation and State, the matchless wisdom that is enshrined in our Constitution, all these need constant effort and tireless vigilance for their protection and support." Once again, the need for action to protect the Constitution is clearly stated while he also acknowledged the separation of powers and its impact on the executive.

In attempting to apply generic characteristics, we might overlook the policy implications of inaugural speeches. The identification of some generic characteristics may help to elucidate portions of inaugural speaking, but critics must take care not to be distracted from some of the other purposes of inaugurals. If the overall purpose of a critical system could be clarified and perhaps recognized as only one way of viewing inaugurals, this might do much to reduce such concerns.

REACTIONS TO THE INAUGURAL

The reception of Coolidge's inaugural was quite favorable. The *Washington Post* wrote,

President Coolidge's inaugural address deserves a high place among state papers. In its comprehensiveness, combined with brevity, it has rarely been equalled by the utterances of Presidents. Within a compass of 3,800 words Mr. Coolidge has compressed a wide variety of topics, and toward each of them he makes his attitude perfectly clear.[25]

The *New York Times*, however, was less effusive: "These essentials of the Inaugural Address undoubtedly indicate the lines along which President Coolidge intends to work during the next four years. The President does no boasting as he puts on the harness. But there is no question that he is putting it on."[26]

In the *Washington Post*, Elbert H. Gary, chairman of the board of the United States Steel Corporation, reacted to the inaugural by calling it "able, plain, comprehensive, specific, and convincing. It will be read with admiration and satisfaction by the peoples of all nations. It contains no basis for reasonable objection by anyone. It is fair and friendly toward all classes and groups of the United States and toward all nations and nationalities."[27] Other critics also reacted favorably to the address. According to William Allen White, Chief Justice William H. Taft wrote in a letter to his son Robert that "Coolidge made an admirable speech."[28] White's personal reaction was similar:

Probably nothing he said or wrote elsewhere represents so perfectly the Coolidge ideal, the Coolidge literary style, which in itself deeply reveals the man; a sentimentally inspiring man, full of good will, a man not without an eye to the political main chance, a man always considering the vote-giving group, shrewdly eloquent about accepted beliefs, never raising debatable issues, a good man honestly proclaiming his faith in a moral government of the universe.[29]

Claude Fuess called Coolidge's inaugural his best speech, for it "turned out to be one of his ablest utterances." Fuess also quoted Taft as saying that the president had acquired "great aptness of expression and brevity and force," but he noted that "some listeners thought it seemed too complacent."[30]

Two critics thought Coolidge attained a measure of eloquence in his address. Fuess believed that "in closing his appeal for economy and peace, Coolidge reached a high level of eloquence."[31] Fuess thought the following passage was eloquent:

America seeks no earthly empire built on blood and force. No ambition, no temptation, lures her to the thought of foreign dominions. The legions which she sends forth are armed, not with the sword, but with the cross. The higher state to which she seeks the allegiance of all mankind is not of human, but of divine origin. She cherishes no purpose save to merit the favor of almighty God.

Additionally, Davis Newton Lott noted that "Coolidge was never noted for his eloquence, but this passage dealing with peace could well rank with the most profound observations of any of his peers."[32] This is the passage that Lott thought was eloquent:

Peace will come when there is realization that only under a reign of law, based on righteousness and supported by the religious conviction of the brotherhood of man, can there be any hope of a complete and satisfying life. Parchment will fail, the sword will fail, it is only the spiritual nature of man that can be triumphant.

SUMMARY

The Coolidge inaugural address was an extension of his campaign speaking. He covered the same issues and used the same or similar language. The inaugural did have passages that fulfill the generic elements of epideictic speaking, but when examined in the political context of the day these same passages also served significant deliberative functions. It appears that any examination of inaugural speaking should be embedded in its political context. More cooperative work between rhetoricians and political scientists might inform this task.[33]

NOTES

1. Donald R. McCoy, *Calvin Coolidge: The Quiet President* (New York: Macmillan, 1967), 261.

2. "Coolidge States Views on Issues in Last Big Speech," *Washington Post*, October 14, 1924, 4.

3. Howard H. Quint and Robert H. Ferrell, *The Talkative President: The Off-the-Record Press Conferences of Calvin Coolidge* (Amherst: University of Massachusetts Press, 1964), 10.

4. *Washington Post*, October 14, 1924, 4.

5. "Smith Denounces Coolidge's Silence on Ku Klux Klan," *New York Times*, October 19, 1924, 1.

6. "Coolidge Believes Election Assured," *New York Times*, October 27, 1924, 3.

7. Claude M. Fuess, *Calvin Coolidge: The Man from Vermont* (Boston: Little, Brown, 1940), 350.

8. McCoy, *Calvin Coolidge*, 262.

9. Mark De Wolfe Howe, ed. *Holmes-Laski Letters, 1916–1935* (Cambridge, Mass.: Harvard University Press, 1953), 671.

10. McCoy, *Calvin Coolidge*, 262.

11. Ibid.

12. Ibid., 4.

13. "Calvin Coolidge Inaugural Address," in *Inaugural Addresses of the Presidents of the United States from George Washington 1789 to Richard Milhous Nixon 1969* (Washington, D.C.: U.S. Government Printing Office, 1969), 217. All subsequent references and quotations from Coolidge's inaugural are to this version.

14. *New York Times*, October 24, 1924, 4.

15. Ibid.

16. Ibid., 4.

17. Ibid.

18. Ibid.

19. Fuess, *Calvin Coolidge*, 353.

20. "The Inaugural Address," *New York Times*, March 5, 1925, 18.

21. Karlyn Kohrs Campbell and Kathleen Hall Jamieson, "Inaugurating the Presidency," in *Form, Genre, and the Study of Political Discourse*, ed. Herbert W. Simons and Aram A. Aghazarian (Columbia: University of South Carolina Press, 1986), 210.

22. "The Inaugural Address," 6.

23. Campbell and Jamieson, "Inaugurating the Presidency," 211.

24. "The Coolidge Inaugural," *Washington Post*, March 5, 1925, 6.

25. Ibid.

26. "The Coolidge Inaugural," *New York Times*, March 5, 1925, 18.

27. "Gary Says Address Is a Masterpiece," *Washington Post*, March 5, 1925, 8.

28. William Allen White, *Puritan in Babylon: The Story of Calvin Coolidge* (New York: Macmillan, 1938), 314.

29. Ibid., 315.

30. Fuess, *Calvin Coolidge*, 361.

31. Ibid., 362.

32. Davis Newton Lott, *The Presidents Speak: The Inaugural Addresses of the*

American Presidents from Washington to Nixon (New York: Holt, Rinehart and Winston, 1969), 218.

33. Richard A. Joslyn, "Keeping Politics in the Study of Political Discourse," in *Form, Genre, and the Study of Political Discourse*, 336.

Chapter Seven

President Herbert Hoover's Inaugural Address, 1929

Carl R. Burgchardt

Herbert Hoover has been one of the most vilified presidents in the history of the United States. The image of a hard-hearted, incompetent, sullen president, barricaded in the White House while innocent citizens begged for bread and slept in shantytowns, is indelibly etched in the popular recollection of a nation. This ignominious stereotype was reinforced for decades after the Great Depression by Democratic party orators who sought to frighten voters about the prospect of putting another "Herbert Hoover" in the White House. These enduring impressions about Hoover are particularly ironic because, on the date of his inauguration to the presidency, March 4, 1929, Hoover's public image was diametrically different. He had been overwhelmingly elected president because the voters believed that he was unparalleled in energy, competence, compassion, and vision. Moreover, he delivered an inaugural address that capitalized on these positive public perceptions. Although he was a diffident public speaker, Hoover crafted an oration that was widely praised.

THE INAUGURAL AS GENRE

How can we account for the relative success of Hoover's inaugural address? Unfortunately, genre theory is not very helpful in reaching a meaningful assessment. Karlyn Kohrs Campbell and Kathleen Hall Jamieson have argued that presidential inaugurals are characterized by four essential elements, and a case could be made that these elements exist in the 1929 inaugural. Hoover probably does "reconstitute the people" in the sense that he pleads with citizens to work together, in conjunction with the federal government, to reform abuses in society. Presumably, Hoover "rehearses traditional values" by cataloging national ideals that the people hold in common. He honors the past by giving his predecessor, Calvin Coolidge, credit for bringing about unprecedented prosperity. Without doubt, Hoover "set[s] forth the principles that will govern [his] tenure in office." Finally, Hoover "enact[s] the presidency" in the sense that he asks for a "mutual covenant" with the people "to commit themselves to the political philosophy enunciated in the address." The mere existence of these four elements, however, does not provide reliable conclusions about the eloquence, appropriateness, or political effectiveness of the discourse. Moreover, as Richard A. Joslyn has suggested, the four elements are probably found in a wide range of political communication other than inaugural addresses. Hence, the presence of the four elements in Hoover's address does not necessarily place his speech in a distinctive genre of presidential inaugurals.[1]

The least satisfactory aspect of the Campbell and Jamieson essay is its claim that presidential inaugurals are epideictic by definition. Although Hoover's speech displays some ceremonial dimensions, it is primarily action oriented rather than contemplative, and its focus is firmly fixed on the future rather than the "eternal present." Furthermore, Hoover's inaugural does not sustain eloquence, put primary emphasis on stylistic amplification, or attempt to "reinvigorate . . . traditional values." An editorial writer for the *New York Times* accurately described the 1929 inaugural as "a cross between one of Mr. Hoover's campaign speeches . . . and a Presidential message to Congress." In this regard, Hoover's oration does not fit Campbell and Jamieson's generic prescription for presidential inaugurals. As further support for this judgment, there is not a single reference to Hoover's speech in the essay "Inaugurating the Presidency."[2]

In order to assess Hoover's inaugural address, one must relinquish genre theory, set aside the events that occurred after the onset of the Great Depression, and focus on the historical moment of March 4, 1929. When this is done, it becomes clear that Hoover's inaugural was not a document prepared primarily for posterity or a timeless piece of political philosophy or literature but, rather, pragmatic discourse tailored for the distinctive political and social context of 1928–1929.

The major thrusts of Hoover's speech were fitting for the rhetorical situation facing him on Inauguration Day. The American public voted for him with the expectation that he was a pragmatic man of action, an engineer, a businessman, and an extraordinary administrator who believed deeply in helping people. Hoover's inaugural address was designed primarily to validate the public image of himself that had been cultivated by the 1928 campaign. He matched public expectations by giving a speech that featured pragmatic policy and confirmed the voters' hopes for continued prosperity and peace. This content was reinforced by a contemporary style, logic, and method of arrangement.[3]

THE 1928 CAMPAIGN

During the 1928 campaign, Hoover gave relatively few orations. He presented a lengthy acceptance speech, six campaign addresses at different sites around the country, and a short radio talk to the nation. In these speeches, Hoover advocated taxation reform and business regulation to maintain a competitive system, sweeping reform of the judicial system, reorganization of the federal government for efficiency and economy, and policies to help agriculture and labor. Moreover, he called for free and universal education and to preserve equality of opportunity. Above all, Hoover projected an optimistic tone that the United States was entering a new age of economic prosperity and moral development.[4]

Hoover tried to finesse the issue of Prohibition by referring to it as "a great social and economic experiment, noble in motive" but imperfect in implementation. Although many citizens were adamantly opposed to ending the experiment, Hoover created the impression that he would reform the abuses of enforcement, and several newspapers urged their readers to vote for Hoover in order to make Prohibition more palatable. During the campaign, Hoover clearly stood for continuation of the Eighteenth Amendment; his opponent, Al Smith, stood for repeal. Smith, however, focused most of his rhetoric on reforming federal agricultural policy and attacking Republican favoritism to big business. In actuality, Smith did not have many effective issues to use against Hoover. Both favored governmental reorganization, tariff revisions, and nonintervention in Latin America. While Hoover did not attack Smith for his Catholicism and opposition to Prohibition, Republican underlings did. On the other hand, Republican rhetoricians featured Hoover as the candidate who could maintain prosperity, the Eighteenth Amendment, and separation of church and state. In the contest between Hoover and Smith, many perceived the Republican as the more liberal and proactive candidate.[5]

Hoover crushed Smith at the polls, winning 444 electoral votes to Smith's 87, and beating Smith by over 6 million votes. In accounting for Hoover's victory, journalists stressed Smith's Catholicism and opposition to Prohibition as major liabilities for the Democrat. Even more significant, though, were the twin issues of Republican prosperity and peace. The press speculated that no Democratic candidate could have defeated a Republican in 1928.[6]

More important than Hoover's oratory was his brilliantly conducted public relations campaign, which was a strong precursor of the image management techniques so prevalent in the United States since the

1960s. Hoover's staff convinced editors and journalists to run flattering stories and opinion pieces about him. Moreover, they distributed thousands of press releases and bulletins that cultivated an image of Hoover as a master of technology, an efficiency expert, and a great humanitarian. Adulatory stories in newspapers recounted his meteoric rise from a poor orphan to a globetrotting, adventurous entrepreneur, to a celebrated savior of the starving and suffering peoples of the world. In short, Hoover was characterized as a new kind of politician, possessing exceptional competence, knowledge, and integrity.[7]

On the day of Hoover's inauguration, the public expected to behold a heroic figure who was particularly well suited for the zeitgeist of the late 1920s. The majority believed that he could be counted on to continue the unrivaled prosperity and peace enjoyed under Republican administrations since 1921. Moreover, Hoover was perceived by many as a progressive; he was popular with intellectuals, educated citizens, and liberal groups. In addition, the public viewed his background as a mining engineer and an organizational expert as an asset. Many thought that, as a practical man of action, an engineer was above politics, and "Hoover's training appeared to give him special powers to do anything."[8]

Significantly, the public did not expect Hoover to be a philosopher, orator, or revolutionary but rather a superb administrator. The public had voted not to overturn the political system but to secure more of the same, only done better. Hoover was the engineer who could make the great economic engine of the United States run more smoothly. By implication, then, Hoover's inaugural address did not have to trumpet new ideas, lead the United States in a dramatically new direction, or establish the new president as a brilliant rhetorical performer. Hoover merely had to validate the public image of the plain-spoken, humanitarian organizer who could take a fundamentally sound status quo and improve it.

THE INAUGURAL ADDRESS

Delivery

Hoover was inaugurated on the rainy afternoon of March 4, 1929. Up to one hundred thousand people were on hand to listen to the address through strategically placed loudspeakers, and at least 63 million more heard the speech through the technological marvel of radio, an innovation that elicited much comment in the press. William Howard Taft administered the oath of office on the east side of the Capitol. The Bible used in the ceremony was open to Proverbs, chapter 29, verse 18— "When there is no vision the people perish; but he that keepeth the law happy is he"—a thematically appropriate quotation for an address that would focus strongly on law enforcement and Hoover's vision of efficient government.[9]

After completing the oath of office, Hoover began speaking in a resonant, tenor voice. He used few gestures during the course of the speech and looked up from the manuscript only occasionally. He did not have much vocal variety but read the speech in even tones at a fairly fast rate. A reporter for the *Washington Post* presented an accurate overall view of Hoover's delivery:

President Hoover, in a plain black overcoat, his head bare, took the rain on his face and spoke for better than half an hour, the battery of the microphones picking up his rather low voice and making a Demosthenes of him, the words rolling out from the hidden horns to the farthest of the ranked thousands. . . . Eyes unlifting from the yellow pages of the book in which his inaugural address had been printed in large type, he read away with the methodical efficiency of a well-oiled machine, hardly stopping for the bursts of cheering, which were especially thick during his statements on enforcement of the eighteenth amendment.

The miserable weather conditions created sympathy for Hoover, and the drenched audience did not seem to mind the speaker's efforts to terminate the oration quickly. In the words of one observer, "If the rain was uncivil to Mr. Hoover, at least Mr. Hoover made the best of it."[10]

Deliberative Focus

The major features of Hoover's inaugural were aimed directly at voter expectations developed during the campaign. The most obvious characteristic of the speech was its strong policy orientation. The deliberative focus of the inaugural satisfied audience expectations that Hoover, the efficiency expert, would take action to make government function better. It is important to note, though, that these proposals were a continuation of campaign rhetoric.[11]

The major policy direction of the speech was established in the second paragraph, when Hoover announced that he would "express simply and directly the opinions which I hold concerning some of the matters of present importance."[12] This was not ceremonial language but the discourse of someone addressing practical problems of the moment. Thus, Hoover evidently perceived the speech as a response to the immediate situation rather than discourse for posterity.

The first main section of the body announced that in most respects the nation was doing very well, but a few areas needed improvement. The most serious problem to consider was "disregard and disobedience of the law," which he called "the most malignant of all . . . dangers" facing the country. Later he referred to this problem as "the most sore necessity of our times."

In amplifying the problem, Hoover noted that crime was increasing and confidence in justice diminishing. In seeking the causes of the problem, Hoover used a systematic method that is sometimes called "elimination order." He stated that lawlessness was not caused by moral decay, by the impotence of the federal government, or by Prohibition, although Prohibition was a partial cause. The real culprit, he concluded, was ineffective organization. His solution for this defect was to "critically consider" the structure of law enforcement, to redistribute it functions, simplify procedures, add special tribunals, and provide for "better selection" of juries and "more effective organization" of investigatory agencies. Hoover next addressed possible fears audience members might have about reforming the federal justice system. Judicial reform, he argued, was not a new topic. Indeed, reorganization had been advocated for years by "statesmen, judges, and bar associations." He urged that necessary reform be delayed no longer and that action be undertaken immediately.

Having discussed general problems of inefficiency in the federal judiciary, Hoover next took up the particular case of Prohibition, an issue of intense interest to large numbers of the public. He admitted that "undoubted abuses" had occurred under the Eighteenth Amendment and then identified the causes: problems with the justice system, caused partly by states that did not accept their responsibility for enforcement and partly by state and local officials who did not honor their oaths of office to enforce the law, and the fact that many citizens purchased illegal alcohol, thus providing a stimulus to criminal behavior. The first step in stopping the abuses was for men and women to stamp out crime by serving as good examples. Hoover proposed to establish a national commission to investigate the structure of the federal system of jurisprudence, study methods of enforcement of the Eighteenth Amendment, and investigate the causes of abuse. As an interim move, Hoover pledged to transfer enforcement activities from the Treasury Department to the Justice Department.[13]

The section of law enforcement was the longest and most elaborately developed of the speech, comprising about one-fifth of its total length. Hoover specifically identified it as the most pressing issue facing the nation and gave it organizational primacy by discussing it first. In subsequent sections, Hoover proposed additional policies, although these were not developed in as much detail. For example, the middle of the speech addressed world peace. He advocated briefly the national policies of naval reductions and participation in the World Court. The final section of the speech outlined what he considered to be the mandates of the election. In particular, he favored legislation on agricultural relief and tariff revision, and he announced that he was calling for a special session of Congress to act on these matters. He promised to enact other mandates from the election: economy in public expenditures, regulation of business to prevent domination in the community, prevention of government from owning enterprises that would compete with private citizens, expansion of public works, and promotion of government activities that would aid education and the home.

Arrangement

Approximately one-third of the inaugural was devoted to an explicit discussion of policy issues. Much of the rest of the address outlined Hoover's political principles, the goals of his administration, and values that Americans held in common. This material was integrally connected to his policy propositions. Study of the arrangement of the speech reveals that Hoover first established a general proposition that the audience would likely accept; then he made a specific policy proposal. Although he did not construct formal syllogisms, the logic was distinctly deductive or enthymematic. For example, in order to justify proposed reforms in law enforcement, he first established the proposition that justice should be swift and sure. Since justice currently was not swift and sure, there was a need for change. His proposal would restore justice to its ideal condition. He used a similar pattern to support his other domestic and foreign policy proposals. Although Hoover articulated ideals, values, and political vision, these concepts were intertwined with concrete plans of action.

Not only did the substance of the speech validate the public image of a pragmatic organizer and efficiency expert, but the systematic structure of the oration suggested it as well. In arguing for change, Hoover identified a problem, discovered the causes of the problem, proposed one or more solutions, answered possible objections, and urged immediate action. That organizational pattern, along with his reliance upon deductive or enthymematic logic, reinforced the image of the methodical engineer. Theodore Joslin, a close political adviser to Hoover, characterized Hoover's presidential rhetoric in the following way: "Scientific preciseness governed all of his writing, once the effort approached final form. An engineer by training, he built his public utterances as he would drive a mine shaft or construct a bridge." Fortunately for Hoover, this logical, systematic approach was appropriate for the rhetorical situation.[14]

Style

Herbert Hoover's style reinforced the image of the pragmatic man of action. Although it may have been unconscious, his language reflected the mentality of an engineer. In opening the speech, Hoover said that he would "survey" the state of the nation at home and abroad, a term suggesting the systematic approach of a functional problem solver. In assessing the optimistic future of the nation, he used the construction metaphor of "building a new civilization." If citizens and government officials did not meet their responsibility, self-government would "crumble," employing the metaphor of the collapsing edifice. In addition, Hoover described the ideals of justice as "rigid and speedy" and "rigid and expeditious." Such language derives from a mechanical model and suggests an unvarying and precise operation—a type of justice that conforms to scientific principles. This peculiar choice of language smacks of construction materials and efficiency ratings. To correct lawlessness, Hoover said the nation must "critically consider the entire Federal machinery of justice." The machine metaphor was not coincidental, for Hoover thought of government as a mechanism that could be made to run more productively. He wanted to "redistribute," "simplify," "add," and provide for "more effective organization." He referred to "standards" and "structure" of federal law enforcement. Hoover argued that individual judges and attorneys were not the cause of law enforcement problems. The problem, therefore, was not with the parts but with the "system" that is "ill adapted to present-day conditions." Most important, Hoover did not want justice to fail because it was "inefficiently organized."

Tone

Another way Hoover met the expectations of a nation on Inauguration Day was by maintaining an extremely optimistic tone throughout the address. In the introduction, Hoover praised national progress since the war. The United States had played a strong role in the recovery and progress of the world. Currently, the nation had more freedom and less poverty than ever before. Indeed, said Hoover, "We are steadily building a new race—a new civilization great in its own attainments"—and all of this progress had occurred under Republican administrations. Hoover credited his immediate predecessor, Calvin Coolidge, for maintaining upward progress.

Such a statement posed a minor dilemma for Hoover. If things were so wonderful under Coolidge, why not continue the status quo? Hoover chose the metaphor of the healthy man to justify his reform program: "But all this majestic advance should not obscure the constant dangers from which self-government must be safeguarded. The strong man must at all times be alert to the attack of insidious disease." In other words, Coolidge had left a healthy body politic, and Hoover was simply trying to maintain this good health and ward off diseases that continuously threaten the well-being of democracies. Considering that Hoover disapproved of Coolidge's approach to government and considered him far too conservative, this was a particularly deft rhetorical stroke.

After Hoover had completed his reform proposals, he noted that impetus for change came from the desire to improve something that was already outstanding: "The questions before our country are problems of progress to higher standards; they are not the problems of degeneration." Hoover concluded the speech much as he had begun it, with an extremely optimistic view of the potential of the nation: "I have no fears for the future of our country. It is bright with hope."

Progressive Image

Hoover had been presented to the electorate as a progressive figure in the 1928 election, and he validated that image in the speech. For example, he showed a strong faith in moral suasion to bring about social change. In his discussion of Prohibition, he pleaded with citizens not to purchase illegal alcohol. Indeed, he said, "No greater national service can be given by men and women of good will" than to serve as noble examples. Throughout the speech Hoover expressed the importance of the individual responsibility of citizens in a democratic society. Without personal initiative, democratic government would crumble. In the speech Hoover also placed faith in expert, nonpartisan commissions to solve problems and make government work more efficiently. Finally, he voiced his belief that education was central in making representative government work, to provide leadership and prevent the establishment of unyielding class stratification. All of these themes contributed to the composite picture of a progressive rather than a conservative.[15]

Advocate of World Peace

For those citizens who voted for Hoover as a means of maintaining world peace, he did not disappoint. The most moving part of the speech occurred during the section on international affairs. He pledged non-aggression against neighbors in the Western Hemisphere, supported armament reductions, and argued for participation in a world court. In order to justify these positions, Hoover spoke feelingly of the costs of war: "It is impossible, my countrymen, to speak of peace without profound emotion. In thousands of homes in America, in millions of homes around the world, there are vacant chairs." In one of the few places where he used a personal pronoun, Hoover stated, "I covet for this administration a record of having further contributed to advance the cause of peace." In this regard, Hoover satisfied the vast majority of the electorate who, in the aftermath of World War I, fervently wanted to avoid military conflict.

OUTCOME

According to the available evidence, Herbert Hoover succeeded in validating the image of himself that he had cultivated in his campaign. He pleased prohibitionists by pledging to enforce the Eighteenth Amendment, yet to those who favored repeal, he promised an investigation into the abuses of enforcement. Individualists and businessmen approved of his policy of preventing government from interfering with business. Internationalists and foreign audiences liked his advocacy of peace and world cooperation. Moreover, nothing happened during the address to undermine the tremendous support Hoover enjoyed in the press. Editorials from around the country praised his fine moral character, his abilities, and his legislative program. Most agreed with the *New York Herald Tribune*: "The President's inaugural address glowed with courage, confidence, and statesmanship." Hoover created an overriding impression of competence, and that was the most important outcome, because the public wanted a competent administrator to make the vast engine of prosperity run even more efficiently. This notion was echoed by the *Washington Star Herald*, which praised Hoover's "earnest inaugural address" and noted that the president "is an engineer, and knows that work is done by machinery, not by words, loud or soft."[16]

CONCLUSION

If one considers Hoover's speech as timeless and applies formalistic standards of literary judgment, there is much to criticize. But if one considers Hoover's speech as strategic discourse, inextricably linked to a specific rhetorical situation, a speech that needed primarily to satisfy audience expectations, then a much more positive judgment emerges. On the basis of recorded reactions to the speech, Hoover succeeding in delivering a fitting response to the rhetorical situation. The public did not vote for Hoover because of his oratorical ability but because he was the sort of person it desired to administer the national government. Hoover's inaugural was earnest, humane, systematic, and unambiguous, and it promised reform on a number of fronts. In sum, it reinforced the image of the compassionate man of action.

In some respects Hoover succeeded too well in bolstering a heroic image. Prior to taking office, he admitted that he was distressed by

the exaggerated idea the people have conceived of me. They have a conviction that I am a sort of superman, that no problem is beyond my capacity. . . . If some unprecedented calamity should come upon the nation . . . I would be sacrificed to the unreasoning disappointment of a people who expected too much.

Rarely has a politician been so prescient about his own fate.[17]

NOTES

1. Karlyn Kohrs Campbell and Kathleen Hall Jamieson, "Inaugurating the Presidency," in *Form, Genre, and the Study of Political Discourse*, ed. Herbert W. Simons and Aram A. Aghazarian (Columbia: University of South Carolina Press, 1986), 206, 209–10, 211, 212; Richard A. Joslyn, "Keeping Politics in the Study of Political Discourse," in *Form, Genre*, 303.

2. Campbell and Jamieson, "Inaugurating the Presidency," 216–19.

3. This chapter uses the theoretical perspective articulated by Lloyd F. Bitzer. For a complete discussion of exigencies, rhetorical situations, and fitting responses, see his "The Rhetorical Situation," *Philosophy and Rhetoric* 1 (1968): 1–14.

4. David Burner, *Herbert Hoover: A Public Life* (New York: Alfred A. Knopf, 1978), 201; David Hinshaw, *Herbert Hoover: American Quaker* (New York: Farrar, Straus, 1950), 145; Edgar Eugene Robinson and Vaughn Davis Bornet, *Herbert Hoover: President of the United States* (Stanford, Calif.: Hoover Institution Press, 1975), 20, 22; Richard Norton Smith, *An Uncommon Man: The Triumph of Herbert Hoover* (New York: Simon & Schuster, 1984), 105. Hoover's campaign speeches can be found in *Public Papers of the Presidents of the United States: Herbert Hoover* (Washington, D.C.: U.S. Government Printing Office, 1974), 497–611.

5. Herbert Hoover, "Acceptance of the Nomination," in *Public Papers*, 511; Burner, *Herbert Hoover*, 203–5; Martin L. Fausold, *The Presidency of Herbert C. Hoover* (Lawrence: University Press of Kansas, 1985), 24, 29; Robert Sobel, *Herbert Hoover and the Onset of the Great Depression, 1929–1930* (Philadelphia: J. B. Lippincott Company, 1975), 20; Robinson and Bornet, *Herbert Hoover*, 19.

6. Fausold, *Presidency of Hoover*, 30; Sobel, *Herbert Hoover*, 21; Burner, *Herbert Hoover*, 207.

7. Craig Lloyd, *Aggressive Introvert* (Columbus: Ohio State University Press, 1972), 153, 186; Harris Gaylord Warren, *Herbert Hoover and the Great Depression* (New York: Oxford University Press, 1959), 3–4; Fausold, *Presidency of Hoover*, 22, 24. See, for example, *New York Herald Tribune*, August 12, 1928; *Chicago Daily Tribune*, August 13, 1928; *Kansas City Times*, August 13, 1928. All of the newspaper references in this chapter were taken from files of the Herbert Hoover Presidential Library, West Branch, Iowa.

8. Warren, *Herbert Hoover*, 3, 6; Robinson and Bornet, *Herbert Hoover*, 15, 20, 21, 24, 37; Smith, *Uncommon Man*, 106; Hinshaw, *Herbert Hoover*, 167; Burner, *Herbert Hoover*, 207. See *New York Times*, February 17, March 3, 6, 1929; *Washington (Iowa) Democrat-Independent*, February 21, 1929; *Burlingame (California) Advance Star*, March 4, 1929; *Washington Star*, March 2, 6, 1929; *Washington Times*, March 4, 5, 1929; *San Francisco Recorder*, March 5, 1929; *Florida Times Union*, March 6, 1929.

9. Fausold, *Presidency of Hoover*, 39; Robinson and Bornet, *Herbert Hoover*, 30; *Washington Herald*, March 5, 1929; *San Francisco Chronicle*, March 5, 1929.

10. *Washington Post*, March 5, 1929. My assessment of Hoover's delivery is based partially on audio and visual recordings of excerpts of the 1929 inaugural. This resource can be found in the Herbert Hoover Presidential Library.

11. Robinson and Bornet, *Herbert Hoover*, 30–31.

12. Herbert Hoover, "Inaugural Address," in *Public Papers*, 1–12. All subsequent references to Hoover's inaugural come from this source.

13. Hoover's proposal to transfer enforcement activities from the Treasury Department to the Justice Department was inadvertently left out. However, the advance copy contained this proposal and was published in the press. Later, Hoover stated that he had intended to add this point during delivery of the speech. See *New York World*, March 5, 1929.

14. Theodore Joslin, *Hoover Off the Record* (Garden City, N.Y.: Doubleday, 1934), 44–45.

15. Fausold, *Presidency of Hoover*, 14–15, 17–18; Burner, *Herbert Hoover*, 192.

16. Warren, *Herbert Hoover*, 52; Fausold, *Presidency of Hoover*, 40, 62; *New York Herald Tribune*, March 5, 1929; *Washington Star Herald*, March 5, 1929. See also *Cambridge* (Massachusetts) *Sentinel*, March 9, 1929; *Washington* (Iowa) *Democrat-Independent*, March 7, 1929; *New York Evening Post*, March 4, 1929; *New York Times*, March 5, 1929; *New York World*, March 5, 1929; *St. Louis Globe Democrat*, March 5, 1929; *Sheboygan* (Wisconsin) *Press*, March 4, 1929; *Washington Evening Star*, March 5, 1929; *Washington News*, March 5, 1929; *Washington Post*, March 5, 1929.

17. Herbert Hoover, quoted in Burner, *Herbert Hoover*, 211.

Chapter Eight

President Franklin D. Roosevelt's First Inaugural Address, 1933

Halford Ryan

Franklin Delano Roosevelt's First Inaugural Address is one of his premier persuasions. FDR believed it contained all of the elements of his New Deal. Samuel Rosenman ranked the speech among FDR's foremost: "This was one of the President's truly great speeches, not only in form and substance but in accomplishment"; and Harry Hopkins thought the speech FDR's best: "For myself I think his first inaugural address was the best speech he ever made. . . . With that one speech, and in those few minutes, the appalling anxiety and fears were lifted, and the people of the United States knew that they were going into a safe harbor under the leadership of a man who never knew the meaning of fear."[1]

WRITING THE RHETORIC

The following drafts are in the Roosevelt Library at Hyde Park, New York: a first draft, on legal paper, in FDR's handwriting; a second draft, a typed copy of the first with a variety of emendations; a typed third draft, which includes the emendations from draft 2 and additional revisions; and a final typed reading copy from which FDR delivered his speech.[2]

The existence of Roosevelt's handwritten draft, in conjunction with a note that he had attached to it (the note stated that he wrote the first draft at Hyde Park on February 27, 1933), implies that he created his own inaugural address, but although he wrote out this first draft, he was not its author. Rather, Raymond Moley composed it.

Moley related how he prepared the first draft, how FDR copied his draft in longhand at Hyde Park, and how Moley tossed his own draft into the fire, with the words, "This is your speech now," after FDR had finished copying Moley's draft.[3] Moley's version is independently verified by the drafts. Instead of FDR's written draft filling each successive page, there are lacunae on pages 3, 5, and 7, suggesting that FDR took more pages to write than did Moley or that FDR's ten pages could be reduced to eight pages if FDR had written his text seriatim on each page; indeed, Kenneth Davis contended that FDR's copying of Moley's draft "was done with deliberate *intent* to deceive posterity"[4] [emphasis in original].

As for the famous fear statement—"the only thing we have to fear is fear itself"—it, too, has been attributed to FDR. The phrase, however, was Louis Howe's handiwork. Howe, FDR's personal secretary, dictated a beginning paragraph for the third draft in which the phrase appears de novo, but Frank Freidel complained that Howe's source has eluded researchers.[5]

Only one major relevant revision appears on the handwritten draft (FDR's copy of Moley's draft). In the second paragraph, Moley wrote of leadership in past national crises and how the people's support of that leadership "on every occasion has won through to." FDR excised the quoted phrase and substituted "is an essential to victory."[6] FDR's phrase is more concise, and it links leadership with victory in a military-like sense.

I pass by emendations on the second draft (the first typed one) because they are not in FDR's bold, printlike handwriting.

The third draft (the second typed one) is replete with Roosevelt's handwriting. In the paragraph that contained his fear statement, Howe had written, "nameless, unreasoning, unjustified terror which paralyzes the needed efforts to bring about prosperity once more." With a definite emphasis on warlike words, FDR produced, "which paralyzes *needed* efforts *to convert retreat into advance*" [hereafter, emphasized words indicate FDR's emendations]. Later, the text read: "The standards of the money-changers stand indicated"; however, FDR wished to denigrate the bankers further and wrote, "*Practices* of the *unscrupulous* money-changers stand indicated." *Practices* sullies the loftiness of "standards," and *unscrupulous* speaks for itself. Treating the bankers in the same vein a bit later, FDR changed, "They know of no other ways than the ancient rules" to, "They know *only* the rules *of a generation of self-seekers*." FDR cast additional ridicule on the bankers: "The moral stimulation of work must no longer be submerged in the sham of evanescent profit scouring," became, "The moral stimulation of work *no longer* must be *forgotten* in *the mad chase of* evanescent profits."[7] FDR took particular pains (pleasure?) to denigrate the bankers more than Moley had in his draft, and later I demonstrate why.

In the latter part of his address, FDR turned to his personal leadership as president. In a number of places in this draft, FDR strengthened or clarified Moley's language in order to enhance the action orientation of his intended presidency. Several examples illustrate the point. "Because without such discipline no progress can be made, or any leadership really led" became "Because without such discipline no progress *is* made, *no* leadership *becomes effective.*" The future tense of Moley's thought was brought into the present by FDR's change, which stressed the immediacy of his leadership, and *effective* looked for vigorous results; moreover, FDR's use of asyndeton in his phrases verbally underscored the parallelism of progress under a productive leadership. "I am prepared under my constitutional duty to indicate the measures" became "I am prepared under my constitutional duty to *recommend* the measures." *Recommend* has a stronger sense of positive advocacy than *indicate*, for FDR emphasized his leadership by recommending, rather than merely indicating, to Congress his measures for fighting the Great Depression. Interestingly, FDR deleted *sword of* in the following passage: "With this pledge taken, I assume unhesitatingly the sword of leadership of this great army of our people." Perhaps *sword* sounded too militaristic, and perhaps he wanted to accentuate his personal leadership rather than a symbolic gesture. In any event, FDR's emendations manifested the active, personal leadership with which he would assume the presidency, for he clearly strengthened Moley's draft in those respects.[8]

The fourth draft, his reading copy, contained only one emendation. While waiting in the Senate Committee Room for the inaugural ceremonies to begin, FDR added in longhand an opening sentence: "This is a day of consecration." When he delivered the speech, he ad-libbed *national* before "consecration."[9]

One might have wished that FDR had authored his First Inaugural—but he did not. One might also have wished that he had invented the famous fear statement—but he did not. Nevertheless, Roosevelt did make important emendations on three of the four drafts, and these changes indicated his desire to use bellicose words to evoke military-like associations in his audience. He paid special attention to the bankers by utilizing language that purposefully defamed them and their practices. He also managed his language to strengthen his presidential role, for he would act immediately to lead the nation through its crisis.

MARCH 4, 1933: THREE RHETORICAL TECHNIQUES COALESCE

The Scapegoat Technique

By inauguration day, almost five thousand banks had failed, and twenty-two states had closed their banks. The spiraling effects of stock losses, foreclosures, and, ultimately, bank failures had at their epicenter the bankers and brokers. Rexford Tugwell pointed the finger: "The financial establishment was being blamed for what had happened"; Finis Farr concurred: "It was true that most of the guilt belonged to the money changers, who probably had something to do with the Stock Exchange"; and William Leuchtenburg noted that FDR's delivery matched the mood of his words: "Grim, unsmiling, chin uplifted, his voice firm, almost angry, he lashed out at the bankers."[10]

FDR's coup in his inaugural was to make Wall Street the scapegoat. The scapegoat has its derivation in Jewish antiquity, when the people symbolically placed their sins on a goat's head and then allowed the goat to escape into the wilderness, thus relieving them of their guilt. The efficacy of his using the scapegoat technique ensued from his ability to channel Americans' anxieties and frustrations from themselves to the moneychangers. His inaugural plainly indicted Wall Street for the depression: "The rulers of the exchange of mankind's goods have failed through their own stubbornness and their own incompetence, have admitted their failure, and have abdicated. Practices of the unscrupulous moneychangers stand indicted in the court of public opinion, rejected by the hearts and minds of men." And, again, "Yes, the money-changers have fled from their high seats in the temple of our civilization. We may now restore that temple to the ancient truths [Applause]."[11] This was the first ovation that FDR received from the 150,000 people in the immediate inaugural audience (approximately 50 million listened on the radio). (Ironically, the famous fear statement, which FDR spoke very early in the address, did not evoke an audience response.) In order to stop a return to the "evils of the old order," FDR announced his banking reforms: "There must be a strict supervision of all banking and credits and investments [Applause]. There must be an end to speculation with other people's money [Applause]. And there must be a provision for an adequate but sound currency [Applause]." To these ends, Congress enacted the Emergency Farm Mortgage Act on May 12 and the Home Owners Loan Act on June 13.

Roosevelt struck a responsive rhetorical chord with his scapegoat technique. Editors from Universal Films and Pathe News included his attack on the bankers in their newsreels. The *Christian Century* chronicled, "The 'false moneychangers' deserve all the condemnation that can be heaped upon them"; the *Nation* observed that Roosevelt dealt the moneychangers a "verbal scourging"; and *News-Week* noted, "It was an assault on the bankers, against whom the voices of the distressed are raised in an ever-swelling chorus as the depression endures."[12]

FDR used the scapegoat technique to blunt opposition from those laissez-faire sympathizers who might attack his New Deal banking and investment measures, and he sought support from all those victimized by Wall Street. The *Times* (London) observed that FDR was "likely to rouse the opposition of a good many vested interests," but, according to Basil Rauch, Roosevelt disarmed his banking critics: "The bankers were in a chastened mood.... They had lost the cohesion of a vested group."[13] Available evidence from the inaugural audience, contemporary newsreels, newsprint media, and later commentators warrants FDR's success in obtaining his persuasive end.

Military Metaphor

Knowing that his program would need mass backing and that the New Deal would bring broad and even radical departures from conducting government as it had been until 1933, FDR used military metaphor to garner that support. Leuchtenburg concluded that FDR purposefully responded to the depression with military metaphor: "Roosevelt's inaugural address ... reflected the sense of wartime crisis.... President Roosevelt sought to restore national confidence by evoking the mood of wartime."[14]

FDR deployed an advance guard of military metaphor in the early parts of his address: "retreat into advance," "victory," "direct recruiting," and "emergency of war." But when he directly urged compliance with and acceptance of his New Deal leadership in the latter three-fourths of his address, his language was replete with military metaphor:

If we are to go forward, we must move as a trained and loyal army, willing to sacrifice for the good of a common discipline, because without such discipline no progress can be made, no leadership becomes effective. We are, I know, ready and willing to submit our lives and our property to such discipline because it makes possible a leadership which aims at the larger good. This I propose to offer, pledging that the larger purposes will bind upon us, bind upon us all a sacred obligation, with a unity of duty hitherto evoked only in times of armed strife. With this pledge taken, I assume unhesitatingly the leadership of this great army of our people dedicated to a disciplined attack upon our common problems.

This great American army, organized under the personal leadership of its new commander in chief, would wage war on the depression. In fact, a clergyman from Yonkers, New York, had urged in a letter to FDR that he call for a "mobilization as if the United States were at war."[15] FDR did not disappoint: The repetition of *discipline* four times and *leadership* three times, and other value-laden words, such as *duty, sacred obligation,* and *armed strife,* reinforced desires that yearned for action against the depression. If Paul Conkin was correct when he argued that "the situation invited a surrender of power to some leader," then FDR's military metaphor facilitated Americans' surrender of power and liberty, much as one does in the real army, to their commander in chief.[16]

The effect-oriented responses from private persons and the press were favorable to FDR's warlike images. From all quarters came support for FDR's bid for quasi-military leadership, and that support itself was often couched in Roosevelt's infectious military metaphor. Republican Alfred M. Landon of Kansas affirmed, "If there is any way in which a Republican governor of a midwestern state can aid the President in the fight, I now enlist for the duration of the war" (Landon let his enlistment lapse when he ran against FDR in 1936). Myron C. Taylor, chairman of United States Steel Corporation, declared, "I hasten to re-enlist to fight the depression to its end." Moreover, James Hagerty wrote, "In the phraseology which ran all through his speech he indicated that he regarded the United States as in an economic war."[17]

Leading newspapers also championed the new commander in chief's rhetoric. The Atlanta *Constitution* applauded Roosevelt's "straight-from-the-shoulder attack"; the Birmingham *News-Age Herald* labeled the inaugural "a clarion call for national unity in the face of a crisis"; the Cleveland *Plain Dealer* portrayed the address as "fighting words, fit for a time that calls for militant action"; the Des Moines *Register* thought "it is the rallying of the country to renewal of a courageous and sustained war on the depression"; the New York *Daily News*, which had not endorsed Roosevelt in the election, nevertheless pledged itself "to support the policies of FDR for a period of at least one year; longer if circumstances warrant"; and the *Times* (London) remarked on Roosevelt's warlike language, "What is important to note is the spirit which inspired it throughout. A high and resolute militancy breathes in every line."[18]

This use of military metaphor could hurt FDR if the audience misperceived his intent, however. Therefore, in what seems to have been an effort to reassure Americans that they had little to fear of a nascent executive dictatorship in his New Deal, FDR hastened to allay any fears of the audience: "Action in this image, action to this end, is feasible under the form of government which we have inherited from our ancestors. Our constitution is so simple, so practical, that it is possible always to meet extraordinary needs by changes in emphasis and arrangement without the loss of essential form." Wary listeners might have challenged FDR's assertion that "changes in emphasis and arrangement" can ensue without a "loss of essential form," but Farr believed the claim sounded fine to about 99 percent of FDR's listeners, and, anyway, there was little time to raise that issue because FDR's confident voice marched forward.[19]

Adolf Hitler's Fuehrer principle was fresh in some Americans' minds, however, and they were not so easily beguiled. Partially indicative of this thinking was William Randolph Hearst's *New York Mirror*, which headlined its March 6 issue: *ROOSEVELT ASKS DICTATOR'S ROLE*.

Edmund Wilson, editor of the *New Republic*, believed that FDR's military metaphor signaled a dire warning: "The thing that emerges most clearly is the warning of a dictatorship," and Rauch recalled that, even among liberals, the military metaphor caused some concern: "Liberals were later to profess they found the germs of fascism in the First New Deal. Perhaps they found cause for suspicion in the evocation of the 'regimented' moods of wartime."[20]

Indeed, Herr Hitler readily appreciated the efficacy of Roosevelt's inaugural militancy as evidenced by the language that he selected for his congratulatory cable:

The Reich Chancellor is in accord with the President that the virtues of sense of duty, readiness for sacrifice, and discipline must be the supreme rule of the whole nation. This moral demand, which the President is addressing to every single citizen, is only the quintessence of German philosophy of the State, expressed in its motto "The Public Weal Before Private Gain."

And Benito Mussolini's *Il Giornale d'Italia* perceived in FDR's inaugural a reaffirmation of its views:

President Roosevelt's words are clear and need no comment to make even the deaf hear that not only Europe but the whole world feels the need of executive authority capable of acting with full powers of cutting short the purposeless chatter of legislative assemblies. This method of government may well be defined as Fascist.

Franklin D. Roosevelt, however, was not a Hitler or Mussolini, and so he made a change on the third draft by adding *present* to the following thought: "They have made me the *present* instrument of their wishes." His change suggests that he had a more reasonable and limited conception of his presidency. *Present* implies a four-year term and does not preclude another president four years later.[21]

Although some contemporary and later critics were concerned with FDR's bellicose language, Roosevelt's military metaphor successfully evoked in the American people a patriotic duty and discipline to support the new president's quasi-military generalship in combating the depression. Lest this warlike image smack too much of an incipient dictatorship, FDR took pains to assure his audience that the Constitution would survive; mere changes in emphasis would not affect its essential form.

Carrot-and-Stick Technique

"The new Congress," wrote Walter Lippmann, "will be an excitable and impetuous body, and it will respect only a President who knows his own mind and will not hesitate to employ the whole authority of his position."[22] As a rhetorical president, Roosevelt had enlisted the country in his army with the military metaphor; he had used the scapegoat technique to subdue Wall Street; he had a favorable press; now he had only to deal with the Congress.

Accordingly, FDR resorted to the carrot-and-stick approach to move the Congress to follow his executive leadership. His carrot was a clever cajoling of Congress to act either on its own or in tandem with him:

And it is to be hoped that the normal balance of executive and legislative authority may be wholly equal, wholly adequate, to meet the unprecedented task before us. But it may be that an unprecedented demand and need for undelayed action may call for temporary departure from that normal balance of public procedure. I am prepared under my constitutional duty to recommend the measures that a stricken nation in the midst of a stricken world may require. These measures, or such measures as the Congress may build out of its experience and wisdom, I shall seek within my constitutional authority to bring to speedy adoption.

If the carrot were not motivation enough, the stick would be:

But in the event that the Congress shall fail to take one of these two courses, in the event that the national emergency is still critical, I shall not evade the clear course of duty that will then confront me. I shall ask Congress for the one remaining instrument to meet the crisis: broad executive power to wage a war against the emergency, as great as the power that would be given to me if we were in fact invaded by a foreign foe.

The tumultuous applause that immediately followed—and it was the greatest applause in the speech—could not have been mistaken by members of Congress.[23] Eleanor Roosevelt thought the applause was "a little terrifying. You felt that they would do *anything*—if only someone would tell them *what* to do [emphasis in original]."[24] The Dallas *News* supported FDR's carrot-and-stick technique by suggesting, "If Congress fails him, the country will strongly back him in his demands for virtual war powers," and the conservative Boston *Transcript* even sustained FDR: "The President's program demands dictatorial authority. This is unprecedented in its implications, but such is the desperate temper of the people that it is welcome."[25]

In hindsight, the Congress was anything but intransigent, but FDR did not know that when he fashioned his speech. Although the carrot-and-stick technique admittedly did not directly cause Congress to cooperate, it nevertheless served a vital function. Within the framework of the rhetorical presidency, where speaking is governing, President Roosevelt conveyed to the people and to the Congress that he was prepared to use the stick if it were necessary. Notice that if a recalcitrant Congress did not cooperate with Roosevelt, it certainly would not grant him broad executive powers. But this logic was lost in the rush of Roosevelt's rhetoric, for Alfred Rollins believed that if FDR had not demonstrated his ability to act and to lead, he might have failed on Inauguration Day: "What Roosevelt did do, with monumental success, was to preserve the faith which vague commitment or partial action might have shattered."[26]

FDR's FIRST: AN UNGENERIC INAUGURAL?

In his First Inaugural, Roosevelt did unify and reconstitute the people. Nevertheless, he separated the bankers from the rest of the people with the scapegoat technique, so not all citizens were unified and reconstituted on an equal footing.

FDR did rehearse communal values, but these mores were more resonant with Progressive or Wilsonian principles, for Roosevelt would move the country forward by returning to the verities of yesteryear rather than the tried-but-found-wanting Republicanism of the Harding-Coolidge-Hoover era.

FDR did communicate his political principles. These broke with past executives' laissez-faire doctrines, because FDR's New Deal would restructure a United States in the midst of the depression.

FDR did clearly communicate his appreciation of the powers and limitations of the presidency vis-à-vis the Congress. On the surface, the carrot-and-stick functioned as lip-service to the separation of powers doctrine. But implicit in the technique was FDR's willingness to test the Constitution, which he claimed could survive with "changes in emphasis and arrangement without the loss of essential form."

Yet FDR's First was clearly deliberative, clearly action oriented. The scapegoat device prepared the way for action against Wall Street by enlisting the people behind Roosevelt and against the moneychangers. The military metaphor recruited the audience to enroll in FDR's battle to fight the Depression. And the carrot-and-stick technique encouraged the Congress to work with the president. Action, not contemplation, was FDR's object on March 4, 1933: "These three devices could not serve a useful function or make rhetorical sense if they were not fashioned and employed to actuate the American people and especially the Congress to support his New Deal," and, as Cleveland Rodgers realized, FDR's First Inaugural "first won for him the support of the great masses of people and put behind his efforts the full force of an overwhelming public opinion."[27]

CONCLUSION

Closing remarks are best left to Franklin Delano Roosevelt, for his three rhetorical techniques coalesced in his inaugural's conclusion:

The people of the United States have not failed. In their need they have registered a mandate that they want direct, vigorous action. They have asked for discipline and direction under leadership. They have made me the present instrument of their wishes. In the spirit of the gift, I take it.

NOTES

1. *The Public Papers and Addresses of Franklin D. Roosevelt*, ed. Samuel I. Rosenman (1928–1936, 5 vols.; New York: Random House, 1938), 2:16; Samuel I. Rosenman, *Working with Roosevelt* (New York: Harper, 1952), p. 89; Harry L. Hopkins, Foreword to *Nothing to Fear*, ed. B. D. Zevin (Boston: Houghton Mifflin, 1946), viii.

2. Inaugural Address, 1933, Master Speech File, Box 0610, Roosevelt Library, Hyde Park, New York. The second draft was typed on Tuesday, February 28. The third draft was retyped on Wednesday, March 1. The reading copy was typed on March 3. Hereafter, references to the FDR Library holdings on the First Inaugural will be cited as MSF.

3. Raymond Moley, *The First New Deal* (New York: Harcourt, Brace & World, 1966), 114.

4. MSF, first handwritten draft, 1–10; Kenneth S. Davis, "FDR as a Biographer's Problem," *American Scholar* 53 (Winter 1983–1984): 102.

5. Frank Freidel, *Franklin D. Roosevelt Launching the New Deal* (Boston: Little, Brown, 1973), 203.

6. MSF, first handwritten draft, 1.

7. MSF, draft 3, typed, 1–4.

8. MSF, draft 3, typed, 10–11.

9. MSF, reading copy, 1–2.

10. Rexford G. Tugwell, *Roosevelt's Revolution* (New York: Macmillan, 1977), 6; Finis Farr, *FDR* (New Rochelle, N.Y.: Arlington House, 1972), 182; William E. Leuchtenburg, *Franklin D. Roosevelt and the New Deal: 1932–1940* (New York: Harper & Row, 1963), 41.

11. Most printed texts, which relied on the advanced text to the press, are in error. For an accurate text, with insertions of audience applause, see my *American Rhetoric from Roosevelt to Reagan*, 2d ed. (Prospect Heights, Ill.: Waveland Press, 1987), 2–6. All subsequent quotations from FDR's First Inaugural are from this authoritative inaugural speech text.

12. Universal Film MP 77–5, and Pathe News 201–29–1, FDR Library; "The Inaugural Address," *Christian Century*, March 15, 1933, 351; "The Faith of Roosevelt," *Nation*, March 15, 1933, 278; "Roosevelt Takes Oath in Crisis," *NewsWeek*, March 11, 1933, 9.

13. "The President's Speech," *Times* (London), March 6, 1933, 13; Basil Rauch, *The History of the New Deal: 1933–1938* (New York: Creative Age Press, 1944), 61.

14. William E. Leuchtenburg, "The New Deal and the Analogue of War," in *Change and Continuity in Twentieth-Century America*, ed. John Braeman, Robert H. Bremner, and Everett Walters (Columbus: Ohio State University Press, 1964), pp. 104–5.

15. Letter, February 24, 1933, PPF 10, Box 1, FDR Library.

16. Paul Conkin, *The New Deal* (New York: Crowell, 1967), 30.

17. Quoted in Cabell Phillips, *From the Crash to the Blitz: 1929–1939* (London: Macmillan, 1969), 107; "Leaders Here Praise Address as 'Strong,' " *New York Times*, March 5, 1933, 6; James A. Hagerty, "Roosevelt Address Stirs Great Crowd," *New York Times*, March 5, 1933, 2.

18. "Comments of Press on Roosevelt's Inaugural Address," *New York Times*, March 5, 1933, 6; *Daily News* quoted in Phillips, *From the Crash to the Blitz*, 107; "The President's Speech," 13.

19. Farr, *FDR*, 182.

20. *New York Mirror* quoted in ibid., 191; Wilson quoted in William Manchester, *The Glory and the Dream* (Boston: Little, Brown, 1973), 77; Rauch, *The History of the New Deal: 1933–1938*, 59.

21. Hitler quoted in John Toland, *Adolf Hitler* (Garden City, N.Y.: Doubleday, 1976), 1:340–41; Mussolini quoted in Freidel, *Franklin D. Roosevelt Launching the New Deal*, p. 208; MSF, draft number 3, typed, 13.

22. Lippmann quoted in James T. Patterson, *Congressional Conservatism and the New Deal* (Lexington: University of Kentucky Press, 1967), 1.

23. Freidel, *Franklin D. Roosevelt Launching the New Deal*, 205. Pathe News and Universal Films both included this important segment (see n. 12).

24. Joseph P. Lash, *Eleanor and Franklin* (New York: Norton, 1971), 360.

25. "Comment of Press on Roosevelt's Inaugural Address," 6; quoted in Phillips, *From the Crash to the Blitz: 1929–1939*, 107.

26. Alfred B. Rollins, Jr., *Roosevelt and Howe* (New York: Knopf, 1962), 366.

27. Halford R. Ryan, *Franklin D. Roosevelt's Rhetorical Presidency* (Westport, Conn.: Greenwood Press, 1988), 107; Cleveland Rodgers, *The Roosevelt Program* (New York: Putnam, 1933), 16.

Chapter Nine

President Franklin D. Roosevelt's Second Inaugural Address, 1937

Michael Weiler

Franklin Roosevelt first won the American presidency in 1932 at the height of the Great Depression. Four years later, though weaknesses persisted,[1] the American economy had improved dramatically.[2] Roosevelt's second presidential campaign, in 1936, emphasized this contrast. "For twelve years," he recalled, "this nation was afflicted with hear-nothing, see-nothing, do-nothing government." But since 1933, "you have had an administration which instead of twirling its thumbs has rolled up its sleeves. We will keep our sleeves rolled up."[3]

His landslide victory over Kansas governor Alf Landon convinced Roosevelt that the public vigorously supported the New Deal. From this premise, he concluded that efforts to remove the chief barrier to its successful operation and expansion, the anti–New Deal majority on the U.S. Supreme Court, would be greeted with equal enthusiasm.

On February 5, 1937, Roosevelt sent to Congress a proposal two years in the making but kept under wraps until then: a plan to allow the president to appoint an additional justice to the Court for every sitting justice seventy years of age or older to a maximum of fifteen justices in all.[4] The intent of this "court-packing" scheme was obvious to everyone. Because six members of the Court were then seventy or older, Roosevelt could have ensured by new appointments a pro–New Deal majority on the Court.

Oddly, however, his rationale for the proposal did not acknowledge its manifest purpose, emphasizing instead the need for new justices in order to handle the crush of cases allegedly inundating the "nine old men." This transparently disingenuous argument was soon dispatched, and as opposition to the court plan grew, Roosevelt switched to the more candid but, as it proved, fatally belated strategy of condemning past Court decisions that had overturned parts of the New Deal and warning that if the situation was not reversed, a full and durable economic recovery could not be achieved.[5]

Roosevelt's mistaken rhetorical strategy was only one reason the court plan ultimately foundered, however. His failure to consult with congressional leaders, even of his own party, prior to announcing the plan caused resentments and disunity in the Democratic ranks, which were to persist long afterward.[6] Also, Roosevelt had underestimated the ease with which public conservatism regarding changes in major government institutions could be mobilized against the scheme. Finally, and perhaps most important, the switch of Justice Owen Roberts from an anti–New Deal to pro–New Deal position, especially on the vote upholding the constitutionality of the Wagner Act, together with the subsequent retirement of conservative justice William Van Devanter, convinced even many of Roosevelt's supporters that the war for the New Deal had been won without packing the Court.

Coming as it did on January 20, 1937, Franklin Roosevelt's Second Inaugural occupies an uneasy position between his overwhelmingly successful second presidential campaign and his dismally unsuccessful effort to pack the Supreme Court. Substantively, the address belongs quite clearly to the rhetoric of the former; though it lacks a partisan political tone, it restates, albeit more broadly, the themes of the presidential campaign and does not treat at all (except for one heavily veiled hint)[7] the court-packing initiative to come. Yet, formally at least, the address is not the last speech of an electoral campaign but one of the first of a new presidential term.[8] Accordingly, at least one critic has suggested that Roosevelt should have used the occasion of the inaugural to prepare the public for his court-packing proposal, stating candidly his real reasons for wanting reform. To have done so, by this view, might have generated public support strong enough to overcome the plan's other substantial political liabilities.[9]

From this perspective, Roosevelt's Second Inaugural is as significant for what it did not say as for what it did. Had the public been given what would have amounted to, in effect, an extra sixteen days' notice of the court-packing bill, perhaps its fate would have been different. This possibility, nevertheless should not divert us from confronting the speech on its own terms, for the Second Inaugural is noteworthy for its positive message as well as for its omissions. It failed to say everything, but it said a good deal. It stands as the eloquent articulation of a distinctive political philosophy, one seldom expressed as forcefully— indeed, one seldom heard of at all from major party politicians today. In the case of this inaugural address, the rhetorical road not taken did not make *all* the difference.

ROOSEVELT'S SECOND INAUGURAL ADDRESS:
CAPITALISM MADE MORAL

More than any other period before or since, the early years of the Great Depression in the United States threatened to undermine public faith in the legitimacy and survivability of industrial capitalism and the liberal political system undergirding it. In the early 1930s, even mainstream opinion leaders wondered whether economic disaster at home coupled with the political successes of fascism and communism abroad meant that the twilight of liberal capitalism had been reached.

In this sense, the first four years of the Roosevelt presidency were as much a test of an economic and political system as they were a record of the performance of a political leader and his party. Roosevelt's New Deal was not just a political program; it was a prescription for liberal capitalism's malaise. That, at least, was how Roosevelt, running for reelection in 1936, wanted American voters to evaluate the apparent results of his New Deal initiatives. The New Deal had worked its cure on the bodies economic and politic, and the doctor should be given his due.

Not everyone agreed. Republican businessmen wondered whether New Deal prescriptions had not altered the patient beyond recognition, mutating the American policy into the very form (fascism or socialism, depending on the version) from which it was supposed to be saved. Roosevelt acknowledged such accusations during the campaign and then brushed them aside. "Some of these people," he said, "really forget how sick they were. . . . All of the distinguished patients wanted two things—a quick hypodermic to end the pain and a course of treatment to cure the disease. They wanted them in a hurry; we gave them both. And now most of the patients seem to be doing very nicely. Some of them are even well enough to throw their crutches at the doctor."[10]

Enough people believed in 1936 that Roosevelt had saved the American system to provide him with an electoral majority in every state but two. His Second Inaugural was in a sense a postscript to the 1936 campaign, but it was also more. Rather than simply reviewing the accomplishments of the New Deal as he had done throughout much of the campaign, Roosevelt used the inauguration ceremony to state in a more reflective, less partisan way the political philosophy that underlay it. Amid the rhetorical trappings suitable to the occasion could be found a distinctive political doctrine: in effect, a theory of more capitalism.

Its philosophical tone notwithstanding, the Second Inaugural is structurally a deliberative address. Although much of it consists of a narration of the past and a description of the present, its purpose is to suggest at least the outlines of future action. That action is implied rather than specific, but the political philosophy on which it must be based is presented coherently. Thus, the address answers, and by implication raises, four questions: two dealing with the past—Why was the New Deal necessary? and What has the New Deal accomplished?—the third with the present—What remains to be done?—and the last with the future— What new approach will be needed?

The programs of Roosevelt's first term summarized by the label "New Deal" represented for the United States an unprecedented degree of federal government initiative in the economic sphere, particularly in the area of social welfare legislation. Although the federal government had intervened in economic affairs in the past, the intervention had been primarily to aid corporate business interests. The New Deal, by contrast, attempted to regulate some kinds of corporate business activity and to affect the distribution of economic resources in the direction of greater benefits for the least advantaged.[11]

In a political society ideologically grounded on principles of liberal capitalism, these new emphases—regulation of big business and benefits to the most needy—required justification. In his Second Inaugural, Roosevelt offered two: the complexities of the modern industrial age and the social irresponsibility of greedy men.

In his defense of the New Deal as the appropriate solution for economic depression, Roosevelt noted "the need to find through government the instrument of our united purpose to solve for the individual the ever-rising problems of a complex civilization. Repeated attempts at their solution without the aid of government," he recalled, "had left us baffled and bewildered." Now, however, having gone through the hard school of the depression, "nearly all of us recognize that as intricacies of human relationships increase, so power to govern them must also increase."

These references to the complexities of twentieth-century industrial capitalism are the specific contents of a familiar line of argument: New problems require new solutions. Roosevelt's second justification for government action in the private sphere, however, addressed a very old problem, one with which liberal theorists have long had to grapple: the tendency of human beings to prefer more to less and to beggar their neighbors in order to get it.

The Second Inaugural contains several vivid references to such miscreants. "We have always known," said Roosevelt, "that heedless self-interest was bad morals; we know now that it is bad economics." Although the overwhelming majority of Americans are "men and women of good will," there are still those "private autocratic powers" whom only government can control. Their greed and the extraordinary means they possess for serving it made necessary a crusade "to drive from the temple of our ancient faith those who had profaned it."

The social irresponsibility of greedy men is a problem as old as politics itself, but in the context of modern industrial capitalism it is a new problem as well. By virtue of capitalism's tendency to concentrate the control of more and more economic resources in fewer and fewer hands, the power of the few to disadvantage the many is considerably strengthened. These powerful "economic royalists," as Roosevelt referred to them elsewhere, could be controlled for the common good only by a power equal to theirs: the government.[12]

In Roosevelt's view, the New Deal amounted to a refusal to leave to economic "winds of chance and hurricanes of disaster . . . the problems of our common welfare," a determination to find "practical controls over blind economic forces and blindly selfish men." In the context of the economic emergency of his first term, the New Deal had succeeded. This improved economic climate, the primary theme of Roosevelt's electoral campaign, received little mention in his inaugural. "Our progress out of the depression is obvious," he noted quickly. "But," he added, "that is not all that you and I mean by the new order of things." Beyond economic recovery, "we have made the exercise of all power more democratic; for we have begun to bring private autocratic powers into their proper subordination to the public's government. The legend that they were invincible—above and beyond the processes of democracy—has been shattered."

The abuses of the greedy and powerful had been curbed. More than this, the New Deal had established the beginnings of a new civic order, one based on the social responsibility of all citizens to one another. "Out of the collapse of a prosperity whose builders boasted their practicality," Roosevelt observed, "has come the conviction that in the long run economic morality pays. We are beginning to wipe out the line that divides the practical from the ideal; and in so doing we are fashioning an instrument of unimagined power for the establishment of a morally better world."

In emphasizing the moral side of the New Deal, Roosevelt made clear that so far only the foundations for this "morally better world" had been laid. Much remained to be done. Indeed, his discussion of the job ahead occasioned the best-remembered, most eloquent passages of the address. "Our present gains," he noted, "were won under the pressure of more than ordinary circumstances. Advance became imperative under the goad of fear and suffering. The times were on the side of progress."

In 1936, however, seven years after the depression's onset and after four years of the New Deal corrective, the danger was that complacency would replace urgency, that recognition of the need for change would give way to paralyzing conservatism. "Comfort says, 'Tarry a while,' " warned Roosevelt. "Opportunism says, 'This is a good spot.' Timidity asks, 'How difficult is the road ahead?' " To be seduced by these siren voices would be not only to squander opportunities for future progress but to risk the undoing of progress already made. Indeed, Roosevelt observed, "dulled conscience, irresponsibility, and ruthless self-interest already reappear. . . . Prosperity already tests the persistence of our progressive purpose."

Although the potential of the United States to do good for its own citizens and for all peoples of the world was almost limitless, that potential remained largely unfulfilled. "I see a great nation," said Roosevelt, "upon a great continent, blessed with a great wealth of human resources. . . . I see a United States which can demonstrate that, under democratic methods of government, national wealth can be translated into a spreading volume of human comforts hitherto unknown, and the lowest standard of living can be raised far above the level of mere subsistence."

Despite this vast potential, however, a sobering reality obtained, one that called not for standing pat but for mounting a new crusade. "Here is the challenge to our democracy," Roosevelt said:

I see tens of millions of citizens—a substantial part of the whole population— who at this very moment are denied the greater part of what the very lowest standards of today call the necessities of life. I see millions of families trying to live on incomes so meager that the pall of family disaster hangs over them day by day. . . . I see one third of a nation ill-housed, ill-clad, ill-nourished.

What was to be done? Roosevelt offered no specific programs. Instead, he discussed the political principles on which any comprehensive solution had to be based. "The test of our progress," he insisted, "is not whether we add more to the abundance of those who have much; it is whether we provide enough for those who have too little." "We are determined," he added, "to make every American citizen the subject of his country's interest and concern; we will never regard any faithful law-abiding group within our borders as superfluous."

Social justice, then, would have to be the foundation of the nation's future. To meet the economic emergency of depression was one thing; to root out the structural inequalities in the nation's economic system was another. "In our personal ambitions," Roosevelt observed, "we are all individualists. But in our seeking for economic and political progress as a nation, we all go up, or else we all go down, as one people." With characteristic optimism, Roosevelt said, "It is not in despair that I paint this picture" of social and economic injustice. "I paint it for you in hope— because the nation, seeing and understanding the injustice in it, proposes to paint it out."

· It may seem odd to identify as deliberative an address so bereft of specific policy proposals and specific arguments to justify them. I do so, however, because, as my reading of its arguments has suggested, the

Second Inaugural is oriented essentially toward the future. It presents a problem, partially solved in the past but still compelling in the present. It explains the causes of that problem and suggests in general the kind of solution (although not its specifics) that will be needed to solve it completely. Out of this process of deliberation emerges not only the conceptual outlines of such a solution but a remarkably cogent though brief statement of the political philosophy of New Deal liberalism.

It is not coincidental that this philosophy should emphasize social morality, for it addresses the central problematic of liberal capitalism: How can an economic system based on the pursuit of individual self-interest be made compatible with a politics of civic responsibility? More simply, how can capitalism be made moral?

THE GENESIS OF ROOSEVELT'S SECOND INAUGURAL ADDRESS

The Second Inaugural was composed in four drafts, the first based on a draft of a complete speech written by Donald Richberg. Subsequent drafts were the joint product of Richberg, Samuel Rosenman, Thomas Corcoran, and the president himself.[13] Rosenman, Roosevelt's chief speech writer throughout his administration, has stressed the president's high degree of involvement in the composition of virtually every major speech he gave. The president acted typically as an equal partner in the compositional process during both conceptualization and editing stages.[14]

According to Rosenman, the original drafts of the Second Inaugural "show probably more work, corrections, inserts, substitutions and deletions by the President than any of the other speeches [whose drafts are housed at the Roosevelt Library in Hyde Park, New York]."[15] Certainly Roosevelt's contributions were considerable. It was he who personified comfort, opportunism, and timidity in such memorable fashion. It was he who changed the phrase "private economic power" to the more pointed and personal "private autocratic powers." And it was he who summarized the nation's job to be done in the famous passage, "one-third of a nation, ill-housed, ill-clad, ill-nourished."[16]

The original drafts of the Second Inaugural illustrate Roosevelt's preference for simple, unadorned, direct language. For example, the third draft refers to "six million families—twenty-five million people—trying to live on incomes of less than $20.00 a week. Their current resources are so meager that the pall of family disaster hangs over them day by day." Roosevelt's editing reduced these two sentences to, "I see millions of families trying to live on incomes so meager that the pall of family disaster hangs over them day by day."[17]

Although his refinements tended toward economy in most cases, Roosevelt could add words for emphasis; in the third draft, "We all go up and down together," becomes in the fourth, "We all go up, or else we all go down, together."[18] In this case as in many others, his instincts were unerring. The line as finally written was one of six on which the audience applauded during the speech's delivery.

Although major substantive changes in the drafts are few, there are indications that Roosevelt sought to strengthen his emphasis on social justice, especially as it related to his program past and future, and to sharpen his criticism of the socially irresponsible. In two early sentences of the third draft, "without the aid of government" and "without that aid," respectively, are added to his explanation of how the depression occurred, thus highlighting the importance of government power in solving it.[19] "Uncurbed self-interest" in the third draft becomes "heedless self-interest" in the fourth, the change suggesting motivation and thus directing blame at human agents rather than at a political condition.[20]

Throughout the drafts, there are numerous indications of an engaged and critical mind, attentive to detail, seeking the most potent mix of arguments and style. Though a collaborative effort, it can be said of this speech what is seldom true of presidential rhetoric today: It was Franklin Roosevelt's Second Inaugural Address.

THE DELIVERY OF THE ADDRESS

It rained hard throughout most of Roosevelt's Second Inaugural. Audio tape recordings of the speech feature the tattoo of the rain on Roosevelt's microphone as he carried on bare-headed and apparently undaunted for the seventeen minutes the Second Inaugural took to deliver. Only after the speech was over and the national anthem begun did the rain slacken and the sky lighten, leading one radio commentator to wonder whether the improving weather conditions suggested good things for the nation's future.

Roosevelt's delivered the inaugural in a firm, penetrating, and even youthful voice. His habit prior to speaking was to emphasize various words by underlining them or, in some cases, by penning hieroglyphics suggestive of their meanings. *"Without* the *aid* of *government"* received such emphasis on both the reading draft and in Roosevelt's delivery of it. So did *"private, autocratic"* powers. At the place where the draft read, "Hard-headedness will not so easily excuse hard-heartedness," Roosevelt drew a little head and heart to remind him not to transpose the two references.[21]

Roosevelt's first audience ovation came fully halfway through the speech when, after describing the principles of social justice on which the New Deal was founded, he said, "For these reasons, I am justified in believing that the greatest change we have witnessed has been the change in the moral climate of America." Similarly enthusiastic responses occurred when, after painting his picture of the shameful poverty and depravation that he still saw, Roosevelt predicted that the nation would "paint it out," and when, a line later, he predicted the nation would "carry on" despite the blandishments of comfort, opportunism, and timidity.

The philosophical tone of his message and the relative sobriety of the occasion restrained him from using much dramatic variation of voice. He did, however, ham it up a bit when relating what comfort, opportunism, and timidity had to say.

In sum, Roosevelt's delivery was characteristically assured and polished. He made few slips and recovered quickly and easily when he did. He was emphatic yet not overly demonstrative. He spoke very much like a skilled speaker on an occasion significant for the tradition of the orderly and democratic conferral of power it represented but undistinctive in its individual historical consequences.

CONCLUSION

Karlyn Kohrs Campbell and Kathleen Hall Jamieson have identified presidential inaugurals as a rhetorical genre and suggest that most inaugurals to a greater or lesser degree contain four generic elements.[22] All four of these characteristics are appropriate in some sense to the description of Roosevelt's Second Inaugural, yet it is important to understand what that sense is lest the rhetorical significance of the address be misunderstood.

Roosevelt's frequent references to "the nation" and his lavish use of the collective pronouns *we, our,* and *us* are proof of his desire to constitute his audience as a unified group. But we should not forget that the identity of this group was based, in his version, as much on who was excluded as who was included. "The people" emphatically did not include socially irresponsible, blindly selfish men whose abuses caused the depression. These moneychangers were to be driven from the national temple. Roosevelt's constitution of the audience had a divisive, exclusive dimension that must be accounted for in any account of its rhetorical power.

Roosevelt certainly did rehearse communal values from the past, but, significantly, they were primarily from the recent past—his first term. Although he claimed to have discovered "no wholly new truth" in bringing forth the New Deal, he did boast of "writing a new chapter in our book of self-government. It was the *"new* materials of social justice"* [emphasis mine] used to fashion his programs that he wished to emphasize. Thus, except for a few perfunctory references, Roosevelt did not rehearse communal values deriving from American political traditions so much as he brought to the forefront the new structure of social morality erected in his first presidential term.

The moral structure was the principle on which Roosevelt proposed to found his second term. Locating its provenance and describing its implications for the future was what his address was all about. Campbell and Jamieson's third characteristic of inaugural addresses is thus central to an appreciation of the rhetoric of the Second Inaugural. In saying so, however, it is important to emphasize that this third characteristic, because of its relative importance in the address, becomes the primary element. Others, of necessity, become secondary.

This hierarchy certainly applies to the fourth characteristic: references to the limits and requirements of executive power. Indeed, beyond ritualistic mention of the accountability of the president to the public, there is little in the address about limits at all. The requirements of power are discussed in the context of the necessity of federal action to curb the excesses of economic activity. And this discussion, in turn, is part of the larger theme of a moral capitalism and its prerequisites. Therefore, it may be questioned whether, in these particular rhetorical circumstances, this emphasis of the positive uses of executive power to the virtual exclusion of its negative aspects (and therefore the need to limit its use) meets the spirit of Campbell and Jamieson's fourth generic criterion.

The picture of a generic inaugural that emerges from Campbell and Jamieson's schema is one of an address "urging contemplation not action."[23] In a sense, this is an accurate picture of the Second Inaugural. Its lack of specific proposals and its philosophical tone suggest that it should be placed firmly within epideictic rather than deliberative bounds. Yet the address's problem-solution structure belies such an easy categorization. More important, when considered in its historical context, as an address of transition from one highly action-oriented presidential term to what from all appearances would be another, the Second Inaugural becomes, at least by implication, a prophecy of future action based on an approach rooted in the recent past.

NOTES

1. William E. Leuchtenburg, *Franklin D. Roosevelt and the New Deal* (New York: Harper & Row, 1963), 194.

2. James MacGregor Burns, *Roosevelt: The Lion and the Fox* (New York: Harcourt, Brace & World, 1956), 266–67.

3. From Roosevelt's campaign speech at Madison Square Garden, October 31, 1936, quoted in Samuel I. Rosenman, *Working with Roosevelt* (New York: Harper & Brothers, 1952), 134.

4. Leuchtenburg, *Franklin D. Roosevelt and the New Deal*, 232.

5. See Burns, *The Lion and the Fox*, 301–2.

6. See Leuchtenburg, *Franklin D. Roosevelt and the New Deal*, 238–39.

7. The hint is contained in the following passage: "The essential democracy of our nation and the safety of our people depend not upon the absence of power, but upon lodging it with those whom the people can change or continue at stated intervals through an honest and free system of elections. The Constitution of 1787 did not make our democracy impotent." Quoted from "Franklin D. Roosevelt: Second Inaugural Address," in *Inaugural Addresses of the Presidents of the United States: From George Washington 1789 to George Bush 1989* (Washington, D.C.: U.S. Government Printing Office, 1989), 274–78. All subsequent inaugural citations are from this text. Not surprisingly, few people took this as a negative reference to the Supreme Court. See Frank Freidel, *Franklin D. Roosevelt: Rendezvous with Destiny* (Boston: Little Brown, 1990), 226.

8. Roosevelt's Annual Message to Congress, January 6, 1937, preceded the Second Inaugural.

9. See Halford Ross Ryan, *Franklin D. Roosevelt's Rhetorical Presidency* (Westport, Conn.: Greenwood Press, 1988), 90–91.

10. From a campaign speech in Chicago, October 14, 1936. Quoted in Rosenman, *Working with Roosevelt*, 117.

11. We should remember, however, that the welfare system the New Deal initiated was limited in scope and its income redistribution effects relatively minor. See Theda Skocpol, "The Limits of the New Deal System and the Roots of Contemporary Welfare Dilemmas," in *The Politics of Social Policy in the United States*, ed. Margaret Weir et al. (Princeton, N.J.: Princeton University Press, 1988), 293–311.

12. According to Samuel Rosenman, Roosevelt's first use of the term was in his acceptance address at the 1936 Democratic National Convention. *Working with Roosevelt*, 106.

13. Ibid., 142.

14. Ibid., 1–12.

15. Ibid., 142.

16. Ibid., 143.

17. Second Inaugural Address, third draft, 7, President's Personal File (hereafter cited as PPF) 1820 (Speech Collection), Franklin D. Roosevelt Library, Hyde Park, New York.

18. Second Inaugural Address, third draft, 9, and fourth draft, 9, PPF 1820.

19. Second Inaugural Address, third draft, 1, PPF 1820.

20. Second Inaugural Address, third draft, 4, and fourth draft, 4, PPF 1820.

21. Rosenman, *Working with Roosevelt*, 144.

22. "Inaugurating the Presidency," in Herbert W. Simons and Aram A. Aghazarian, eds., *Form, Genre, and the Study of Political Discourse* (Columbia: University of South Carolina Press, 1986), 205.

23. Ibid.

Chapter Ten

President Franklin D. Roosevelt's Third Inaugural Address, 1941

Michael Weiler

Franklin Roosevelt's Third Inaugural is surely among the easiest of American presidential inaugurals to classify, for it is, first to last, an epideictic speech: its tense is the present; its business is to define democracy, and, given that definition, to praise the people who through their faith and will preserve and extend democracy.

Most inaugurals touch on such themes, and some quite heavily. But Roosevelt's Third Inaugural is remarkable for the single-sightedness and coherence of its treatment. There is no talk of policy, no direct references to current political crises, almost nothing to divert the hearer from the address's focus on the essence of democratic government.

Because it treats a topic of such enduring importance and because its treatment is so little tainted by circumstantial argument—or, for that matter, by political partisanship—the Third Inaugural, almost without changing a word, could have been delivered at virtually any time and on any suitable occasion in American history. But, in fact, it was delivered on January 20, 1941. Roosevelt had just won an unprecedented third term as president. Dwarfing this political feat, however, was the inexorable movement of the United States toward war, a war that had already engulfed most of Europe and much of Asia.

The Third Inaugural must be understood, therefore, not as an isolated paean to democracy but as a speech situated in the midst of a world war and the domestic politics arising from it. Yet here is an address that makes only the most oblique reference to the momentous events surrounding it, that assiduously avoids linking its discussion of democracy to the need for the United States to prepare for war. How do we locate such an apparently detached rhetorical moment within the discourse of its time?

The Roman orators of antiquity often inserted in their addresses to the senate or the courts a *digressio*: material unnecessary to the logical development of the address that interrupted its organizational pattern. The digression was a refreshing and often entertaining diversion from the lengthy and elaborate arguments of the speaker's case and gave him an opportunity to dazzle with his eloquence, but these were not the only purposes it could serve.[1] Properly conceived, a digression could encourage one's hearers to reflect on the broader philosophical and historical issues implicit in the rest of the presentation but lost perhaps in its welter of detail.[2] It was hoped that an audience thus enlightened would return to the case in a frame of mind more favorable to the speaker's position.

If digressions can appear within speeches, then perhaps they can appear also within discourses composed of several speeches. This is how I propose to approach Franklin Roosevelt's Third Inaugural. This address should be analyzed not as separate from Roosevelt's political discourse of the period but as an integral part of that discourse, meant to serve its larger purpose in a distinct yet significant way.

That purpose was to prepare the American people for participation in a war that many of them, even as late as January 1941, believed they could avoid. The Third Inaugural, unlike Roosevelt's speeches before and after it, did not even mention war, much less the role the United States should play in it. Instead, the address talked about the essence of democracy. But it described that essence in such a way as to suggest, albeit indirectly, the course in the war that the United States ought to and would be forced eventually to take.

PRELUDE: THE BATTLE AGAINST ISOLATIONISM

The first two terms of the Roosevelt presidency represent for most Americans the struggle against and ultimate triumph over economic depression. But they coincided also with the rise of fascism in Hitler's Germany and fanatic militarism in Japan and with the ever-increasing belligerence of these two powers. Roosevelt, understandably preoccupied with domestic affairs, found himself increasingly alarmed about developments abroad.

Germany and Japan were bent on world conquest. Even as early as 1933, there was little doubt in Roosevelt's mind of that. He rapidly became convinced, moreover, that the United States, with its vast economic power and military potential, would at some point and in some substantial way be forced, in order to save the world from fascism, to join the forces opposing it.[3] Yet his rhetoric generally failed to reflect the sense of crisis and especially the sense of mission that he felt privately and that many in his administration shared.

His fear of alienating powerful members of Congress was the reason. Isolationist sentiment was strong in both parties. To arouse it was to risk the defeat not only of his foreign policy but of the New Deal. Accordingly, throughout the 1930s and even, to an extent, up to the Japanese bombing of Pearl Harbor, Roosevelt "sought some way to choke fascist expansion that would not involve a head-on fight with the isolationists."[4]

This balancing act produced, as one historian has labeled it, "a policy of pinpricks and righteous protest" but little else.[5] Roosevelt believed that the sheer weight of events would eventually bring the American public around to the realization that the United States had to take a more active role in supporting those nations allied against Germany, Italy, and Japan.[6] His rhetorical strategy was to exploit those events as best he could, making sure that his appeals for a more partisan and activist policy in the war did not outrun them. This approach minimized domestic political fallout but at the cost of chaining U.S. policy to the glacial pace of public opinion. As James MacGregor Burns put it, "Each time in the race between aggression and American opinion, victory went to the former."[7]

It was not until 1940 that events of the war effected a change in public opinion significant enough to allow Roosevelt to abandon all pretense of neutrality.[8] The astonishingly rapid fall of France and the vicious air assault on Britain were convincing evidence that the United States should use its industrial might to arm the Allies, but Americans still hoped that the United States need not itself become a belligerent. Roosevelt was quick to appeal to both public views.

In June, at the University of Virginia, Roosevelt pledged that "we will extend to opponents of force the material resources of this nation; and, at the same time, we will harness and speed up the use of those resources in order that we ourselves in the Americas may have equipment and training equal to the task of any emergency and every defense."[9] In late December, in one of his fireside chats, Roosevelt suggested that "we must be the great arsenal of democracy."[10] In both speeches, however, he was careful to disclaim any intention of involving the nation directly in war. "This is not a fireside chat on war," he assured the nation on December 29. "It is a talk on national security; because the nub of the whole purpose of your President is to keep you now, and your children later, and your grandchildren much later, out of a last-ditch war for the preservation of American independence."[11]

Roosevelt's argument for each new step in the campaign to arm the Allies was that timely aid was the best way to keep the United States out of war. He may have believed this "only in his most optimistic moments," but he felt obliged to say so nonetheless.[12] Roosevelt's Third Inaugural occurred amid these tireless efforts to increase U.S. aid to the Allies in ever more substantial ways without arousing at home a politically paralyzing fear of war. The address is part of this discourse and, in its distinctive way, speaks to this purpose.

ROOSEVELT'S THIRD INAUGURAL: THE SPIRIT OF DEMOCRACY

The thesis of the Third Inaugural is straightforward: "The life of a nation is the fullness of the measure of its will to live."[13] Roosevelt referred here to democratic nations. He argued that democracy's survival rests not on chance or fate but on the strength of the collective will of its citizens.

The address was structured simply. A brief introductory section linked the present and past. "In Washington's day," Roosevelt recalled, "the task of the people was to create and weld together a nation. In Lincoln's day the task of the people was to preserve that Nation from disruption from within. In this day the task of the people is to save that Nation and its institutions from disruption from without." There followed a transition to the thesis statement: "To us there has come a time, in the midst of swift happenings, to pause for a moment and take stock—to recall what our place in history has been, and to discover what we are and what we may be. If we do not, we risk the real peril of inaction."[14]

Roosevelt moved next to the substance of his argument, an argument from definition.[15] He argued for democracy and, by implication, for actions that would preserve it not by specifying those actions but by describing the essence of the democratic system they would defend. He began with a brief confutation: Democracy's demise is not inevitable. "There are men who believe," he acknowledged, "that democracy, as a form of Government and a frame of life, is limited or measured by some kind of mystical and artificial fate that, for some unexplained reason, tyranny and slavery have become the surging wave of the future—and that freedom is an ebbing tide."[16] Why was this not so? Roosevelt offered two proofs, one inductive and one deductive. Inductively, he presented the success of the New Deal as an example used to justify the conclusion that defenders of democracy could take their fate in their own hands; they could act to save their political system. "Eight years ago," Roosevelt recalled, "when the life of this Republic seemed frozen by a fatalistic terror, . . . we acted. We acted quickly, boldly, decisively." The New Deal, then, was powerful evidence that democracy's future was bright.

As a deductive proof of democracy's strength, Roosevelt began with the premise that the willingness of citizens to fight for and preserve their political system rested on the relative benefits the system provided. Because democracy provided the greatest benefits, its citizens would be the most stalwart and successful in its defense. "Democracy is not dying," Roosevelt insisted:

We know it because democracy alone, of all forms of government, enlists the full force of men's enlightened will. We know it because democracy alone has constructed an unlimited civilization capable of infinite progress in the improvement of human life. We know it because, if we look below the surface, we sense it spreading on every continent—for it is the most humane, the most advanced, and in the end the most unconquerable of all forms of human society.

Roosevelt was then ready to confirm his thesis: The essence of democracy is to be found in the will of its people to preserve and extend it. He began with an extended metaphor comparing a democratic nation to a human being. "A nation, like a person," said Roosevelt, "has a body—a body that must be fed and clothed and housed, invigorated and rested, in a manner that measures up to the objectives of our time." Likewise, "A nation, like a person, has a mind—a mind that must be kept informed and alert, that must know itself, that understands the hopes and needs of its neighbors." More than body and mind, however, "a nation, like a person has something deeper, something more permanent, something larger than the sum of all its parts. It is something that matters most to its future—which calls forth the most sacred guarding of its present. It is a thing for which we find it difficult—even impossible—to hit upon a single, simple word. And yet we all understand what it is—the spirit—the faith of America."

Roosevelt moved to a historical argument for regarding the spirit of democracy as its most important element. He touched briefly on the manifestation of that spirit in "the ancient life of early peoples," in "the middle ages," and in "the Magna Charta," but he was concerned chiefly with the American spirit from the Mayflower Compact to the present day, a history he reviewed quickly. Then he returned to his body-mind-spirit scheme. "It is not enough," said Roosevelt,

to clothe and feed the body of this Nation, and instruct and inform its mind. For there is also the spirit. And of the three, the greatest is the spirit. Without the body and the mind, as all men know, the Nation could not live. But if the spirit of America were killed, even though the Nation's body and mind, constricted in an alien world, lived on, the America we know would have perished."

Although Roosevelt noted the difficulty of defining the spirit of America precisely, we know that its two chief elements are faith and will. Without the faith of the people in democracy's survival and their determination to see that it does survive, the material prosperity and political freedom that are part of democracy's promise are but empty vessels. In the present circumstances, how should the people demonstrate their faith? How should they exercise their will? The final paragraphs of the address suggested the answer. Roosevelt avowed:

That spirit [of democracy]—that faith, speaks to us in our daily lives in many ways often unnoticed, because they seem so obvious. . . . It speaks to us from the other nations of the hemisphere, and from those across the seas—the enslaved as well as the free. Sometimes we fail to hear or heed these voices of freedom because to us the privilege of freedom is such an old, old story.

Here was the first suggestion that the spirit of American democracy has ramifications beyond American shores. It is still not clear, however, just what the voices of freedom were saying. Were they urging the United States to come to their aid because democracy is indivisible or simply exhorting us to keep the spirit of democracy strong at home so as to avoid their fate? The next passage of the address did little to resolve this question. Roosevelt quoted the "words of prophecy" of George Washington, "words almost directed, it would seem, to this year of 1941":

"The preservation of the sacred fire of liberty and the destiny of the republican model of government are justly considered . . . deeply, . . . finally, staked on the experiment entrusted to the American people." If we lose that sacred fire, if we let it be smothered with doubt and fear—then we shall reject the destiny which Washington strove so valiantly and so triumphantly to establish. The preservation of the spirit and faith of the nation does, and will, furnish the highest justification for every sacrifice that we may make in the cause of national defense.

These last paragraphs of the address, viewed alone, could be read as a justification for isolation as much as for involvement in the struggle of the Allies against fascism. Nothing suggested that "the experiment entrusted to the American people" could not be carried on separately from the squabbles of less-favored nations elsewhere. But such a reading is scarcely relevant in the rhetorical circumstances of January 1941. For several months and with increasing intensity and specificity, Roosevelt had urged Americans to support military aid to the Allies. The "destroyers-for-bases" agreement with Great Britain had been concluded and announced the previous September. Steel and scrap iron to Japan had been embargoed later the same month. In December, Roosevelt had announced his Lend-Lease initiative and had submitted it to Congress, the most far-reaching measure yet for helping the Allied cause. Finally, the "Four Freedoms" message to Congress of January 6 had provided an ideological justification for the president's policies.[17]

In this political environment, it could not have required any great ingenuity on the part of Roosevelt's audience to discern with what specific measures the spirit of democracy was to be associated. The faith of the people in democracy had to become a faith in its survivability not just at home but in those nations battling valiantly against the Axis. The will of the people to preserve democracy had to be turned toward preserving it, not just in the United States but around the world. Indeed, as Roosevelt had argued continually and would continue to insist, democracy's future in America depended directly on how democracy fared abroad.

THE GENESIS OF THE THIRD INAUGURAL

By the time of the preparation of the Third Inaugural, Roosevelt's chief speech writers were Samuel Rosenman, Robert Sherwood, and Harry Hopkins. Because Hopkins was out of the country and Sherwood was ill, Rosenman had the most to do with the early drafts of the address. Sherwood sent some material in advance and arrived later to polish the final drafts.[18]

The second draft of the address was the product of Rosenman's synthesis of two first drafts, one handwritten by Roosevelt himself and the other by Archibald MacLeish. The address went through seven drafts in all, with Roosevelt making handwritten corrections on the fourth, fifth, and sixth.[19] Thus, the final address reflected both considerable direct input from the president and considerable effort from all others concerned.

MacLeish's draft stated the thesis that was to survive in the final version and noted the need for stocktaking.[20] The rest of the draft, however, talks mainly of the American past, recent and distant. The successful fight against the depression is detailed and placed in the larger context of the history of the American republic.[21] The second draft (Rosenman's synthesis), however, reflected a less historical, more philosophical approach. The body-mind-spirit scheme is added, and the rehearsal of past glories, especially of recent years, is reduced. The word *soul* is substituted for *spirit*, and the discussion of it as an element of democracy is brief. There is considerable emphasis on domestic concerns and none at all, even indirectly, on foreign.[22]

From the third draft on, the soul of democracy receives increasing emphasis. In the fourth draft, *spirit* is substituted for *soul*, the sections discussing the body and mind of democracy are shortened, and the development of the spirit as the crucial element of democracy is lengthened.[23] It was Roosevelt who preferred these changes, even over the objections of Rosenman and Felix Frankfurter, an occasional consultant to the composition process.[24]

The fifth and sixth drafts show the emergence for the first time of references, albeit cautious ones, to wartime issues. To the fifth, Roosevelt added "the real peril of inaction" line.[25] In the sixth, the reference to national security was sharpened. Democracy as "the highest, the supreme motive for defense"[26] becomes democracy as "the highest justification for every sacrifice that we may make in the cause of national defense."[27] The latter version draws attention implicitly to Roosevelt's rearmament policies; the former does not.

The sequence of drafts suggests two things about Roosevelt's intentions. First, he appears to have been determined to develop his "essence of democracy" theme fully and coherently. Accordingly, he placed the greatest emphasis on his definition of democracy's elements and in particular on its most important element, the spirit of democracy. Second, Roosevelt wanted to link, however gently, his remarks about democracy to the need to prepare for war. Accordingly, he cited the real peril of inaction ("isolation" as delivered), and he talked of sacrifices in the cause of national defense. In the circumstances, these references were enough to place the address for the audience within the context of his wartime rhetoric before and after it.

CONCLUSION

As with most other epideictic speeches, at least those intended for more than mere entertainment, Franklin Roosevelt's Third Inaugural has an explicit-contemplative and an implicit-active dimension. Explicitly, the speech encourages the audience to reflect on the philosophical foundations of their political system; implicitly, it asks them to consider what the nature of that system implies for the policies their nation ought to be pursuing in the world and to prepare themselves for the rigors such policies will require. To expect an audience to experience a speech in the first of these dimensions but not in the second is to suggest that its members can step out of the world in which they live. Especially in times of great trouble, this is impossible for most people to do.

It would be a mistake, therefore, to analyze the Third Inaugural as a text isolated from the larger political discourse of which it was a part, for this larger discourse was an important element in January of 1941. It makes more sense to ask what place in that discourse the address occupied. I have described it as a philosophical digression from the main body of arguments that Roosevelt used to move the American people toward war. In this sense, it was a case of the pursuit of foreign policies by other than the usual deliberative means.

These other means are the same as two of those identified by Karlyn Kohrs Campbell and Kathleen Hall Jamieson in their study of the generic characteristics of American presidential inaugural addresses.[28] In particular, Roosevelt in the Third Inaugural "unifies the audience by reconstituting its members as 'the people' " and "rehearses communal values drawn from the past."[29] Actually, he accomplishes the first by doing the second: the people are defined by the democratic tradition they share.

The explicit dimension of the address amounts to a rehearsal of communal values, but it is also something more. Roosevelt's definitional approach was designed to add new insight to his audience's understanding of the democratic values on which their nation was based, to render those values in a newly vivid, compelling form. His address was as much a rethinking of values as a rehearsal of them. It was as if he was rediscovering via a fresh interpretation the forgotten meanings of the lead character's major soliloquy in an old play.

A third characteristic, the setting forth of political principles upon which the new administration will be based,[30] is present implicitly to the extent that Roosevelt's praise of democracy suggests his commitment to it, but there are no explicit pledges of this sort in the speech. Democracy by its nature requires the spirited commitment of all. Without it, there is no democracy.

Roosevelt was disappointed at the tepid response to his Third Inaugural.[31] He, more than most other presidents, and certainly more than most recent presidents, took political philosophy seriously and felt qualified to talk seriously about it. Indeed, he may have been the last in a distinguished line of American philosopher-presidents stretching from Jefferson and Madison through Lincoln and on to Woodrow Wilson. Moreover, Roosevelt could, as on this occasion, deliver his philosophy straight. Perhaps his twentieth-century American audience lacked a taste for abstract discussions of democracy largely unrelieved by contemporary, concrete reference. Or perhaps the inaugural was the wrong occasion. Whatever the case, the Third Inaugural does not appear to have made a major public impression.[32]

I have suggested, however, that the speech should not be evaluated in isolation, and this should be true as well for the appraisal of its reception. For such a purpose, a digression is not something to be separated from the discourse of which it is a part any more than one would attempt to measure separate responses to a narration or peroration within a speech. If, by the use of this philosophical interlude, Roosevelt was able to increase the effectiveness of his efforts to prepare the nation for war, then the Third Inaugural served its purpose admirably. Whether it did so is impossible to determine. Locating the address in its larger discursive context, however, at least clarifies its purpose and strategic potential.

NOTES

1. See Marcus Tullius Cicero, *De Inventione*, trans. H. M. Hubbell (Cambridge, Mass.: Harvard University Press, 1968), 55, 57.

2. See Quintilian, *The Institutio Oratoria* (X, i, 31–34), trans. H. E. Butler (London: William Heinemann, 1921), 2:19–23. Quintilian objected to digressions for entertainment purposes only, insisting that they be germane to the speaker's case. See ibid. (IV, iii), 2:121–31.

3. William E. Leuchtenburg, *Franklin D. Roosevelt and the New Deal* (New York: Harper & Row, 1963), 210–11, 214–15.

4. Ibid., 211.

5. James MacGregor Burns, *Roosevelt: The Lion and the Fox* (New York: Harcourt, Brace & World, 1956), 385.

6. Ibid., 400.

7. Ibid.

8. Previously, Roosevelt's rhetoric, in condemning the Axis powers and in praising those who opposed them, had, by implication at least, attacked the isolationist stance. But it was not until 1940 that he could justify candidly the substantial military aid he had wanted for so long to provide the Allies.

9. "Address at University of Virginia" June 10, 1940, in *Public Papers and Addresses of Franklin D. Roosevelt: 1940 Volume*, (New York: Macmillan, 1941), 264.

10. "Fireside Chat on National Security," December 29, 1940, in *Public Papers and Addresses*, 643.

11. Ibid., 633.

12. See Frank Freidel, *Franklin D. Roosevelt: A Rendezvous with Destiny* (Boston: Little, Brown, 1990), 361.

13. "Franklin D. Roosevelt: Third Inaugural Address," in *Inaugural Addresses of the Presidents of the United States: From George Washington 1789 to George Bush 1989* (Washington, D.C.: U.S. Government Printing Office, 1989), 279–82. All quotations from the speech hereafter are from this source.

14. In delivery, Roosevelt actually said "the real peril of isolation" first and then added the manuscripted "the real peril of inaction." Samuel Rosenman reports that after the speech the president described how he delivered both versions, adding, "all of which improved it." See *Working with Roosevelt* (New York: Harper and Brothers, 1952), 270–71.

15. See Richard M. Weaver, "Abraham Lincoln and the Argument from Definition," in *The Ethics of Rhetoric* (South Bend, Ind.: Regnery/Gateway, 1953), 86.

16. Rosenman, *Working with Roosevelt*, 270, claims that the phrase "surging wave of the future" was chosen as a sly reference to Ann Lindbergh's book, *The Wave of the Future*, a defense of isolationism, Halford Ross Ryan disputes Rosenman's version, however. See *Franklin D. Roosevelt's Rhetorical Presidency* (Westport, Conn.: Greenwood Press, 1988), 95.

17. See Freidel, *Franklin D. Roosevelt*, 361.

18. Rosenman, *Working with Roosevelt*, 268.

19. Ibid., 268–70.

20. See "Third Inaugural Address: Draft from MacLeish," President's Personal File (hereafter, PPF), 1820 (Speech Collection), 1, Franklin D. Roosevelt Library, Hyde Park, New York.

21. Ibid., 1–5.

22. Third Inaugural Address: Second Draft, PPF, 1820.

23. Third Inaugural Address: Fourth Draft, PPF, 1820.

24. Rosenman, *Working with Roosevelt*, 269–70.

25. Third Inaugural Address: Fifth Draft, 1, PPF, 1820.

26. Ibid., 8.

27. Third Inaugural Address: Sixth Draft, 8, PPF, 1820.

28. "Inaugurating the Presidency," in *Form, Genre, and the Study of Political Discourse*, ed. Herbert W. Simons and Aram A. Aghazarian (Columbia: University of South Carolina Press, 1986), 203–25.

29. Ibid., 205. Campbell and Jamieson's fourth generic characteristic of inaugurals, the acknowledgment of the responsibilities and limits of executive power, does not apply to the Third Inaugural.

30. Ibid.

31. Rosenman, *Working with Roosevelt*, 271.

32. See Halford Ross Ryan's discussion of the speech's reception. *Franklin D. Roosevelt's Rhetorical Presidency*, 91–96.

Chapter Eleven

President Franklin D. Roosevelt's Fourth Inaugural Address, 1945

Daniel Ross Chandler

President Franklin D. Roosevelt achieved in his Fourth Inaugural his rhetorical objective that "the form of this Inauguration be simple and its word brief."[1] The occasion appeared almost austere. Convinced that conducting the inaugural ceremonies at the White House rather than at the Capitol was more consistent in consummating the country's war efforts since such ceremonies would be scaled down, low-key, and somber, Roosevelt terminated the long-standing tradition of holding the stately activities upon the steps of the Congress. The assembled audience that heard his Fourth Inaugural was among the smallest ever. And with the exception of Washington's Second Inaugural, Roosevelt's Fourth was the shortest in American history. A sophisticated patrician who struggled to surmount the poliomyelitis that paralyzed his legs but strengthened his spirit, Roosevelt sat in his wheelchair taller than many enemies could stand. The president heroically lead a perplexed people through a problematic period pervaded by a devastating economic depression and catastrophic world war, sometimes assuming sweeping executive powers that prompted his opponents to criticize him as a virtual dictator. Roosevelt became neither an embittered cynic nor a caustic skeptic, but he remained an unconquerable optimist who acknowledged, like Charles Dickens, that the worst of times are the best of times.

Like his great contemporary Winston Churchill, Roosevelt headed an English-speaking nation that was inspired to heroic heights when a gifted speaker employed language effectively and eloquently. Elected to an unprecedented fourth term, the president had served twelve eventful years; subsequently an amendment to the U.S. Constitution limited a president's term to eight years. Emphasizing public service and encouraging social responsibility, he wielded a charismatic leadership and commanded his rhetorical presidency so powerfully that Chicago clergyman Preston Bradley commented, "Franklin Roosevelt could have remained a playboy and could have wined and dined and traveled his way through life without a worry, but he did not; he chose another way; and that's why the common people love him."[2] Dying in office almost five months following his fourth inauguration and less than a month before the Germans surrendered during World War II, a larger-than-life Roosevelt imparted an immortality that prompted some countrymen to observe that Franklin Roosevelt dead might be stronger than Roosevelt alive. The president's Fourth Inaugural confirms James Barber's conclusion that personality determines performance, and this conviction was especially evident when Roosevelt referred to a previous inaugural address by reminding the American people that they had nothing to fear but fear itself and by inspiring his countrymen with his unyielded affirmation that confidence emanates from conviction.[3] Amid the enshrouding, encumbering darkness, a perceptive president discerned within an illuminating light the radiant, unprecedented opportunities for achieving enduring peace and nurturing human progress. The seeds that Roosevelt planted with rich rhetoric produced a bountiful harvest and ripened fruit during the crucial decades following his death.

AN INTELLECTUAL GENESIS OF ROOSEVELT'S GERMINAL IDEAS

Roosevelt's Fourth Inaugural is distinguished from its predecessors by a philosophical perspective—an embattled president's courageous attempt to discover meaning and discern purpose within and transcending contemporary conflicts. The speech reflected Roosevelt's untiring, undiminished efforts to exert persuasive presidential leadership during an especially turbulent time.

A significant idea expressed in the address is the president's affirmation of America's "essential democracy" and the nation's imperfect but improvable Constitution. Clearly acknowledging and effectively expressing his philosophy of government, the president professed correctly that the current crisis challenged the nation's "essential democracy" and that although the Constitution was imperfect, nevertheless this governmental system constituted the finest that the founding fathers could formulate.

Another important idea appearing in the president's address was attributed by Roosevelt to a former Groton schoolmaster who taught that life will not always run smoothly—sometimes humanity will ascend toward towering heights before sliding downward—but that the trend within civilization remains upward or forward. Sensing social progress and attempting to diminish widespread apprehension, Roosevelt explained that a line drawn through the middle of the peaks and the valleys inevitably reveals human progress.

Finally, a third fundamental idea was articulated when Roosevelt quoted the preeminent American philosopher Ralph Waldo Emerson as saying that the only way to have a friend is to be a friend. The president employed the quotation to encourage international cooperation and to promote worldwide community. One could translate Emerson's wisdom as, as a nation gives, so the country receives.

GENERIC ELEMENTS IN THE ADDRESS

Analyzing how presidential inaugural addresses exhibit generic elements emanating from their character and the nature of the occasion, Karlyn Campbell and Kathleen Jamieson concluded that the president demonstrates his comprehension of democratic principles, understands the limitations that characterize democratic government, and exercises a rhetorical leadership serving as the symbolic head of state.[4] In his Fourth Inaugural, Roosevelt unified his diverse audience with a common conviction and courage-inspiring conviction that "it is America's purpose that we shall not fail." The chief executive effectively demonstrated his understanding of presidential leadership during a time of "supreme test" and "historic importance" when he articulated his administration's anticipation of "total victory in war," followed by an honorable and durable peace. Roosevelt recounted and rehearsed the historic communal values inherent within a democracy where the American people strive persistently for perfection and learn from their mistakes, and he contended convincingly that these errors must never result from a faintness of heart or abandonment of moral principle. Consistent with his conclusion that the trend toward higher civilization remains forever upward, he claimed that although the Constitution is an imperfect instrument, this fundamental law of the land provided "a firm base upon which all manner of men, of all races and colors and creeds, could build a solid structure of democracy."

The inaugural ceremony provided an appropriate occasion for teaching the lessons that the president had learned from extensive historical experience. Roosevelt said that history produces certain insight; that Americans cannot live alone, at peace; and that the welfare of the United States requires securing goodwill from foreign nations. Like an adroit professor stressing an essential concept, Roosevelt admonished the American citizenry that his people "must live as men and not as ostriches, nor as dogs in the manger." Consistent with his conclusion was his conviction that Americans must acknowledge their citizenship within the world community.

The address, however, contained neither an acknowledgment nor any appreciation of the powers and limitations that circumscribe the executive functions within American democracy. In a real sense, Roosevelt's moving the inaugural ceremonies from the halls of Congress to the White House, coupled with the ascendant powers that he wielded as commander in chief, rhetorically reinforced and symbolized dramatically the conspicuous absence of this generic element. A time-tested titan who dwarfed the Senate and the House of Representatives, Roosevelt seemed to some critics to approximate a dictator who was willing to transgress constitutional limitations imposed upon his presidential authority by renouncing and repudiating the regulations imposed by the Congress and the Supreme Court.

Roosevelt's Fourth Inaugural was neither as memorable nor as outstanding as his First Inaugural, which was not simply the president's finest inaugural address but was a superb specimen representing exceptional presidential discourse. Neither was the Fourth as significant as the Second, during which the president surveyed his contested and controversial New Deal programs. However, Roosevelt's Fourth resembled his First, which marked an innovation in intellectual content and rhetorical style of inaugural public addresses. Both the First and the Fourth indicated that because agreement occurs most easily at higher levels of intellectual abstraction, a speaker's concepts must become generalized to convince or persuade a diverse audience within a pluralistic society. Confronting widespread economic depression and worldwide military engagements required that Roosevelt diminish his emphasis upon America's greatness while stressing the historic faith that is essential in perpetuating that greatness.[5]

The principal rhetorical purpose pervading Roosevelt's Fourth was inspirational. In this sense, the speech was more contemplative than deliberative. The president reported that the nation's war efforts were progressing toward an eventual victory, that the coming success would promote human civilization, and that Americans' confidence in victory was sustained by the correctness of the country's objectives. What appeared astounding was Roosevelt's undiminished optimism about the long-range progress of human civilization. The president's vision was not restricted by the short-range perspective from a contemporary catastrophe. Indeed, Roosevelt examplified how a classical education equips an aspiring speaker with an essential philosophical predisposition, an expanded historical perspective, and a familiarity with the world's great literature.[6]

ROOSEVELT'S DELIVERY

Self-confident, gregarious, and exuberant, Roosevelt developed a rhetorical delivery that projected competence, dynamism, and authority.

The president's resonant tenor voice was usually modulated carefully and controlled conscientiously in rhythmic cadences and emphatic phrases that evoked sensations of strength and sincerity. His charm bespoke enormous confidence and unshaken conviction. Employing carefully crafted phrases and instantly intelligible sentences, Roosevelt achieved a crystal-clear certainty and dramatic emphasis within his listening audiences, although his hearers embraced diverse political persuasions.

Films recording Roosevelt's Fourth Inaugural preserved in his presidential library at Hyde Park, New York, indicate that even with a diminished dynamism and subdued enthusiasm, Roosevelt remained effective.[6] Roosevelt's Fourth Inaugural was delivered more slowly and deliberately, suggesting that the gallant warrior had grown older and was afflicted with a lingering illness as he faced the stress and strain of the war. Resembling a sacrificial martyr persevering in a holy cause or sacred calling, the dying president suffered hypertension, hypertensive heart disease, and cardiac failure.[8] Roosevelt's delivery remained a powerful force asserting the president's undiminished authority, nurturing a communicative intimacy among the president and his people, and inspiring a country's respect for a war-torn warrior.[9] During his Fourth Inaugural, Roosevelt digressed skillfully from his manuscript in an effective effort to articulate his thoughts more precisely and adapt to the audience more directly. The president was impressive with a slower speaking rate, decisive phrasing, and deliberate emphases.

THE EVOLUTION OF THE ADDRESS

Franklin D. Roosevelt mastered the rhetorical-communicative techniques that characterize a persuasive politician preceding his campaign for the presidency of the United States. As an archetypical contemporary American president, he successfully transformed the nation's highest elective office from an aloof Olympus towering above the American people into an interpersonal intimacy uniting the citizenry into a community warmed by his charisma, especially with folksy fireside chats. Not the first chief executive who effectively employed professional speech writers, Roosevelt utilized these competent professionals and virtually institutionalized the practice. He acknowledged openly the assistance he received from Samuel Rosenman, Robert Sherwood, Donald Richberg, Harry Hopkins, Louis Howe, Tommy Corcoran, and Archibald MacLeish. Recognizing the enormous communicative power inherent in radio, Roosevelt had used the newly emerging communicative medium while governor of New York with an astonishing persuasive impact, and his awesome political career became inextricably linked with the progressive development of mass media broadcasting.

Using the nation's airwaves to disseminate important inspirational speeches and strengthen his interpersonal intimacy among his constituency, Roosevelt communicated confidence and certainty during his Fourth Inaugural when he deliberately talked with citizens through the technological environs that ensued when families gathered around a radio. Roosevelt had accurately anticipated and appreciated the communicative potential inherent within radio when he presented the first televised presidential speech during the 1939 New York World's Fair. With consummate skill, he elevated the presidential news conference and fashioned that communicative forum into an important instrument for exerting political persuasion. In a manner subsequently employed by Ronald Reagan, Roosevelt adapted public speeking effectively to appeal directly to the American people for their crucial support.[10]

Recognizing that considerable controversy surrounds the authorship of Roosevelt's Fourth Inaugural, Halford Ryan contended convincingly and correctly that a critic should distinguish between a speaker's thoughts and the ideas contributed by another writer.[11] Critical rhetorical analysis produces the conclusion that Roosevelt's Fourth Inaugural was derived solely from a working draft submitted by Robert Sherwood. This conclusion is confirmed by the rich rhetorical resources contained in the collections at the Franklin D. Roosevelt Library at Hyde Park.[12]

Although Roosevelt's Fourth Inaugural grew directly from his germinal ideas, the president's final reading draft was derived from Sherwood's manuscript. The primary sources crucial in confirming the authorship are ten specific speech manuscripts, the carbon copies of these manuscripts, and the final reading copy. The anatomy that appears in analyzing this accumulated material indicates that Roosevelt initially contributed the drafts containing his random thoughts, that a draft from this material was written by MacLeish, that two drafts were composed by Rosenman, that two drafts were submitted by Sherwood, and that three specific drafts provided the foundation from which the final reading copy was derived. Rosenman reported that MacLeish, Sherwood, and he submitted drafts to Roosevelt and that the president used these three drafts and his own composition in the final draft, which is shorter than any of the three submitted by his professional speech writers.[13] However, Rosenman was misleading, for Ryan discovered that Roosevelt's final reading copy was developed during three stages of rhetorical invention and that the manuscript was predicated upon Sherwood's draft.

In the process of rhetorical composition, Roosevelt initially stated his own thoughts; he directed his three speech writers to construct their drafts; and then he selected Sherwood's submission as the draft used in composing the final reading copy. The two elementary drafts initially composed by the president and assigned to his speech writers contain these fundamental ideas: an affirmation concerning human progress that Roosevelt attributed to a schoolmaster, his conviction that America's "essential democracy" would survive although the Constitution was imperfect, and an assertion that confidence is derived from conviction, sustained by an Emersonian admonition that having a friend entails being a friend. Roosevelt quoted himself when he recalled from his First Inaugural that the only thing that all Americans have to fear is fear itself. The germinal ideas doubtless flowed from the historical-rhetorical situation that the president confronted during his Fourth Inaugural. Roosevelt sensed correctly that the occasion required that he assert confidence during a time of uncertainty and assurance during a decade of supreme test. These qualities were not simply demanded by the situation but were inherent within Roosevelt's dynamic, powerful, commanding personality. The Fourth Inaugural was a reflection and expression of Roosevelt himself. Examining the drafts submitted by these presidential speech writers reveals the rhetorical process through which Roosevelt's final reading draft was composed.

MacLeish's five-page manuscript contained a detailed discussion describing the nation's war effort and a section envisioning a future pervaded with freedom.[14] With a single exception, no clearly discernable indication of MacLeish's manuscript appears in the final reading manuscript.

Rosenman's original handwritten draft was developed into a typewritten original manuscript from which two carbon copies were produced.[15] Rosenman used Roosevelt's thought about confidence coming from conviction, and he skillfully amplified this statement. The quotation from Roosevelt's schoolmaster was diminished, but the president's thought concerning the improvement or perfection of the U.S. Constitution was strengthened. Rosenman revised the president's statement about "fearing fear" by simplifying an awkward rhetorical construction and making the thought more clearly evocative of Roosevelt's statement that appeared in the First Inaugural. With the single exception of the quotation that Roosevelt attributed to his Groton schoolmaster, the three specific instances in which Rosenman revised Roosevelt's statements constituted an improvement in expressing the president's thought. However, a minimum of Rosenman's manuscript is evident in Roosevelt's final reading manuscript. In Roosevelt's Fourth Inaugural Rosenman's revision of the "fearing fear" statement is absent. The statement concerning the perfection or imperfection of the Constitution does not resemble Rosenman's construction. The president restored the quotation from his teacher, and the "confidence from conviction" affirmation was restored partly to Roosevelt's original statement. Hence, Rosenman's manuscript deviated substantially from Roosevelt's basic draft.

Sherwood composed an undated handwritten manuscript from which were made a typed original and two carbon copies.[16] All the germinal thoughts given initially by the president appear in Sherwoods's manuscript. Sherwood accepted but rewrote and reduced the statement about the Constitution, utilized the schoolmaster's quotation, changed and diminished the impact of the statement about "fearing fear," and employed the president's assertion about confidence emanating from conviction. With the sole exception of the statement attributed to the schoolmaster, Sherwood's alterations of language changed the meaning and the emphasis of the president's germinal thoughts and created a version in which Roosevelt's original statement was diminished.

The final reading draft was developed from Sherwood's manuscript. Distinguishing Roosevelt's dictated emendations from Sherwood's statements remains difficult because these changes were made in Sherwood's handwriting. Evidently Roosevelt accepted these emendations during a process of rhetorical invention during which Sherwood's copy ceased to be Sherwood's and became instead the president's manuscript. Roosevelt's "confidence from conviction" statement was restored.

A new draft was developed from this working manuscript. This new draft indicates that the manuscript was revised extensively. Brevity was achieved by eliminating excessive verbage, pessimistic words were replaced with more optimistic choices, and the statements were tightened with an economy of language. A fresh second draft was typed from the emendations appearing on the typewritten "new draft," and from this draft a typewritten, triple-spaced final reading copy was prepared.

CONCLUSION: ROOSEVELT'S RHETORICAL PROPHECY

Roosevelt's Fourth Inaugural Address constituted a religious statement that expressed powerfully a country's testament of historic faith. The president acknowledged the deity in a manner consistent with the continuous profession articulated by presidents who served since Abraham Lincoln and that observers such as Charles LaFontaine identified as a national theology.[17] Roosevelt successfully engaged, as a significant motivational source, an American civil religion that exists separately from the nation's religious institutions but that appears as a glorification of the state. This enduring sentiment, enunciated in Roosevelt's Fourth Inaugural, identifies national purpose, promotes public cohesion, strengthens social responsibility, and provides a sustained inspiration. A rhetorical statement such as Roosevelt's constitutes no blatant demagoguery threatening religious orthodoxy or the established institutions with a tendency toward secular humanism; instead, these statements strengthen the nation's commitment to freedom and peace by placing these cherished verities within a cosmic frame of reference. What Duncan Howlett described as "the fourth American faith"[18] was presented during the 1950s as a religious pluralism that comprised a socioreligious subculture emphasizing essential commonalities and providing a religious way of belonging. This persuasion, as A. Powell Davies stated, emphasized universality, championed individual intellectual freedom, practiced democratic processes in human relationships, professed a disciplined search for truth, and asserted allegiance to universal human community.[19] As a distinctive religious persuasion expressed through presidential discourse, this "fourth faith" was articulated appropriately when Roosevelt employed the occasion to engage this historic tradition and these symbols to strengthen American idealism and aspirations.[20]

Serving as the country's highest elected secular priest and presenting a customary ceremonial address, Roosevelt concluded with a providential benediction. Reverently the president recognized how Almighty God had blessed America by providing the people with stout hearts and strong hands; he inspired his countrymen with a reference to a faith that had become "the faith of all peoples in an anguished world." The president prayed for the vision to perceive a better life for his country and all humanity and to promote His will of peace upon the earth. Roosevelt's steadfast resolve promised that he would dedicate his strength with an uncompromised determination and undiminished conviction to serving with dignity the finest that was discernable within himself and his fellow citizens. He promised to practice peace beyond the tempest of resounding armies and the tumult of clashing camps. Believing that the historic past is not a single source of illuminating inspiration, Roosevelt insisted that his audience should cherish their traditions, aspirations, and idealism while awaiting patiently to hear new sounds from silent sources that had not yet spoken.

Roosevelt's Fourth Inaugural served a prophetic function. The president perceived so clearly the existing situation that he envisioned the promising future. The Fourth Inaugural evidences the president's capacity for rhetorical prophecy, an ability that appears when a speaker fathoms so deeply the potential within current events that he or she discerns the impending developments that eventually transpire in the future. Roosevelt's unswerving conviction in the inevitability of human progress and a better future provided an unconquerable spirit in which the president inspired his war-weary countrymen. Realizing that the United States and the Allied nations were passing precariously through a perplexing period of supreme testing, Roosevelt contended with confidence that the successful and honorable fulfillment of rightful responsibilities would result in a service of great historic significance. Roosevelt stressed a present possibility latent within a crisis, a chance for bequeathing humanity an enduring legacy that men, women, and children would honor throughout the passing centuries. Hence, Roosevelt developed a rhetorical transcendence that inspired his people when he articulated their unquenchable aspirations to reach a higher plane of human civilization and to promote social progress. Optimistically he challenged the citizens by proclaiming that America's purpose was to succeed. Roosevelt specified and justified the unyielding purpose undergirding the nation's military endeavor, an honorable and enduring peace. Employing rhetorical paradox, the commander in chief professed that fighting for complete victory was required for establishing eventual peace. The president cultivated courage among the American people by claiming that the mistakes that might be committed must result not from faintness of heart or abandoning moral principle. Eventually peace would be procured "only if we proceed with the understanding and the confidence and the courage which follow from conviction." Roosevelt's Fourth Inaugural was inspiring, futuristic, and prophetic.

NOTES

1. Franklin Delano Roosevelt, "Fourth Inaugural Address," in *American Rhetoric from Roosevelt to Reagan*, ed. Halford Ross Ryan (Prospect Heights, Ill.: Waveland Press, 1987), 26. Hereafter, all quotations are from this authoritative text of FDR's Fourth Inaugural.

2. Preston Bradley, "A Tribute to President Roosevelt," *Liberalist* 22 (1945): 3.

3. See James D. Barber, *The Presidential Character: Predicting Performance in the White House* (Englewood Cliffs, N.J.: Prentice-Hall, 1972).

4. Karlyn Kohrs Campbell and Kathleen Hall Jamieson, "Inaugurating the President," *Presidential Studies Quarterly* 15 (1985): 394–411.

5. Leo Finkelstein, Jr., "The Calandrical Rite of the Ascension to Power," *Western Journal of Speech Communication* 45 (1981): 51–59.

6. See Bruce A. Kimball, *Orators and Philosophers: A History of the Idea of Liberal Education* (New York: Teachers College Press, 1986), 1–204.

7. Film MP–78–1, number 3, Franklin D. Roosevelt Library, Hyde Park, New York.

8. John Gunther, *Roosevelt in Retrospect* (New York: Harper and Brothers, 1950), 364.

9. Barnet Baskerville, *The People's Voice: The Orator in American Society* (Lexington: University Press of Kentucky, 1979), 179.

10. James W. Ceaser, Glen E. Thurow, Jeffrey Tulis, and Joseph M. Bassette, "The Rise of the Rhetorical Presidency," in *Essays in Presidential Rhetoric*, ed. Theodore Wendt and Beth Ingold (Dubuque, Iowa: Kendall/Hunt, 1983), 3–22.

11. Halford Ross Ryan, "Roosevelt's Fourth Inaugural Address: A Study of Its Composition," *Quarterly Journal of Speech* 67 (1981): 157–66.

12. Among these primary sources are a succession of manuscripts that culminates in final reading copies upon which the president sometimes contributed concluding emandations. These drafts are enriched by using the sound recordings, motion picture films, and indexed photography files. This invaluable collection for rhetorical research contains mail that registers public response to the

president's speeches, insightful oral histories, diaries written by Roosevelt's contemporaries, and a compilation of scholarly theses and dissertations in which scholars have analyzed Roosevelt's public addresses. Franklin D. Roosevelt, "Some Thoughts for Inaugural Speech," January 6, 1945, Papers of Franklin D. Roosevelt, Master Speech File, number 1570, Fourth Inaugural Address, January 20, 1945, Franklin D. Roosevelt Library; Franklin D. Roosevelt, "Other Thoughts for Inaugural Speech," January 13, 1945, Fourth Inaugural File, 1–3; First Draft, Fourth Inaugural Address of the President, January 20, 1945, Fourth Inaugural File, 1–3; Final Reading Copy, Fourth Inaugural Address of the President, White House, January 20, 1945, Fourth Inaugural File, 1–2; and a verbatim transcription in *The President's Fourth Address, From the South Portico of the White House, January 20, 1945, about 12:06 p.m., and Broadcast Nationally*, Fourth Inaugural File, 1–3.

13. Samuel I. Rosenman, *Working with Roosevelt* (New York: Harper and Brothers, 1952), 516–17.

14. Archibald MacLeish, draft of Fourth Inaugural, Fourth Inaugural File, original typewritten and carbon copy, 1–5.

15. Samuel I. Rosenman, typewritten draft of Fourth Inaugural, Fourth Inaugural File, 1–4.

16. Robert Sherwood, handwritten draft for Fourth Inaugural, Fourth Inaugural File, 1–3.

17. Charles V. LaFontaine, "God and Nation in Selected U.S. Inaugural Addresses, 1789–1945," *Journal of Church and State* (1976): 39–60, 503–21.

18. Duncan Howlett, *The Fourth American Faith* (Boston: Beacon Press, 1968), 29–61. See Stow Persons, *Free Religion: An American Faith* (New Haven: Yale University Press, 1947).

19. A. Powell Davies, *American Destiny: A Faith for America* (Boston: Beacon Press, 1942), 29–30; and Davies, *America's Real Religion* (Boston: Beacon Press, 1965), 45.

20. See James David Fairbanks, "The Priestly Functions of the Presidency: A Discussion on the Literature of Civil Religion and Its Implications for the Study of Presidential Leadership," *Presidential Studies Quarterly* 11 (1981): 214–32.

Chapter Twelve

President Harry S. Truman's Inaugural Address, 1949

Halford Ryan

President Harry S. Truman beat Governor Thomas E. Dewey of New York by running against the "Do-Nothing Eightieth Congress" in the 1948 election. The Republican-controlled House and Senate were loath to pass the president's domestic agenda, so Truman ran frontally against the Congress and incidentally against Dewey.

But the president's forte was foreign policy. Addressing a joint session of Congress on March 12, 1947, Truman delivered his so-called Truman Doctrine speech that committed the United States to containing communism. Thus, the political auguries of Truman's administration and of the 1948 campaign impinged on the inaugural address by anyone skilled enough to read them.

THE GENESIS OF HARRY TRUMAN'S INAUGURAL ADDRESS

George Elsey's prescient reading of the auguries had a profound impact on the inaugural development. Elsey, an assistant to Clark Clifford, who was Truman's special counsel, endorsed the inaugural purview in a November 16, 1948, memorandum to Clifford:

I suggest that the State of the Union Message be confined insofar as possible to domestic matters and that all foreign policy issues be reserved for the Inaugural Address. . . . No other occasion in the foreseeable future offers the President so great an opportunity to speak to the entire world . . . and I believe that his words on January 20 should match the dignity and responsibility of that role [leader of the free world].[1]

Elsey's perception was preeminently rhetorical. Whereas it would be difficult for Truman on Inauguration Day to discuss divisive domestic issues, Truman could address a united country on foreign affairs, for anticommunism was growing as the Soviets expanded in Europe. Thus Elsey had Truman break cleanly with his 1948 campaign and focus instead on foreign issues, for which he had some prior successes with the people and Congress.

Elsey charted the course, but it was another task to compose a speech. Clifford notified the State Department that he could use some help on the inaugural,[2] and Joseph Jones obliged. Jones, a speech writer in the State Department, sent a January 6, 1949, draft and a January 11, 1949, revision to David Lloyd, who had joined the Truman speech team at Clifford's behest and helped with the inaugural. These drafts were evidently rejected by Clifford in conference with Lloyd.[3]

Early in this process, President Truman agreed to Elsey's memorandum of November 16, 1948. Elsey noted that the speech was "not to exceed 15 minutes @ 120 words = 1800 words"; that it should be "exceedingly simple in language and concrete not abstract"; and that the "President stated that the Inaugural would be on Foreign Policy."[4]

Then the process took a fortuitous turn. Benjamin Hardy, a junior officer in public affairs at the State Department, read Clifford's call for suggestions from the State Department. Hardy presented his idea through normal diplomatic channels, but the State Department was uninterested. Persevering, he contacted George Elsey, in what Elsey later characterized as an "entirely unofficial and off-the-record visit."[5] Hardy gave Elsey an outline of Point Four, and Elsey then conferred with Clifford, who immediately appropriated the idea. Clifford remarked in chiasmas: "We had a speech in search of an idea, Hardy had an idea in search of a speech."[6] Hardy's germinal ideas were:

1. Political institutions
   a. UN [United Nations]
   b. Respect for the rights of all peoples
2. Economic betterment
   a. ERP [European Recovery Program, or Marshall Plan]
   b. World trade
   c. Technological development
3. ~~Military Security~~ [in original] Preservation of Law and Order
   1. Regional defense pacts
   2. Military aid and advice to other nations
   3. Our own military strength

Fourth, we will join with other nations in reducing barriers to international trade because world trade is one of the foundations of world peace.[7]

These four points, only slightly modified, were the innervating components of the speech as delivered.

A first draft, unsigned and undated, was written. A second draft, January 14, 1949, finally had Hardy's four points in it.[8] Point Four proceeded on a third draft on January 15, 1949. Lloyd, Clifford, Elsey, Charlie Ross, and Matt Connelly all gathered in the Cabinet Room as President Truman read aloud the draft.[9]

Clifford sent Dean Acheson at the State Department a fourth draft, dated January 16. Acheson offered a suggestion that was used in the final address. His insert was an example of the classical concept of apophasis, or affirmation by denial. If Acheson did not wish "to draw issues," then why make the point? The apophasis neatly masked his real intent:

I state these differences, not to draw issues of belief as such, but because the actions resulting from the Communist philosophy are a result [in original] threat to the efforts of free nations to bring about world recovery and lasting peace.[10]

The president made some insignificant emendations on a fifth draft, dated January 20, 1949. On the reading copy, which was twenty-four pages long, Truman underlined words, but he emphasized so much verbiage that his practice made little sense for vocal pacing.[12]

PRESIDENT TRUMAN'S INAUGURAL ADDRESS: SUPERNATION RHETORIC

Prior to the end of World War II, the people of the United States and their presidents were committed to a public philosophy of a reified nation. Among the many aspects of this ideology was one that conceived the nation as the embodiment of freedom and justice for the American people; consequently, American domestic issues tended to dominate in pre–World War II inaugurals.[12]

After World War II, according to Dante Germino, a new kind of supernation rhetoric emerged: "The rhetoric of inaugurals stressed . . . the new rote of the quasi-apocalyptic transformation of the world in a final battle with demonic communism."[13] Two ideas characterized this rhetoric: (1) the president depicts the supernation in Manichaean terms, which is "to view one's own side as the repository of all goodness and the other of all evil"; and in using this kind of rhetoric, (2) the president distorts the meaning of freedom:

The result has been the arbitrary division of the world into that of the "free" and the "enslaved," even though a majority of the countries with whom the United States has made alliances can scarcely be called "free" in the American public philosophy's understanding of freedom. Instead of being defined in relation to that philosophy, freedom becomes defined as non-Communist.[14]

Since HST was the first president to deliver an inaugural after World War II, his speech is an archetype of supernation rhetoric. The thesis is that Truman made a break with historical inaugural addresses by focusing entirely on foreign issues.

President Truman sounded the leitmotif of supernation rhetoric in the second sentence of his inaugural address: "I accept it [the presidency] with a resolve to do all that I can for the welfare of this Nation and for the peace of the world."[15] Hence, Truman enacted the president-as-the-speaker-of-the-free-world role that Elsey envisioned in his memorandum. Truman declared: "It is fitting, therefore, that we take this occasion to proclaim to the world the essential principles of the faith by which we live, and to declare our aims to all peoples."

At their face value, the "essential principles of faith" were traditional exponents of nation rhetoric. Although Truman delivered the following words, they could just as appropriately be spoken by any previous chief executive:

The American people stand firm in the faith which has inspired this Nation from the beginning. We believe that all men have a right to equal justice under law and equal opportunity to share in the common good. We believe that all men have a right to freedom of thought and expression. We believe that all men are created equal because they are created in the image of God. From this faith we will not be moved.

The anaphora of "We believe" communicated some stylistic elegance to an otherwise pedestrian patriotism.

Yet a classical Aristotelian enthymeme—a truncated rhetorical syllogism in which the audience completes the logic of the argument without the orator's proving all of the premises—was at work in Truman's nation rhetoric. In the historical context of Soviet expansionism, democratic principles, such as equal justice under law and freedom of thought and expression, assumed a salience that transcended traditional lip-service to domestic verities. Truman invited domestic and foreign audiences to complete his enthymeme by reasoning thus: since communism subverts U.S. values, communism is bad; therefore, communism should be contained.

If some obdurate listeners did not perceive Truman's drift, he reiterated it in subsequent paragraphs, which also signaled the transition to supernation rhetoric. "The United States and other like-minded nations," Truman averred, "find themselves directly opposed by a regime and a totally different concept of life." Truman's enthymeme was so clear that he did not have to identify the Soviet Union and its communist philosophy.

Truman used the stylistic device of antithesis to juxtapose communism with democracy. Four pairs of antithetical units starkly communicated Manichaean dichotomies:

1. Communism believes "that man is so weak" that he "requires the rule of strong masters," but democracy believes "that man has the moral and intellectual capacity . . . to govern himself."
2. Communism "subjects" individuals to invidious state controls, whereas democracy protects "the rights of the individual."
3. Communism "maintains that social wrongs can be corrected only by violence," whereas democracy achieves "social justice . . . through peaceful change."
4. "Communism holds that the world is so widely divided into opposing classes that war is inevitable," but "democracy holds that free nations can settle differences justly and maintain a lasting peace."

The anaphora of "communism" and "democracy," which juxtaposed each of the four thought units, verbally reinforced the opposites. Truman reinforced the antithesis:

These differences between communism and democracy do not concern the United States alone. People everywhere are coming to realize that what is involved is material well-being, human dignity, and the right to believe in and worship God. [And then he used Acheson's insert:] I state these differences, not to draw issues of belief as such, but because the actions resulting from the Communist philosophy are a threat to the efforts of free nations to bring about world recovery and lasting peace.

By now, most listeners would have appreciated Truman's point, but he was not yet finished with his verbal portraiture of communist perfidy. Continuing in the Manichaean vein, he warranted more evidence. The antithesis was present in the form of an enthymeme: the audience easily supplied what nation was the opposite of the United States. The listing had four paragraphs that began with the anaphora of "We have":

1. "We have sought no territory." Free peoples of the world would recall the Berlin blockade in 1948.
2. "We have constantly and vigorously supported the United Nations." Americans would remember that the Soviet Union often used its veto power to stymie world peace.
3. "We have made every effort to secure agreement on effective international control of our most powerful weapon." The fact that the Soviet Union vetoed

in the Security Council in 1946 a plan for international control of atomic energy warranted Truman's claim.[16]

4. "We have encouraged ... the expansion of world trade on a sound a fair basis." The 1947 Geneva agreement had produced the General Agreement on Tariffs and Trade.

The Manichaean enthymeme marched forward. "Almost a year ago, in company with 16 *free nations* [author's emphasis] of Europe, we launched the greatest cooperative economic program in history." Truman alluded to the Marshall Plan, and he allowed in supernation rhetoric that "we have saved a number of countries from losing their liberty."

The Manichaean juxtapositions, used once in four units of clear antithesis and once in four units of implied antithesis, were masterful rhetorical enthymemes. Truman's supernation rhetoric presented the evidence, and Americans supplied the inferences.

As a U.S. solution to combat Soviet perfidy, Hardy's outline remained remarkably intact. His first point was political institutions, with the United Nations as a subpoint. Truman pledged: "First, we will continue to give unfaltering support to the United Nations." Hardy's other subpoint, "respect for the rights of all peoples," became more narrowly defined by Truman as "lands now advancing toward self-government under democratic principles."

Hardy's second point, economic betterment with subpoints of the ERP, world trade, and technological development, remained complete, except for the technology part. "Second," HST enumerated, "we will continue our programs for world economic recovery." He spoke of the "European recovery program," and reducing trade barriers, for "economic recovery and peace itself depend on increased world trade."

Hardy's third point was preservation of law and order, which included regional defense pacts, military aid, and U.S. military strength. It was a serviceable blueprint, for Truman announced: "Third, we will strengthen freedom-loving nations against the dangers of aggression." Truman acknowledged that a "collective defense arrangement," which would be known as the North Atlantic Treaty Organization (NATO), was close to fruition. Truman sold the fledgling NATO alliance with supernation rhetoric while employing the fallacy of *petitio principii*. Without proving that the United States was faced with imminent belligerence, he assumed that premise and then argued that the aggression could be deterred by giving "unmistakable proof of the joint determination of the free countries to resist armed attack from any quarter. . . . [Then] the armed attack might never occur." The inaugural audience's "applause was perhaps the strongest" for this appeal.[17]

Hardy's fourth point was the reduction of trade barriers to international trade and peace. Of the four points, this one was redirected in the final address toward technological aid to developing countries; however, the theme of international trade and peace were still apparent. "Fourth," Truman proclaimed, "we must embark on a bold new program for making the benefits of our scientific advances and industrial progress available for the improvement and growth of underdeveloped areas." Truman listed the miserable living conditions of more than half the people in the world, and then offered U.S. "technical knowledge" that was "inexhaustible." This aid, however, was circumscribed. The problem was worldwide, including communist countries, but the solution was limited to anti- or noncommunist nations because U.S. aid would be made "available to peace-loving peoples." Later in his address, Truman again assured Americans that "our aim should be to help the free peoples of the world." He summarized his four points with a Manichaean appeal:

Democracy alone can supply the vitalizing force to stir the peoples of the world into triumphant action, not only against their human oppressors, but also against their ancient enemies—hunger, misery, and despair. On the basis of these four major courses of action we hope to help create the conditions that will lead eventually to personal freedom and happiness for all mankind.

The conclusion of Truman's inaugural could be termed a classical peroration, an ending of unusual elegance and force. Truman constructed a series of five sentences that began with the anaphora of "We are aided by." Truman proclaimed:

We are aided by all who wish to live in freedom from fear. . . . who want relief from lies and propaganda. . . . who desire self-government. . . . who long for economic security. . . . [and]who desire freedom of speech, freedom of religion, and freedom to live their own lives for useful ends.

To bolster the Manichaean rhetoric that recurred throughout the speech, Truman waxed biblically: "Our allies are the millions who hunger and thirst after righteousness." To motivate Americans to battle against evil, the president preached that it would "test our courage, our devotion to duty, and our concept of liberty." And, as if to verify the cliché that God is a being mentioned in the last sentence of a political speech, Truman intoned: "With God's help, the future of mankind will be assured in a world of justice, harmony, and peace."

TRUMAN'S DELIVERY

Although Elsey's November 16, 1948, memorandum noted that the inaugural should be 1,800 words and fifteen minutes long, it lasted twenty minutes and contained about 2,200 words. Hence, HST delivered the speech at 110 words per minute (wpm) in a conscious effort to slow his usual 150 wpm rate in order to dignify the occasion.[18]

Truman delivered his speech in his typical fashion. His eye contact was poor because he read his address. He even muffed one of the principal lines in the speech: "From this fai . . . uh . . . faith we will not be moved."[19] His voice was nasal and his vocal pacing uninspired.[20] Although Truman's was the first inaugural to be broadcast by television, Jack Gould noted that his delivery was the "slow movement in the spectacle."[21]

REACTIONS TO THE ADDRESS: FOUR POINTS AND POINT FOUR

Point Four is an example of amphiboly, that is, ambiguous meaning. In this case, the uncertainty is in the number: Should the address be called Four Points or Point Four? Harold Gosnell noted that Truman's foreign policy address "outlined four major policies," and Roy Jenkins noted that the address "was christened Point Four (by the press, not by Truman) and was the beginning of Third World Aid."[22] Although a fine point, the nomenclature of *Point Four* or *Four Points* is notable. *Point Four* captured the limelight, but the *Four Points* were the epicenter of Truman's foreign policy from 1949 to 1953, and all four points were proclaimed in Manichaean, supernation rhetoric.

With regard to the Four Points, the public reaction to Truman's inaugural was favorable. (The Truman Library contains five pro folders and one con folder.) Four Points also prompted international approval, although the Soviets carped predictably in *Tass* that Truman's speech was an "enraged attack" on communism.[23]

The con letters in the Truman Library are the most interesting. A writer from Rochester, Minnesota, discomfited by the Manichaean inaugural, complained that Truman's heated rhetoric was "a declaration of war." In less hyperbole, a writer from Wilton, Connecticut, scored Truman's cold war idealogy:

It is neither true, nor safe to believe, that *all* the virtue is on our side and *all* the evil on our opponents' [emphasis in original]. . . . Finally, I notice that Wall Street, to which you alluded unfavorably in your appeal to the electorate, reacted favorably to this speech, which in itself is an indication that you are off on the wrong boat.

Additionally, a writer from Chicago objected to Truman's helping governments whose only virtue was being anticommunist:

Neither is the support of governments that are fascist and corrupt such as those of Greece and China. Finally, it does not seem that nations are being considered as equals when they are preached to and when they are told that our ways are better than theirs.[24]

These anecdotal letters were mirrored by national figures. Henry Wallace complained that his former boss's speech came "closer to a declaration of war than the inaugural address of any peacetime President in our history." The *New Republic* rejoined Truman's rhetoric with a stinging rebuttal:

In pursuit of our containment of Russia we have made friends with every other dictatorship everywhere—with Chiang, Peron, Franco—if it was only willing to be, or to say it is, anti-Communist. . . . Greece sinks from one level of corruption and incompetence to another, and we do nothing about it, since the corrupt leaders are our allies against Moscow and its friends.[25]

CONCLUSION: GENERIC CONSIDERATIONS

HST's inaugural speech has been assigned the sobriquet of Point Four, but its historical importance and rhetorical efficacy were in its Four Points. Hardy originally gave Elsey four thematic ideas. Their raison d'être ensured peace for the United States under the free world leadership of President Truman. The Manichaean, supernation enthymemes in all four points made little rhetorical sense if they did not seek acquiescence from the audience for supporting the United Nations, economic recovery, military security, and technological aid.

Not epideictic, Truman's inaugural address was essentially deliberative in nature. He laid before the American people and Congress a four-point program for political action. Albeit he understandably did not use Aristotelian terminology, Truman mentioned in his memoirs that his speech was an action-oriented, deliberative inaugural: "I proposed four important major courses of action. . . . Thus was launched what came to be universally known, within a matter of months, as the 'Point Four program,' because it was the fourth of the four important courses of action set forth in the inaugural address." The *New York Times* presciently perceived the president's purpose: "Unlike many of his predecessors, whose inaugural addresses were in the nature of philosophical discourses, the plain-spoken Missourian delivered a major policy statement. It was replete, like virtually all his speeches, with concrete statements and proposals." Truly, Elsey stated that whenever the president gave a political speech, it was "to mold public opinion or persuade congressional leaders."[26]

Truman's inaugural speech conformed only marginally to generic stipulations. He did rehearse communal values, but they were new Manichaean, supernation mores. And he did communicate the guiding political principles for his administration: the Four Points remained cornerstones in American foreign policy against communism until the early 1990s. And Truman did reconstitute the people when, after a fashion in his introduction, he asked for "the help and prayers of everyone of you" and for "your encouragement and for your support."

But significantly, Truman did not mention the powers and limitations of the presidency vis-à-vis the Congress. This rhetorical strategy was purposeful because Elsey wanted Truman to treat domestic issues in the State of the Union and to address foreign issues, the president's strength, in the inaugural. The Manichaean, supernation rhetoric renewed the president's powers, for few congressmen and citizens wanted to be perceived as pro-Soviet during the cold war.

The fourth point's rhetoric, however, was more renowned than its reality. Point Four was passed by Congress in May 1950, more than a year after its dramatic announcement on inaugural day. William Pemberton observed that Truman's "proposal reaped great propaganda rewards, but the much lauded plan never amounted to much except as a publicity device." And when explaining why the fourth point failed to meet expectations, Thomas Patterson said it best:

Hastily announced, originally neglected by the State Department, lost in the turmoil of more dramatic Cold War issues, hampered by limited congressional appropriations, resisted in many parts of the Third World, spurned by American businessmen, and ultimately diverted to military purposes and strategic materials stockpiling, Point Four faltered early.[27]

NOTES

1. George Elsey to Mr. Clifford, November 16, 1948, Papers of George Elsey, Speech File, Box 36, 1–2, Harry S. Truman Library (HSTL), Independence, Missouri.

2. Clark Clifford with Richard Holbrooke, *Counsel to the President: A Memoir* (New York: Random House, 1991), 249.

3. Papers of David Lloyd, Presidential Speech File, Box 13, HSTL.

4. Notes on Inaugural Address, January 27, 1949, Papers of George Elsey, Speech File, Box 36, HSTL.

5. Memorandum for Mr. Clifford, July 17, 1963, Papers of Clark Clifford, Box 39, HSTL.

6. Clifford, *Counsel to the President*, 250.

7. Files of David Lloyd, Box 13, HSTL.

8. Inaugural Address, 1949, Papers of David Lloyd, Presidential Speech File, Box 13, HSTL.

9. Draft of January 15, Papers of George Elsey, Speech File, Box 36, HSTL.

10. Draft of January 16, Papers of George Elsey, Speech File, Box 36, HSTL.

11. President's Secretary's Files, Speech File, Box 48, and Inaugural Address,

Reading Copy, HSTL; Donald L. Wolfarth, "John F. Kennedy in the Tradition of Inaugural Speeches," *Quarterly Journal of Speech* 47 (1961): 130.

12. Dante Germino, *The Inaugural Addresses of American Presidents: The Public Philosophy and Rhetoric* (Lanham, Md.: University Press of America, 1984), 2, 15–19.

13. Ibid., 21.

14. Ibid., 23, 25.

15. *The Public Papers of the Presidents, Harry S. Truman,, 1949* (Washington, D.C.: U.S. Government Printing Office, 1964), 112. All subsequent quotations of Truman's inaugural address are from this speech text.

16. Harry S. Truman, *Memoirs by Harry S. Truman: Years of Trial and Hope* (Garden City, N.Y.: Doubleday, 1956), 2:11.

17. "Truman Sworn in, the 32d President," *New York Times*, January 21, 1949, 2.

18. Robert Underhill, *The Truman Persuasions* (Ames: Iowa State University Press, 1981), 337.

19. Cassette, Inaugural Address, Selected Speeches of Harry S. Truman, 1948–1951, Side 2, HSTL.

20. Underhill, *The Truman Persuasions*, 334–38.

21. "Hail to the Chief," *New York Times*, January 21, 1949, 55; Jack Gould, "10,000,000 Viewers See the Ceremony," *New York Times*, January 21, 1949, 6.

22. Harold F. Gosnell, *A Political Biography of Harry S. Truman* (Westport, Conn.: Greenwood Press, 1980), 441; Roy Jenkins, *Truman* (New York: Harper & Row, 1986), 146.

23. See "President's Talk Encourages Italy" and "Message Praised by British Papers," *New York Times*, January 21, 1949, 6; "World Fair Deal," *Newsweek*, January 31, 1949, 18.

24. PPF 200, Box 326, HSTL.

25. "Wallace Calls Talk of Truman Warlike," *New York Times*, January 21, 1949, 5; "President Truman's Global Plans," *New Republic*, January 31, 1949, 5–6.

26. Truman, *Years of Trial and Hope*, 2:227, 230; Anthony Leviero, "Peace a Major Aim," *New York Times*, January 21, 1949, 1; George Elsey, Oral History Transcript, 17, May, 1974, HSTL.

27. Robert A. Packenham, *Liberal America and the Third World* (Princeton, N.J.: Princeton University Press, 1973), 43; William E. Pemberton, *Harry S. Truman: Fair Dealer and Cold Warrior* (Boston: Twayne Publishers, 1989), 160; Thomas G. Patterson, *Meeting the Communist Threat: Truman to Reagan* (New York: Oxford University Press, 1988), 157.

Chapter Thirteen

President Dwight D. Eisenhower's First Inaugural Address, 1953

Martin J. Medhurst

The election of Dwight D. Eisenhower on November 4, 1952, ended twenty years of Democratic control of the executive branch. Eisenhower ran a campaign based on three main issues: Korea, communism, and corruption (K_1C_2). In each case, Ike argued that the policies being pursued by the Truman administration were injurious to the nation and that nothing short of a complete housecleaning could restore decency and integrity to government. It was a hard-fought campaign that often called forth invective, name calling, and extreme charges on both sides.[1]

When Eisenhower turned from the election to preparations for taking office, however, he left behind the bitterness of the campaign trail, and matters of policy formulation became paramount. From the outset, Eisenhower intended to use every means at his disposal, including public speaking, to press his policy agenda. Foremost on this agenda was finding a quick yet suitable end to the Korean War, the most recent manifestation of a much larger policy concern, the spread of international communism.

Long before his decision to enter elective politics, Eisenhower had been a committed anticommunist. As director of the Allied Zones of Occupation immediately following World War II, chief of staff of the U.S. Army, and Supreme Commander of the newly formed North Atlantic Treaty Organization (NATO) forces, Eisenhower had observed communist tactics at first hand. As president, he would wage cold war against what he considered to be an implacable and immoral foe. That war would officially begin on January 20, 1953, with delivery of his First Inaugural.

Ike's First Inaugural looked forward, not back, and it was rooted in the historical exigencies of the moment. The great urgency of January 1953 revolved around the question: To whom does the future belong? The communist philosophy held that historical evolution was determined by economic forces and that such forces would inevitably lead to the overthrow of capitalist democracies and the ascendancy of communist (scientific socialist) societies. Eisenhower was taking office when the future direction of human governance was a matter of debate. Would the models for the rest of the world be America and Great Britain, or China and the Soviet Union?

Ike determined that his first speech as president would state clearly his belief that "the future shall belong to the free." By making this proclamation, Eisenhower accomplished three objectives. First, he altered his audiences—domestic, international friends, and international foes—to his basic stance and attitude. Second, he announced the broad outlines of the policies that his administration would follow. Third, he made the first in what would be a series of rhetorical attempts to position the United States as a peacemaker in the ongoing cold war—a position that would make the waging of psychological warfare against the Soviet empire more palatable to the American electorate.[2]

DRAFTING THE SPEECH

Work on the inaugural address commenced in mid-November 1952. Although Ike initially turned to his old friend and campaign speech writer C. D. Jackson for compositional assistance, he quickly turned the inaugural assignment over to a man whom he had known for only the previous three months: Emmet John Hughes. Both Hughes and Jackson had joined the general's campaign in late August 1952 to bolster an overworked speech-writing staff. Both worked for the *Time/Life/Fortune* empire of Henry and Clare Booth Luce, and neither planned on a long-term stay in government service. Although Ike liked and trusted Jackson, he soon realized that Hughes was by far the better writer.

The first hint that the inaugural address would be driven by policy considerations occurred on December 8, 1952, when Hughes joined Eisenhower and key members of his cabinet-designate to go over a "summary review" of the address.[3] The location of the meeting was on board the cruiser *Helena,* where Ike and his lieutenants were engaged in strategic planning for the upcoming administration. From the outset, the views of men such as John Foster Dulles, Herbert Brownell, Charles Wilson, Harold Stassen, and Henry Cabot Lodge were to be reflected in the speech. Little is known about what happened on board the *Helena,* but the first complete draft must give some indication of the directions that Hughes received.

Between December 11, when the *Helena* docked at Honolulu, and

January 12, when Eisenhower read the entire address to his cabinet-designate, Hughes produced at least six drafts of the speech.[4] The first draft introduced the theme that would carry through to the day of delivery: freedom. Hughes wrote: "The world and we have come to the midway point of a century of challenge. This, for freedom, has been an age of seige [sic]." Many of the themes that Ike would sound on January 20 are found in this first, undated draft. Also present are several of the policy matters that Ike wished to emphasize: interdependence ("As we confront a common peril, so we can seek only a common safety"), economic and political security ("Assessing realistically the needs of proven friends of freedom, we shall strive . . . to help them achieve economic and political security"), fair trade ("we shall strive to foster everywhere in the world policies that will promote profitable and equitable trade"), and the European Defense Community ("Convinced that rigid nationalism in Europe has become an obsolete and dangerous political luxury, we shall earnestly strive to speed the achieving of true unity on that continent"). The rhetoric was motivated by policy concerns.

In each of the six drafts written between December 11 and January 12, policy matters became more pronounced. In draft 3, for example, the necessity of cold war was plainly stated: "Still in quest of peace, we still must wage war. And it shall continue to be thus—until they who live by the sword will come finally to know that free men, by simple definition and by solemn dedication, never will surrender their faith." Also in draft 3, emphasis was placed on deterrence—"Shunning and abhoring war as a chosen way to meet those who threaten us, we hold it to be the first task of statesmanship to summon all our resources . . . in the task of deterring aggression"—and on military strength—"we view our nation's security as a trust upon which rests the hope of free men everywhere. That trust demands both military strength and economic strength, for neither can long exist without the other." Both deterrence and military strength would become central aspects of Eisenhower's New Look defense posture. By draft 6, Hughes had added a reference to associations of nations—"Knowing that geography and economic advantage combine to suggest regional groupings of free peoples, we hope to help the strengthening of such special bonds the world over"—thus foreshadowing the development of the Southeast Asia Treaty Organization (SEATO) and other regional defense associations. With each successive draft it became clearer that policy was driving the discourse, which is reinforced by Ike's meeting of January 12, 1953, with members of his cabinet-designate.

The January 12 meeting was important because it provides external confirmation of the internal evidence of the drafts.[5] It also provides a key insight into Eisenhower's thinking, not only about the content of the address but also concerning such matters as language use, audience, and tone. For example, immediately after reading the address to the assembled cabinet, Eisenhower noted: "Here is this thing going out to probably one of the greatest audiences that has ever heard a speech. It is going in the papers. Here are thousands out in front of us. You want every person there to carry home with him a conviction that he can do something." We learn two things from this quotation: Ike was indeed concerned with the domestic audience—those who would hear the speech in person or over radio or television, or read it in the newspaper—and that he expected the speech to be a motivation toward action, to "do something."

But we learn much more. When John Foster Dulles spoke, he pointed directly to matters of policy: "You speak about independence? Africa, don't you? How about just saying self-government so that you don't seem to take the African side against the French side?" And again, Dulles said: "There was a reference to developing regional areas but there was no reference toward the United Nations." Dulles was not the only person concerned with policy matters. Secretary of Defense–designate Charles E. Wilson said: "On the trade business, I like to talk about trade as being a two-way street. In other words, you are not giving anything away and we are not pushing out our surpluses on anybody, or anything like that. Trade is a two-way street." And Arthur Summerfield, soon to become the postmaster general, observed: "I thought there might be a point about the availability of our surpluses to these less fortunate nations. This speech is going to be heard all over the world. This is not entirely a selfish plan."

Eisenhower agreed with some of it, but much of the discussion centered around how the speech would articulate U.S. policy. Ike, however, was equally concerned with how the speech would be understood and interpreted. His goal was to reach not only policymakers but common citizens as well. As he told the group: "In this speech I deliberately tried to stay in the level of talk that would make as good reading as possible at the Quai D'Orsay or at No. 10 Downing, but I particularly tried to make the words that would sound good to the fellow digging the ditch in Kansas." Ike was very aware of the language, tone, and sentiment of his address. He was also insistent that the emphasis on American productivity stay in the speech. As he replied to Dulles: "But we must remember also today that unless we can put things in the hands of people who are starving to death we can never lick Communism." As a clear instance of cold war rhetoric, Ike's First Inaugural placed the defeat of communism in titular position.[6]

When Oveta Culp Hobby, secretary of Health, Education, and Welfare, asked about the use of the phrase "trained citizenry," Eisenhower responded at length about the policy implications of the wording:

If we are going to keep down our expenses that are involved in the constant maintenance of very large military organisms we have got to plan carefully for the rapid transition of this whole country from a peace to a war activity. If you are going to do that one of your bottlenecks will be the training of great bodies of citizens. The thing that makes possible the cutting down of an existing force is the existence of a trained citizenry. That is what I was trying to get over.

Robert Cutler, chosen to be Ike's first national security adviser, commented on one of the goals of the speech: "We must strike a note which will make the people who are so pressed down in other countries yearn to be on our side. Peace is not enough to offer those people. It must be a peace where they can grow and develop, not a Pax Americana where we say we will keep the world at peace." Eisenhower heartily agreed.

The January 12 meeting demonstrates that all those who had a hand in the preparation of Eisenhower's First Inaugural were acutely aware of the policy implications of his remarks. What is not very clear from the minutes of this meeting was Eisenhower's growing frustration with the speech and the speech writer.

From several sources, we know that the period from January 13 through January 18 was one of growing frustration for Eisenhower. More than anything, Ike wanted his inaugural address to get across the idea that it was up to each individual, both at home and abroad, to work for peace, by which he meant the triumph of democratic ideals. He wanted the address to be stately and high-minded but also simple and moving to the average citizen. During the discussion with his cabinet, Ike's main complaint had been that the address was too long, but there was more to his discontent than length alone.

The private diary of Emmet John Hughes gives a good deal of insight into the composition processes of the final week. On January 13, Hughes noted in his diary that he spent the afternoon working on the "final" draft of the inaugural and that he was still striving for what Ike called a "more down to earth" emphasis.[7] The next day, Hughes gave Eisenhower the reworked draft, which Ike promised to look over that evening. On January 15, Hughes wrote in his diary: "Many penned changes in draft when we meet. Example of unpredictibility [sic]: beneath first senstence [sic] of 'midway point of century of challenge' he scrawls 'I hate this sentence'—a sentiment never before hinted. Other changes on mss. I rework."

Hughes had already received permission from Ike to leave New York City on January 15 and drive to Washington, D.C., to set up his new home. He arrived in Washington late on January 16 and spent the next day unpacking. While Hughes was away, Eisenhower became increasingly upset with the current draft. On January 16, Ike wrote in his personal diary:

For some weeks I have been devoting harried moments to preparation of my inaugural address—to be delivered next Tuesday. I want to make it a high-level talk. By this I mean I want to appeal to the speculative question of free men more than I want to discuss the material aspects of the current world situation. But how to do it without becoming too sermonlike—how to give it specific application and concrete substance has somewhat defied me.

My assistant has been no help—he is more enamored with words than with ideas. I don't care much about the words if I can convey the ideas accurately. I want to warn the free world that the American well can run dry, but I don't want to discourage any. Above all, I don't want to give the Soviets the idea they have us on the run.[8]

Eisenhower became so upset by the morning of January 17 that he called C. D. Jackson and asked him to produce, in less than twenty-four hours, a new version of the inaugural address. Here is how Hughes recalls the incident:

About 5—CD calls from NY. Ike had called him over this morning to express unhappiness over Inaugural, wants him to give it a "whirl" between now and 930 A.M. tomorrow.

I exploded with frustrated wrath. It8s [sic] manifest impossibility to create new speech at this date. What's wrong with present one? "Oh you know his lecture on the subject of words, words."

Tempted to call Adams—but resist. . . .

Tired and late we go to Mayflower reception and dinner for Nixons. . . . Dulles stops me, asks what [is] this about new Inaugural to be sent down tomorrow. I confess ignorance and dismay; he laughs.

Hughes did not think that Eisenhower's last-minute retreat was any laughing matter. His diary entry for Sunday, January 18, tells what happened:

Get to Shoreham by 915 to be ready for any discussion of Inaugural fiasco—only Dulles there. We phone Anne [sic] Whitman trying to locate missing new Inaugural, locate Helen Weaver (WAC). Stassen appears. Finally Weaver appears with text. Dulles glances at it and says in 10 seconds, "Well, this just doesn't look any good at all." CD text rough, verging on unintelligibility; stresses "change" theme for some odd reason; retains 9 point program and most of peroration. Dulles anxiously calls Brownell over. He reads original and this version, then both call Ike and flatly tell him, "First version is fine and this one just won't do." . . . I remark to Herb how nervous Ike gotten about whole thing of late, he says—"Well, wouldn't you be nervous?" . . . On phone Ike murmurs, "it sounds like I'm giving a sermon." Herb tells him, "in a way that's just what you should give." More phoning back and forth, Hagerty relaying Ike's last tinkering to Mrs. O'Day on one extension, me on the other.

With Eisenhower in New York and his assistants in Washington, D.C., the final draft of the inaugural address was composed over a long-distance telephone line. So involved was Eisenhower in this process that he was an hour late boarding his special train for Washington, D.C.[9]

AN ANALYSIS OF THE TEXT

On Tuesday, January 20, Eisenhower attended church early in the morning. When he returned to his suite at the Statler Hotel, he decided to compose a prayer for delivery at his inauguration ceremony, scheduled for noon. As he later wrote in his memoirs:

Religion was one of the thoughts that I had been mulling over for several weeks. I did not want my Inaugural Address to be a sermon, by any means; I was not a man of the cloth. But there was embedded in me from boyhood, just as it was in my brothers, a deep faith in the beneficence of the Almighty. I wanted, then, to make this faith clear.[10]

Ike's prayer was clearly part of the rhetoric of the inaugural address if for no other reason than it reinforced the ethos of the man. Ike prayed:

Almighty God, as we stand here at this moment my future associates in the Executive branch of Government join me in beseeching that Thou will make full and complete our dedication to the service of the people in this throng, and their fellow citizens everywhere.

Give us, we pray, the power to discern clearly right from wrong, and allow all our words and actions to be governed thereby, and by the laws of this land. Especially we pray that our concern shall be for all the people regardless of station, race or calling.

May cooperation be permitted and be the mutual aim of those who, under the concepts of our Constitution, hold to differing political faiths; so that all may work for the good of our beloved country and Thy glory. Amen.[11]

The prayer pointed to an ultimate reality, and thus paralleled the inaugural address itself, for the speech allowed for no room between good and evil:

The world and we have passed the midway point of a century of continuing challenge. We sense with all our faculties that forces of good and evil are massed and armed and opposed as rarely before in history.

This fact defines the meaning of this day. We are summoned by this honored and historic ceremony to witness more than the act of one citizen swearing his oath of service, in the presence of God. We are called as a people to give

testimony in the sight of the world to our faith that the future shall belong to
the free.

Several dimensions of the opening prayer and opening lines of the
address are noteworthy. First, the notion of time as linear (not eternal
or timeless) is featured: "at this moment," "the midway point of a century," "the meaning of this day," "the future." The very situatedness
of the ceremony at a particular point in time becomes a central aspect
of its rhetoric. Second, the audience is portrayed as active. It is not only
present "to witness" but also "to give testimony." In short, the outcome
of "this century of continuing challenge" may well depend on the actions
undertaken by those listening to the speech. Both features are central
to a proper understanding of the First Inaugural, for the policies that
will be articulated are grounded in the rhetorical situation of the moment;
the central argument depends on a linear view of history; and the audiences addressed—domestic listeners, international friends, and international foes—are all asked to fulfill the role of actors, not merely
spectators.

Eisenhower's main argument was stated in the form of a proposition
of fact: "The future shall belong to the free." The rest of the speech was
an outworking of this basic premise and the unstated conclusion to
which it led: "The future shall belong to us." The argument, in full syl-
logistic form, is: The future shall belong to the free//The free are we//
The future shall belong to us. Having first set up the rhetorical situation
as "a time of recurring trial," Eisenhower moved to establish his minor
premise: "At such a time in history, we who are free must proclaim
anew our faith. This faith is the abiding creed of our fathers. . . . This
faith rules our whole way of life. It decrees that we, the people, elect
leaders not to rule but to serve." Notice that in these passages Eisenhower used the *forms* of epideictic discourse, but he used them for a
distinctly argumentative *function* and purpose: to establish his minor
premise that "the free are we." He continued to establish this minor
premise by contrasting America's faith in freedom to that of its enemies:
"The enemies of this faith know no god but force, no devotion but its
use. They tutor men in treason. They feed upon the hunger of others.
. . . Here, then, is joined no argument between slightly differing philosophies. This conflict strikes directly at the faith of our fathers and the
lives of our sons."

With U.S. soldiers still dying in Korea, Eisenhower's image of the
communist serpent striking at American faith, freedom, and very lives
must have been a powerful appeal. To this point in the speech, Eisenhower was clearly addressing the American people. But the section on
faith and freedom, the minor premise of his extended argument, was
soon expanded to include U.S. allies as well: "The faith we hold belongs

not to us alone but to the free of all the world. . . . We wish our friends the world over to know this above all: we face the threat—not with dread and confusion—but with confidence and conviction. We feel this moral strength because we know that we are not helpless prisoners of history. We are free men." Ike moved to secure the minor premise while at the same time expanding it to include "all free peoples" who had not succumbed to the serpent's wiles.

The next section of the speech was therefore addressed primarily to the friends of freedom as a statement of American *policy* intentions. It is composed of nine "fixed principles," virtually all of which carried direct policy implications:

1. We hold it to be the first task of statesmanship to develop the strength that will deter the forces of aggression and promote the conditions of peace.
2. We shall never try to placate an aggressor by the false and wicked bargain of trading honor for security.
3. Knowing that only a United States that is strong and immensely productive can help defend freedom in our world, we view our Nation's strength and security as a trust upon which rests the hope of free men everywhere.
4. We shall never use our strength to try to impress upon another people our own cherished political and economic institutions.
5. We shall strive to help them [our friends] to achieve their own security and well-being.
6. We shall strive to foster everywhere, and to practice ourselves, policies that encourage productivity and profitable trade.
7. Economic need, military security and political wisdom combine to suggest regional groupings of free peoples. . . .
8. Conceiving the defense of freedom, like freedom itself, to be one and indivisible, we hold all continents and peoples in equal regard and honor.
9. Respecting the United Nations as the living sign of all people's hope for peace, we shall strive to make it not merely an eloquent symbol but a effective force.

Clearly these nine principles not only announced what the United States planned to do but also asked friendly nations to do some things as well: to assume a heavier defense burden, open up markets, join in regional defense groupings, unite as a "free Europe," and cooperate with the United Nations. One paragraph in this section even seemed directed primarily to the Soviet Union. Under point 1, Eisenhower said:

We stand ready to engage with any and all others in joint effort to remove the causes of mutual fear and distrust among nations, so as to make possible drastic reduction of armaments. The sole requisites for undertaking such effort are that—in their purpose—they be aimed logically and honestly toward secure peace for all; and that—in their result—they provide methods by which every participating nation will prove good faith in carrying out its pledge.

This was Eisenhower's opening shot in a campaign of psychological warfare that would be echoed repeatedly during his first term in office in speeches such as "The Chance for Peace," "Atoms for Peace," and "Open Skies." Interestingly, the paragraph addressed to the Soviets appears in none of the six drafts penned by Hughes up through January 14.[12] But even in this late addition, Ike asked the Soviets to make a move toward peace.

As Eisenhower reminded his listeners in the peroration:

These basic precepts are not lofty abstractions, far removed from matters of daily living. They are laws of spiritual strength that generate and define our material strength. Patriotism means equipped forces and a prepared citizenry. Moral stamina means more energy and more productivity, on the farm and in the factory. Love of liberty means the guarding of every resource that makes freedom possible.

In short, the whole speech sought action. As Ike implored, "And so each citizen plays an indispensable role. . . . No person, no home, no community can be beyond the reach of this call. We are summoned to act in wisdom and in conscience, to work with industry, to teach with persuasion, to preach with conviction, to weigh our every deed with care and with compassion. . . . This is the work that awaits us all." The entire speech was a call to act in line with specific policy objectives and was so understood throughout the world.

Various sources of audience reaction testify to how the speech was received. As a security-restricted report on "Foreign Press Reaction to President Eisenhower's Inaugural Address" states: "In most regions there was heavy editorial comment on the Inaugural Address and what it portended for the future of US foreign policy." Excerpts from editorial pages around the world make clear that the inaugural address was viewed by most as a statement of policy. The following extracts are illustrative:

No one, after hearing his speech, will have any ground for fearing that the US under his leadership is likely to abdicate in any significant respect from the responsibilities which the country has assumed under his predecessors. [*Manchester Guardian* (liberal)]

Let it be set down in black and white just how Britain can participate in the EDC's military and economic decisions. [London *Economist* (independent-influential)]

American big business, in the interest of self-preservation, is in the process of being converted to something approaching free trade. [*New York Times*]

As may be expected, communists deprecated the address. On January 22, Radio Warsaw broadcast a commentary by Stefan Arski in which he alleged that Eisenhower tried to "wrap the brutal truth in empty phrases and to disguise the aggressive policy of the US." For Arski, the speech's meaning was simple: when Eisenhower said the United States would try to make the United Nations "an effective instrument," he was referring to "the continuation of the aggression in Korea and the abuse of the UN for the aggressive US aims."[13]

As these extracts clearly indicate, worldwide press reaction, both communist and noncommunist, viewed the speech as articulating matters of policy. So did some of the domestic letter writers. A man from Spring Lake, Michigan, wrote: "The President's inaugural address may have pleased the Eastern Internationalists but it struck a sour note out here in the Middle West. In fact it sounded as tho Acheson had written it. Out here we would like to see the United Nations sent elsewhere; the NATO nations told to fish or cut bait; and the Korean War either won or called off." Most domestic letter writers, however, commented not so much on the content of the address but on the prayer that preceded it. To these listeners, the prayer was a sign of Eisenhower's character. A woman from North Plainfield, New Jersey, wrote: "I liked your opening with a pray [*sic*]. I firmly believe if people took more time out to ask God's help and to thank him for what he has done this world would be a far better world. I first had the privilege to vote back in 1932 and have been very discouraged until today. I feel I have had a small part in helping put in a good man as president." Repeatedly, the domestic letter writers referred to the prayer and what it indicated about Eisenhower's character. It seemed to prove, as one letter writer put it, that "our faith and trust in you will be well founded."[14]

CONCLUSION

Most historians of the Eisenhower presidency agree with Stephen E. Ambrose that Ike's First Inaugural was "devoted exclusively to foreign policy."[15] Charles C. Alexander was even more specific: "Although it was not one of America's great state documents, the speech was important because, virtually ignoring domestic matters, it unequivocally committed the new administration to maintaining the American conception of international order through collective security efforts, founded on 'the basic law of interdependence.' "[16] All of this is true yet seems to miss the equally important point that Eisenhower was arguing a thesis: "the future shall belong to the free." His mode of proving that thesis was to demonstrate that the American people, and those who shared American values, constituted "the free." Ike called upon all free peoples to act on those values by endorsing or adopting certain policies that, he believed, would help to ensure the survival of freedom far into the future.

Although employing many of the linguistic forms associated with classical epideictic discourse, Eisenhower's First Inaugural functioned in a distinctly deliberative fashion to suggest the directions in which the new Republican administration would move. Far from merely "contemplating" or "gazing upon" the discourse, the audience was asked to participate, to act, and to secure a future yet to be determined.[17]

NOTES

1. See Martin J. Medhurst, *Dwight D. Eisenhower: Strategic Communicator* (Westport, Conn.: Greenwood Press, 1992), chap. 2.

2. See Martin J. Medhurst, "Eisenhower's 'Atoms for Peace' Speech: A Case Study in the Strategic Use of Language," *Communication Monographs* 54 (1987): 204–20.

3. Emmet John Hughes, *The Ordeal of Power: A Political Memoir of the Eisenhower Years* (New York: Atheneum, 1963), 49.

4. I isolated six different drafts completed between December 11, 1952, and January 13, 1953. None is numbered or dated, but internal analysis has allowed me to reconstruct the order in which they were produced. There were drafts subsequent to January 13, but none is to be found among the Eisenhower Papers at Abilene, Kansas, or the Hughes Papers at Princeton University. The six drafts from which I am working are in the Emmet John Hughes Papers, Box 2, Mudd Manuscript Library, Princeton University, Princeton, New Jersey.

5. All quotations from the cabinet meeting are from the Whitman File, Cabinet Series, Box 1, "Cabinet Meeting of January 12–13, 1953," Eisenhower Library.

6. See Martin J. Medhurst, Robert L. Ivie, Philip Wander, and Robert L. Scott, *Cold War Rhetoric: Strategy, Metaphor, and Ideology* (Westport, Conn.: Greenwood Press, 1990); Dante Germino, *The Inaugural Addresses of American Presidents: The Public Philosophy and Rhetoric* (Lanham, Md.: University Press of America, 1984), 22–24.

7. All quotations from the diary are from Emmet John Hughes Diary, Hughes Papers, Box 1, Mudd Manuscript Library, Princeton, New Jersey.

8. Dwight D. Eisenhower, *The Diaries of Dwight D. Eisenhower*, ed. Robert H. Ferrell (New York: W. W. Norton, 1981), 225.

9. Robert J. Donovan, *Eisenhower: The Inside Story* (New York: Harper, 1956), 20.

10. Dwight D. Eisenhower, *The White House Years: Mandate for Change, 1953–1956* (Garden City, N.Y.: Doubleday, 1963), 100.

11. All quotations from the prayer and the inaugural address are from the *Public Papers of the Presidents of the United States: Dwight D. Eisenhower, 1953* (Washington, D.C.: U.S. Government Printing Office, 1960), 1–8. For more detail

on Ike's prayer in relationship to the more general practice of clergymen delivering prayers at presidential inaugurations, see Martin J. Medhurst, "God Bless the President: The Rhetoric of Inaugural Prayer" (Ph.D. diss., Pennsylvania State University, 1980), 201–61.

12. Since this paragraph was clearly inserted at some point after January 14 and since it is rhetorically akin to the propaganda offensive launched by Eisenhower shortly after taking office, one is tempted to attribute it to Ike's specialist in cold war propaganda, C. D. Jackson. Could it be a fragment of the substitute address that Jackson prepared for Eisenhower on the night of January 17?

13. The Eisenhower Library has 2,015 pages of responses to the inaugural address, sorted into pro (2,000 pages) and con (15 pages) groupings. See Dwight D. Eisenhower: Records as President, 1953–61, President's Personal File, Boxes 584–586, "PPF 20-C, Inaugural Address Pro/Con," Eisenhower Library. All quotations of foreign reaction are from "Foreign Press Reaction to President Eisenhower's Inaugural Address," Hughes Papers, Box 1, Mudd Library.

14. All quotations from letter writers are from PPF 2-C, Inaugural Address, Pro/Con," Boxes 584–586. Eisenhower Library.

15. Stephen E. Ambrose, *Eisenhower: The President* (New York: Simon and Schuster, 1984), 43.

16. Charles C. Alexander, *Holding the Line: The Eisenhower Era, 1952–1961* (Bloomington: Indiana University Press, 1975), 36.

17. See Karlyn Kohrs Campbell and Kathleen Hall Jamieson, *Deeds Done in Words: Presidential Rhetoric and the Genres of Governance* (Chicago: University of Chicago Press, 1990), chap. 2.

Chapter Fourteen

President Dwight D. Eisenhower's Second Inaugural Address, 1957

Martin J. Medhurst

Dwight Eisenhower's Second Inaugural is similar in many respects to his First. Both emphasize America as the beacon of freedom in the world, both use Manichaean language to contrast the God-fearing free world to the gulag of godless communism, both reject isolationism in any form, both underscore the need for economic democracy, and both understand peace to be secured through strength—economic, military, and spiritual. Furthermore, both are action oriented, though the types of action called for are different. The differences between the addresses, are of emphasis, tone, and focus rather than content or basic orientation. Such differences arose from the changing rhetorical situation.

The situation in January 1957 was far different from that inherited by Eisenhower four years earlier. In 1953, America was at war in Korea; by 1957, peace reigned. In 1953, it was believed that the Soviets could and might launch a military offensive at any moment, thus plunging the globe into another world war; by 1957, Eisenhower knew that American nuclear capability, both qualitatively and quantitatively, far surpassed that of the Soviets. In 1953, Eisenhower enjoyed slim majorities in both houses of Congress; by 1957, Ike faced a Congress controlled by the opposition party. All of these factors and others invited a qualitatively different address in 1957.

Eisenhower had just completed an election rout of Adlai Stevenson, burying the Democratic standard-bearer by over 9 million votes and carrying forty-one of the forty-eight states. Even so, Ike had failed to pull the rest of the Republican ticket into office. The nation liked Ike, not the Republican party. Eisenhower knew that to secure passage of his legislative agenda, a *modus vivendi* would have to be worked out between moderate Republicans and more conservative, predominantly southern Democrats. Without Democratic votes, Eisenhower's agenda would not succeed, for the right wing of his own party could be counted on to oppose many of his initiatives, particularly those involving mutual aid for foreign governments. To Ike, there was nothing more important than the mutual security program, and his Second Inaugural can be read as part of the ongoing campaign to secure passage of the annual mutual security appropriation bill.

Examination of Eisenhower's speeches immediately prior to the Second Inaugural, the drafting process that produced the Second Inaugural, and the speech as delivered all point to the policy motivations that lay behind the address. Such motivations were perhaps less explicit than in Ike's First Inaugural but were nonetheless crucial to understanding why Eisenhower chose to speak as he did and why his comments were aimed not only at the American public but especially at the U.S. Congress.

THE RHETORICAL SITUATION

In the three months immediately preceding the Second Inaugural, several crucial events had taken place. Great Britain, France, and Israel had conspired to seize the Suez Canal from Egypt; the Soviet Union had invaded Hungary to put down a citizens' revolt against communist rule; and Eisenhower had been swept into office in an election landslide. All of these events colored Ike's speaking. Beyond the events themselves was the larger question of what policies to pursue in a world of rapid change, a world where colonialism was dying, nation-states were being born, and communist satellites, especially Poland and Hungary, were itching to break free of the Soviet orbit. Eisenhower's answer was clear: America must do everything in its power to make sure that those who wished to live in freedom could do so, free from the fear of communist subversion. In practical terms, this meant increasing American aid in the form of mutual security funds, especially to those nations in which the United States had a strategic interest.

As these events unfolded, Eisenhower's speeches repeatedly pointed to mutual security as the only road to peace. In his election eve broadcast on November 5, 1956, Ike said:

We understand clearly that no single nation in this world may have peace unless all travel the same road. Because peace is something that must be universal or it doesn't exist.

Now, I know of no single principle that is more important than this one. Because, my friends, everything that happens abroad these days affects us here at home. . . .

So we have a very large stake in the freedom of every people—wherever they may be, just as we do in our own.[1]

Eisenhower followed this with a call for direct action. In his Eisenhower Doctrine speech on January 5, 1957, the president called for action to ensure the freedom and safety of the Middle East. He told the joint session of Congress:

The proposed legislation is primarily designed to deal with the possibility of Communist aggression, direct and indirect. There is imperative need that any lack of power in the area should be made good, not by external or alien force, but by the increased vigor and security of the independent nations of the area. . . .

And as I have indicated, it will also be necessary for us to contribute economically to strengthen those countries, or groups of countries, which have governments manifestly dedicated to the preservation of independence and resistance to subversion. Such measures will provide the greatest insurance against Communist inroads. Words alone are not enough.[2]

Finally, in Eisenhower's 1957 State of the Union address, delivered just eleven days before the Second Inaugural, the president said:

In short, the world has so shrunk that all free nations are our neighbors. Without cooperative neighbors, the United States cannot maintain its own security and welfare, because:

First, America's vital interests are world-wide, embracing both hemispheres and every continent.

Second, we have community of interest with every nation in the free world.

Third, interdependence of interests requires a decent respect for the rights and the peace of all peoples.[3]

From the day of the election forward, Eisenhower used every opportunity to press the idea of mutual security. He realized that with the opposition party's controlling both houses of Congress, his legislative agenda could be in serious trouble, so he used every opportunity to make his case to the public. Eisenhower sincerely believed that there was nothing more crucial to the maintenance of world peace than the annual mutual security appropriations. These were monies that bought worldwide defenses for only a fraction of what it would cost to station American troops around the world. With the oil-rich Middle East in turmoil and traditional allies in disarray, Eisenhower turned to the American people and their representatives to sustain an American peace offensive.

DRAFTING THE SECOND INAUGURAL

Work on Eisenhower's Second Inaugural began shortly after December 6, 1956, for it was on that day that the president, through his personal secretary, Ann Whitman, instructed speech writer Emmet John Hughes as to the theme he wanted developed in the speech. Whitman recorded the directive in her diary: "The President asked me to call Emmet Hughes and tell him this: He wants the Inaugural address based on 'the price of waging peace.' (Emmet is to read the last chapter of Crusade.) The problem of winning peace is not a passive thing, but an active thing. When we are investing in other countries, we are not giving away—it is not charity—it is a security expenditure."[4]

In this directive, Eisenhower was anticipating the congressional battle that lay ahead. He realized that many of his political opponents would argue that mutual aid was simply a giveaway program and that the monies being spent on overseas programs ought to be cut or redirected to domestic concerns. Eisenhower had heard such arguments before, but with the seating of a predominantly Democratic Senate and House, Ike might well have expected such arguments to be raised even more insistently. However the Democratic majority voted, Eisenhower still had to contend with the isolationist elements within his own party. Because Ike could not count on solid Republican backing for his mutual security proposals, the appeal to moderate and conservative Democrats became even more important.

Emmet Hughes, who had left his position as a presidential speech writer in October 1953, was persuaded to return for a brief stint during the election campaign of 1956. By election day, Hughes had once again retreated to his home in New York City, but there was never any doubt that he would be called upon to draft Ike's Second Inaugural, just as he had drafted the First. When the call came from Ann Whitman, Hughes immediately set to work, producing several rough drafts, all unnumbered, before December 18, 1956. Hughes edited these early drafts into a composite document that became draft 1 when it was delivered to Eisenhower on December 18, 1956. Ike hand-edited draft 1, and his changes reveal much, about both the man and the speech.[5]

At the top of the draft, using his familiar black grease pencil, Ike wrote: "*First*: I question rightness of my starting with personal prayer." And at the bottom of the page, he wrote: "Prayer in terms of 'America's prayer.' " Here was Eisenhower the rhetorician at work. He instinctively understood that to start with a personal prayer, as he had done in 1953, would reduce the words to a ritualized gesture and call into question the spontaneity and sincerity of his earlier effort. Instead, he would offer America's prayer, giving voice to the innermost feelings and desires of his fellow citizens. At the end of Hughes's proposed prayer, Ike changed "guide and lead all other peoples who love freedom" to "walk with those who love freedom." Already in draft 1, the emphasis on cooperation, interdependence, and unity was beginning to take shape.

Next to the organizing concepts of "justice, strength, peace, and law," Eisenhower placed a question mark. Hughes had written: "Treasuring peace, we have, first in the Far East, then in the Middle East, steadfastly sought to still the guns of war—and to prove to all peoples of the earth our passion for peace." Eisenhower marked the sentence and below it wrote: "Peace is the sine qua non of existence today + we ought to say it."

Always alert to the implications of language, Eisenhower changed "the prosperity known by the greater Western nations" to "the productivity of the earth," avoiding the offense that surely would have accompanied the original phrasing. Likewise, Ike bracketed, and later eliminated, Hughes's sentence: "The once-sweeping authority of Great Britain and France has fallen back before the onrush of freedom in once-colonial areas." Although Eisenhower agreed with the sentiment, he would not unnecessarily antagonize allies, especially those that had so recently suffered the humiliation of Suez.

As the speech turned to the Soviet Union, Hughes wrote: "The designs of the Soviet Union are transparently clear. It hopes to snare those peoples on all continents struggling for a richer way of life. And it hopes to tear apart the bonds among free nations." Drawing an arrow to the end of this paragraph, Eisenhower added in longhand: "It hopes with false doctrine to snare these peoples with hopes, enticing promises— covering the mail fist." To Ike, the evils of communism were real, as references to Warsaw and Budapest made clear. Instead of referring to the eastern satellites' "deathless love of national freedom," Eisenhower picked up the next sentence and changed it to read: "Occupation armies have failed to crush the love of freedom." Although Hughes's phrase seemed to mean that national freedom would never die, Eisenhower understood that the sacrifices had not been "deathless" and that the use of that descriptor was inappropriate.

Eisenhower cut much of the last three pages of draft 1, including a reference to practicing "justice and equality for men of all races in our nation." He cut several paragraphs on the economic dependence of all nations, noting at the bottom of the page: "I'm not sure you couldn't have 2 or 3 complexes with big enough markets, so we don't have to be in direct contact with every people." On the bottom of the following page, he wrote: "For as spirit of nationalism has separated us, inexorable eco[nomic] developments have made us more dependent. And because eco[nomic development] vital to good, we are as concerned with friends as ourselves."

Circling Hughes's sentence "*We* are the revolutionaries of our time,"

Ike wrote: "Put earlier + Communism is reactionary doctrine. Dictatorship old as pharaohs. Earth cannot prosper under such dead teaching." Bracketing the final prayer, Ike wrote at the bottom of the last page: "We talk not of charity or largesse. These are stern duties demanded by *self-preservation*. We cannot afford to ignore cry of any nation that bears same aspiration as we. Greatest coop[erative] effort in mankind's history is required of us."

The address that Eisenhower delivered on January 21, 1957, was substantively different from this first draft of December 18; nevertheless, the outlines of Eisenhower's thought are clear in his written comments. Concern for other countries was, to Eisenhower, simply another way of protecting oneself. Mutual security funds were part of the national defense, for America's interests lay in the oil fields of the Middle East just as surely as in the oil patches of Texas and Oklahoma.

Eisenhower did not see the speech again until January 7, when Hughes forwarded draft 2 to the White House with a cover note saying, "I'll wait to hear from you what the President may next wish done. I have been having a fearful time getting this much accomplished along with an article on the Soviet Empire for my employers."[6] Hughes had taken seriously Eisenhower's suggestions and had produced a wholly new speech in the interim. Several features of draft 2 stand out.

First, Hughes transformed the opening from a personal prayer to "the prayers of our people." Second, he introduced the notion of "an historic paradox"—the paradox of plenty and comfort at home with peril and material want abroad. Third, he focused the speech on America's relationship to the rest of the world, writing: "This is our home—but this is not our world. For our world is where our full destiny lives—with free men, of all peoples and all nations." This was a theme reiterated throughout draft 2. The specific language carried through to the delivery draft. Wherever possible, Eisenhower sought to reinforce the linkage of America with the whole world. For example, in place of Hughes's sentence, "And we shall never honor that nation which, coveting its neighbor's goods, stifles his freedom," Eisenhower wrote: "We realize that to suppress the rights of any nation invites eventual destruction of our own." Fourth, and most important, draft 2 emphasized the price that must be paid if freedom was to be sustained. In line with Ike's December 6 directive, Hughes wrote: "We know, nonetheless, that this peace we seek cannot come as any cheap gift of history. Great as can be its blessing, high must be its price: in toil patiently sustained, and in sacrifice generously given. And we know that, however great the price, the cost of peace could never be so great as one day of modern war."

Eisenhower liked draft 2, and it became the basis for the speech as delivered. Even so, the address would go through seven more drafts and be subjected to the critical eyes of Gabriel Hauge, Sherman Adams,

John Foster Dulles, and Kevin McCann, among others, before Eisenhower would be satisfied. On January 9, Eisenhower's edited copy of draft 2 was returned to Hughes, now labeled as draft 3. The next day, a page of changes dictated by Eisenhower was sent to Hughes, with several more changes following on January 11. The incorporation of these changes produced draft 4, and it was this draft that was circulated to Hauge, Adams, Foster Dulles, and McCann on January 12.

In a two-page memorandum dated January 14, Hauge pronounced the speech "a tour de force of language" but worried that the "brilliant" expression might overshadow the ideas being expressed. He suggested that the cost-of-peace paragraph "be strengthened and enlarged into the keynote of the talk."[7] On January 15, Adams responded with his own three-page memo, which represented both his views and those of "a small group in the staff." It was from this memo that the phrase "May we pursue right—without self-righteousness" emerged. Adams questioned the use of the term *paradox* to describe the contrast between "plenty" and "peril" and suggested that "the phrase 'fabulous though our fortune be' may be a little braggadocio. We suggest that it read 'fortunate though our lot.' " Eisenhower agreed. Like Hauge, Adams urged that the " 'price of peace' idea be elaborated" and suggested some possible wording, none of which was used. Adams's group concluded its critique by observing: "In a number of passages, today's world situation is depicted perhaps too strongly in terms of crisis and violent contest. Such expressions include 'time of tempest,' 'shadowed by such peril,' 'winds of danger,' 'the blast,' and 'dynamic strength pitted against us.' It is suggested that the tone instead be placed on a slightly lower key."[8] Eisenhower, however, did not wish to lower the key, and the imagery remained. On January 16, McCann responded in a thoughtful, one-page memo in which he questioned both the "paradox" and the idea "of Soviet might as the shadow that divides all the world. If shadows can be divisive," McCann noted, "there are others. The memory of the past, the fear that it will return with its absentee rulers and landlords, prisons for rebels, great estates for a few and starvation patches for millions."[9] The shadow imagery was dropped, but McCann's larger point was barely addressed. Dulles also responded on January 16, urging that international communism and moral law be emphasized. Focusing on the same line that bothered McCann ("The shadow that divides us is the shadow of Soviet might"), Dulles substituted: "The shadow that divides is the shadow of International Communism and the power that it controls." Where Hughes had written, "Yet the Soviet world itself has been shaken by a fierce and mighty force," Dulles substituted, "Yet the world of International Communism has been shaken." Two days later, on January 18, Dulles once again examined the speech, then in draft 7, and in place of the phrase "the building of a peace with justice in a world of law" substituted "the building of a peace with justice where moral law prevails." Clearly, Dulles's changes were primarily ideological in nature. Nevertheless, it was an ideology shared by Dwight D. Eisenhower, who accepted each of Dulles's changes, including a short paragraph dictated by Dulles on the subject of the liberation of captive nations. "We share the aspirations of those nations which, now as captives, covet freedom," wrote Dulles. "They can know the bounteous welcome that awaits them when, as must be, they join again the ranks of freedom."[10]

While Dulles and the White House aides were responding to draft 4, Hughes submitted draft 5 on January 16. In his accompanying cover letter, Hughes wrote:

While it has had the virtue of brevity, I have worried about its sounding too much like a sermon-without-particulars. Specifically, I have feared that 'the price of peace' was really not very plainly stated except as a general exhortation. . . .

I fear that you may not too much like the addition of a couple of paragraphs to the overall length. I can only offer a plea that you consider with some sympathy the possible worth of (1) the slightly longer paragraph on allied unity with its more specific insistence on the working out of common policies (2) the observations on the satellites a couple of paragraphs later which, though said similarly during the campaign seems to me too important substantively to omit here. And there is (3) a return to a modified form of my original ending that alludes once again to our 'prayer.' On behalf of this, I can only argue that it seems to me to give a completeness and coherence to the address as a whole.[11]

Hughes's new draft, along with the comments from Dulles, Adams, Hauge, and McCann, were combined to produce draft 6 early on January 18. As the president worked over the draft during the day, it became draft 7, produced late on January 18. Eisenhower continued to edit draft 7, revising the opening paragraph to read: "May we prove worthy in response to the trust of any friend or the challenge of any foe." Although Ike eliminated the first reference to International Communism by crossing out the word *international*, he later reversed himself. Instead of helping "to build the strength of others," he substituted "the security of others," emphasizing the link between foreign relations and America's own national security. Where Hughes had penned, "And we refuse to despair of the coming of that day when our peoples may freely meet in friendship, and hence our governments in mutual trust and respect," Eisenhower deleted the reference to governments. To Ike, there could be no intercourse between communism and democracy, no mingling of the good with the godless.

Draft 8 was produced on January 19; it added little of a substantive nature but nonetheless heightened the tone of danger and divisiveness.

In longhand, Hughes added references to "this time of trial in which we live," "the aggressive power of International Communism," and "the onrush of new political and economic forces." There seemed to be an intentional effort made to make the language and imagery even more arresting. For example, instead of, "As all these forces of change sweep across the world, any nation, including ours, can ignore them only at its peril," Hughes wrote: "Thus across all the globe, there harshly blow the winds of change. And we—fabulous through our fortune be—know that we can never turn our backs to the blast." Repeatedly language choices were made that accentuated, contrary to the advice of Adams and others, the stark contrasts and dismal dilemmas of the atomic age.

The final draft, produced on January 20, consisted almost entirely of minor word changes. Only one sentence was completely rewritten to emphasize that "only in respecting the hopes and the cultures of others will we practice the equality of all nations." By the evening of January 20, the speech was ready to be produced in large type for Ike's reading copy. The next morning, Eisenhower went over the reading copy, writing out in longhand his salutation and, as was his custom, underlining key words and phrases for vocal emphasis. He made no changes in the reading copy and delivered it as written, with one minor exception. Instead of "the favor of Almighty God," Ike actually said "the blessings of Almighty God."

AN ANALYSIS OF THE TEXT

The Second Inaugural was divided into five sections: (1) opening prayer, (2) peril, (3) purpose, (4) hope, and (5) closing prayer.[12] As in the First Inaugural, Eisenhower opened with a prayer, although in 1957 the prayer was integrated into the speech text and represented "the deepest prayers of our whole people." The prayer served to reinforce Eisenhower's ethos as a good man who was humble, sincere, and God fearing. Ike prayed: "May we pursue the right—without self-righteousness. May we know unity—without conformity. May we grow in strength—without pride in self. May we, in our dealings with all peoples of the earth, ever speak truth and serve justice." The opening prayer set the tone and established the focus of the speech: America's relationship to the world at large.

Eisenhower led into the second section of the speech by referring to "this time of trial through which we pass," a phrase highly reminiscent of his First Inaugural. He then stated his first thesis: "We live in a land of plenty, but rarely has this earth known such peril as today." In this section, Eisenhower developed the contrast (referred to as a paradox in earlier drafts) of American wealth versus world need. After painting a word picture of "America the bountiful," Ike drove home the point:

"Now this is our home—yet this is not the whole of our world. For our world is where our full destiny lies—with men, of all people and all nations, who are or would be free." The wording once again echoed the First Inaugural, with its heavy emphasis on freedom. Eisenhower then turned to examine the peoples and nations and found "want, discord, danger." "From the deserts of North Africa to the islands of the South Pacific," said Eisenhower, "one third of all mankind has entered upon a historic struggle for a new freedom: freedom from grinding poverty." Unlike the First Inaugural, when the only real danger was communist aggression, in the Second Inaugural the dominant focus becomes economic privation and its consequences. One such consequence was communist takeover, and Eisenhower did not hesitate to name the evil. "The divisive force," said he, "is International Communism and the power that it controls. . . . It strives to capture—to exploit for its own greater power—all forces of change in the world, especially the needs of the hungry and the hopes of the oppressed." Unlike the First Inaugural, however, this divisive force is not monolithic, for "International Communism has itself been shaken by a fierce and mighty force: the readiness of men who love freedom to pledge their lives to that love." In particular, Eisenhower cited Budapest and proclaimed that "henceforth it is a new and shining symbol of man's yearning to be free." Having thus sketched the dimensions of the peril that confronted his listeners, Eisenhower made a transition into the third and most important section of the address. Said Ike:

Thus across all the globe there harshly blow the winds of change. And, we—though fortunate be our lot—know that we can never turn our backs to them.
    We look upon this shaken earth, and we declare our firm and fixed purpose—the building of a peace with justice in a world where moral law prevails.
    The building of such a peace is a bold and solemn purpose. To proclaim it is easy. To serve it will be hard. And to attain it, we must be aware of its full meaning—and ready to pay its full price.

Thus did Eisenhower launch into the most crucial portion of the speech. The purpose of America, he said, was to bring peace, justice, and law to the world, but "high will be its cost." In language that he had used before and would use again in his fight for mutual security funds, Eisenhower said:

To counter the threat of those who seek to rule by force, we must pay the costs of our own needed military strength, and help to build the security of others.
    We must use our skills and knowledge and, at times, our substance, to help others rise from misery, however far the scene of suffering may be from our shores. For wherever in the world a people knows desperate want, there must

appear at least the spark of hope, the hope of progress—or there will surely rise at last the flames of conflict.

We recognize and accept our own deep involvement in the destiny of men everywhere.

Here was the heart of Ike's argument: that America must be willing to help others if it hoped to save itself. As he told his listeners, "For one truth must rule all we think and all that we do. No people can live to itself alone. The unity of all who dwell in freedom is their only sure defense." This line of reasoning was the rationale for the whole mutual security program. It was the rationale behind the North Atlantic Treaty Organization, the Southeast Asia Treaty Organization, and the entire cold war strategy from the Truman Doctrine forward. Eisenhower ardently believed that it was only through cooperative effort that World War II had been won; similarly only cooperation and allied unity could prevent World War III. Therefore, Ike saw the wisdom in extending grants and loans not only to America's traditional friends, but especially to those countries just beginning to emerge from colonialism as they sought to build better lives for their peoples. Such countries had raw materials that the industrialized West needed, or they provided strategic air bases or navy ports, or they served as listening posts on the borders of the Soviet Union. They could, Ike knew, be useful in any number of ways to American strategic interests. To Eisenhower, the monies spent on mutual security arrangements with some forty-two countries around the world was the best investment that America could make to ensure its own future well-being. He could not understand how his political opponents, both Democrats and Republicans, could seek year after year to cut such appropriations. Yet that was what they had done in the past and what he expected them to do again in 1957. Eisenhower therefore used the most powerful platform he could command, his own inauguration, to set forth the case for mutual security.

Having thus set forth America's purpose, Eisenhower turned to America's hope. "We cherish our friendship with all nations that are or would be free," said Ike. "We honor the aspirations of those nations which, now captive, long for freedom." Addressing himself specifically to "the people of Russia," Eisenhower wished them well in their efforts to gain more freedoms. He closed section 4 by expressing the hope that "the weight of fear and the weight of arms be taken from the burdened shoulders of mankind," echoing his great speech of April 1953, "The Chance for Peace."

Eisenhower closed his Second Inaugural with another prayer, one, he said, that "carries far beyond our own frontiers, to the wide world of our duty and our destiny." And that, of course, was the crux of the matter: a call for the American people and their representatives to recognize their duty and to do it. Ike prayed: "May the light of freedom, coming to all darkened lands, flame brightly—until at last the darkness is no more. May the turbulence of our age yield to a true time of peace, when men and nations shall share a life that honors the dignity of each, the brotherhood of all."

CONCLUSION

Dwight D. Eisenhower understood that the cost of peace would be high, but to his way of thinking, there could be no cost too high if it preserved the peace. His job was to convince the electorate and their representatives of the rightness of that proposition. To do so, Eisenhower waged a relentless campaign from election eve 1956 to his nationally televised appeal to the American public on May 21, 1957, when he called mutual security "a saving shield of freedom."[13] The Second Inaugural was only part of that ongoing and ultimately unsuccessful campaign,[14] yet it was the most eloquent presentation of Eisenhower's cold war policy, a policy that he shared with the whole world on January 21, 1957.

NOTES

1. Dwight D. Eisenhower, "Radio and Television Remarks on Election Eve, November 5, 1956," in *Public Papers of the Presidents of the United States: Dwight D. Eisenhower, 1956* (Washington, D.C.: U.S. Government Printing Office, 1960), 1088.

2. Dwight D. Eisenhower, "Special Message to the Congress on the Situation in the Middle East, January 5, 1957," in *Public Papers, 1957*, 14, 15.

3. Dwight D. Eisenhower, "Annual Message to the Congress on the State of the Union, January 10, 1957," in *Public Papers, 1957*, 29.

4. Ann Whitman, diary, December 6, 1956, Whitman File, Speech Series, Box 20, "Second Inaugural 1/21/57," Dwight D. Eisenhower Library, Abilene, Kansas.

5. The early rough drafts and completed draft 1 with Ike's handwritten comments on it are found in the Emmet John Hughes Papers, Box 3, Mudd Manuscript Library, Princeton, New Jersey. All quotations from draft 1 are from this source. All quotations from subsequent drafts are from the Hughes Papers, Box 3, or the Whitman File, Speech Series, Box 20.

6. Both the cover note and draft 2 are found in the Whitman File, Speech Series, Box 20, "Second Inaugural 1/21/57," Eisenhower Library.

7. Gabriel Hauge to the President, memo, January 14, 1957, Whitman File, Speech Series, Box 20, "Second Inaugural 1/21/57," Eisenhower Library.

8. Sherman Adams to the President, memo, January 15, 1957, Whitman File, Speech Series, Box 20, "Second Inaugural 1/21/57," Eisenhower Library.

9. Kevin McCann to the President, memo, January 16, 1957, Whitman File, Speech Series, Box 20, "Second Inaugural 1/21/57," Eisenhower Library.

10. John Foster Dulles to the President, January 16, 1957, Whitman File, Speech Series, Box 20, "Second Inaugural 1/21/57," Eisenhower Library. Dulles's edited copy of draft 4 accompanied his cover letter and is also found in this file. For Dulles's editing of draft 7, see John Foster Dulles Papers, Box 116, Mudd Manuscript Library, Princeton, New Jersey.

11. Emmet John Hughes to the President, Whitman File, Administration Series, Box 20, "Emmet, Hughes, 1956–57," Eisenhower Library.

12. The analysis of the speech as delivered is based on the text published in the *Public Papers, 1957*, as corrected by comparison with an audio recording on file at the Eisenhower Library.

13. Dwight D. Eisenhower, "Radio and Television Address to the American People on the Need for Mutual Security in Waging the Peace," in *Public Papers, 1957*, 385.

14. In his memoir, Eisenhower recounted the 1957 battle over the mutual security program, noting that he had requested 3.8 billion but that the Congress had authorized only $3.3 billion and appropriated but $2.7 billion. See *The White House Years: Waging Peace, 1956–1961* (New York: Doubleday: 1965), 144–47.

Chapter Fifteen

President John F. Kennedy's Inaugural Address, 1961

Theodore Otto Windt, Jr.

Among inaugural addresses, John F. Kennedy's speech stands out as a gem of the genre. Rivaled by only a handful of others, Kennedy's address transcended the tired and the trite to reach the exalted plane of eloquence. Lavishly praised both at the time and since, the address marked President Kennedy's emergence as a unique voice in American politics. Previously, his reputation had rested primarily on his literary writings. During the presidential campaign, and especially in his joint television appearances with Richard Nixon, he had added to his luster through his urgent speeches and his quick-witted responses in the debates. But it was the inaugural that established his splendor as a speaker. "The Talk of the Town" section of the *New Yorker* stated: "Whatever the impact of the Inaugural Address on contemporary New Frontiersmen, we find it hard to believe that an Athenian or Roman citizen could have listened to it unmoved, or that Cicero, however jealous of his own reputation, would have found reason to object to it."[1] The writer saw even greater significance beyond a triumph for the speaker. Kennedy's eloquence that day raised hopes "that he has reestablished the tradition of political eloquence."[2] In retrospect, it was as if the whole nation once again turned its attention to presidential speeches, and a new standard was struck because of this single address.

We should remember that words are not so magical in and of themselves that they can cause this kind of reaction among people. There must be an aching need, a linguistic void in the collective psyche that makes people receptive to language and argument. In 1961 this ache, this void existed.

THE POLITICAL ENVIRONMENT

To place Kennedy's address in context, we need to examine three major influences that shaped it: the sterility of American foreign policy at the end of the Eisenhower years, the confusion among Americans about their purpose in an increasingly baffling world, and the 1950s sense of blandness about political life.

Since the announcement of the Truman Doctrine in 1947, American foreign policy had been animated by a bipolar vision of the world, a Manichaean struggle between the forces of light and the forces of darkness.[3] In the 1950s this struggle intensified into a moral crusade. Secretary of State John Foster Dulles succinctly summarized the pragmatic reasons for this moral rhetoric:

Our people can understand, and will support policies which can be explained and understood in moral terms. But policies merely based on carefully calculated expediency could never be explained and would never be understood.[4]

This rhetoric had produced moral posturing rather than pragmatic policies toward the Soviet Union. Indeed, during the decade, there had been few negotiations between the two major powers of any substance. Despite a change in leadership after the death of Stalin, Soviet-U.S. relations remained almost as hardened in place as they had been in 1947. Kennedy told Theodore Sorensen, his chief speech writer, that he did not want his inaugural address to continue the "customary cold war rhetoric about the Communist menace nor any weasel words that Khrushchev might misinterpret."[5] Balancing a fresh flexibility with traditional firmness fused two different but complementary approaches to Soviet-American relations that would be stressed in the sections addressed to the Soviet Union.

The second influence on the address was a by-product of the first. Anticommunism had been so strong over the past decade that Americans had begun to define themselves not by what they stood for but by what they opposed: communism. Implicit in this anticommunism was an equally strong sense of the moral superiority of Americans. In the second half of that decade, however, confusion crept in about American goals and purposes in the world. Sociologist Daniel Bell described the cause of this confusion as an "exhaustion of political ideas in the fifties."[6] That exhaustion, in part, created the general feeling of uneasiness. The final influence on the inaugural, according to Sorensen, was Kennedy's directive "to set a tone for the era about to begin."[7] The Eisenhower era had been viewed as one of gray conformity, or to use the words of Adlai Stevenson, an administration of "the bland leading the bland." Public service seemed a burden to Eisenhower and his appointees. The president often appeared more interested in golf than government. His administration had been one of "normalcy" in that ugly word's most unctuous expression. He seldom seemed excited and thus conveyed an air of disinterestedness even as he spoke platitudinously and in his sometimes deliberately inarticulate fashion about the threats Americans faced and the satisfaction the consumer culture of the 1950s promised. His farewell address to the American people fairly represented this mood. Responding to Kennedy's rhetorical challenges during the campaign, Eisenhower warned against some "spectacular and costly action" that might be taken as a "miraculous solution to all current difficulties." More specifically, he warned that in a dangerous era of confrontation, "there is called for not so much the emotional and transitory sacrifices of crisis, but rather those which enable us to carry forward steadily, surely, and without complaint the burdens of a prolonged and complex struggle."[8]

Kennedy would have none of this advice. He saw the country in peril, and he believed it required a mood of urgency to face it, as well as a new approach to those problems that would be a clear but unstated, departure from the Eisenhower administration. Drawing upon what he thought were the reasons "why England slept" in the years before World War II, Kennedy now resolved to awaken and unite the American people in preparation for the new dangers that lay in the coming decade.[9] His would be a crisis administration, and his inaugural address would be its clarion call into being.

DRAFTING THE INAUGURAL ADDRESS

The story of writing the inaugural address is told directly and succinctly by Theodore Sorensen in his memoir.[10] And certainly he was well placed to tell the story since he was entrusted by the president-elect to develop the speech. Sorensen wrote that Kennedy gave the following directions about the address:

He wanted it short. He wanted it focused on foreign policy. He did not want it to sound partisan, pessimistic or critical of his predecessor. He wanted neither the customary cold war rhetoric about the Communist menace nor any weasel words that Khrushchev might misinterpret. And he wanted it to set a tone for the era about to begin.[11]

Kennedy also requested that Sorensen read previous inaugurals and look especially at Lincoln's Gettysburg address to "study the secret" of its success. Sorensen dutifully did as requested, even to the point of doing a word count of inaugural addresses by twentieth-century presidents. The "secret" of Lincoln's success, according to his study, was that Lincoln relied on single-syllable words as much as possible. The final draft of Kennedy's inaugural contained 951 monosyllabic words, 71 percent of the words in the speech.[12]

In late December Sorensen began gathering materials for the address at his home in Washington while Kennedy relaxed in Palm Springs. On December 23 Sorensen sent a telegram to ten public figures asking for suggestions for the speech. One consistent theme came through the responses: Tell us where the country stands and provide the leadership to tell us where it is going. Adlai Stevenson put it this way: "The main thing, of course, is to create the impression of new, bold, imaginative purposeful leadership; to de-emphasize the bi-polar power struggle; and to emphasize the affirmative approaches to peace."[13] He included a list of eleven topics, two of which were crossed out apparently by someone other than Stevenson. (The two were his proposals to liquidate military bases overseas "as fast as progression toward disarmament makes this possible" and to "hint" at a reexamination of U.S. policy toward the People's Republic of China.)[14]

The actual drafting of the address began only a week before the inaugural after Sorensen flew to Palm Springs to work directly with the president-elect. An early outline contained a tribute to Eisenhower; an "inventory of where we stand, what we need, and what this Administration is inheriting"; "the gold crisis"; "the domestic slump"; a section on the "kind of government it will be"; and a "call for sacrifice on the New Frontier."[15] Dissatisfied with attempts to weave domestic issues into the address, Kennedy decided to "drop the domestic stuff altogether" and concentrate solely on foreign policy.[16] By January 17 as the two were flying back to Washington, Kennedy produced a workable handwritten draft that the two reworked on the flight.[17] It was completed on the next day.

The draft had part of its genesis in campaign speeches, ideas, and phrases that were recast in more compact form for the occasion. Sorensen noted that the phrase "a new generation of Americans" came from Kennedy's acceptance speech in Los Angeles and had been used in a variety of campaign speeches; that the statement, "For man holds in his mortal hands the power to abolish all forms of human poverty and all forms of human life," also came from the acceptance speech; and that the famous line "Ask not" came from a televised speech on September 20.[18] The idea of an Alliance for Progress in Latin America was first voiced on October 18, 1960, in a speech in Tampa, Florida.[19] In addition to drawing from phrases in campaign speeches, the draft circulated among Kennedy advisers and others. John Kenneth Galbraith suggested that *joint ventures* be replaced with *cooperative ventures*. Dean Rusk recommended that the challenge to the rest of the world be changed from "what you can do for freedom" to "what we together can do for freedom." The most celebrated change came from Walter Lippmann, who advised that the communist bloc be described as an "adversary" rather than an "enemy," thus implying a change in the metaphor governing Soviet-U.S. relations from the war metaphor to a diplomatic metaphor. This substitution was consistent with the later line, "Let us never negotiate out of fear, but let us never fear to negotiate." Had *enemy* been used, the negotiation line would have been inconsistent, for one does not negotiate with enemies until they are defeated, and a number of other lines about cooperation either would have to be changed or would sound contradictory. Concerned at the last minute that in his decision to concentrate on foreign issues he might be accused of neglecting the central domestic issue, civil rights, the president-elect added a commitment to human rights "at home and around the world."[20] Although these substantive changes, some given by advisers, led to questions about his authorship of the address, the fact remains that this was Kennedy's speech. He had sought advice from others; he had worked with his speech writer, Sorensen; but he had handwritten an early draft, and he had developed its final form. Kennedy was its architect even as some improved the exact lines of the rhetorical edifice and others placed a few bricks or added some mortar.

THE INAUGURAL ADDRESS, JANUARY 20, 1961

Inauguration Day was cold. Servicemen had joined with city workers to remove the eight inches of snow that had fallen the night before. At the appointed time for the ceremony, the temperature stood at 22 degrees. After taking the oath of office, John Kennedy removed his topcoat and began his address. Firm of voice, more deliberate than previously in presentation, his animated delivery seemed to exemplify the vigor that he had so often touted during the campaign.

The address can be divided into five sections, each flowing into the next through skillful transitions that make them seem as though each is the natural consequence of what came before. The opening section began with his celebration of the occasion:

We observe today not a victory of party but a celebration of freedom, symbolizing an end as well as a beginning, signifying renewal as well as change. For I have sworn before you and Almighty God the same solemn oath our forebears prescribed nearly a century and three-quarters ago.[21]

These concise, elegant words carried with them twin organizational themes that guided the address. Kennedy developed the celebration of a specific oath of office by extending the oath motif into a series of pledges and invitations to the American people, to their allies and friends, and eventually to "those who would make themselves our adversary." Near the end of the address he returned to this theme by asking Americans and others throughout the world for a reciprocal oath of cooperation and participation. The second theme—"an end as well as a beginning," "renewal as well as change"—permeates the address. Contending that the "world is very different now" than in the past, Kennedy wove these two strands into a tapestry of willingness to face the new challenges of the new world by first reminding his auditors of their precious heritage and then of the new leadership forged in that heritage but more than willing to go beyond it to confront the new world:

We dare not forget today that we are the heirs of that first revolution. Let the world go forth from this time and place, to friend and foe alike, that the torch has been passed to a new generation of Americans—born in this century, tempered by war, disciplined by a hard and bitter peace, proud of our ancient heritage—and unwilling to witness or permit the slow undoing of those human rights to which this nation has always been committed, and to which we are committed today at home and around the world.

Let every nation know, whether it wishes us well or ill, that we shall pay any price, bear any burden, meet any hardship, support any friend, oppose any foe to assure the survival and the success of liberty.

The rapid rhythmic effect was achieved through the parallelism of construction, the omission of conjunctions (asyndeton), and the alliteration. But the stylistic urgency was consistent and strengthened by the substance of a new generation taking up the torch and moving vigorously in a new direction. That substance was further heightened by the audience's awareness that the oldest president in American history was now being replaced by the youngest elected president in American history.

The second section is an extension of the first, Kennedy's pledge to the American people transformed into a series of pledges to allies and friends around the world. These pledges to "old allies," to "new states," to "people in the huts and villages of half the globe struggling to break the bonds of mass misery," to "our sister Republics south of our border" were presented with parallel constructions as introduction to each, thus pointing specifically to each promise to each different group. These promises stressed both renewal and change. The most remarkable change, a direct departure from the Eisenhower years, was to the emerging nations and peoples. Kennedy pledged to remove them from the superpower confrontations:

We pledge our word that one form of colonial control shall not have passed away merely to be replaced by a far more iron tyranny. We shall not always expect to find them supporting our view. But we shall always hope to find them strongly supporting their own freedom.

And again:

We pledge our best efforts to help them help themselves, for whatever period is required, not because the Communists may be doing it, not because we seek their votes, but because it is right.

But even as he articulated this new approach to nations far from home, he voiced a warning about nations nearer to home. Speaking of the turmoil in Latin and South American countries, Kennedy issued a veiled warning to the Soviet Union and Cuba:

But this peaceful revolution of hope cannot become the prey of hostile power. Let all our neighbors know that we shall join with them to oppose aggression or subversion anywhere in the Americas. And let every other power know that this hemisphere intends to remain the master of its own house.

This litany of pledges concluded appropriately with the United Nations. Echoing Lincoln, he described it as "our last best hope," a place intended to replace armed conflict with cooperative negotiation as a means of resolving differences. The placement of remarks about the United Nations at the end of this section prepared the way for the transition to the third section of the address.

From pledges to allies, Kennedy turned to invitations to antagonists:

Finally, to those nations who would make themselves our adversary, we offer not a pledge but a request: that both sides begin anew the quest for peace, before the dark powers of destruction unleashed by science engulf all humanity in planned or accidental self-destruction.

Clearly, Kennedy renewed the charge that the Soviets were responsible for the cold war but urged them to join with him in changing its course by new cooperative action. In a particularly striking paragraph, the new president called upon these adversaries to "begin anew, remembering on both sides that civility is not a sign of weakness, and sincerity is always subject to proof. Let us never negotiate out of fear, but let us never fear to negotiate." For foreign listeners, Kennedy's emphasis on negotiation stuck an especially responsive chord.[22] These stirring words suggested a distinct change in attitude from moral condemnation of the Soviet Union to political accommodation based on negotiations, an opening to the development of a post-Eisenhower cold war rhetoric—or so it was celebrated at the time.

The remainder of this section enumerated a variety of cooperative efforts that the new president believed should provide the basis for pushing "back the jungle of suspicion." Again invoking a parallel form, "let both sides," to introduce each, Kennedy listed a series of joint ventures—realistic arms control proposals, exploration in space, medical research, and encouragement for the arts and commerce. Such cooperative efforts, Kennedy hoped, would culminate in "a new world of law, where the strong are just and the weak secure and the peace preserved." This open invitation to negotiation and cooperation was firmly based in traditional American values. The implicit assumption was that if such a cooperative venture could be established with the Soviet Union, it would, as if by osmosis, evolve to the point that it would accept those values.

The fourth section drew together the topics of all that had gone before and returned to Kennedy's conception of the presidency, its opportunities and limitations:

All this will not be finished in the first one hundred days. Nor will it be finished in the first one thousand days, nor in the life of this administration, nor even in our lifetime upon this planet. But let us begin.

In your hands, my fellow citizens, more than mine, will rest the final success or failure of our course. Since this country was founded, each generation of Americans has been summoned to give testimony to its national loyalty. The graves of young Americans who answered the call to service surround the globe.

Now the trumpet summons us again—not as a call to arms, though arms we need, not as a call to battle, though embattled we are—but as a call to bear the burden of a long twilight struggle, year in and year out, "rejoicing in hope, patient in tribulation"—a struggle against the common enemies of man: tyranny, poverty, disease and war itself.

Can we forge against these enemies a grand and global alliance, North and South, East and West, that can assure a more fruitful life for all mankind? Will you join in that historical effort?

In the long history of the world, only a few generations have been granted the role of defending freedom in its hour of maximum danger. I do not shrink from this responsibility—I welcome it. I do not believe that any of us would exchange places with any other people or any other generation. The energy, the faith, the devotion which we bring to this endeavor will light our country and all who serve it—and the glow from that fire can truly light the world.

Kennedy concluded this majestic march of language with the climax of his speech, the climax presented in two contrapuntal sentences that capture the essence of his address:

And so, my fellow Americans: ask not what your country can do for you—ask what you can do for your country.

My fellow citizens of the world: ask not what America will do for you, but what together we can do for the freedom of man.

These noble sentiments, smartly stated, addressed both audiences—domestic and foreign—in a spirit of cooperation, sacrifice, and idealism. They formed the climatic moment.

Having reached the high point of his address, Kennedy closed on a calmer note:

Finally, whether you are citizens of America or citizens of the world, ask of us here the same high standards of strength and sacrifice which we ask of you. With a good conscience our only sure reward, with history the final judge of our deeds, let us go forth to lead the land we love, asking His blessing and His help, but know that here on earth God's work must truly be our own.

The closing was classic. In *The Attic Orators*, R. C. Jebb wrote that the conclusion to an eloquent speech resolves the tumult that has gone before into a final serenity:

The very end is calm; not so much because the speaker feels this to be necessary if he is to leave an impression of personal dignity, but rather because the sense of an ideal beauty in humanity and in human speech governs his effort as a whole, and makes him desire that, where this effort is most distinctly viewed as a whole—namely at the close—it should have the serenity of a completed harmony.[23]

Kennedy achieved that "completed harmony" through the grace of humility found in these moving words and through the change to accept personal responsibility for human actions that concludes the address.

CONCLUSION: KENNEDY'S SPEECH AND THE GENRE OF INAUGURAL ADDRESSES

Kennedy's speech fits within the general characteristics of the genre of inaugural addresses. His address "unifies the audience by reconstituting its members as the people, who can witness and ratify the ceremony."[24] From his opening words ("We observe today not a victory of party but a celebration of freedom") to his mighty exhortation ("Ask not. . . ."), the new president stressed the unity of the American people on this ceremonial occasion. Their ratification of his presidency was directly requested through his rhetorical questions asking them to join him in the "historic effort" upon which he and they were about to embark. Clearly he sought to reconstitute the people in a cast different from the placid people of the decade just ended and from the leadership during that decade. But even as he sought this, he did so within a celebration of "communal values of the past."[25] The "torch has been passed to a new generation," he declared, but that generation was "proud of its ancient heritage and unwilling to witness or permit the slow undoing of those human rights to which this nation has always been committed." So too throughout the speech, new initiatives were placed within the context of traditional values whose general nature were reaffirmed even as they sometimes were specifically redefined by the president.

Three themes emerge from the speech, three that seem to herald the Kennedy administration as distinctly different from Eisenhower's in its guiding political principles. The primary theme is cooperation among peoples and nations. Even as he reaffirmed commitments to old allies and the United Nations, he sought to reconstitute relations among nations on the basis of cooperation rather than neglect or confrontation. To Latin American countries, he restated his call for an alliance for progress; to newly emerging nations and "peoples in the huts and villages of half the globe," he pledged to remove them from superpower confrontations and to work with them toward free societies and to breaking "the bonds of mass misery"; and finally to the Soviet Union, he issued an invitation to cooperative ventures and to negotiations.

His second theme, almost as prominent as the first, was his call to sacrifice—to sacrifice for country, to sacrifice for freedom. Statements about sacrifice, both those committed in the past and those that may be called for in the future, abound. They are summarized in the justly famous line: "Ask not what your country can do for you; ask what you can do for your country." Indeed, as Kathleen Jamieson pointed out, this memorable phrase "forecast the philosophy and tone of the Kennedy administration and at the same time provided a prism through which the Kennedy presidency could be viewed and judged."[26]

But for critics and historians, it was the third theme that came closer to characterizing the Kennedy administration. Just as Kennedy sought to reconstitute the people and relations among nations, so too he sought to reconstitute the world in which Americans lived. The idealism of cooperation and sacrifice were counterbalanced by an acute sense of cosmic urgency about the state of the world, in stark contrast to the placid composure of the Eisenhower administration. This third theme of crisis was expressed in these ominous words: "In the long history of the world, only a few generations have been granted the role of defending freedom in its hour of maximum danger." These words were not a rhetorical flourish but were consistent with the other two themes. If his call for cooperation were rebuffed by the Soviets, then sacrifice would be required of Americans to face the hard decisions of the very different world where "man holds in his mortal hands the power to abolish all forms of human poverty and all forms of human life." Although people would remember his calls for cooperation and sacrifice, it would be the aura of crisis that permeated and directed his administration.[27]

Finally, Kennedy certainly marked his understanding of the opportunities presented by the presidency ("I do not shrink from these responsibilities—I welcome them") as well as its limitations ("All this will not be finished in the first one hundred days" and "In your hands, my fellow citizens, more than mine, will rest the final success of railure of our course"). The address stresses the opportunities as befitting a new administration, but only two years later, both the president and his speech writer were stressing the limitations of presidential power.[28]

Kennedy's inaugural address both fulfills and transcends the characteristics of the genre. Nonetheless, two qualifications seem warranted. Campbell and Jamieson contend that these addresses urge "contemplation, not action, focusing on the present while incorporating past and future."[29] If we interpret "contemplation" as an essentially relaxed or passive activity, surely that was not the purpose or the impact of the speech. Kennedy's speech was vigorous and sought to instill a new vigor in Americans. But if we interpret "contemplation" not as a quiet meditative act but rather as an active disciplining of the mind to steel our resolve to face the future, then we might well say that it is a contemplative speech, one that reorients the mind in different directions although it does not call for specific policy actions. More to the point, Kennedy's eye was on the future and the past. The present is only a fleeting moment in the address. Bolstered by principles that define our ancient heritage, Kennedy sought to redefine relations for the new administration entering a new decade. One major part of the idealism so many saw in the address came from his vision of future cooperation and sacrifice.

One final remark seems needed. On January 20, 1961, John F. Kennedy presented one of the most forceful inaugural addresses in American history. But this analysis is necessarily incomplete. The very act of dissecting eloquence diminishes it, for eloquence is an organic and living whole that resists all efforts to reveal the secrets of its power. Before its power, the critic eventually stands tongue-tied. Daniel Webster stated this sentiment best:

True eloquence, indeed, does not consist in speech. It cannot be brought from far. Labor and learning may toil for it, but they will toil in vain. . . . It must exist in the man, in the subject, and in the occasion. . . . It comes, if it come at all, like the outbreaking of a fountain from the earth, or the bursting forth of volcanic fires, with spontaneous, original, native force. . . . The clear conception outrunning the deductions of logic, the high purpose, the firm resolve, the dauntless spirit, speaking on the tongue, beaming from the eye, informing every feature, and urging the whole man onward, right onward to his object—this, this is eloquence.[30]

So it was with John F. Kennedy as he presented his classic address—
with "firm resolve" and a "dauntless spirit."

NOTES

1. "Talk of the Town," *New Yorker*, February 4, 1961, 23.

2. Ibid., 24.

3. See Lynn Boyd Hinds and Theodore Otto Windt, Jr., *The Cold War as Rhetoric: The Beginnings, 1945–1950* (New York: Praeger, 1991).

4. *Department of State Bulletin* 22 (1955): 164.

5. Theodore C. Sorensen, *Kennedy* (New York: Harper & Row, 1965), 240.

6. Daniel Bell, *The End of Ideology: On the Exhaustion of Political Ideas in the Fifties* (New York: Free Press, 1960).

7. Sorensen, *Kennedy*, 240.

8. Dwight D. Eisenhower, "Farewell to the American People January 17, 1961," in *The President and the Public: Rhetoric and National Leadership*, ed. Craig Allen Smith and Kathy B. Smith (Lanham, Md.: University Press of America, 1985), 311.

9. On the influence of his senior thesis, *Why England Slept*, and his other early experiences, see Theodore Windt, "The Public Presidency: A Psychological Inquiry into John F. Kennedy," *Politics and Psychology: Contemporary Psychodynamic Perspectives*, ed. Joan Offerman-Zuckerberg (New York: Plenum Press, 1991), 83–98.

10. Sorensen, *Kennedy*, 240–43.

11. Ibid., 240.

12. Edward P. J. Corbett, "Analysis of the Style of John F. Kennedy's Inaugural Address," in *Essays in Presidential Rhetoric*, ed. Theodore Windt and Beth Ingold, 2d ed. (Dubuque, Iowa: Kendall/Hunt, 1987), 100. I am using Corbett's analysis for most matters of Kennedy's style in this speech. His essay is invaluable.

13. Stevenson to Sorensen, Sorensen File, Box 62, JFK Library, Boston.

14. Ibid.

15. "Possible Themes for the Inaugural," n.d., Sorensen File, Box 62, JFK Library.

16. Sorensen, *Kennedy*, 242.

17. Ibid., 243. See the handwritten, untitled draft by Kennedy dated January 17, 1961, Sorensen File, Box 62, JFK Library.

18. Sorensen, *Kennedy*, 241. A variety of other sources have been cited for this most memorable phrase. Among the most intriguing is that it came from Rev. George St. John, headmaster of Choate, the preparatory school Kennedy attended. He is credited with having admonished students: "Ask not what your school can do for you; ask what you can do for your school." Cited by Karlyn Kohrs Campbell and Kathleen Hall Jamieson, *Deeds Done in Words* (Chicago: University of Chicago Press, 1990), 229. They cite as their source Walter Scott, "Walter Scott's Personality Parade," *Parade*, December 15, 1968, 2.

19. *The Speeches of Senator John F. Kennedy Presidential Campaign of 1960* (Washington, D.C.: U.S. Government Printing Office, 1961), 1159–66.

20. Sorensen gives credit for these changes on p. 243. Galbraith wrote that he contributed other phrases to the speech, including "let us begin." But I was unable to verify this in the JFK archives. See John Kenneth Galbraith, *Ambassador's Journal* (Boston: Houghton Mifflin, 1969), 16.

21. John F. Kennedy, "Let Us Begin," in *Presidential Rhetoric: 1961 to the Present*, ed. Theodore Windt, 4th rev. and exp. ed. (Dubuque, Iowa: Kendall/Hunt), 9. All subsequent quotations come from this version, 9–11.

22. See, for example, "U.N. Delegates Praise Speech; Acclaim the Quest for Peace," *New York Times*, January 21, 1961, 10.

23. R. C. Jebb, *The Attic Orators* (New York: Russell & Russell, 1962), 1:ciii–civ.

24. Campbell and Jamieson, *Deeds Done in Words*, 15.

25. Ibid.

26. Kathleen Hall Jamieson, *Eloquence in the Electronic Age: The Transformation of Political Speechmaking* (New York: Oxford University Press, 1988), 95.

27. See, for example, Theodore Otto Windt, Jr., "The Crisis Rhetoric of President John F. Kennedy: The First Two Years," and "The Crisis Rhetoric of President John F. Kennedy: The Final Year," in *Presidents and Protesters: Political Rhetoric in the 1960s* (Tuscaloosa: University of Alabama Press, 1990), 17–87; Montague Kern, Patricia W. Levering, and Ralph B. Levering, *The Kennedy Crises: The Press, the Presidency, and Foreign Policy* (Chapel Hill: University of North Carolina Press, 1983); and Michael R. Beschloss, *The Crisis Years: Kennedy and Khrushchev, 1960–1963* (New York: Edward Burlingame Books, 1991).

28. See Kennedy's foreword to and the book by Theodore C. Sorensen, *Decision-Making in the White House* (New York: Columbia University Press, 1963).

29. Campbell and Jamieson, *Deeds Done in Words*, 15.

30. Quoted in Donald C. Bryant, *Rhetorical Dimensions in Criticism* (Baton Rouge: Louisiana State University Press, 1973), 133.

Chapter Sixteen

President Lyndon B. Johnson's Inaugural Address, 1965

Kurt Ritter

When Lyndon B. Johnson took the presidential oath of office as he stood on the east front of the Capitol building on January 20, 1965, the scene naturally evoked in the national memory John F. Kennedy's inauguration four years earlier. Only fourteen months prior to Johnson's inaugural address, the nation had been shocked by Kennedy's assassination. Such comparisons, while inevitable, were not desired by Johnson. He was painfully aware that he lacked Kennedy's charisma and skill as a television orator. Having been elected in his own right, Johnson sought to cast his presidency in terms that transcended his predecessor. A month prior to his inauguration, LBJ's longtime aide Horace Busby had recommended that Johnson capitalize upon the circumstance that he had been elected in the 175th year of the American presidency. "Adoption of the 175-year theme," Busby suggested, "would, as no small benefit, eliminate adverse comments or unwelcome pressures for associating the late President Kennedy with your Inauguration."[1]

Busby was correct in believing that Johnson's inauguration would compete with the memory of Kennedy. Even as Americans wrote to Johnson congratulating him on his inaugural address, they prefaced their remarks with expressions of grief over Kennedy's death. Among the 40 million viewers who watched Johnson's address on television was a woman from Abilene, Texas, who felt compelled "to sit down right now, immediately after your Inaugural speech to tell you how I feel." Before praising Johnson, however, she explained: "Perhaps I should start by saying that as an ardent supporter of Mr. Kennedy in 1960 & deeply grieved as millions of others by his tragic death, I wondered that sad day what Mr. Johnson would be like."[2] Similar letters poured into the

White House from across the nation. These Americans recognized that Johnson's address lacked Kennedy's flair. As one remarked: "It was a speech as unalike [sic] that of your predecessor as one could imagine. Not fiery, not bombastic—not filled with rhetoric and bravado, it was nevertheless a speech that will be long remembered." Such letters concluded with the sentiment that Johnson's "inaugural address was one that fully vindicated and earned for you the love and trust of all the American people."[3] Echoing this theme, a Michigan resident who described herself as "a mother Democrat," assured LBJ: "As much as we loved our late President Kennedy, we love you equally as much."[4]

The success of Johnson's speech was not achieved through a stirring presentation. Never effective on television, Johnson delivered his inaugural address at a painfully slow pace. Television news commentators found the address "a very well-written speech and perhaps [it] reads almost better than it is delivered by Mr. Johnson."[6] Lyndon Johnson eclipsed the memory of Kennedy's inauguration with a speech that reached far back into the American experience. It drew on America's oldest rhetorical form to unite national values with LBJ's national policies. His inaugural address can be read as a secular jeremiad that provided a moral justification for his Great Society domestic policies and his expansion of the Vietnam War. So effective was his address that television commentators like Walter Cronkite and Eric Sevareid of CBS mentioned Kennedy not at all. Once Johnson had concluded his speech, Cronkite remarked: "Eric, this was a rather powerful appeal to the people." Sevareid responded: "Yes, . . . this was a statement of faith, a personal testament in the accents of the great American tradition and the basic tenets of this country and its now rather long history. . . . He has called back the hallmarks of American life, which are justice, liberty and union, and he has reminded us—and reminded the world—that this is a nation of believers."[6]

Yet the news commentators sensed that Johnson's speech was not merely a sermon on national values; it advocated Johnson's philosophy of activist government. Turning to Cronkite, Sevareid noted that "again and again, Walter, he came back to the—the point that human beings are the masters of their own fate. . . . He's been trying to tell us that a secret has been discovered in this generation; that is, that we can all progress together."[7] Like Sevareid and Cronkite, the American public also understood Johnson's inaugural address as a statement of civil religion—a secular sermon that exhorted Americans to action at home and abroad. Indeed, even scholars noticed the religious quality in Johnson's speech. When Robert N. Bellah wrote his seminal essay on American civil religion in 1967, he cited Johnson's inaugural address, as well as those by Washington, Jefferson, Lincoln, and Kennedy.[8]

Johnson's address followed the pattern of the jeremiad, which for three centuries had been a principal vehicle for expressing America's special identity. The jeremiad, a type of sermon in which the preacher exhorted the congregation to "get right with God," survived the death of New England's puritan theocracy to become perhaps "the most American of all rhetorical modes."[9] Ministers using it spoke as scolding prophets as they presented jeremiads that included the following features: (1) an assumption that Americans were God's chosen people with a special mission, a special destiny, and therefore a special responsibility; (2) a general theme of sin-repentance-reform; and (3) the application of religious doctrine to secular, even political affairs. By Johnson's day, the contemporary political jeremiad had moved far from its religious origins. Indeed, Sacvan Bercovitch, a leading scholar of the American jeremiad, has noted that it is a "distortion of religious discourse for secular purposes."[10] While the Puritan jeremiad exhorted the people to correct belief and action, the political jeremiad exhorts the people to support policies that advance the work of America's divine mission—policies that uphold America's covenant with its destiny and with its God.[11]

LYNDON JOHNSON'S JEREMIAD

The key rhetorical move in constructing a jeremiad is to define the American covenant; Johnson devoted his inaugural to this question. Borrowing words from John Steinbeck, LBJ urged "this generation" to use its national heritage as a guide in a changing world—to rely on "the unchanged character of our people and their faith. They came here— the exile and the stranger, brave but frightened—to find a place where a man could be his own man. They made a covenant with this land."[12] Although Johnson alternately characterized the American covenant as being with God, with earlier generations, and with the land, he consistently defined the requirements of the contract throughout his address as "justice," "liberty," and "union."[13]

These three categories were developed in terms of the jeremiad. In each area, Johnson set up tests that America would have to satisfy if it was to fulfill its national covenant. *Justice* became a code word for domestic programs of social welfare and civil rights.[14] It required America to eradicate poverty, feed the hungry, tend the ill, and more. A month before the inauguration, one of LBJ's staff members had urged that civil rights be used as "a speech-and-action theme—possible even for the Inaugural Address."[15] When Johnson delivered the speech, he declared: "Justice requires us to remember: when any citizen denies his fellow, saying: his color is not mine or his beliefs are strange and different, in that moment he betrays America." Johnson made liberty the centerpiece of his address and devoted it largely to foreign policy. "Liberty" required self-government and individual rights on a global scale and victory over "tyranny and misery" everywhere in the world. Finally, union required that Americans achieve a sense of national community—that they transcend divisions between "capitalist and worker, farmer and clerk, city and countryside." Johnson drew his address to a close by turning again to the words of John Steinbeck:

I do not believe that the Great Society is the ordered, changeless, and sterile battalion of the ants. It is the excitement of becoming—always becoming, trying, probing, falling, resting, and trying again. . . . In each generation—with toil and tears—we have to earn our heritage again.

In the tradition of the jeremiad, LBJ urged Americans to rely on old principles as he offered new policies: "You must look within your own hearts to the old promises and the old dreams. They will lead you best of all."

CRAFTING THE INAUGURAL ADDRESS

We can safely assume that Johnson's speech writers and advisers did not self-consciously create a jeremiad. Hence, it is instructive to examine how the inaugural address acquired this form. Serious work on the inaugural began amazingly late. Despite suggestions and outside drafts sent to the White House in November and December 1964, LBJ appears to have had his first extended discussion about the inaugural address while flying from Washington to Texas on January 14, 1965, just six days before the inauguration.[16]

Two days later, LBJ's best speech writer, Richard Goodwin, produced an initial draft that was submitted to the president through presidential aides Horace Busby and Jack Valenti.[17] The LBJ White House had inherited Goodwin along with John Kennedy's other speech writers when Johnson assumed office in 1963. In contrast, Busby and Valenti were Johnson's men. Multiple drafts followed from Goodwin; within four days, he was on draft 9. Working parallel to Goodwin over this period was Busby, a seasoned political writer. Between these two men, LBJ's inaugural took shape between January 16 and 20. In the early stages of writing, it had a superficial theme of change, but as it moved through successive drafts the notion of a national covenant that would guide the nation through a new and changing world quickly came to dominate the speech.

In various drafts, both Busby and Goodwin followed the jeremiadic pattern, but because Busby's draft was not dated it is unclear whose writing introduced this form to the inaugural. Possibly the speech's broad theme of America's historic mission derived from Paul Horgan, then a leading writer about the American Southwest. His suggestions for Johnson's inaugural centered on "the American genius" for "growth—change—advance," and he observed that "along every step toward the way of advance and innovation, there is a prophetic vision which has told us what we are to fulfill."[18] In the early pages of his second draft, Goodwin summarized the jeremiad in three brief paragraphs that stressed the conditional nature of America's covenant:

The Constitution I have just sworn to defend has stood for almost two centuries. Under its generous rule we have become a nation, great, mighty, and prosperous. And we have kept our freedom.

But that success does not guarantee our future. The fact we have grown does not mean we continue to grow. The fact we are free does not mean we will remain free. We have not been chosen by God for greatness. We have been allowed by Him to seek greatness with the sweat of our hands and the strength of our spirit. And we will retain that heritage only as long as we are willing to earn it again.

For without the resolve of the people, the vision will perish.[19]

In his draft, Busby wrote:

We draw our strength as a nation from the covenant of our forefathers made with the land. Conceived in justice, written in liberty, nourished by union, that covenant was meant one day to encompass all of man.[20]

Working with the same material, Goodwin added the crucial element in his second draft: the nation's reward for fidelity to the America dream:

We made a covenant with that land. It was conceived in justice, written in liberty, nourished by union and meant one day to encompass mankind. In proportion that we have been true to it we have prospered.[21]

The jeremiad theme thus provided the basic structure of the speech. Even in the preliminary drafts, it was introduced early in the address, was developed in terms of America's obligation to remain faithful to justice, liberty, and union in a changing world, and was used to close the speech with a prophetic voice:

If we fail it will not be because we were not strong enough or rich enough. We will have forgotten in abundance what we learned in hardship: that democracy rests on faith, that freedom always asks more than it gives, and that the judgment of God is harshest on those who are young and most favored.[22]

In his third draft (dated January 17, just three days before the inauguration), Goodwin moved the explanation of the jeremiad from the introduction of the address and consolidated it in an abbreviated form with the jeremiadic material in the conclusion. The fundamental organization and logic of the speech remained unchanged, but this editorial change meant that the speech's introduction no longer gave a preview of the jeremiad's true function as the organizing principle of the speech.[23]

SPEECH WRITING AND POLICYMAKING

It is instructive to follow Johnson's frantic aides and writers as each tried to accomplish two conflicting tasks: to produce a successful speech for the inaugural ceremony and to set forth policy statements that would support the presidential adviser's agenda for the administration. There was no genuine question of divided loyalties to LBJ at this point in his administration, but a reading of the speech files in the Lyndon Baines Johnson Library makes it clear that these aides viewed important speeches as opportunities to influence national policy. These were ambitious and capable men who measured their success in terms of proximity to the president and influence on him. To influence the drafting of the inaugural address was to rise in stature and power.

The seventeen drafts of the inaugural address examined for this study (as well as related memoranda offering suggestions) testify to the dynamic, fluid nature of inaugural speech writing. Garry Wills has noted that the jeremiad is "less a genre of oratory than a style of thought."[24] Since the jeremiad became the organizing principle of the address early in the speech-writing process, its mode of thought favored certain changes in arrangement and style and discouraged others. This constraint influenced the policies that were ultimately emphasized in Johnson's inaugural.

As the speech-writing process moved forward, the discussion of foreign policy became more central to the address. Originally foreign policy was not defined as part of the covenant (justice, liberty, union). Instead, it was placed as a fourth and final section of the address under the heading "Change and the World."[25] In the final hectic hours of revision, the foreign policy discussion found its way into the heart of the address. Goodwin's ninth (and final) draft kept foreign affairs in a separate section, but the address was under constant revision once it moved out of Goodwin's hands. Lady Bird Johnson recalled that "even as we were getting dressed to come to the ceremony itself, he [LBJ] had been arranging the part about liberty, justice, and union—Jack Valenti bounding in and out of the room like a rubber ball—taping over certain phrases on the teleprompter [script]. I wouldn't have interrupted them if the building had been on fire."[26]

Through this process, the discussion of America's global mission was inserted into the middle of the address under the heading "Liberty." In the end, four of the six paragraphs in the "liberty" section dealt with foreign policy. Good composition required this reorganization. Had foreign policy remained in a separate section of the speech, it would have been outside the covenant—an afterthought standing apart from the logic of the speech. At some level, the White House advisers sensed that the foreign policy statement had to be woven into the basic fabric of the speech—into the jeremiad itself.

This editorial change placed American foreign policy at the heart of the American covenant. In a passage that provided an unnerving prophecy of America's defeat in the Vietnam War, Johnson urged that if America failed liberty anywhere in the world, it would violate its covenant:

The American covenant called on us to help show the way for the liberation of man. . . . Change has brought new meaning to that old mission. We can never again stand aside, prideful in isolation. Terrific dangers and troubles that we once called "foreign" now constantly live among us. If American lives must end and American treasure be spilled, in countries we barely know, that is the price that change has demanded of conviction and of our enduring covenant.

By moving this passage to the section on liberty, LBJ and his speech writers made international intervention an obligation that had to be fulfilled, lest (in Johnson's words later in his inaugural) America feel "the judgment of God [which] is harshest on those who are most favored."[27]

The influence of the jeremiad can also be detected in the language that Johnson and his advisers selected for the inaugural. In the earliest drafts, the choice of words was consistent with the uncompromising and moralistic nature of the jeremiad. Goodwin declared on behalf of Johnson:

There are no longer any merely "foreign" troubles or "foreign" dangers. They live among us. There is no way back from this responsibility. For great nations, retreat is the signal for decline. And if American lives must end . . .[28]

This passage was entirely consistent with the recommendations of Johnson's foreign policy advisers. The day before the inaugural, McGeorge Bundy urged LBJ to include "a couple of strong sentences on our commitments and engagements abroad." He went on to explain that Scotty Reston of the *New York Times* had called Bundy "to ask me about the 'new isolationism.' " Bundy's prescription was "to take out insurance against criticism on this by some pretty strong language in the inaugural."[29]

Yet when confronted with strong language in the passage on American interventionism, Bundy tried to weaken it. Elsewhere in the White House, Bill Moyers was troubled by the same passage. Both Bundy and

Moyers recommended inserting several sentences that mentioned America's partnership with "two score allies," its hopes to "work in friendliness with four score nations more," and its desire to "seek no enemies at all." Using phrasing suggested by Bundy, Moyers also expanded the passage to include a declaration that rang faintly of Kennedy's inaugural address: "Let us here commit ourselves to make America the enemy of war and want—and partnership of all progress—and the friend of ordered freedom—at home and around the world."[30]

These additions were integrated into subsequent typed drafts of the inaugural address but were cut out of the speech as it moved from the eighth to the ninth draft. Why were Bundy's and Moyer's efforts to no avail? Because their suggested passages were not in the language of the jeremiad. The American jeremiad assumes a special role for America. In such a formula, there is little room for "partnerships" with other nations—certainly not with dozens of nations. To speak of "two score" and "four score" allies, to imply that the American mission could be constrained by other nations, and, worst of all, to suggest that the American mission could be shared with other nations would have been heresy to American civil religion.

Goodwin's original passage stating that Americans must die in far-off lands was his most blunt: If American lives must end, and American treasure be spilled, *in countries we cannot name* [emphasis added], that is the price that change has demanded of conviction." Bundy attempted to replace the offensive phrase with "where freedom is in danger," but then recommended that the phrase simply be deleted. Yet the jeremiad would not yield; it required the unqualified language of moral absolutes. Moyers suggested that the offending words be replaced with the phrase, "in countries we could not name a few years ago," but his alternative was also rejected. Goodwin tried to moderate his own language, with only limited success. In his final two drafts, Goodwin was able to retain the original structure and meaning of the sentence without sending Americans to spill their blood in totally unknown lands. Those lands became "countries we hardly know," and finally, "countries we barely know."[31]

THE JEREMIAD AND NATIONAL POLICY: WHAT THE AUDIENCE HEARD

An examination of the public reaction files to Johnson's inaugural address reveals that Americans heard the religious themes in LBJ's speech; moreover, they understood that the religious motive of the address supported specific public policies. The nation's clergy were most likely to apprehend LBJ's jeremiad. A Methodist minister in central California rushed to his typewriter, explaining: "I am writing to you a few minutes after hearing your historic Inaugural Address. . . . We make much of our formal separation of Church and State in this country, but thank God you and other leaders feel very deeply the union of faith and practice which government must put into action." On the other side of the country, a rabbi praised Johnson's speech for its "sermonic tone" and preached his next sermon on "President Johnson's First Inaugural Address." Echoing Johnson's theme, the rabbi declared to his congregation in Virginia: "America seems to be God's chosen Nation. Let us not embarrass our God because of His choice, by our own fault; our own fallibility; or own feebleness. Let us not deviate nor detour from the heritage of our forefathers. . . . It is our covenant with them and with our God."[32]

This response was not limited to the clergy. Ordinary citizens in California, Kansas, Texas, Florida, and elsewhere praised Johnson's inaugural for its "spiritual quality" and described the speech as "a prayer for tomorrow"—as "a Prayer—calling for our hearts, our hands and our minds." Telegrams carried similar messages: "Your Inaugural speech is like a prayer for us"; "President Kennedy was our Moses but you are our Joshua."[33]

These viewers did not hear Johnson's inaugural as a ceremonial speech detached from national policy. They clearly understood that his moral message carried practical implications. In Chicago a woman expressed her disappointment that Johnson had not connected the nation's values to the need for "law and order." Anticipating a political issue that would dominate domestic politics in the latter half of the 1960s, she first pledged her support for "our successful attainment of the Great Society" and then raised her objection about the inaugural: "You pledged your administration to fight against poverty, hunger, disease, ignorance and injustice, but I am disappointed that crime was not added to this. . . . We boast about liberty and freedom in our country, but are we justified to do so when decent citizens are not safe on our streets, on public transportation, and in their homes? Law and order is rapidly breaking down."[34] Not all viewers were so kind. Those inclined to view Johnson as "a master of deceit" found his use of religion blasphemous and his policies flawed. The very vehemence of such attacks, however, reflects how widely the American audience recognized the policy implications and religious origins of LBJ's secular jeremiad.[35]

CONCLUSION

Johnson's inaugural was heard as a policy prayer expressing his convictions and aspirations for the nation. As a prayer, its success did not rest primarily on oratorical delivery. In fact, Johnson's lack of skillful delivery seemed to reinforce the impression that the inaugural address reflected his beliefs. As television news commentators remarked, Johnson's "rhetoric was not forced or contrived. It was simply stated. . . . Even though Mr. Johnson is not an orator . . . this was given by a man of an obvious enormous self-confidence and personal strength."[36] One citizen was even convinced that Johnson had dismissed his speech writers: "Congratulations on the splendid address you just delivered. It is nice to have at least one person in Washington do his own thinking and prepare his own address. I never did like the idea that ghost writers are used to render their own thoughts. Your speech was sincere and from your heart."[37]

Perhaps the impact of Johnson's inaugural address was best expressed in a letter from a young woman in Pennsylvania. Writing immediately after the inaugural ceremony, she recounted that when LBJ took the oath "and the band played 'Hail to the Chief,' all I could do was cry and think of the late President Kennedy and the disappointments and failures of past years." But after Johnson's address, she explained, "I realized again the importance of looking to the future and *believing* in what we can do as individuals and as a nation. I have always been one of the 'believers' you mentioned, but I needed my faith in the leadership of America renewed." When the ceremony concluded with a second rendition of "Hail to the Chief," she "was moved to tears a second time—only this time because I realized the great future and destiny of our country."[38]

The jeremiad theme provided Johnson with twin advantages: It linked his presidency not to John Kennedy but to the origins of the very concept of America, and it provided a historic justification for his policies to advance justice, liberty, and union. It helped him urge action based upon America's values rather than merely inviting contemplation of those values.

The jeremiad is part of the fabric of American political discourse. It influences the logic, the structure, and the tone of political rhetoric. In Lyndon Johnson's inaugural, it influenced the manner in which broad presidential policies were advocated. The power of the jeremiad rests in its ability to tell Americans who they are and what they should aspire to do. At some level, presidents and their speech writers sense this function of the jeremiad, which means that it will probably continue to appear in presidential inaugurals.

NOTES

1. Horace Busby to the President, memo on the "Theme for the Inauguration," December 9, 1964, Folder PP6 (12/1/64–12/31/64), Box 71 (GEN PP), Papers of LBJ, Lyndon Baines Johnson Library, Austin, Texas. All archival materials cited in this chapter are from the Johnson Library.

2. Mrs. P. A. Ravella to President Johnson, January 20, 1965, folder SP1/Pro-Con/R, Box 58 (GEN SP1), Papers of LBJ. The size of the television audience comes from Robert E. Kintner (NBC-TV) to Bill Moyers, January 22, 1965, Folder PP6 (1/26/65–1/29/65), Box 72 (EX PP6), Papers of LBJ.

3. Mrs. Theodora Ostroff to President Johnson, January 23, 1965, Folder SP1/Pro-Con/O, Box 57 (GEN SP1), Papers of LBJ.

4. Frieda Ann Dechert to President Johnson, February 1, 1965, Folder SP1 Pro-Con/D, Box 56 (EX SP1), Papers of LBJ.

5. Videotape of the Inaugural Address, Audio-Visual Department, Johnson Library; transcript of CBS-TV inauguration day coverage, January 20, 1965, Folder SP1 Inaugural Address (11/23/63–2/28/65), Box 56 (EX SP1), Papers of LBJ.

6. Transcript of CBS-TV inauguration day coverage, January 20, 1965.

7. Ibid.

8. Robert N. Bellah, "Civil Religion in America," *Daedalus* 96 (1967): 8.

9. J.G.A. Popcock, *The Machiavellian Moment: Florentine Political Thought and the Atlantic Tradition* (Princeton, N.J.: Princeton University Press, 1975), 513.

10. Sacvan Bercovitch, "The America Jeremiad: Continuity and Change in the Rhetoric of the National Mission" (paper presented to the Speech Communication Association, New York, November 14, 1980), 6.

11. For discussions of the jeremiad, see Perry Miller, *The New England Mind: From Colony to Province* (Cambridge: Harvard University Press, 1953), 27–39; Sacvan Bercovitch, *The American Jeremiad* (Madison: University of Wisconsin Press, 1978); David Howard-Pitney, *The Afro-America Jeremiad: Appeals for Justice in America* (Philadelphia: Temple University Press, 1990); Kurt Ritter, "American Political Rhetoric and the Jeremiad Tradition: Presidential Nomination Acceptance Addresses, 1960–1976," *Central States Speech Journal* 31 (1980): 153–71; and Kurt Ritter and David Henry, *Ronald Reagan: The Great Communicator* (Westport, Conn.: Greenwood Press, 1992), 36–60.

12. "Inaugural Address of President Lyndon B. Johnson As Actually Delivered," 2, Inaugural Address Folder (1–20–65), Statements of LBJ. All subsequent quotations are from this document. For Steinbeck's contributions to the inaugural address, see Eric F. Goldman to Mrs. Johnson (teletype), January 16, 1965, and the attached document "John Steinbeck Material for Reading at the Inauguration," Inaugural Address Folder (1–20–65), Statements of LBJ.

13. Johnson's three categories were related to three themes that had been included in inaugural addresses from 1789 onward: the promised land, liberty, and empire. See Kurt Ritter and James R. Andrews, *The American Ideology: Reflections of the Revolution in American Rhetoric* (Annandale, Va.: Speech Communication Association, 1978), 40–68.

14. For the most thorough study of Johnson's rhetoric on domestic policy, see David Zarefsky, *President Johnson's War on Poverty: Rhetoric and History* (University, Ala.: University of Alabama Press, 1986).

15. Bob Hunter to Douglass Cater, December 22, 1964, Folder SP1 Inaugural Address, Box 56 (EX SP1), Papers of LBJ.

16. President's Daily Diary, 9:15 P.M., January 14, 1965.

17. President's Daily Diary, 12:10 P.M., January 16, 1965.

18. "Paul Horgan's Comments," Inaugural Address Folder (1–20–65), Files of Bill Moyers, White House Aides' Files. This material may have reached Johnson's

speech writers via White House aide Douglass Cater, who had served briefly with Horgan on the faculty of Wesleyan University.

19. Goodwin Inaugural Draft 2, p. 2, Inaugural Address Folder (1–20–65), Statements of LBJ.

20. Busby Preliminary Inaugural Draft, p. 3, Inaugural Draft Folder, Files of Horace Busby, White House Aides' Files.

21. Goodwin Draft 2, p. 3.

22. Goodwin Inaugural Draft 2, p. 8.

23. Goodwin Inaugural Draft 3, p. 5, Inaugural Address Folder (1–20–65), Statements of LBJ.

24. Garry Wills, *Under God: Religion and American Politics* (New York: Simon and Schuster, 1990), 68.

25. Goodwin Inaugural Draft 2, p. 7.

26. Lady Bird Johnson, *A White House Diary* (New York: Holt, Rinehart and Winston, 1970), 226.

27. "Inaugural Address of President Lyndon B. Johnson As Actually Delivered," p. 2. For the most complete study of Johnson's rhetoric on the Vietnam War, see Kathleen J. Turner, *Lyndon Johnson's Dual War: Vietnam and the Press* (Chicago: University of Chicago Press, 1985).

28. Goodwin Inaugural Draft 2, p. 7.

29. McGeorge Bundy to the President, January 19, 1965, Inaugural Address Folder (1–20–65), Statements of LBJ.

30. Marginal notes by McGeorge Bundy on Goodwin Inaugural Drafts 4 and 5, Inaugural Address Folder (1–20–65), President's Speech File, National Security Files; and marginal notes by Bill Moyers on the same two drafts, Inaugural Address Folder (1–20–65), Files of Bill Moyers. See also McGeorge Bundy to Richard Goodwin, January 18, 1965, President's Speech File, National Security Files.

31. Goodwin Inaugural Drafts 2, 3, and 4, Inaugural Address Folder (1–20–65), Statements of LBJ; and Goodwin Inaugural Drafts 5, 6, 8, and 9, Inaugural Address Folder (1–20–65), Files of Bill Moyers.

32. Robert Sanford to President Johnson, January 20, 1965, Folder SP1/Pro-Con/S, Box 58 (GEN SP1), Papers of LBJ: and Emmet Allen Frank, "President Johnson's First Inaugural Address," January 22, 1965, 5–6, Folder SP1/Pro-Con/F, Box 57 (GEN SP1); both in Papers of LBJ. See also "The Source of President Johnson's Eloquence," *Reconstructionist*, February 5, 1965, 5.

33. Ruth L. Oliver to President Johnson, January 21, 1965, Folder SP1/Pro-Con/O; Charles G. Geltz to President Johnson, January 21, 1965, Folder SP1/Pro-Con/G; Thomas F. Jones, January 20, 1965, Folder SP1/Pro-Con/A-K; Elizabeth and Homer Hendricks to President Johnson (telegram), Folder SP1/Pro-Con/A-K; Lola M. Nelson to President Johnson (telegram), January 20, 1965, Folder SP1/Pro-Con/N: all in Boxes 56 (EX SP1) and 57 (GEN SP1), Papers of LBJ.

34. Mrs. Robert Lyons to President Johnson, January 21, 1965, Folder SP1/Pro-Con/L, Box 57 (GEN SP1), Papers of LBJ.

35. For example, see John W. Prestridge to the *Tyler (Texas) Courier-Times*, January 30, 1965, attached to W. Marvin Watson to E. B. Germany, Feb. 9, 1965, Folder SP1 Inaugural Address (11/23/63–2/25/65), Box 56 (EX SP1), Papers of LBJ.

36. CBS transcript.

37. Chester M. Way to President Johnson, January 23, 1965, Folder SP1/Pro-Con/W, Box 58 (GEN SP1), Papers of LBJ.

38. Susan G. Dix to President Johnson, January 20, 1965, Folder SP1/Pro-Con/D, Box 56 (EX SP1), Papers of LBJ.

Chapter Seventeen

President Richard Nixon's First Inaugural Address, 1969

Hal W. Bochin

Richard Nixon was so proud of the favorable responses, both in the United States and abroad, to his first inaugural address that he suggested in a memo to presidential assistant John Ehrlichmann: "A pretty good collection of one-line quotes—such as appears in the advertisement of a hit play or the cover of a book—could be attached to the mail-out of the RN Inaugural Address when one is made."[1] Nixon had good reason to be pleased with the reaction to his address. For the time being, at least, he had united the country behind his leadership.

Defeated in 1960 by the narrowest margin in the popular vote for president in the twentieth century, Nixon was elected in 1968 by only a slightly greater plurality. In a three-man race with Hubert Humphrey and George Wallace, Nixon captured 43.4 percent of the popular vote, compared to Humphrey's 42.7 percent and Wallace's 13.5 percent. Put another way, 56 percent of the electorate voted against the winning candidate. Nixon's Republican party did not fare much better, gaining four seats in the House and five seats in the Senate. Thus, Nixon faced a Congress dominated by his political rivals, 243–192 in the House and 58–42 in the Senate. He became the first first-term president elected in 120 years without a majority of supporters in either house.[2]

The newly elected president faced a number of other significant challenges as well. The Vietnam War, which had led to Lyndon Johnson's decision not to seek reelection, continued. Popular opinion on the issue divided the country; especially among college-age youth, ending the war was the number one priority, and they had shown themselves willing to take to the streets in defiance of the police to put across their views. Racial conflict, which manifested itself in urban rioting every summer, rocked the nation's stability. Overseas, the Arab-Israeli conflict threatened to draw the United States and the Soviet Union into a military confrontation. Most important, if he hoped to unite the country, Nixon first had to reshape his own image.[3]

To many of his constituents, Nixon was best remembered for his overly aggressive congressional campaigns against Jerry Voorhis and Helen Gahagan Douglas. Called "Tricky Dick" by his opponents, he was pictured in Herblock cartoons emerging from a gutter. The chief tormentor of Democrats as Eisenhower's vice president, he was seen to take the low political road while Ike maintained the high ground. To many, Nixon would always be the "sore loser" of the 1962 California gubernatorial election. Even the appearance of a "new Nixon" in the 1968 presidential campaign had done little to lessen his reputation for going for the jugular. Handicapped by this negative image, Nixon faced a unique challenge in his first official act as president, the presentation of his inaugural address. Although he had won the election, he still had to persuade a large portion of the country that he was no longer a partisan but a president and that he deserved, at least for the moment, the entire country's support. This he accomplished. In recognizing Nixon's significant achievement, however, we should keep in mind William Norwood Brigance's distinction between a successful speech and a great one: "The first is judged by its attainments, the second by its qualities."[4]

PREPARATION OF THE INAUGURAL

Almost from the day of his election, Nixon started to prepare his inaugural address. He asked each of his three major speech writers, William Safire, Patrick Buchanan, and Raymond Price, to have ready a suggested draft of the speech by the first of the year. At the wedding reception of Julie Nixon and David Eisenhower on December 22, 1968, Nixon greeted Safire in the receiving line with: "Let's get the suggestions for the inaugural in by January 5."[5] Even his daughter's wedding could not keep him from thinking about the speech.

To learn to talk like a president, Nixon read the inaugural addresses of all the past presidents and discovered that all could be classified into three general categories: those that called for unity, those that called for sacrifice, and those that deliberately sought to strike a note of confidence for a troubled people. At the first meeting with his writing staff to discuss the inaugural, Nixon shocked them all by asking if they were familiar with the inaugural address delivered by James K. Polk in 1845. None was. Nixon liked it because it was short, and he recommended it to his writers as a model they could follow. Polk's address had one paragraph that was especially applicable to Nixon's political situation. Following the Tennessee Democrat's upset victory over Henry Clay, Polk had written: "Although in our country the Chief Magistrate must almost of necessity be chosen by a party and stand pledged to its principles and measures, yet in his official action he should not be President of a part alone, but of the whole people of the United States."[6]

In discussing his predecessors' speeches, Nixon said that his favorites were Lincoln's Second, "a great one," Wilson's First, and FDR's First. He thought Theodore Roosevelt's was "damn good." He liked Kennedy's because it had "some good phrases" and caught the mood of the country and of the man who delivered it. He reported that some of his advisers, remembering the success Truman had in presenting his Four Point program in the 1949 inaugural, wanted him to call for a specific action in his speech. They suggested, for example, that he could invite a Russian cosmonaut to join the American astronauts on their planned trip to the moon. Nixon, however, rejected such advice because it would "stick out too transparently as gimmickry." He saw the inaugural as a place to signal direction, to suggest priorities, not to discuss specific proposals.[7] In the typology of Karlyn Campbell and Kathleen Jamieson, he sought "contemplation not action."[8]

On January 15, 1969, Rosemary Woods and Ray Price joined Nixon at his home in Key Biscayne, Florida, where Price and the president-elect spent the next few days collaborating on the last drafts of the speech. Woods, Nixon's longtime personal secretary, took dictation as Nixon read from his longhand drafts of the speech, typed them, and returned them for revision. She was also charged with typing the final copy. As they began the final phase of writing the speech, Nixon told Price that his goal was not to turn out a "blockbuster" but rather to say what he believed and to do what he could to heal a divided country. Price recognized that in writing the speech, Nixon was defining the goals of his administration. One important goal concerned the role of the federal government vis-à-vis the individual.[9]

Nixon noted that the start of his presidency would also mark the start of the final third of the century. The middle third had seen a sharp increase in the power of the federal government in Washington and a concomitant loss of power at the state and local levels. Nixon hoped that the final third would be characterized by a shift in direction, a shift in "the flow of power away from Washington and back closer to the people themselves." In offering this hope, Nixon was repeating one of the main issues that had made him a political candidate in the first place. In 1946, speaking to the Committee of 100, who attempted to find a Republican congressional candidate they could support, Nixon expressed exactly the same view.[10]

Among those who offered advice on the inaugural were the evangelist Billy Graham and Paul Keyes, the head writer for the popular "Laugh-In Show" on television. Both were old friends, and both offered advice that Nixon heeded. Graham urged a "strong spiritual emphasis" to the speech, and Keyes suggested a passage from the prayer of St. Francis, which Nixon eventually used: "Where peace is unknown, make it welcome; where peace is fragile, make it strong; where peace is temporary, make it permanent."[11]

Presidential advisers Daniel Patrick Moynihan and Henry Kissinger also offered suggestions that Nixon accepted. Moynihan, the presidential assistant for urban affairs, responded to Nixon's request for topics for the inaugural by writing that three groups needed special recognition by the president: the black poor, the educated youth, and the white working class. Poor urban blacks especially needed reassurance from Nixon that he would not turn away from the Civil Rights Acts of 1959, 1964, and 1965. Moynihan reaffirmed in his memo what an urban task force had already told Nixon: "The rumor is widespread that the new government is planning to build concentration camps."[12]

In answer to Moynihan, Nixon combined his reassurances to the black community with the theme he had chosen for the inaugural ceremonies, "Forward Together." He said, "No man can be fully free while his neighbor is not. To go forward at all is to go forward together." Perhaps remembering Lyndon Johnson's successful quoting of words from the black anthem, "We Shall Overcome," Nixon took words from the second verse: "This means black and white together." He added, "The laws have caught up with our conscience. What remains is to give life to what is in the law; to insure at last that as all are born equal in dignity before God, all are born equal in dignity before man."[13]

Nixon also added a section at the behest of Henry Kissinger, his assistant for national security, who reminded Nixon that Soviet representatives had been promised a public signal that Nixon did indeed desire to negotiate differences between the two countries. Price took little from Kissinger's three-page memorandum, for he found most of it to be "typical boilerplate rhetoric," but the final version of the inaugural contained a strong reaffirmation that the Nixon administration was ready to negotiate with the Soviets. Nixon said: "After a period of confrontation we are entering an era of negotiation. Let all nations know that during this Administration our lines of communication will be open." Nixon, however, rejected as too bellicose Kissinger's proposed statement on Vietnam: "We ask no more than that the people of that nation be allowed to determine their own fate free of external force. We shall settle for nothing less."[14]

Perhaps the best remembered section of the inaugural first appeared in one of Price's early drafts, in which he urged that we, as a nation, should "lower our voices." Nixon liked the idea, and the final version contained these words: "The simple things are the ones most needed today. . . . To lower our voices would be a simple thing." Although many commentators later ascribed the genesis of this passage to Nixon's Quaker background, and this may have been what made it appealing to Nixon, Price was the one who suggested the idea.[15]

In reviewing the final drafts with Price, Nixon made it clear that he wanted to avoid saying anything that might embarrass outgoing President Johnson. He had long felt that Kennedy's line, "The torch has been passed to a new generation," had been a not-so-subtle attack on the elderly Eisenhower, and he was determined not to say anything at which Johnson might take offense.[16]

Not until midnight Saturday were Nixon and Price satisfied that the speech was ready. On Sunday morning, however, Nixon telephoned Price to discuss an introduction that would invite the public to share the "majesty of the moment" with him. He wanted it done gracefully, without his appearing "self-celebrating." Price returned to his typewriter, and, after consulting with Nixon a number of times by telephone, they agreed on the introduction that Nixon used: "I ask you to share with me today the majesty of this moment. In the orderly transfer of power, we celebrate the unity that keeps us free."

Nixon's reading copy of the speech indicates that he made only a few stylistic changes between the time the manuscript was typed and the speech was delivered. The sentence, "In throwing wide the horizons of space we have opened our eyes to the horizons of earth," was changed to, "In throwing wide the horizons of space we have discovered new horizons on earth." In two places he dropped the word *here* from in front of *on earth.* He added "to uphold and defend the Constitution of the United States" after "I have taken an oath today in the presence of God and my countrymen."[17] All of the stylistic changes helped sharpen the language of the speech.

THE INAUGURAL SPEECH

On Monday, January 20, 1969, Richard Nixon stood on a platform built over the steps at the east front of the Capitol and repeated the presidential oath administered by Chief Justice Earl Warren. He rested his left hand on two family Bibles, held by his wife, Pat Nixon, and opened to the second chapter, fourth verse, of Isaiah: "And they shall beat their swords into plowshares and their spears into pruning hooks." The temperature hovered in the mid-thirties, but a strong wind made it seem even colder, and the dark gray sky threatened rain.

Nixon's last-minute introduction worked well. He asked the audience to share with him "the majesty of this moment," a moment "of beginning, in which courses are set that shape decades or centuries." The United States was eight years from its two hundredth anniversary as a nation and close to the beginning of the third millennium, and Nixon declared: "What kind of nation we will be—what kind of world we will live in . . . is ours to determine by our actions and our choices." This sentence served as a transition into the body of the speech, where Nixon described his hopes for America's future, the problems facing the country, their causes and solutions, and the relationship between the United States and the other nations of the world. Rather abruptly, Nixon hit his first major theme, the search for peace: "The greatest honor history can bestow is that of peacemaker. This honor now beckons America." This was part of the description of what America could be, but it takes a number of readings of the speech to see how this sentence fits with what came before. The reason for the confusion was that Nixon's transition prepared the audience for a description of the nation. A section beginning "We will be at peace" would have been more appropriate.

Following the call to be a peacemaker, "our summons to greatness," Nixon listed five achievements of the "second third of this century" and followed with an examination of what was wrong with the country. The United States suffered from a "crisis of spirit." The solution lay within ourselves, and Nixon declared: "The simple things are the ones most needed today if we are to surmount what divides us and cement what unites us." Developing Price's idea further, Nixon suggested: "We cannot learn from one another until we stop shouting at one another—until we speak quietly enough so that our words can be heard as well as our voices." He promised that government would listen to all those who had grievances and that "we will set as our goal the decent order that makes progress possible and our lives secure." (This is the only mention of law and order, one of Nixon's main campaign themes, in the address.) In a sentence that reflected his desire to limit federal control of the individual, he warned: "We are approaching the limits of what government alone can do." Instead, he suggested that the "energies of our people," all of our people, would be needed because "to go forward at all is to go forward together."

Throughout the speech, Nixon used the word *government* in two distinctly different senses: to refer to the federal government system, including the federal bureaucracy ("government has passed more laws, spent more money"), and synonymously with himself as president ("For its part, government will listen. We will strive to listen in new ways—to the voices of quiet anguish"). All the presidential actions Nixon described in the speech were seemingly autonomous; he never suggested that they might require congressional approval or be restricted by constitutional limitations. In fact, Nixon completely ignored the other branches of government and any other potential restrictions on presidential power.[18]

Having analyzed what needed to be done at home, Nixon offered another transition: "As we learn to go forward together at home, let us also seek to go forward together with all mankind." Again Nixon returned to the theme of peace and said: "We are entering an era of negotiations," and he invited those who "would be our adversaries to a peaceful competition . . . in enriching the life of man." In a series of statements beginning with the personal pronoun *I* Nixon reassured his American audience about the common humanity of those in foreign countries—"I have seen the hunger of a homeless child"—and he reassured the citizens of foreign countries about America's goodwill—"I know the heart of America is good." Having spoken directly to both groups, Nixon reached the climax of his speech, where he made a "sacred commitment": "I shall consecrate my office, my energies, and all the wisdom I can summon to the cause of peace among nations." Nixon concluded by looking at the "world as God sees it." He returned to the concept of "moment" presented in the introduction and suggested that, at this moment, "our destiny lies not in the stars but on earth itself, in our own hands and our own hearts."

NIXON'S DELIVERY

A sample of comments by speech professionals reveals unanimity in their descriptions of Nixon's delivery. His oral presentation was "undemonstrative but firm." "There were no vocal pyrotechnics, no oratorical tricks, no obvious demonstrative dramatics. It was a no nonsense delivery, business-like, unwavering, to the point, sensible." He displayed "little of the raucous voice [he was known for]." In short, his delivery strongly supported his message. As one listener put it: "He personified the man who had lowered his voice."[19]

Nixon's manuscript shows that he worked hard on his oral presentation. The most important two or three words in each sentence were underlined for vocal emphasis. Lines were drawn under each major sentence of the speech to remind the speaker to pause. Since the typescript is in outline form, it was easy for him to give proper emphasis to various ideas. Generally Nixon had little eye contact with his audience, for he was tied to his manuscript. A major exception occurred when he spoke the words of his "sacred commitment" directly to the television camera.

REACTIONS TO THE INAUGURAL

Nixon's presidential demeanor, his attempt to unite the country (he used *we* sixty-six times in the speech), the abstract language that no one could disagree with, his quotations from the allusions to Democratic presidents, his emphasis on peace, and his special recognition of groups that had not supported him in the election, including the young, whom he described as "better educated, more committed, more passionately driven by conscience than any generation in our history," combined to offer even the most skeptical critic the image of a concerned president.[20] In the terminology of Campbell and Jamieson, he clearly "reconstituted 'the people,'" restated traditional values, and enunciated the principles that would guide his administration.[21] An additional factor that supported Nixon in the presidential role was the ease with which he donned the mantle of high priest in America's civil religion. After noting that Nixon did not lay out specific programs or proposals, one reporter offered this characterization: "His rhetoric possessed a flowery, metaphorical, and sermon like quality." In support he offered the following example from Nixon's speech: "We have endured a long night of the American spirit. But as our eyes catch the dimness of the first rays of dawn, let us not curse the remaining dark. Let us gather the light."[22]

Newsweek called the inaugural "a short, general, and often eloquent homily aimed at the common sense and common decency of Middle America." *Time* agreed: "The speech he fashioned was a short, hortatory sermon on hope—a call for peace in the world (without saying how it would be wrought) and a summons to citizen involvement at home (without telling the citizens exactly what to do)." James Reston of the *New York Times* applauded Nixon's conversion from campaigner to president: "The hawkish, political, combative, anti-Democratic Nixon of the past was not the man on the platform today." He noted that Nixon had reached out to many who had opposed his election—"progressive Democrats, the young, the blacks, and the Soviets." Reston concluded that Nixon's speech "could have been written by Ted Sorensen or Arthur Schlesinger, Jr., or Senator J. W. Fulbright, and delivered by the Kennedys or even Gene McCarthy."[23]

Political leaders of both parties, columnists, and editorial writers praised Nixon's address. In recording various responses, the *New York Times* found it "remarkable" that "the speech drew much the same reaction from widely separated political factions." Chairman of the Senate Foreign Relations Committee and leading critic of the Vietnam conflict J. William Fulbright called the address "a very superior speech and very hopeful for a more rational foreign policy." Similar words of praise came from Senator Eugene McCarthy, who described it as a "good address, pretty well generalized as an inaugural address should be." Senator Henry M. Jackson, Democrat of Washington, said: "It was an excellent statement of the finest aspirations of our people." Congressman Charles S. Joelson, a liberal Democrat from Paterson, New Jersey, reported: "I tried very hard to listen with a nonpartisan ear. If John F. Kennedy had said it, I would have thought it magnificent." Senator Edward Brooke, Republican of Massachusetts and the only African-American in the Senate, called the speech "a message of hope . . . very sound and inspirational." At the same time, conservative Senator John L. Sparkman of Alabama described it as "a speech of confidence and hope."[24]

As expected, Republicans praised the president. Nelson Rockefeller, Nixon's primary opponent for the Republican nomination, said of the speech: "I thought the whole thing was excellent and positive, just great." House GOP leader Gerald Ford of Michigan, said: "The speech struck just the right note for this moment in history." One Yankee Congregationalist, a Senate Republican who preferred to remain anonymous, commented: "There was more religion in that speech than in all five prayers [preceding the speech] put together."[25]

Columnists of various political persuasions found the contemplative tone of Nixon's address appropriate for the audience and the times. Noting the lack of specific proposals in Nixon's address, Joseph Kraft decided "that there are just now special circumstances which make it sensible to be clear about goals and obscure about how to reach them." He continued: "The needs of the moment . . . demand a man who can speak in homilies. . . . Mr. Nixon was speaking in homilies. But they were the right homilies." Flora Lewis argued that the times called for moderation and deliberation rather than for sweeping promises and stirring appeals: "So it would be wrong to begin the Nixon era with complaints about lack of excitement, lack of radiant vision, lack of whirlwind drive beyond the horizon. That is not what the country chose, and it is quite possibly not what the country needed." Mary McGrory, never a fan of Nixon, may have summed up the position of most liberal columnists best: "There's no dancing in the streets, but there's an acceptance that Richard Nixon has rarely known in his controversial career." When Gallup asked the nation in late January, "Do you approve or disapprove of the way Nixon is handling his job as President?" 59 percent said they approved and only 5 percent disapproved.[26]

NIXON'S STYLE

Although it was very effective, Nixon's First Inaugural cannot be considered a great speech because of its lack of originality, its structural problems, and its uneven style, which ranged from banal to eloquent.

Nixon so often used the words of others to embellish his thoughts that the speech suffers from a lack of originality. He directly quoted FDR's description of the economic problems of 1933: "They concern, thank God, only material things." He alluded to the reply of Cassius to Brutus in Act I, scene 2 of *Julius Caesar*: "The fault, dear Brutus, is not in our stars but in ourselves." He quoted directly from an essay by the poet Archibald Macleish describing the view of the Apollo astronauts: "Riders on the earth together, brothers on that bright loveliness in the eternal cold." He recalled Woodrow Wilson: "Make the world safe for democracy." From Lincoln's First Inaugural, he borrowed the last six words, "the better angels of our nature." The Book of Malachi provided him with the phrase, "with healing in its wings." Philip Tompkins noted that Nixon even turned to Lyndon Johnson's inaugural for inspiration. Nixon's line, "Until he has been part of a cause larger than himself, no man is truly whole," reminds the listener of what Johnson had said four years earlier: "Men want to be part of a common enterprise—a cause greater than themselves." It is probably not coincidental that Nixon sought inspiration most often from the man who had defeated him in 1960:

JFK: "Let the word go forth, to friend and foe alike."
Nixon: "Let this message be heard by strong and weak alike."

JFK: "Let every nation know."
Nixon: "Let all nations know."

JFK: "To those nations who would make themselves our adversary. . . . "
Nixon: "Those who would be our adversaries, we invite to a peaceful competition."

JFK: "We dare not tempt them with weakness, for only when our arms are strong beyond doubt can we be certain beyond doubt that they will never be employed."
Nixon: "But to all those who would be tempted by weakness, let us leave no doubt that we will as strong as we need to be, for as long as we need to be."

The ideas are similar, and in a number of cases the language is similar as well. Finally, a lack of originality can be seen in Nixon's use of such tired phrases as, "This is our summons to greatness"; "I believe the American people are ready to answer this call"; "I know the heart of America is good"; "I speak from my own heart"; "We have endured a long night of the American spirit"; and "Let us not curse the remaining dark."[27]

Structurally, the speech was not a typical Nixon effort. He did not enumerate his important points. His transitions were weak because what followed a transition statement was often not what the listener expected. The speech had many short paragraphs, but the president offered little to connect them. The peace theme reappeared in every section of the speech, but Nixon never developed it beyond a few lines, and it did not act to unify the speech.

Two major stylistic problems also limited the inaugural's potential for greatness: He badly overused devices that, if used sparingly, could have been quite effective, and he chose to be abstract, a tactic that may have helped to unite his audience. He carried it to an extreme, however, so what he meant exactly often became unclear. Two examples warrant the problem. What did Nixon mean when he said, "I do not offer a life of inspiring ease. I do not call for a life of grim sacrifice. I ask you to join in a high adventure"? What is the listener supposed to think? What is the nature of this adventure, and how can it solve the problems Nixon has raised? Similarly, what did the president mean when he promised, "We shall plan now for the day when our wealth can be transferred from the destruction of war abroad to the urgent needs of our people at home"? This might be seen as a commitment to end the war in Vietnam or to cut back on military spending, but it comes after the statement that our problems are not the result of a lack of "material things" and that they can best be solved by looking within ourselves. A close reading also reveals that the promised day is not imminent; only the planning for it is. Throughout the speech, Nixon provided abstract concepts without development and did not reduce them to a level that an audience could readily understand.

The second problem involved the overuse of antitheses and aphorisms. Kennedy's best-remembered line, "Ask not what your country can do for you, ask what you can do for your country," must have had an extraordinary influence on Nixon. He used the same device repeatedly, so much so that it lost much of its effectiveness. These examples illustrate the kind of sentence he overused: "We cannot expect to make everyone our friend, but we can try to make no one our enemy"; "Our destiny offers not the cup of despair, but the chalice of opportunity"; "So let us seize it not in fear but in gladness." William Buckley referred to such phrases as "the rhetorical blight of Sorensen; those false antitheses which are substituted for analytical invigoration."[28] Nixon also offered a plethora of aphorisms: "Greatness comes in simple trappings"; "The way to fulfillment is in the use of our talents"; "Peace does not come from wishing for it"; and, perhaps worst, "The American dream does not come to those who fall asleep." What in moderation could have been effective failed through excessive use.

On the other hand, a number of lines worked well. In addition to the sections on lowering our voices and going forward together, Nixon offered such striking statements as: "The essence of freedom is that each of us shares in the shaping of his own destiny"; "We find ourselves rich in goods, but ragged in spirit; reaching with magnificent precision for the moon, but falling into raucous discord on earth"; and "Those who have been left out, we will try to bring in. Those left behind, we will help to catch up." Such sentences reminded Jon Ericson of "superbly constructed floats in a mediocre parade."[29]

CONCLUSION

In a statement issued from Walter Reed Army Medical Center where he was recovering from a series of heart attacks, Dwight Eisenhower summarized the mood Nixon was trying to create in his inaugural address: "No longer are we partisans in a presidential campaign. Now we are Americans together." With a large number of Americans, Nixon's strategy of quietly appealing for unity at home and for peace in the world succeeded. One editorial writer noted: "If one of the purposes of the ceremonial transfer of power in Washington is to persuade people to give the new President a chance at national leadership, the inauguration was a success. To that end Mr. Nixon's demeanor and eloquent words notably contributed."[30] Significant problems with style and structure, however, prevented Nixon's successful speech from attaining greatness.

The honeymoon period following the inaugural did not last long. Nixon's failure to end quickly American involvement in Vietnam brought steadily increasing criticism from Congress, the media, and vocal elements of the citizenry. Stung by the criticism and by what he considered to be disloyalty from some members of his administration, who leaked classified material to the press, he began to act out the presidential role he had implied in his inaugural address. Nixon became the president who was the government, acting without regard for constitutional limitations. In the words of Theodore White, Nixon came to believe he was "the sole custodian of America's power," and under the guise of protecting national security he authorized the wiretaps and surveillances that eventually culminated in Watergate and his resignation.[31]

NOTES

    1. Bruce Oudes, ed., *From: The President* (New York: Harper & Row, 1989), 12.

    2. Zachary Taylor faced the same situation in 1849. Stephen E. Ambrose, *Nixon: The Triumph of a Politician* (New York: Simon and Schuster, 1989), 221.

    3. Phillip K. Tompkins, "Nixon's Search for Peace," in Jon L. Ericson and Robert Forston, eds., *Public Speaking as Dialogue* (Dubuque, Iowa: Kendall/Hunt, 1970), 135.

    4. Tom Wicker, "Number 37 Is Ready," *New York Times Magazine*, January 19, 1969, 21; William N. Brigance, "What Is a Successful Speech?" *Quarterly Journal of Speech Education* 11 (November 1925): 372.

    5. Robert B. Semple, "2 Nixon Aides Fly to Florida," *New York Times*, January 16, 1969, 26.

    6. William Safire, *Before the Fall* (New York: Da Capo Press, 1975), 110–11.

    7. Raymond Price, *With Nixon* (New York: Viking Press, 1977), 42. Although

the Nixon Museum is open, the library is not. Thus, Price remains the best source for information about the preparation of the speech.

8. Karlyn Kohrs Campbell and Kathleen Hall Jamieson, "Inaugurating the Presidency," in Herbert W. Simons and Aram A. Aghazarian, eds., *Form, Genre, and the Study of Political Discourse* (Columbia: University of South Carolina Press, 1986), 205.

9. Semple, "2 Nixon Aides," 26; Price, *With Nixon*, 44.

10. Price, *With Nixon*, 46; Hal W. Bochin, *Richard Nixon, Rhetorical Strategist* (Westport, Conn.: Greenwood Press, 1990), 12.

11. Price, *With Nixon*, 45.

12. Ibid., 43.

13. Quotations from the inaugural address are taken from Richard Nixon, *Public Papers of the Presidents of the United States* (Washington, D.C.: U.S. Government Printing Office, 1971), 1–4.

14. Price, *With Nixon*, 43–44.

15. "New President Pleads for Unity," *Christian Science Monitor*, January 21, 1969, 11.

16. Price, *With Nixon*, 42–43.

17. Ibid., 49; "RN's Copy, Inaugural Address," typescript, President's Personal File, Box 46, Nixon Presidential Materials Project, National Archives.

18. Nixon made a *pro forma* statement that he would uphold and defend the Constitution.

19. Anthony Hillbruner, "The Ambience of the Forty-Sixth Inaugural," in Ericson, *Public Speaking*, 99; Robert Cathcart, "The Nixon Inaugural Address," in Ericson, *Public Speaking*, 133.

20. Phillip K. Tompkins, "Nixon's Search for Peace," 138.

21. Campbell and Jamieson, "Inaugurating the Presidency," 205.

22. Robert B. Semple, "A Role for the Disaffected and Young Pledged," *New York Times*, January 21, 1969, 22.

23. "With Lowered Voice, Enter Mr. Nixon," *Newsweek*, February 3, 1969, 16; "Let Us Go Forward Together, *Time*, January 27, 1969, 17; James Reston, "From Partisan to President of All," *New York Times*, January 21, 1969, 1, 22.

24. John W. Finney, "Congress Hails Goals Set Forth by Nixon," *New York Times*, January 21, 1969, 23.

25. Finney, "Congress Hails," 23; "Rockefeller Calls Speech 'Positive—Just Great,' " *New York Times*, January 21, 1969, 23.

26. Joseph Kraft, "A Time for Homilies," *Los Angeles Times*, January 22, 1969, 2:9; Flora Lewis, "Nixon at the Helm," *Los Angeles Times*, January 23, 1969, 2:9; Mary McGrory, "New President Is Installed," *America*, February 1, 1969, 125; *Gallup Opinion Index*, Report 44 (February 1969): 1.

27. Tompkins, "Nixon's Search for Peace," in Ericson, *Public Speaking*, 135; Garry Wills noted these and other similarities between the Nixon and Kennedy inaugural addresses in *Nixon Agonistes* (Boston: Houghton Mifflin, 1970), 403–4.

28. William F. Buckley, "The Inaugural: Minus and Plus," *Los Angeles Times*, January 24, 1969, 2:8.

29. Jon M. Ericson, "The Inaugural Address of Richard Nixon," in Ericson, *Public Speaking*, 124.

    30. "Day of Rejoicing for Eisenhower," *New York Times*, January 21, 1969, 22; James A. Wechsler, *New York Post* editorial reprinted in Ericson, *Public Speaking*, 142.
    31. Theodore H. White, *Breach of Faith* (New York: Dell Publishing, 1976), 420.

Chapter Eighteen

President Richard Nixon's Second Inaugural Address, 1973

Thomas A. Hollihan

The 1972 presidential election was one of the most one-sided contests in the nation's history. Richard M. Nixon was reelected to office with more than 60 percent of the votes, carrying forty-nine of the fifty states. His Democratic challenger, Senator George McGovern, was unable to carry even his home state of South Dakota. Only Massachusetts and the District of Columbia failed to support the president. Despite the electoral landslide, however, the January 20, 1973, inaugural was not a joyous event. In fact, most accounts of Nixon's Second Inaugural speech and of the festivities that accompanied the address acknowledge that the mood in the nation's capital that day was as dark and foreboding as the cold, gray, January weather.[1]

Approximately $4 million was spent on the 1973 inaugural festivities in an attempt to create a memorable celebration.[2] More than fifty thousand invited guests observed the speech and danced away the evening at several different inaugural balls. Some two hundred thousand spectators lined Pennsylvania Avenue for a parade consisting of hundreds of horses, more than thirty floats, and marching bands representing almost every state in the nation.[3] In keeping with the tenor of the times, as the president spoke, the shouts of antiwar protestors could be faintly heard from some three blocks away.[4]

The nation was intensely divided as President Nixon began his second term. He had promised just prior to the November election that the Vietnam War was almost over, but he had been unable to deliver on this promise. The Paris Peace Talks had stalemated, and in December the president, without consulting the Congress and without explanation to the American people, ordered a massive increase in bombings over

North Vietnam. Members of Congress immediately protested. Democratic Senator William Fulbright announced that the Democrats now had the votes to pass the long-threatened resolution to cut off all funds for the war.[5] Even many members of the president's own party had reached their limits. Republican Senator William Saxbe of Ohio lamented that the president "appears to have left his senses on this issue."[6] *Newsweek* declared that the public was so completely stunned by the new bombings that the prevailing mood was one of "discouragement and demoralization," even among the antiwar protestors who seemed to have given up.[7]

A morose attitude could even be found among the president's closest advisers and cabinet members. The president's first action following his election-night victory parties had been to request the resignations of all senior-level appointees. Although he did not accept all of these resignations, he communicated that he wanted a drastic change in personnel. Herbert Klein, his director of communications, declared: "After being with Nixon on mornings after the election in almost every race since 1946, I found this post-election act the most disheartening, most surprising, and most cruel of all. . . . The 1972 act might be looked at as efficient, but it was ungrateful and it was bitterly cold."[8] President Nixon himself later acknowledged in his memoirs that this move was a mistake: "I did not take into account the chilling effect this action would have on the morale of people who had worked so hard during the election and who were naturally expecting a chance to savor the tremendous victory instead of suddenly having to worry about keeping their jobs."[9]

Following the demands for the resignations of his cabinet and staff members and during the time of the Christmas bombings, the president locked himself away from the public and the press. He made no public statements and left the explanations for his actions to staff members. The press howled in protest. *Newsweek* declared: "It's not simply the furor over the bombing, or the suspense over the peace talks or even the presence in town of so many recently ousted and still disgruntled members of the first Nixon administration. Rather it's the realization that if the recent past is any guide to the political future, then the nation faces four more years of an increasingly reclusive, sometimes vindictive, and disturbingly uncommunicative Chief Executive."[10] The *New Republic* called Nixon the "most aloof President in history."[11]

In one of the few interviews that he gave to the press following his reelection but before his Second Inaugural, the president acknowledged that he had not been in high spirits. Despite his one-sided victory, he nonetheless felt a sense of a "letdown."[12] Perhaps this letdown came because Nixon understood that he had just completed his last political campaign. He gave something of a glimpse into his character when he stated: "I believe in the battle, whether its the battle of a campaign or the battle of this office, which is a continuing battle. It's always there wherever you go. I, perhaps, carry it more than others because that's my way."[13] In his memoirs, he also admitted that this second inaugural ceremony was a difficult one for him, attributing his personal disappointment to the fact that he had hoped to be inaugurated in peacetime but that, against his wishes, the war had dragged on.[14]

What should have been a time of profound celebration was thus a somber event. A president who had just claimed a huge landslide but could not claim the affection of the American people—indeed, at this point not even the affection of his closest aides and advisers—and who was himself depressed and isolated was about to present a speech designed to set a tone for the second term. Given how that second term turned out—the crisis of Watergate and the forced resignation from office—it seems that the speech did set the tone for Nixon's embattled second term.

THE PREPARATION OF THE SPEECH

President Nixon, unlike most other political figures, was committed to the preparation of his own speeches. Although he worked with a small staff of speech writers, he was personally responsible for the generation of his own ideas and for most of the language chosen for the text.[15] His Second Inaugural was no exception. Although the president asked for some assistance from his aides, especially requesting that they read the inaugural addresses given by Theodore Roosevelt in 1905 and Franklin Delano Roosevelt in 1937 and 1941, the president merely scanned the material that they provided him and wrote his own speech.[16]

In his memoirs, President Nixon recalled how he awoke the morning of the speech and, "before going downstairs, I stopped in the Lincoln Bedroom in the spot where the Emancipation Proclamation was written and where I understood Lincoln's desk was located and bowed my head for a moment, and prayed that I might be able to give the country some lift, some inspiration and some leadership in the rather brief inaugural that I had prepared."[17] If the president's goal truly was, as he declared, to inspire the public, his speech was a failure.

THE SPEECH

President Richard Nixon's Second Inaugural was bland and almost melancholy, with few of the lofty platitudes that distinguish effective and memorable inaugural speeches. If there was a unifying theme of the speech, it was that the U.S. government and the American people had reached too far and had attempted to achieve too much. Now it was time, the president solemnly said, to redefine our goals and our policies, both foreign and domestic.[18]

Although the speech was delivered in the deep, dark shadow of the Vietnam War, the president did not refer to Vietnam by name. Instead, he referred to the nation standing on "the threshold of a new era of peace in the world."[19] There was no great celebration that the long war was about to be finished; instead, the president lectured: "Let us resolve that this era we are about to enter will not be what other postwar periods have so often been; a time of retreat and isolation that leads to stagnation at home and invites new danger abroad." Furthermore, he argued that "the peace we seek in the world is not the flimsy peace which is merely an interlude between wars, but a peace which can endure for generations to come."

The president held that the United States had to change fundamentally its foreign policy conceptions and objectives. Only twelve years earlier, in his inaugural address, President John F. Kennedy had declared: "Let every nation know, whether it wishes us well or ill, that we shall pay any price, bear any burden, meet any hardship, support any friend, oppose any foe, in order to assure the survival of the success of liberty."[20] Now President Nixon, whom Kennedy had defeated by a razor-thin margin in the election of 1960, was firmly in control. He had just been reelected by a landslide, and he was eager to put an end to the Kennedy policies. Nixon declared: "The time has passed when America will make every other nation's conflict our own, or make every other nation's future our responsibility, or presume to tell the people of other nations how to manage their own affairs." Instead, he observed, "Just as we respect the right of each nation to determine its own future, we also recognize the responsibility of each nation to secure its own future." The president's sternest remarks, however, were not about foreign policy but rather about domestic policies. Again, the president was eager to communicate that it was time to reject the policies of his Democratic predecessors, Kennedy and Lyndon Johnson. In his inaugural address, President Kennedy had urged Americans: "Ask not what your country can do for you, ask what you can do for your country."[21] In the most widely quoted statement from this speech, President Nixon recast Kennedy's language into: "In our own lives, let each of us ask not just what will government do for me, but what can I do for myself?" In short, the president declared that people needed to be self-sufficient and that they should not count on governmental programs or assistance to help resolve their problems.

The president was most explicit in his criticisms of Johnson's Great Society programs: "Just as building a structure of peace abroad has required turning away from old policies that have failed, so building a new era of progress at home requires turning away from old policies that have failed." Nixon was especially critical of attempts to usurp the power from local government: "Abroad and at home, the time has come to turn away from the condescending policies of paternalism—of Washington knows best." Individuals would have to do more for themselves. The image that the president suggested was one of too many people who had become lazy and were eager to feed at the public trough, a people who were looking for handouts rather than using initiative. He observed,

That is why I offer no promises of a purely governmental solution for every problem. We have lived too long with that false promise. In trusting too much in government, we have asked of it more than it can deliver. This leads only to inflated expectations, to reduced individual effort and to a disappointment and frustration that erode confidence both in what government can do and in what people can do. Government must learn to take less from people so that people can do more for themselves.

The president communicated little sympathy for those persons who required governmental assistance: "Let us remember that America was built not by government, but by people—not by welfare, but by work—not by shirking responsibility, but by seeking responsibility." While it is customary during inaugural addresses to emphasize the politics of unity and to devise rhetorical strategies that emphasize people coming together, President Nixon instead practiced the politics of division. Nixon's America was a nation composed of essentially two kinds of people: those who worked, contributed, paid their own way, and through their efforts built a great nation; and those who were lazy, did not work, shirked responsibility, and lived off the generosity of others—this from the president who had gone into the Lincoln Bedroom that morning in the hopes of finding a message to inspire the American people.

Paradoxically, the president pleaded for political tolerance: "As America's longest and most difficult war comes to an end, let us again learn to debate our differences with civility and decency." Yet his own remarks demonstrated little tolerance. Nixon willingly used the politics of divisiveness in his comments about American youths: "Our children have been taught to be ashamed of their country, ashamed of their parents, ashamed of America's record at home and its role in the world. At every turn, we have been beset by those who find everything wrong with America and little that is right." Nixon extended no olive branch in this speech to those who had passionately opposed his policies on Vietnam and had marched in the streets to end the war. Those who opposed him, who worked against his reelection, and were still chanting in the streets of Washington to end the war had been taught to hate and not to respect their nation, their parents, and their president. The president was quite openly wrapping himself in the American flag and asserting that to oppose him and his policies was to oppose and hate the nation.

Near the end of his speech, the president cited a litany of achievements about which he claimed Americans could be justly proud. Using parallel structure and seeking to build to a dramatic conclusion, the president ticked off these accomplishments:

Let us be proud that our system has produced and provided more freedom and more abundance, more widely shared than any other in the history of man. Let us be proud that in each of the four wars in which we have been engaged in this country, including the one we are now bringing to an end, we have fought not for selfish advantage, but to help others resist aggression. Let us be proud that by our bold new initiatives, and by our steadfastness for peace with honor, we have made a breakthrough toward creating in the world what the world has not known before—a structure of peace that can last, not merely for our time, but for generations to come.

Although this rhetoric was designed to engage audiences and involve them directly and emotionally with the speech's theme, the language was not particularly memorable or inspirational, and Nixon's lack of enthusiasm in the delivery of the text caused these words to fall short of having the profound effect that he most certainly desired.

THE INAUGURAL AS RHETORICAL GENRE

In his Second Inaugural, President Nixon demonstrated his awareness of the ceremonial importance of the occasion. The speech detailed the nation's achievements, commemorated the contributions of previous generations, and closed with a prayer asking for God's help that he might be guided to make decisions that would keep our nation "a bright beacon of hope for all the world." In his last sentence he declared: "Let us go forward from here confident in hope, strong in our faith in one another, sustained by our faith in God who created us, and striving always to serve his purpose."

Despite the tenor of the closing paragraphs, the speech could not be considered primarily epideictic in focus. Instead, this speech was a call to action, and the president offered a blueprint for the policy moves that would be forthcoming in his second term. America's role in the world would change; the nation henceforth would seek to influence and lead other nations to act in their own interest rather than simply acting ourselves in their behalf. And the role of the federal government would shrink as state and local governments and citizens themselves would be empowered to make their own decisions and to remedy their own problems.

President Nixon used the occasion of his second inauguration to assert that he would not be idle during his second term; there would be no "stagnation," for America was going to move forward, and "the shift from old policies to new will not be a retreat from our responsibilities, but a better way to progress."

REACTIONS TO AND ASSESSMENTS OF THE SPEECH

The reactions to President Nixon's Second Inaugural are remarkable for their consistency. The *Nashville Tennessean* opined: "It must have seemed to many that the address was in keeping with the chilly and overcast day. It held little sunlight. Its words were gray and flat and slightly ominous."[22] The *Winston-Salem Journal* editorialized: "One could detect in President Nixon's inaugural last Saturday a sullen, uneasy, even pessimistic tone. . . . One sensed in the President a brooding melancholy air."[23] The *Toledo Blade* commented: "President Nixon's Second Inaugural Address, delivered in an unimpassioned almost desultory manner, contained little of the sort of inspirational rhetoric calculated to lift the nation's spirits."[24] The *Nation* magazine commented that the inaugural was "tidy, profitable, and banal. Its dominant quality was variously described as 'clouded,' 'strange,' and 'dreary.' Everyone was well-behaved, included the peace marchers. But the inaugural ceremonies and even the President's address evoked little, if any emotions." The same essay also declared that even the president's supporters and invited guests seemed to be "satisfied" with the president but definitely not "jubilant," and that although the speech was interrupted by applause, it was "perfunctory."[25] Even the conservative *National Review* admitted that the rhetoric was "banal," although it did insist that the speech represented a significant departure from the failed past policies of the Great Society.[26]

Many of the newspaper and magazine stories written immediately after the speech contrasted this speech with President Nixon's First Inaugural. Columnist John Osborne noted that in the previous address, Nixon had promised to listen "to the injured voices, the anxious voices" and to "lead us forward together." In this speech, Osborne declared, the president seemed a "harder and colder man," who had no kind words, and who instead asserted that "all Americans must forego the false promise of governmental solutions."[27] John Herbers, writing in the *New York Times*, also commented on the fact that "absent from the address was the gesture to liberals that he had made four years ago. . . . Rather, Mr. Nixon reinforced his post-election image as a President in isolation and loneliness governing in DeGaulle fashion for the long judgments of history."[28] The *Chicago Sun-Times* noted the change in President Nixon's attitude toward America's youth, commenting:

Four years ago, he said, "I believe in them. We can be proud that they are more educated, more committed, more passionately driven by conscience than any generation in our history." Saturday he said, "Our children have been taught to be ashamed of their country, ashamed of their parents, ashamed of America's record at home and of its role in the world."[29]

The *Wall Street Journal*, almost alone in its praise for the speech, editorialized that "the President was quite right to say that today's outlook is hopeful compared with that of four years ago," and that while "many of course consider this [Nixon's assertion that government cannot solve all human problems] a heartless philosophy, by and large, clearly, federal efforts to solve social problems have not worked. And clearly the problem-solvers have overspent federal income."[30]

CONCLUSION

Accepted political wisdom tells us that inaugural speeches, even second inaugurals, are supposed to signal new beginnings. The inaugural ritual is supposed to signal a new period of unification, where the body politic is brought back together after a divisive political campaign. Despite the one-sided Nixon win in 1972, the body politic had seldom been more divided than it was during this campaign. If ever there was a need for inaugural rhetoric aimed at unifying and healing this deep public rift, 1973 was that time. Instead, the rhetoric in this inaugural was divisive, and the rift was, if anything, intensified. Political columnist Mary McGrory was on hand for the inaugural festivities, and in a perceptive column she commented: "They had absolutely nothing to say to each other, the celebrators and the demonstrators. The two opposing tides of America, the invited and the uninvited, surged past each other on Constitution Avenue as the parade was ending and the protest was winding down. They eyed each other, but they did not speak."[31]

In what may be recognized as one of the more prescient statements on record, the *New Republic*, in the anonymous column signed TRB, editorialized: "The funny thing is that under other circumstances I would say that the man who got the third largest landslide in history three months ago is in political trouble. The mood is different from anything I can remember. Congress is really sore. My bones keep sending me signals, and I keep dismissing them as ridiculous, but I am not sure anymore."[32]

President Nixon was, of course, in deep political, legal, and perhaps personal and emotional trouble. The Vietnam Peace Accords would be signed within a few days of his second inauguration ceremonies, but the joy over the end of the war would be insufficient to unify the public. Instead, the continuing news stories on the Watergate break-in and cover-up would increasingly occupy the public's attention and the president's time. President Nixon, who professed his need for and love of the battle, would become engaged in the most embittered and drawn-out battle of his political career. It is likely that the trajectory of events was already too well set to have had its course changed by anything that the president might have said in his Second Inaugural. It does seem clear now, however, that this speech did nothing to lessen the president's problems or to satisfy his critics. It cannot be considered to have been an effective or successful address.

NOTES

1. Typical of the press accounts emphasizing the negative mood in the capital and in the speech itself are: Mel Elfin, "Nixon: The Cocoon of Power," *Newsweek*, January 22, 1973, 19; "Scenes: Something for Everybody," *Time*, January 29, 1973, 12; and "The Clockwork Inaugural," *Nation*, February 5, 1973, 162.

2. "Step Right Up, Folks," *Nation*, January 22, 1973, 100.

3. "Nixon's Own 'Ask Not' . . . ," *Newsweek*, January 29, 1973, 22.

4. R. W. Apple, Jr., "Nixon Inaugurated for Second Term," *New York Times*, January 21, 1973, A40.

5. "Congress and the War," *New Republic*, January 6, 1973, 11.

6. William Saxbe, cited by Richard Nixon, *RN: The Memoirs of Richard Nixon* (New York: Grosset & Dunlap, 1978), 738.

7. "What Went Wrong," *Newsweek*, January 1, 1973, 8.

8. Herbert G. Klein, *Making It Perfectly Clear* (Garden City, N.Y.: Doubleday, 1980), 364.

9. Nixon, *RN*, 768.

10. Elfin, "Nixon," 19.

11. "Near the Breaking Point," *New Republic*, January 6, 1973, 6.

12. Cited by Elfin, "Nixon," 19.

13. Cited by "Nixon's Continued Quest for Challenge," *Time*, January 22, 1973, 11.

14. Nixon, *RN*, 751.

15. For a discussion of Nixon's approach to speech writing, see Hal W. Bochin, *Richard Nixon: Rhetorical Strategist* (Westport, Conn.: Greenwood Press, 1990), 89–90. In his recent book, Richard Nixon, *In the Arena* (New York: Simon and Schuster, 1990), the former president offers an extended argument to explain why he believed it was important that he write his own speeches: "Why should any leader think an issue through, prepare a speech, and then commit it or an outline to memory if no one is going to pay any attention. So he hands the task over to his eager young writers, and a vicious circle soon develops. If policy statements become less important, a leader will spend less time on them. But thinking a speech through helps a leader to think his policy through, so when a speech ceases to be his own, so does the policy. In the end, the public suffers, and so does the leader, because he has no reason to force himself to use his imagination and memory to the hilt" (149–50). See also 210–17 for an extended discussion of how the president prepared for speeches.

16. "The Pageantry and Festivities of Inauguration 1973," *U.S. News and World Report*, January 22, 1973, 19–20.

17. Nixon, *RN*, 752.

18. All references to the Second Inaugural are from "A Transcript of President Nixon's Second Inaugural Address to the Nation," *New York Times*, January 21, 1973, A40.

19. The announcement of the Paris Peace Accords, the treaty that would signal the end of armed conflict, would not come until Secretary of State Henry Kissinger and North Vietnamese emissary Le Duc Tho reached their final agreement two days after the inauguration. See John Osborne, "Four Days," *New Republic*, February 3, 1973, 19–20.

20. Cited by John Herbers, "The Second Inaugural," *New York Times*, January 21, 1973, 42.

21. Cited by ibid.

22. *Nashville Tennessean*, January 23, 1973; *Editorials on File*, January 16–31, 1973, 155.

23. *Winston-Salem Journal*, January 23, 1973; *Editorials on File*, January 16–31, 1973, 157.

24. *Toledo Blade*, January 22, 1973; *Editorials on File*, January 16–31, 1973, 154.

25. "The Clockwork Inaugural," *Nation*, February 5, 1973, 162.

26. "Counterrevolution," *National Review*, February 16, 1973, 192.

27. John Osborne, "Four Days," *New Republic*, February 3, 1973, 19.

28. Herbers, "Second Inaugural," 42.

29. *Chicago Sun Times*, January 22, 1973; *Editorials on File*, January 16–31, 1973, 154.

30. *Wall Street Journal*, January 22, 1973; *Editorials on File*, January 16–31, 1973, 153.

31. Mary McGrory, cited by "The Clockwork Inaugural," 162.

32. "To the Battle Stations," *New Republic*, January 20, 1973, 4.

Chapter Nineteen

President Gerald R. Ford's Inaugural Address, 1974

Bernard L. Brock

Gerald R. Ford was the first president to assume office following the resignation of a president in danger of impeachment, a difficulty that was compounded by the fact that Ford earlier had become vice president following Spiro T. Agnew's resignation under a cloud of scandal.

Ford's unique entrance to the presidency deprived him of delivering a traditional inaugural address. His short remarks following his oath of office, coupled with his more formal "Address to the Joint Session of Congress," are generally considered his official inaugural statement. Robert Hartmann, Ford's long-time adviser and speech writer, viewed the informal remarks as the inaugural, while the formal statement was received by the public as the inaugural.[1] Gerald Ford's address to Congress was especially appropriate since he was the first president to assume office without a vote of the American people. He had been appointed by President Nixon, but he had been approved by the House of Representatives. In a real sense, his inaugural was an address to Congress, which had elected him president, but Ford was also mindful of the American people, whom he would lead.

THE RHETORICAL SITUATION

Gerald Ford faced a nation deeply divided by almost twenty years of internal turmoil over the civil rights movement, the Vietnam War, and Watergate.

Initially, the civil rights movement divided the nation over how quickly equal rights should be granted blacks. This question was partially answered by the enactment of the 1964 Civil Rights and 1965 Voting

Rights acts. However, the division became deeper with the birth of the black power movement and the civil disturbances in 1967, and many people were angered by the movement's threat of violence.

Then the divisions over civil rights were transferred to the Vietnam War. President Richard Nixon inherited from his predecessor, Lyndon Johnson, a nation troubled over the Vietnam War. The hawks felt the United States had a responsibility to assist South Vietnam to pursue democratic values and to oppose the extension of communist North Vietnam that was receiving aid from the People's Republic of China and the Soviet Union. The doves saw American intervention as immoral because they viewed the conflict as a civil war that had been going on for years. Peace groups led demonstrations against the war that disrupted governmental and political processes and had even resulted in violence.[2]

The Watergate scandal ultimately attached this division to the highest seat of government. The 1972 reelection of Richard Nixon was conducted within the climate of the division over Vietnam, and Nixon essentially viewed the campaign as a vote for or against American foreign policy in Vietnam. As a result, his campaign drew upon all the available tools to defend and win the election. Watergate started as a break-in at the Democratic Headquarters in Washington, D.C., but escalated into illegal activities executed by the Committee to Re-elect the President, which Nixon himself covered up in part. Ultimately, the nation became bogged down and depressed as each new revelation was aired on nightly television and in newspaper headlines.

THE INFORMAL INAUGURAL

On August 9, 1974, the thirty-eighth president of the United States needed to restore a divided and depressed nation. Ford assumed office with less than a week's notice, so he was not able to bring the planning process of the presidency to bear upon his address and how to heal the nation. As a result, his long-time adviser and friend Robert Hartmann drafted his informal remarks.

Ford's remarks following his oath of office were especially concerned with the problems of tradition and continuity, since his selection and the informal inaugural itself were a break from tradition. Ford chose to appeal to traditional and constitutional values as he acknowledged his unique situation:

The oath that I have taken is the same oath that was taken by George Washington and by every President under the Constitution. But I assume the Presidency under extraordinary circumstances, never before experienced by Americans. This is an hour of history that troubles our minds and hurts our hearts.[3]

Concerned that he had not been elected in the usual manner, Ford immediately described his broad base of support and the political principles upon which it was based:

Those who nominated and confirmed me as Vice President were my friends and are my friends. They were of both parties, elected by all the people and acting under the Constitution in their name. It is only fitting then that I should pledge to them and to you that I will be the President of all the people.

Ford strategically assumed the role of the statesman and identified with all the people, as well as both political parties. He announced his request to address Congress "to share . . . my views on the priority business of the Nation and to solicit your views"; this request provided him the opportunity for his later formal address.

Ford's first task was to communicate that the nation was essentially unaffected by the divisions that civil rights, Vietnam, and Watergate had caused and that the nation would remain on course. Ford stated:

To the people and the governments of all friendly nations, and I hope that could encompass the whole world, I pledge an uninterrupted and sincere search for peace. America will remain strong and united, but its strength will remain dedicated to the safety and sanity of the entire family of man, as well as to our own precious freedom.

I believe that truth is the glue that holds government together, not only our Government, but civilization itself. That bond, though strained, is always the best policy in the end.

Ford not only affirmed a united nation but one that was still dedicated to peace throughout the world. Further, with these remarks, Ford forecast the theme of his more formal address.

Before concluding these remarks, Ford nevertheless had an important task. Maintaining continuity with tradition had been important, but almost more important was severing himself from the turmoil of the Nixon administration. He did this by seeking a new beginning when he announced, "My fellow Americans, our long national nightmare is over." Hartmann reported that this line had been cut but that he pleaded to retain it because he saw the importance of this dramatic new beginning.[4]

The "nightmare" line was retained, but it was immediately followed by a direct and sympathetic reference to Nixon: "In the beginning, I ask you to pray for me. Before closing, I ask again for your prayers, for Richard Nixon and for his family." Just weeks later, Ford's popularity would be undermined by his pardon of Nixon and by Ford's failure to separate himself at least rhetorically from Nixon.

Ford then closed his informal inaugural with an appeal to God and the American people:

I now solemnly reaffirm my promise I made to you last December 6: to uphold the Constitution, to do what is right as God gives me to see the right, and to do the very best I can for America. God helping me, I will not let you down.

The public response to the new president and his remarks was immediately supportive, as reflected by editorials in the news media.[5] The *Cleveland Press* was encouraged by his message, "There was something simple and touching and very encouraging about the behavior of Gerald Ford on the day he became the 38th President of the United States." It added, "He called it not an inaugural address, not a fireside chat, not a campaign speech, but 'just a little straight talk among friends' and promised it to be the first of many." The *Chicago Tribune* predictably communicated strong acceptance of Ford and compassion for Nixon:

The few words spoken by President Ford after taking his oath of office were well chosen, dignified, and encouraging. Mr. Ford was generous to Mr. Nixon and even offered a prayer for the Nixon family. Yet his words and his attitude reflected a simple straightforwardness that has not been seen around the White house for at least a decade.

The *Houston Post* echoed the positive response to Ford: "honest, open, friendly, without trace of affectation and seeming to embody the most solid virtues of the traditional American ethic." Finally, the *Seattle Times* not only praised Ford but picked up the line Hartmann had fought to include:

But it is not only freedom from what Mr. Ford called "our long national nightmare" that exhilarates the country at this historic juncture. The new President has the qualities needed to restore confidence in government.

Ford's informal inaugural had gotten his presidency off to a strong start.

THE FORMAL INAUGURAL

Gerald Ford's formal inaugural address followed three days after his initial statement. Ford received help from his staff in preparing the speech. Hartmann supervised the team that prepared the formal address and adapted the language to Ford's style. Milton Friedman developed the major domestic policy portion of the speech, and Henry Kissinger was responsible for the foreign policy section. Then Ford interacted with the team in the final stages. A copy of Ford's original manuscript reveals that he made only minor changes in the final draft. The greatest change was the deletion of two sentences on the first page. After acknowledging a "warm welcome" from Congress, Ford struck, "I hope it will be just as genuine when my Presidency ends. It will be, if we work together."[6] These words raised an unnecessary question about whether Congress and the president would work well together, and they also drew attention away from the important focus—the beginning of Ford's presidency. His eighteen-page reading copy revealed few words or phrases either inserted or crossed out in Ford's own handwriting.

In his formal address Gerald Ford again enacted the role of the statesman by appealing to and seeking support from the broadest national and foreign audiences. He made a strong Jacksonian move to be president of all the people and then attempted to transfer his acceptance to his conservative values. In the address, he stated his philosophy of leadership, set forth his domestic legislative priorities, and then supported President Nixon's foreign policy.

Ford correctly sensed the urgency of the situation and adopted the strategy of immediately calling for action: "We have a lot of work to do." He sought the healing of the nation by working with both Congress and the people. He then emphasized the importance of this action by contrasting it with his own address: "I am not here to make an inaugural address. The nation needs action, not words." Ford continued this approach of placing himself in the background by identifying with the people and Congress: "It's good to be back in the People's House." Yet even as he sought oneness, he separated himself from Congress. "But this cannot be a real homecoming," he said. "Under the Constitution, I now belong to the Executive Branch." Ford continued to pursue unity by presenting his "motto towards Congress," "communication, conciliation, compromise and cooperation." "But this must be a two-way street," he added. Ford's strategy was especially effective because it contrasted dramatically with the aloofness of his predecessor, who had become isolated from the nation during the Watergate upheaval. In declaring his unity with the people and Congress, Ford wisely distanced himself from the fallen Nixon and communicated his appreciation of the limitations to executive power.

Ford nevertheless continued to assume the role of statesman with the strategy of subtly separating himself from Congress. He did this by emphasizing that the people were more important than Congress: "As President, I intend to listen. But I also intend to listen to the people themselves—all the people—as I promised them last Friday. I want to be sure we are all tuned in to the real voice of America." Ford made it clear that the Congress is not necessarily the "real voice of America." Further, he indicated that his door would be open to congressmen, "if you don't overdo it." Ford would be a friend of Congress, but he would not let it take advantage of him. Thus, he stressed his powers as well as his executive limitations.

Ford's next task, to set forth the philosophy and style of his administration, was accomplished with a play on words involving his name: "Only eight months ago, when I last stood here, I told you I was a Ford, not a Lincoln. Tonight I say I am still a Ford, but I am not a Model T." Ford, the statesman, established that he was conservative but not reactionary, and then he elaborated on some of his "old-fashioned ideas," which were communal values:

I believe in the basic decency and fairness of America. I believe in the integrity and patriotism of the Congress. And while I am aware of the House rule that one never speaks to the galleries, I believe in the First Amendment and the absolute necessity of a free press.

Ford wisely appealed to traditional American values and in the process further separated himself from Nixon, since these were all values that had been violated by the Watergate scandal.

Not wanting to be stereotyped as a conservative, Ford moved rhetorically to the political middle. He accepted "the direction of the nation's movement" forward; he allowed that in high school he "headed the Progressive Party ticket"; and he used an automobile metaphor to motivate the people to join with him "in getting this country revved up and moving." His phrasing echoed John Kennedy's slogan, "Get the country moving again," when he ran against the more conservative Eisenhower.

Ford's judgment "that the State of the Union is excellent. But the state of our economy is not so good," enabled him to discuss the problem of the economy. Ford immediately focused on inflation and placed the blame on government as he pledged "to bring the Federal budget into balance by fiscal 1976." At this point Ford made a strategic change in his prepared manuscript. He omitted a line in which he admitted favoring federal projects for Grand Rapids in his home state while opposing "wasteful Federal boondoggles" in other states and instead said that he had always stood "against unwarranted cuts in national defense. This is no time to change that nonpartisan policy." Ford, knowing that budget cuts would be in order, attempted to head off significant reduction in defense in the name of nonpartisan policy. In one of the more overt appeals to action in his address he continued this statesman-like strategy by requesting the people's support for budgetary restraint in the November elections:

Support your candidates, Congress and Senators, Democrats or Republicans, conservative or liberal, who consistently vote for tough decisions to cut the cost of government, restrain Federal spending and bring inflation under control.

Ford presented the statesmanlike image of taking the political high road by remaining nonpartisan in pursuing the road of fiscal restraint. He also communicated some of the political principles that would guide his administration.

Ford then applauded Congress for steps it had already taken: authorizing a study of inflation and convening an economic conference of national leaders. He strategically carried the idea further and proposed "that this summit meeting be held at an early date and in full view of the American public." Ford clarified that dealing with inflation was his top priority, "Inflation is our domestic public enemy No. 1," and he recited action-oriented steps he would take in dealing with it.

Having established his philosophy and priorities for leadership, Ford tried to persuade Congress to accept his leadership. He did this by raising the specter of presidential veto:

Tonight is no time to threaten you with vetoes. But I do have the last recourse and am a veteran of many a veto fight in this very chamber. Can't we do the job better by reasonable compromise?

He extended his position by indicating that he brought "no legislative shopping list" but that he would mention a few examples like the "Elementary and Secondary Education Bill," "proposals for better health care financing," and "the Trade Reform bill." In discussing the problems facing the country in specific terms, Ford established his credibility as a knowledgeable leader and continually stressed that he and Congress should work together to solve problems and keep spending down.

Next, Ford strategically emphasized continuity as he embraced Nixon's foreign policy. Because he had not been identified with foreign policy, it was critical to establish his credibility in this field. Furthermore, during the Watergate scandal, the nation had experienced a long vacuum in leadership. By stressing continuity with President Nixon's foreign policy, Ford was able to assure leaders in other countries that their relationships with the United States would not change significantly. He did this by specifically addressing foreign audiences throughout the world:

To our allies of a generation, in the Atlantic community and Japan, I pledge continuity in the loyal collaboration on our many endeavors.

To our friends and allies in this hemisphere, I pledge continuity in the deepening dialogue to define renewed relationships of equality and justice.

To our allies and friends in Asia, I pledge a continuity in our support for their

security, independence, and economic development. In Indo-China, we are
determined to see the observance of the Paris Agreement on Vietnam and the
cease-fire and negotiated settlement in Laos. We hope to see an early compromise
settlement in Cambodia.

Ford continued this strategy by addressing the Soviet Union, the People's Republic of China, and nations of the Middle East. Finally, he
pledged to all nations of the world "a stable international structure of
trade and finance which reflects the interdependence of all peoples."
   Throughout most of the address, Ford carefully separated himself from
Richard Nixon and successfully distanced himself from Watergate and
all that it represented, but he could not afford to offend Republicans
who still respected Richard Nixon and admired him for his expertise in
foreign policy. Ford wisely identified with the Nixon administration in
that area by establishing continuity for leaders throughout the world
and by gaining acceptance from loyal Nixon supporters.
   Having handled both domestic and foreign policy, Ford the statesman
needed to close the address on a high point. He elevated himself to a
"higher plane of public morality" and humanized himself by admitting
a second mistake as he again separated himself from Nixon:

I once told you that I am not a saint, and hope never to see the day that I cannot
admit having made a mistake. So I will close with another confession.
   Frequently along the tortuous road of recent months, from this chamber to
the President's House, I protested that I was my own man.
   Now I realize that I was wrong.
   I am *your* man, for it was your carefully weighed confirmation that changed
my occupation.
   I am the people's man, for you acted in their name, and I accepted and began
my new and solemn trust with a promise to serve all the people, and to do the
best I can for America.

Ford closed with the appeal that with God's guidance, "nothing can
stop the United States of America." He had opened his inaugural calling
for action and he appropriately closed on the same note.

FORD'S STYLE AND DELIVERY

Ford's style and delivery were both plain. He saw himself as a person
of the people and was uncomfortable with a more elevated style. This
preference for the plain style was announced early in the address with
a line he had used favorably in the past: "Only eight months ago, when
I last stood here, I told you I was a Ford, not a Lincoln." However, this
time he did not just repeat it. He added a new wrinkle: "Tonight I say

I am still a Ford, but I am not a Model T." This clever addition allowed him to make the point humorously that he was not too conservative.

Ford's preference for a plain style was reflected in another line he had used over and over again: "They know that a government big enough to give you everything you want, is a government big enough to take from you everything you have." This line makes a bid for eloquence, but its lack of rhythm and balance makes it awkward. Hartmann indicated that, early in his political career, Ford had originally heard this line spoken by Harvard McClain at the Economic Club in Chicago and had liked it. Since then, he had used it sufficiently to make it his own, and he especially enjoyed using it because it received a positive response from the audience and a negative one from the press. He found that he could insert the line any time he needed to get a reaction from the audience, and it had become part of his style.

Ford's most eloquent line came early in the address and had been penciled in on the final draft, "As President, within the limits of basic principles, my motto towards Congress is communication, conciliation, compromise, and cooperation. But this must be a two-way street." Ford's alliteration had a pleasant ring to it, but it was followed by a flat line rather than one that would elevate the earlier thought.

Ford's plain delivery was characterized by a generally slow cadence and monotony in pacing and vocal quality. At times his slow delivery was even halting. Yet this plain style was perceived as credible. People did not feel he was trying to sell them something. This, too, separated him from Nixon, who had the image of a used car salesman.

Under the circumstances Ford's delivery was effective. Democrats and Republicans alike appreciated Ford's plain style because he had touched the hearts of many people. One letter he received focused specifically on his plain style: "Thank you for no Kennedy epigrams, no Johnson corn, no Nixon deviousness." Another person specifically said that he liked Ford's "straight talk."[7]

REACTIONS TO THE ADDRESS

The response to Ford's inaugural address was overwhelmingly favorable. His immediate audience, the joint session of Congress, received him well by interrupting for applause thirty-two times, and the public communicated their approval by flooding the White House with letters congratulating and praising the speech's substance and style.[8] Many agreed that inflation was the nation's greatest problem, so he received letters defending General Motors, attacking labor unions as the cause, and recommending wage and price controls. Women attacked him for sexism when he referred to "women's liberationists" in a list of groups he would represent, and Asians protested at not being included in his list.

Most reactions, however, were general and positive. They ranged from liking his "open door" policy and "willingness to listen" to a speech that made them "feel good about America." Comments repeated in the letters included "uplifting," "heartwarming," "reassuring," "common sense approach," and "honest and fair."

Media response to the address was favorable. The *Houston Chronicle* exclaimed, "President Ford touched all the right buttons," and they pointed to his being "a man who just simply says what he means" and "that he intends to be the president of 'all the people.' "The *St. Louis Globe-Democrat* and the *Wall Street Journal* praised Ford for making dealing with soaring inflation his highest priority, while the *Los Angeles Times* was pleased he had not presented specific solutions for the nation's problems. Finally, the *Washington Post* was reassured by Ford's message of continuity with Nixon's foreign policy, and they saw him as working better with Congress than Nixon had.[9]

Ford's inaugural addresses certainly won for him the hearts and minds of the American public. His acceptance was reflected in his 71 percent approval rating in a Gallup Poll survey shortly following his speech.[10]

CONCLUSIONS

Ford's inaugural address was paradoxical in both substance and form. He opened with a call for action but presented no outline of any plan for action. Further, Ford's leadership style of letting problems solve themselves, both prior to and during his presidency, was inconsistent with an action orientation in this address.

Another paradox was Ford's desire for both continuity—for national stability and credibility in his leadership—but new beginning and separation of the Nixon administration, for the same two reasons. Initially, his high approval rate suggested that his contradictory strategy worked, but he undermined its success and credibility when the pardon identified him too closely to Richard Nixon and his family.[11]

Stylistically the address was also paradoxical. Ford had chosen the high road of the statesman, which called for a style more akin to that of John Kennedy. But Gerald Ford, essentially a plain man, demanded a plain style. In the long run, this was a wise choice because he could have never been comfortable with a high style.

Ford's inaugural address was a success. He had risen to the occasion created by the crisis of a divided country and as a statesman was able to end "our long national nightmare," but Ford's natural plain approach and inherent conservative tendencies precluded his maintaining the more elevated style and nonpartisan road of the statesman. The response to his speech revealed he had let in a light that restored confidence in government. However, soon Ford's pardon of Richard Nixon and Ford's own failed WIN (whip inflation now) campaign undermined his credibility. Nevertheless, the public's belief in Ford's basic goodness was never eroded.

NOTES

1. I interviewed Robert Hartmann by telephone on October 12, 1991, regarding the speech.

2. For an understanding of the Vietnam War, see Stanley Karnow, *Vietnam: A History* (New York: Penguin Books, 1984).

3. Ford's informal remarks were taken from *Weekly Compilation of Presidential Documents* 10 (32): 1974, 1023–25.

4. Hartmann interviews.

5. All media references are from *Editorials on File*, August 1–15, 1974, 994–1010.

6. All quotations from the formal address for the joint session are taken from a copy of Gerald Ford's original manuscript. Office of Editorial Presidential Speeches and Statements, Reading Copy, 8/12/74, Presidential Address to Congressional Joint Session, Box 1, Ford Library, University of Michigan.

7. Responses to both addresses were obtained from the Subject File SP2–3–1, Joint Session of Congress, 8/12/74, Boxes 5–8, Ford Library.

8. *Editorials on File*, 994.

9. Ibid.

10. *Gallup Poll, vol. 1, 1972–1975* (Wilmington, Del.: Scholarly Resources 1978), 369.

11. For a discussion of the Nixon pardon, see Bernard Brock, "Gerald Ford Encounters Richard Nixon's Legacy: On Amnesty and the Pardon," in *Oratorical Encounters: Critical Studies and Sources*, ed. Halford Ryan (Westport, Conn.: Greenwood Press, 1988).

Chapter Twenty

President Jimmy Carter's Inaugural Address, 1977

Craig Allen Smith

Former governor Jimmy Carter of Georgia defeated President Gerald Ford by running as an outsider. He had won the Democratic nomination by distancing himself from traditional Democrats, and he won the presidency by emphasizing honesty, integrity, optimism, and "a government as good as its people." His support was broad but shallow, and he was least popular among northeastern liberals and southern conservatives.[1] He unseated by only fifty-seven electoral votes (a scant 2.1 percent of the popular vote) an incumbent never voted for by anyone beyond southwestern Michigan—one, moreover, who had pardoned Richard Nixon and Vietnam-era draft evaders, sponsored a disastrous swine flu inoculation program, pronounced Eastern Europe free of Soviet domination, and dropped Vice President Nelson Rockefeller in favor of the abrasive Senator Robert Dole of Kansas. Carter attained the presidency largely by seeming consistently the least objectionable available candidate, a difficult mandate from which to lead.

President Carter wrote his own address but not without assistance. Carter Library files contain multipage January memorandums and drafts from some twenty people (including Zbigniew Brzezinski, Pat Caddell, Joseph Califano, Gerald Rafshoon, Theodore Sorenson, and Cyrus Vance). They variously suggested that Carter emphasize human rights, government reorganization, the end of the Vietnam and Watergate era, achievement, and an American renewal.[2]

The first draft of the speech embodied several of the suggested themes and phrasings, and it eventually became the address. This draft appears to have been created by copying promising suggestions from the correspondence onto file cards, sorting and numbering the cards, typing them into a draft, and polishing it through four drafts. A document titled "First draft/inaugural" dated "12/27" and revised on January 8 predated all of the advisory correspondence. Although it experienced only one revision, this discarded speech is in several ways the better speech. Certainly, it is more vigorous and presidential than Carter's inaugural. The authors of the two documents were apparently unaware of their parallel activities.[3]

Carter addressed inadequately the generic demands of the inaugural because he misconstrued it as a personal moment, a conclusion suggested by the coordinated management of meaning (CMM) theory.[4] Critics traditionally consider the speaker, the occasion, and the audience when analyzing a message, but CMM seeks to discern specific levels of rules that guide the coordination of meaning and to this end has identified six kinds of rules: (1) content rules governing semantics, (2) speech act rules differentiating statements from questions, (3) situational rules defining episodes or situations, (4) relational rules governing communities or relationships, (5) life-script rules guiding the idiosyncratic personal behaviors of an individual, and (6) cultural patterns affecting society at large.

From this perspective of all public addresses being governed by a set of speech act rules, Campbell and Jamieson have identified four specific situational rules that define presidential inaugurals—the inaugural unifies the audience, rehearses communal values, sets forth the political principles that will govern the administration, and demonstrates that the president understands the requirements and limitations of the office.[5] Each president brings to the inaugural moment a set of personal life-script rules from which to unite a broad range of cultural patterns in the new administration. Any inaugural address is the result of a series of rhetorical choices made according to these four sets of rules, and analysts who employ one set of rules risk underestimating the configurative power of the other sets.

THE CARTER INAUGURAL: SITUATIONAL RULES

Carter responded to many of the generic rules. He reconstituted the American people "in terms of both spirituality and human liberty . . . [with an] obligation to take on those moral duties which, when assumed, seem invariably to be in our own best interests."[6] Carter's people were moral, wise, confident, proudly idealistic, and quietly strong. The people witnessed the investiture and participated in their own inauguration: "This inauguration ceremony marks . . . a new spirit among us all. . . . A President may sense and proclaim that new spirit, but only a people can provide it."

Carter illustrated the change from previous administrations with two dramatic gestures. First, he sought to end a decade of polarizing accusations. In his first sentence, he thanked Ford "for all he has done to heal our land" and paused to shake Ford's hand, thereby prolonging heartfelt applause for the presidency itself. Carter's words functioned only to frame the symbolic gesture: He neither mentioned Ford's name nor specified what had been done to heal the country. Precisely because the people were left to complete the tribute themselves, the handshake conveyed unambiguous national solidarity. Following the speech, Carter dramatically illustrated a change from the suspicions and security concerns of previous administrations by walking with his family along the 1.2-mile parade route. Carter's walk was a deliberate rhetorical statement:

I remembered the angry demonstrators who had habitually confronted recent Presidents and Vice Presidents, furious over the Vietnam war and the later revelations of Watergate. I wanted to provide a vivid demonstration of my confidence in the people as far as security was concerned, and I felt a simple walk would be a tangible indication of some reduction in the imperial status of the President and his family. . . . I wanted it to be a dramatic moment.[7]

It was. News coverage featured the first couple smiling and waving in pictures that belied the thinness of the new president's base of support.

Second, Carter reaffirmed traditional American values and attributed them to the reconstituted people. Some of Carter's observations are indeed unifying and fully consistent with the inaugural genre:

Our Government must at the same time be both competent and compassionate. . . . We know that the best way to enhance freedom in other lands is to demonstrate here that our democratic system is worthy of emulation. . . . We will not behave in foreign places so as to violate our rules and standards here at home. . . . We will be ever vigilant and never vulnerable. . . . We are a proudly idealistic nation, but let no one confuse our idealism with weakness.

But rather than venerating the past, Carter ignored it, other than to say that "we cannot dwell upon remembered glory." The only shared recollections were ambiguous references to "the American dream" and "our recent mistakes." Previous presidents were honored only with references to "my predecessor" and "our first President." And the only reference to overcoming difficulties was that "when we have stood briefly, but magnificently, united . . . no prize was beyond our grasp."

Beyond that, Carter attributed to his people shared values that may not have been so widely shared. The following statements seem more like arguable claims than shared premises:

We are now struggling to enhance equality of opportunity. . . . Our commitment to human rights must be absolute. . . . Our national beauty preserved. . . . We have learned that *more* is not necessarily *better*, that even our great Nation has its recognized limits, and that . . . we cannot afford to do everything.

Surely such statements had the potential to stir disagreement. Indeed, "Watching the sea of approving faces," wrote Carter, "I wondered how few of the happy celebrants would agree with my words if they analyzed them closely."[8] It seems plausible that the audience, numbed by the frosty air and uncomfortable delivery, would indeed have had great difficulty analyzing Carter's message. But the inaugural ceremony invited applause, polite cheers, and smiles from those fortunate enough to have tickets. Although the inaugural as broadcast, taped, and photographed suggested public support for Carter and his ideational content, much of that applause and approval may have been situationally and culturally motivated.

Carter followed the third inaugural rule by setting forth the political principles that would guide his administration. Such principles might best be instrumental rather than terminal so that the president can define the style of his presidential leadership. This Carter did not do. He said:

I join in the hope that when my time as your President has ended, people might say this about our Nation:

- —that we had remembered the words of Micah and renewed our search for humility, mercy, and justice;
- —that we had torn down the barriers that separated those of different race and region and religion, and where there had been mistrust, built unity, with a respect for diversity;
- —that we had found productive work for those able to perform it;
- —that we had strengthened the American family, which is the basis of our society;
- —that we had earned respect for the law and equal treatment under the law, for the weak and the powerful, for the rich and the poor; and
- —that we had enabled our people to be proud of their own Government once again.

By stressing terminal rather than instrumental goals, Carter emphasized substance over process, thereby inviting history and his critics to assess his results.

Carter's focus on the accomplishments highlights the absence of one fundamental principle: constitutionalism. Constitutional references can provide rhetorical reassurance to the new president's former opponents, thereby facilitating the unification of the people under his leadership.[9] But nowhere does the address pay homage to constitutional duties and procedures, as do most other addresses in the genre.

Carter's inaugural, then, reconstituted the people, reaffirmed some traditional values while largely ignoring opportunities to invoke shared recollections, and oriented his presidency toward results rather than constitutional procedures. On these dimensions alone, his inaugural deviated considerably from the situational rules of the genre. On these dimensions alone, it would seem at best a satisfactory inaugural.

THE CARTER INAUGURAL: RELATIONAL RULES

The most grievous failing of Carter's speech as a presidential inaugural is that he failed to enact the presidential role. Presidents are not required to speak at their inaugural ceremonies, but the moment invites verbalization. In that moment "a candidate" becomes president. This involves a two-dimensional transformation. First, the individual must reconceptualize himself. No longer can he act as a private citizen or candidate could act. Every presidential behavior will be politically meaningful to others because of the symbolic potency of the presidency. The inaugural address is as good a time as any other for the president to take on the role. This did not happen for Carter, as he confided to his diary later that day:

Even though I had been preparing to be President, I was genuinely surprised when in the benediction, the Bishop from Minnesota referred to "blessings on President Carter." Just the phrase, "President Carter," was startling to me.[10]

Perhaps he would have been less startled had his address enabled him to perform the role.

The second level is the public's transformation: from old president to new, from partisan candidate to president of all the people. The essential point is that citizens and their presidents are bound together not by speech act, episodic, personal, or even cultural rules but by relational rules. Like employers and employees, parents and children, presidents and citizens have expectations of one another. Role violations undermine these relationships, as when an employer seems parental or a parent bossy. Citizens need to see that their new president is aware of the presidential job description and that he has been well cast in the role.

"If an inaugural address is to function as part of a rite of investiture," write Campbell and Jamieson, "presidents must speak in the public role of president." This role has four major dimensions. First, new presidents should avoid self-references that illuminate neither the presidency nor the American experience. Consider in this light Carter's third sentence, "As my high school teacher, Miss Julia Coleman, used to say, 'We must adjust to changing times and still hold to unchanging principles.' " This sentence not only fails to illuminate either America or the presidency, it diminishes through attribution an observation that might otherwise have seemed profound.[11] Because Carter invoked no other personal experiences, the address provided little sense of his personal insight into either the presidency or his followers.

Second, we are accustomed to hearing presidents characterize their leadership as constitutional, but Carter never mentioned legal-constitutional procedures or constraints on the presidency—this fresh on the heels of Watergate and Vietnam. Instead he suggested modes of being. "You have given me a great responsibility," he observed, "to stay close to you, to be worthy of you, and to exemplify what you are." These responsibilities, although necessary and admittedly beyond the reach of some of his predecessors, insufficiently defined the presidential role.

Third, inaugurals normally evidence humility and place the nation under God's care. This was Carter's specialty. Absent references to former presidents or the Constitution, Carter invoked the Book of Micah: "What doth the Lord require of thee, but to do justly, and to love mercy, and to walk humbly with God." Carter staked out the low ground, telling his followers that "your strength can compensate for my weakness, and your wisdom can help to minimize my mistakes." He claimed "no new dream to set forth today, but rather urge[d] a fresh faith in the old dream;" although a "President may sense and proclaim that new spirit, . . . only a people can provide it." Even his goals, if accomplished, "will not be my accomplishments—but the affirmation of our Nation's continuing moral strength and our belief in an undiminished, ever-expanding American dream."

Fourth, presidents need to use the inaugural to perform the chief executive's role—by donning its vestments, swiveling in its chair, and exercising its prerogatives. Instead Carter characterized himself as humble, weak, prone to errors, and dependent on his people. "He did little to project leadership qualities," wrote Dan Hahn, "or to extend to the people the security which a strong, charismatic president provides."[12]

In short, Carter did not try to "function as a leader" in the inaugural. Few of the role expectations characterized his speech.[13] He disavowed any new dream for America, acknowledged his unspecified weaknesses, deferred to the people, ignored legal-constitutional constraints, and essentially left himself no role in the governmental process.

Viewed as epideictic discourse that completed the investiture of relational role responsibilities, the Carter inaugural was disappointing. It only faintly reconstituted the people, it articulated few traditional values, it outlined few shared political principles, and it did not enact the presidential role. The address failed to satisfy situational and relational needs because Carter followed a different set of rules.

THE CARTER INAUGURAL: LIFE-SCRIPT RULES

An alternative approach to an inaugural address is to view it as the new president's moment in time, his reward for reaching the pinnacle. It is the briefest of honeymoons in which to speak one's mind in an atmosphere of euphoria, unworried about disapproval. Like an Academy Award acceptance, it can reveal the human side of one who postures publicly as a vocation. Thus viewed, the inaugural is not investiture epideictic but very personal epideictic, governed by personal life-script rules. Such was Jimmy Carter's approach to his inaugural.

As Campbell and Jamieson identified features characteristic of inaugural discourse, others have identified features characteristic of Jimmy Carter's approach to political and rhetorical life. Most important here are the prepresidential regularities that helped Carter to prepare his address, although some observations about Carter's rhetorical career do help to contextualize this moment. Nine characteristics recur in the research literature on Jimmy Carter.

1. *Carter's pragmatic realism required him to be persuasive.* His worldview emphasized practical problem solving through comprehensive programs.[14] Carter's "hydraulic worldview" enhanced his appetite for blueprints, long-range strategies, and "big pictures."[15] He was disinclined to offer either new visions or radical reforms, preferring to make existing systems work "more efficiently, economically, and justly."[16] But this technical kind of reform encounters bureaucratic opposition and excites few supporters. To accomplish it, a leader needs extraordinary legislative relationships, obvious public support, or both, and both require an ability to persuade.

2. *Carter was adept neither at forging nor maintaining legislative coalitions.*[17] His relations with Georgia legislators and party leaders were troubled because his young, inexperienced staff was insufficiently attentive to political etiquette, his brand of reform challenged entrenched interests without benefit of any natural constituency, and he cloaked his willingness to compromise in an uncompromising rhetoric of spiritually mandated technical comprehensiveness that frustrated legislators.[18] Carter forged coalitions by speaking to a variety of organized groups.[19] He reached specific and effective compromises in a way that fostered an impression of stubbornness, which discouraged further cooperation.[20]

3. *Carter disliked oratory, disvalued rhetorical embellishment and rehearsal, and preferred that facts speak for themselves.*[21] When he did speak he rarely bent to situational or audience demands, saying instead what he felt

needed to be said. His prepresidential rhetoric was said to contain "no applause lines, little detail on issues, no rhetorical flourishes" from one who "is not an eloquent man."[22] He valued instead sincerity, truthfulness, and expertise. His expressed indignation had helped him periodically, as when he attracted national attention by calling on President Nixon to resign.[23]

Carter's rhetorical resources were expertise and research. He was a quick study who became "an expert on many unimportant matters."[24] In Georgia, he "came to the fore by studying an emerging issue and becoming an expert on it before anyone else."[25] He preferred simple words that could be understood by any citizen, but by simplifying his language he inadvertently simplified his ideas.[26]

4. *Carter enacted Southern-style politicking in a non-Southern way.* Carter's "good ol' boy" style deemphasized issues and treated voters as friends and neighbors,[27] but without the characteristic southern oratorical style:

He writes and speaks without embellishment. Though verbally agile, he uses words as instruments only, to convey facts, points, arguments. . . . In a particularly un-Southern way, his speeches have no rhythm. Big words pop out in unexpected places. Complex formulations intrude when he is trying to be simple. Parallels don't parallel. . . . He is a long way from either the verbosity or the eloquence of the "Southern" use of language.[28]

Carter is the only Democrat since Lyndon Johnson in 1964 to win a plurality, much less a majority, of the South's electoral votes. But that style is ill suited to the formal epideictic of presidential inaugurals.

5. *Carter frequently made explicit personal references to his devout Christianity, references atypical of American political discourse.*[29] His religiosity animated his denunciations of Vietnam and Watergate-era politicians and thus underscored and energized his criticism. It also energized his belief that "trust and confidence flowed from actions, but successful actions flowed from trust and confidence."[30]

6. *"The people" were an almost mystical source of goodness, morality, strength, and inspiration.*[31] Carter idealized everyday people as a source of public goodness, and close family and neighbors were a source of personal strength.[32] Carter's conception of "the people" enabled them not only to escape blame for Vietnam and Watergate-era embarrassments but to perceive themselves as both the victims and the source of recovery.

7. *Carter tended to express his thoughts as lists of topics without priorities.*[33] Unlike Kennedy's calls that he admired, Carter did not attempt to structure needs and solutions into arguments supporting a program.[34] Speech writer James Fallows reported that

Carter thinks in lists, not arguments; as long as the items are there, their order does not matter, nor does the hierarchy among them. . . . Whenever he edited a speech, he did so to cut out the explanatory portions and add "meat" in the form of a list of topics.[35]

Fallows went on to observe that "the only thing that finally gives coherence to the items of his creed is that he happens to believe them all."

8. *Carter was inclined toward hyperbole, superlatives, and the use of absolutes.*[36] Carter and the people he admired had succeeded when they set impossible standards for themselves and others. Barber wrote of Carter's character, "Perfection was to be held in *mind*. . . . But in the realm of action [becoming], where results counted, one always had to settle for less."[37]

9. *Carter's conception of leadership was narrowly idealistic.* He was disinclined to enact the role of public leader, preferring the persona of humble citizen.[38] One account of Carter's ideal president suggests a leader

speaking with a clear voice to the people, setting a standard of ethics and morality and excellence and greatness and calling on the American people to make sacrifices for the greater good and answering difficult questions and proposing new, bold programs and intelligent foreign policies and secure defense policies.[39]

Missing from this account of presidential leadership are several important qualities—social unification, political legitimation, conflict resolution, and public mobilization—which would later characterize the Reagan administration.

All nine of these Carter tendencies characterized his inaugural address. Carter's pragmatic realism required him to be persuasive because he assumed the presidency bent on making the system work more efficiently, more economically, and more mercifully by challenging the insiders who controlled the system without obvious signs of public support. Moreover, the problems he had experienced forging and maintaining legislative coalitions in Georgia would be magnified in Washington by both the diversity of domestic interests and his stance as an outsider. These problems combined to make Carter's inaugural address the crucial moment of his administration, for on it hinged his future coalitional prospects.

But because Carter disliked oratory and disvalued rhetorical embellishment and rehearsal, his prospects for delivering an outstanding epideictic address were poor. He read previous inaugurals, notably Wilson's First, but his personal orientation rendered him unable to see in those speeches the generic characteristics so apparent to Campbell and Jamieson. Unaware of the generic rules, he could hardly be expected to satisfy them.

Carter preferred to let facts speak for themselves, but what facts are appropriate for an inaugural? Empirical facts appropriate for deliberative and forensic discourse are less appropriate to epideictic than are unifying recollections. Good epideictic would have mixed the references to George Washington, the Bicentennial, "the moral duties which, when assumed, seem[ed] invariably to be in our best interests," the American dream, those "special times when we have stood briefly, but magnificently, united," and "the passion for freedom." Characteristically, Carter invoked these facts and allowed each to speak to his listeners for itself. To do so is to ignore the essence of epideictic discourse, which uses language to enhance the salience of shared recollections. Thus did Carter's orientation toward facts undermine his speech.

Carter had won election with non-Southern Southern politicking, and he continued it in his inaugural. This style explains his atypically personal references to his teacher and to his mother's Bible. It explains the startling pattern of references to his own shortcomings in the speech of presidential investiture. And it accounts for the frequent references to his Christianity, which are unusual in the genre. Inaugural addresses are, perhaps even primarily, occasions for civic piety but not for the personal piety that was heard from Carter.[40]

Carter's people were good and moral and a source of strength and inspiration for him, and that theme pervaded his inaugural. Indeed, his inaugural presumed that Americans shared his confidence in them by investing in them the responsibility for his presidency. William Safire captured succinctly the contradiction: "After campaigning for three years on the theme that Government must be as good as its people . . . he now changes that into an apology that he's no better than us, and therefore we can't expect much."[41]

Carter tended to express his thoughts as lists of topics without priorities. The brief inaugural enunciated an unordered list of six things people might say about our nation after his presidency. There is also a series of nine statements, ("We must again . . . , We know . . . , We recall . . . , We cannot dwell . . . , We cannot afford . . . , We reject . . . , We have already found . . . , We have learned . . . , We cannot afford") that invite some kind of arrangement. Although they follow the statement that "the American dream endures," an absence of transitional devices undermines the passage's coherence.

There are instances of Carter's inclination toward hyperbole in the inaugural. Although a president may proclaim a new spirit, "only" people can provide it. Moral duties, when assumed, "invariably" seem to be in our interest. But there are fewer absolutes than one might expect in an inaugural. The genre calls for timelessness, an eternal present, in which absolutes and hyperbole can—in the right places—be good.

This moderated hyperbole results largely from Carter's narrow conception of leadership as programmatic rather than rhetorical. The discourse is so passive and humble that the speaker does not sound like a leader—which was precisely Carter's intent. Since Carter's ideal leader is programmatic rather than symbolic, it would be wrong to distract followers with glimpses of the imperial presidency.

Carter could, and did, sound presidential when it suited him. Consider the assertive, confident tone and the sense of historic destiny evident in the following portions of the speech announcing his candidacy:

We have dared to dream great dreams for our nation. We have taken quite literally the promises of decency, equality, and freedom, of an honest and responsible government. . . . Our commitment to these dreams has been sapped by debilitating compromise, acceptance of mediocrity, subservience to special interests, and an absence of executive vision and direction. . . . [The Second Continental Congress] reached for greatness. . . . [Sitting in one of their chairs] I wondered to myself: Were they more competent, more intelligent, or better educated than we? Were they more courageous? Did they have more compassion or love for their neighbors? Did they have deeper religious convictions? Were they more concerned about the future of their children than we? I think not. . . . It is now time to stop and to ask ourselves the question which my last commanding officer, Admiral Hyman Rickover, asked me and every other young naval officer who serves or has served in an atomic submarine. For our nation— for all of us—that question is "Why not the best?"[42]

Here Carter sounded like a leader because he aspired to become a leader, and he could not be elected president without sounding like one. But he humbled himself in the inaugural precisely because he had become president. At the very moment when history sought evidence that the candidate had become president, Carter's life script compelled him to assure his God, his people, and even himself that he would not be changed.

This inaugural address was pure Jimmy Carter. It evidenced all nine of the characteristics culled from the literature on Congress with the exception of hyperbole, which gave way to his spirituality based need for humility.

CONCLUSION

What, then, should be said of Jimmy Carter's inaugural address? First, the politics of the moment and Carter's political style made his inaugural moment a crucial one in the translation of his electoral coalition into a governing coalition. Second, the address accomplished few of the goals that most inaugurals need to do, and those few it did only moderately well. Third, the address served as Jimmy Carter's personal moment in history when he accepted the office and preached to the congregation.

Fourth, the inaugural choices set Carter's presidency back severely by undermining the public's, Washington's, and even his own grasp of the fact that he was indeed president.

The Carter inaugural illustrates that a president can ignore generic constraints, instead treating the inaugural ceremony as a personal moment to share his own thoughts and feelings with history and his people. But to do so is to ignore the single greatest opportunity for translating the electoral coalition into a governing coalition.

NOTES

1. James Wooten, *Dasher: The Roots and Rising of Jimmy Carter* (New York: Summit Books, 1978), 38.

2. See letters from January 1977 in "Inaugural Speech Drafts" [2], Box 2, Staff Secretary: Handwriting File, Domestic Policy through Inaugural, Jimmy Carter Library, Atlanta, Georgia.

3. "Inaugural Speech Drafts" [1], Jimmy Carter Library.

4. Craig Allen Smith and Kathy B. Smith, eds., *The President and the Public: Rhetoric and National Leadership* (Lanham, Md.: University Press of America, 1985), xv–xx. On CMM, see, for example, Vernon E. Cronen, W. Barnett Pearce, and Linda M. Harriss, "The Coordinated Management of Meaning: A Theory of Communication," in *Human Communication Theory*, ed. Frank X. Dance (New York: Harper & Row, 1982).

5. Karlyn Kohrs Campbell and Kathleen Hall Jamieson, *Deeds Done in Words: Presidential Rhetoric and the Genres of Governance* (Chicago: University of Chicago Press, 1990), 14–36.

6. Jimmy Carter, "Inaugural Address of President Jimmy Carter," *Weekly Compilation of Presidential Documents*, January 22, 1977, 2. All subsequent references to the speech are to this version of the text (1–4) read in the light of the videotape broadcast by C-SPAN, January 18, 1989.

7. Jimmy Carter, *Keeping Faith: Memoirs of a President* (New York: Bantam Books, 1982), 18.

8. Ibid., 21.

9. Campbell and Jamieson, *Deeds Done in Words*, 22–23.

10. Carter, *Keeping Faith*, 22.

11. Campbell and Jamieson, *Deeds Done in Words*, 24.

12. Dan F. Hahn, "The Rhetoric of Jimmy Carter, 1976–1980," *Presidential Studies Quarterly* 14 (Spring 1984): 270.

13. Campbell and Jamieson, *Deeds Done in Words*, 23–27.

14. Richard W. Leeman and Martin W. Slann, "James Earl Carter," in *American Orators of the Twentieth Century*, ed. Bernard K. Duffy and Halford R. Ryan (Westport, Conn.: Greenwood Press, 1987), 40; Wooten, *Dasher*, 38.

15. James David Barber, *The Presidential Character: Predicting Performance in the White House*, 3d ed. (Englewood Cliffs, N.J.: Prentice-Hall, 1985), 419.

16. Gary M. Fink, *Prelude to the Presidency: The Political Character and Legislative Leadership Style of Governor Jimmy Carter* (Westport, Conn.: Greenwood Press, 1980), 167.

17. Barber, *Presidential Character*, 425–26, 436; James Fallows, "A Passionless Presidency." *Atlantic Monthly* 243 (May 1979): 45.

18. Fink, *Prelude*, 168–69, 176–77; Fallows, "Passionless Presidency," 39.

19. Leslie Wheeler, *Jimmy Who? An Examination of Presidential Candidate Jimmy Carter: The Man, His Career, His Stands on the Issues* (Woodbury, N.Y.: Barron's, 1976), 103–4.

20. Fink, *Prelude*, 172–76; Hahn, "Rhetoric," 281–82, notes that Carter was even perceived as "inflexible and mean."

21. Leeman and Slann, "James Earl Carter," 43; Wooten, *Dasher*, 19; Fallows, "Passionless Presidency," 44.

22. R. W. Apple, *New York Times*, 27 October, 1975, 17; and Lewis H. Lapham, *Harper's Magazine*, August 1976, 11, quoted by Hahn, "Rhetoric," 265.

23. Wheeler, *Jimmy Who?* 106. Hahn, "Rhetoric," 329, reminds us that "Carter was considered a masterful communicator when he took office. . . . But by midterm his presidency was in trouble and before it ended he was perceived as a poor communicator." Leeman and Slann, "James Earl Carter," 38, conclude that "the oratory that served him so well as a first-term campaigner was inappropriate for him as president."

24. Leeman and Slann, "James Earl Carter," 43. Jimmy Carter as quoted by Barber, *Presidential Character*, 425.

25. Wheeler, *Jimmy Who?* 101.

26. Fallows, "Passionless Presidency," 43.

27. Hahn, "Rhetoric," 274, based on George McMillan, "Grins and Grits," *New York Times*, April 9, 1976, 37.

28. William Lee Miller, "The Yankee from Georgia," *New York Times*, April 9, 1976, 18, quoted by Hahn, "Rhetoric," 275.

29. Leeman and Slann, "James Earl Carter," 40; Barber, *Presidential Character*, 435.

30. Hahn, "Rhetoric," 278.

31. Leeman and Slann, "James Earl Carter," 40.

32. Barber, *Presidential Character*, 419.

33. Leeman and Slann, "James Earl Carter," 43–44; Wooten, *Dasher*, 17; Hahn, "Rhetoric," 284; Fallows, "Passionless Presidency," 42.

34. Hahn, "Rhetoric," 284.

35. Fallows, "Passionless Presidency," 42.

36. Leeman and Slann, "James Earl Carter," 44–45; Hahn, "Rhetoric," 277; Wooten, *Dasher*, 33.

37. Barber, *Presidential Character*, 418–19.

38. Leeman and Slann, "James Earl Carter," 45.

39. Wooten, *Dasher*, 47–48.

40. See for example, Roderick P. Hart, *The Political Pulpit* (West Lafayette, Ind.: Purdue University Press, 1977); David Fairbanks, "The Priestly Functions of the Presidency: A Discussion of the Literature on Civil Religion and Its Implications for the Study of Presidential Leadership," *Presidential Studies Quarterly* 11 (Spring 1981): 214–32; and Dante Germino, *The Inaugural Addresses of American Presidents: The Public Philosophy and Rhetoric* (Lanham, Md.: University Press of America, 1984).

41. William Safire, "Pedestrian Inaugural," *New York Times*, January 21, 1977, 23.

42. Jimmy Carter, "Why Not the Best," *A Government as Good as Its People* (New York: Simon and Schuster, 1977), 43, 49–50.

Chapter Twenty-One

President Ronald Reagan's First Inaugural Address, 1981

David Henry

Rhetorical critics attended more closely to Ronald Reagan's oratory throughout his presidency than to that of perhaps any other occupant of the White House. Yet few of Reagan's presidential speeches received the attention accorded the First Inaugural. Assessments tied the text's significance variously to its place in the "rhetoric phase" of the Reagan presidency, its merging of traditional deliberative and ceremonial objectives, and its parallels to Thomas Jefferson's inaugural.[1] Still other judgments focused on Reagan's unique contribution to the established genre of inaugural discourse, the inaugural event as a case study in the ancient rites of augury and investiture, and the ceremony's function in relation to the release of American hostages from Iran.[2] While each critique explains an important facet of Reagan's oratory generally and the First Inaugural in particular, reflection on the speech's place in Reagan's presidential discourse reveals one dominant conclusion: Ronald Reagan's First Inaugural embodied the traits that defined his tenure as the nation's consummate rhetorical president.

As conceptualized by James Ceaser, Glen Thurow, Jeffrey Tulis, and Joseph Bessette, the rhetorical presidency that evolved in the twentieth century evinces three central characteristics. First, exhortations in the name of a national common purpose and an idealized history replaced deliberate debate and rational discussion as the dominant mode of public discourse. Second, the rapid expansion of mass communication dramatically altered the form of that discourse, extended analyses of complex issues giving way to brief phrases easily captured on the evening news or in concise televised campaign messages. And finally, presidential campaigns, once played out fully from primaries to election day every four years, became virtually continuous activities for incumbents and challengers alike. Roderick Hart noted the impact of the rhetorical presidency's evolution on political communication: "The presidency has been transferred from a formal, print-oriented world into an electronic environment specializing in the spoken word and rewarding casual, interpersonally adept politicians." As a consequence, Hart contended, "public speech no longer attends the process of governance, it *is* governance."[3]

Critical studies of Ronald Reagan's rhetoric reflect a remarkably precise fit between the orator and the requirements of a rhetorical president, as four traits recur: (1) Reagan was expert in exploiting, if not arranging, the occasion and the setting of his speeches; (2) he often merged the content of the text with powerful national symbols; (3) the themes advanced were consistent over the course of his public speaking and political career; and (4) the stories he favored in his narratives, if occasionally incorrect in detail, served as the dominant form of textual proof. In addition, Reagan was incomparable in working all of these features to his advantage in the mass media, particularly television.[4] Although extant scholarship illumines Reagan as a rhetorical president during his tenure,[5] analysis of the First Inaugural reveals the speech's foundational role in establishing the parameters of his contribution to the institution.

THE RHETORICAL CHALLENGE

Opinion surveys reflected modest public expectations of the newly elected president. Looking for some hint of how Reagan would improve on the uninspired economic and foreign policies of his Democratic predecessor and campaign opponent, Jimmy Carter, voters wanted reassurance and plans for modest progress as the inaugural ceremony approached. Reagan anticipated public sentiment, for in revising the final draft, he rendered a text that one adviser called "upbeat and vintage Reagan—a slice of his conservative philosophy that has been as constant as the North Star for the last 16 to 20 years." The president himself referred to his speech as "an agenda. I had things that I wanted to accomplish. I began outlining all that with my inaugural address."[6]

That he had needed to explicate that agenda had been clear to his advisers shortly after the election. Yet there were concerns about whether the president recognized the urgency of laying out a program or was even certain of what program he wanted to advance. Although he had campaigned brilliantly against the incumbent Carter, it was not clear that Reagan and his aides had a keen sense of how to convert their electoral success to a plan for governing. Less than two weeks before the inauguration, an anonymously quoted senior adviser observed, for example, "I don't think he's come to grips with his impending presidency. He's still on cloud nine celebrating the fact that he won." What was needed, in the words of Richard Wirthlin, Reagan's pollster, was "an attempt to keep clearly in mind our general objectives and to prioritize and sequence some of them." Essential to the sequencing process was the centrality of "imagery."[7]

Although imagery's key role made the traditional epideictic functions of the inaugural critical to the speech's planning, the conversion of campaign themes to Reagan's own desire to articulate his agenda endowed the speech with decidedly deliberative features as well. The result is a speech text in which Reagan, as Hart contended, placed his signature on the address. Hart delineated Reagan's signature within the larger archetype of the inaugural genre, calling the speech a generic hybrid that is "part inaugural, part campaign speech."[8] What distinguishes the First Inaugural even further is the president's skillful use of symbols and narratives in constructing arguments fitting for the speech's archetypal and signature features.

SYMBOLS, NARRATIVE, AND ARGUMENT

Certainly the symbols and stories for which he had become famous populated Reagan's inaugural,[9] but the speech is substantively noteworthy for both the issues addressed and their emphasis in the text.[10] In one widely received interpretation, presidents characteristically inaugurate their terms by reconstituting "the people," enunciating broad political principles, enacting the office of the presidency, and fulfilling the occasion's ceremonial requirements.[11] With its placement of the people at the center of his call for a new beginning and with the integration of the country's most revered presidents into the argument as symbolic warrants for his philosophy, Reagan's speech surely worked in those directions. Its significance derived even more, though, from its merging of the ostensibly symbolic features with specific policy issues: the economy and renewed military stature in particular. The speech's structure made possible the subtle integration of the ceremonial with the substantive.

Reagan worked at the epideictic level initially by alluding to the solemnity of the moment, confirming the nation's faith in its constitutional tradition, and thanking President Carter "and your people for all your help in maintaining the continuity which is the bulwark of our Republic."[12] He then turned to the economy, the issue that would form the focal point of the first one-third of his tenure. The "business of our nation goes forward," Reagan declared, and he proceeded to define that business:

These United States are confronted with an economic affliction of great pro-
portions. We suffer from the longest and one of the worst sustained inflations
in our national history. . . . Idle industries have cast workers into unemployment,
human misery and personal indignity. Those who do work are denied a return
for their labor by a tax system which penalizes successful achievement and keeps
us from maintaining full production. But great as our tax burden is, it has not
kept pace with public spending. For decades we have piled deficit upon deficit,
mortgaging our future and our children's future for the temporary convenience
of the present. To continue this long trend is to guarantee tremendous social,
cultural, political and economic upheavals.

The president's faith in America's tradition of heroism and selflessness
assured him that the impending economic crisis would be resolved
swiftly and rightly. First, he intoned, the people needed to recognize
that in "this present crisis, government is not the solution to our problem; government *is* the problem"—a problem, in Reagan's view, to
which "we the people" constituted the only plausible solution. "All must
share in the productive work of this 'new beginning,' " he maintained,
"and all must share in the bounty of a revived economy." The new
beginning would be created by the American heroes one could see
"every day going in and out of factory gates," creating new jobs, producing "enough food to feed all of us and then the world beyond."
These heroes' "patriotism is quiet but deep. Their values sustain our
national life." Though he had "used the words 'they' and 'their' in
speaking of these heroes," Reagan concluded, "I could say 'you' and
'your,' because I'm addressing the heroes of whom I speak—you, the
citizens of this blessed land."

Freedom, a symbolic force that consistently underscored the president's articulation of the administration's foreign policy goals, under-
girded his commitment to renewed military strength. Just as economic
renewal enabled the nation to "renew ourselves here in our land," Reagan assured his listeners, "we will be seen as having greater strength
throughout the world. We will again be the exemplar of freedom and a
beacon of hope for those who do not now have freedom." The president
continued, turning his attention to the international audience: "To those
neighbors and allies who share our freedom, we will strengthen our
historic ties and assure them of our support and firm commitment." As
for "the enemies of freedom, those who are potential adversaries, they
will be reminded that peace is the highest aspiration of the American
people. We will negotiate for it, sacrifice for it; we will not surrender
for it, now or ever."

Reagan concluded by pulling together the concepts of American heroism and the country's destiny as a savior of freedom. "Above all," he
said solemnly, "we must realize that no arsenal or weapon in the arsenals
of the world is so formidable as the will and moral courage of free men

and women. It is a weapon our adversaries in today's world do not have. It is a weapon that we as Americans do have. Let that be understood by those who practice terrorism and prey upon their neighbors."

Reagan wove together the ceremonial and deliberative functions of his text in a skillfully crafted peroration that reasserted the administration's policy goals on both the domestic and foreign policy fronts.[13] Reagan's conclusion first called attention to the memory of America's legendary presidents. He then cast his citizen-hero in their image. A World War I soldier whose actions on the battlefield embodied the principles for which the founding fathers stood served as the means for doing so. The president and his advisers had decided to present the inaugural address for the first time from the west portico of the Capitol. The setting not only served symbolically to reinforce the administration's commitment to the new beginning pledged in the election campaign, but from this perspective Washington, Jefferson, and Lincoln could be called upon as intimate participants in the ceremonies. Reagan attended serially to each presidential memorial. He then observed that "beyond those monuments to heroism is the Potomac River, and on the far shore the sloping hills of Arlington National Cemetery, with its row upon row of simple white markers bearing crosses or Stars of David. They add up to only a tiny fraction of the price that has been paid for our freedom."

The story of Martin Treptow, a story that well fit Reagan's affinity for narratives grounded in high-order principles and ideals, served to illustrate that price. One of his longtime supporters from California, Preston Hotchkiss, had written to Reagan about Treptow shortly after the election. As the president explained in his speech, during World War I Treptow left his job as a small town barber in 1917 to join "the famed Rainbow Division" in France. There, "on the Western front, he was killed trying to carry a message between battalions under heavy artillery fire." Reagan knew immediately that Treptow offered a model illustration of the country's selflessness and willingness to sacrifice on behalf of the common good. He thus added Treptow to the draft of the inaugural address that had been provided by Kenneth Khachigian.

An accomplished speech writer who had served in the Nixon White House, Khachigian knew well both Reagan's affinity for the emotional story and his occasional laxness in double-checking his facts. Khachigian reminded Reagan that reporters would doubtless investigate the president's statements quite thoroughly, and it would thus be wise to attend carefully to details. With Reagan's agreement, Khachigian checked on the Treptow story, discovering that it was accurate, save for one important exception: Martin Treptow was buried in Bloomington, Wisconsin, over a thousand miles away from the Arlington National Cemetery.[14] Reagan nevertheless remained determined to take advantage of both the moral provided by the Treptow story and the inaugural setting's proximity to Arlington. Khachigian thus recast Treptow's introduction in the inaugural narrative. "Under one such marker," the president announced after paying homage to those buried at the national cemetery, "lies a young man, Martin Treptow." Reagan thus adjusted the data to fit the story without actually claiming that Treptow was buried at Arlington.

Reagan told his audience that Treptow had left behind a diary with the heading, "My Pledge." Under the heading the soldier had written: "America must win this war. Therefore I will work, I will save, I will sacrifice, I will endure, I will fight cheerfully and do my utmost as if the issue of the whole struggle depended on me alone." The president averred that current domestic and foreign crises did "not require of us the kind of sacrifice that Martin Treptow and so many thousands of others were called upon to make." Yet, he maintained, they did demand "our best effort and our willingness to believe in ourselves and to believe in our capacity to perform great deeds, to believe that together we can and will resolve the problems which confront us. After all, why shouldn't we believe that? We are Americans."

The First Inaugural reflected substantively the traits that would serve Reagan well as a rhetorical president. He attached his most illustrious predecessors to his cause, praised the innate heroism of the American public, and illustrated his ceremonial theme with a representative narrative, a discursive form of which he was particularly fond. At the same time, the text's unique interplay of ceremonial and deliberative functions makes equally clear the centrality of first principles in the president's discourse, for beyond fulfilling the occasion's epideictic requirements, Reagan preached to the nation the need to narrow its attention to two overriding substantive issues. Casting economic recovery and a revival of U.S. military stature as his primary goals, he used "freedom" both to define the pragmatic objectives of those policies and as the abstract ideal that urged their adoption as Americans embarked on their new beginning. Essential to the strategy for advancing his themes was his use of the mass media, particularly television.

MEDIUM AS MESSAGE

Reagan was not the first president to recognize television's power, of course, but he clearly understood the medium's potential uses far better than any of his predecessors. The man and the medium matched perfectly,[15] and Reagan's First Inaugural is appreciated fully only when its manner of presentation is taken into account. As Kathleen Jamieson noted, where most of his "predecessors constructed speeches suitable for the print media of the nineteenth century, Reagan's was written to be spoken and seen through the electronic media of the twentieth century."[16]

Presentation of the address from the Capitol's west portico reflected television's importance, since the monuments to Washington, Jefferson, and Lincoln would be integral to the speech setting. Having received Reagan's final revisions the day before the inauguration, Khachigian passed an advance copy of the text to Mark Goode, the administration's television liaison. Goode contacted all three networks, which then readied to match the visual images projected with the words Reagan uttered.[17] Hence, as Reagan said, "This is the first time in our history that this ceremony has been held . . . on the West Front of the Capitol," network cameras framed the appropriate view for the television audience. "Standing here, one faces a magnificent vista, opening up on this city's special beauty and history. At one end of this open mall are those shrines to the giants on whose shoulders we stand."

NBC directors returned their television picture to President Reagan as he described each of the national memorials and the heroes they honored. ABC, rather than moving quickly to Reagan, initially changed its video angle to focus on the Jefferson Memorial. Perhaps most innovative were the CBS producers. They blended the visual and verbal messages most completely, merging shots of the appropriate monument with the audio of Reagan's text. From the Washington Memorial, for "a man of humility who came to greatness reluctantly," the camera turned to the monument to Jefferson, because "the Declaration of Independence flames with his eloquence." The Lincoln Memorial concluded the series: "whoever would understand in his heart the meaning of America will find it in the life of Abraham Lincoln."

Reagan's depiction of the Arlington National Cemetery, "with its row upon row of simple white markers bearing crosses or Stars of David," concluded the blending of verbal and visual script. As the president called attention to Arlington, each network accompanied the speech text with a different visual image. NBC focused on the address itself, featuring a close-up of Reagan, shifting to his wife gazing beatifically at her husband as he spoke, and then cutting back to the original shot of Reagan speaking. CBS initially showed Robert E. Lee's home at the Arlington National Cemetery and then dissolved to the president. ABC's producers took the most complete advantage of the visual potential. As Reagan mentioned Arlington, cameras turned gradually from a head-and-shoulders shot of the president to show the cemetery's rolling hills. And as Reagan closed the description of the cemetery and the heroes who lay below its markers, ABC again slowly moved to the head-and-shoulders shot of Reagan. During the sequence, the television image on ABC twice merged seamlessly with Reagan's television persona, achieving a visual unity between the president and his heroic predecessors.

In Jane Blankenship's judgment, the performance was "the epitome of careful, even perfect execution of preplanned choices. The President and his staff seemed to produce and direct most of this part of the [inaugural] show."[18] Ken Khachigian had written, and Reagan had edited, the speech to meet the needs of the medium. With the help of television directors, Reagan created a video event that reinforced the message that America required "our best effort and our willingness to believe in ourselves and to believe in our capacity to perform great deeds, to believe that together with God's help we can and will resolve the problems which now confront us." With a catch in his voice characteristic of much of his television speechmaking in the following eight years, he concluded: "And after all, why shouldn't we believe that? We are Americans."

REAGAN AND THE RHETORICAL PRESIDENCY

Ronald Reagan's First Inaugural address took the rhetorical form to a new level. Using the power of television to help tell the story, he employed narratives as substance, populated the narratives with legendary Americans and citizen-heroes, and promoted identification between the culture's heroic figures and his own political agenda in foreign and domestic policy. Television served not only to certify the speech's claims but to unify past, present, and future as he spoke. Although some of these features are obviously characteristic of other inaugurals as well, the uniqueness of Reagan's text resides in the speech's initial effect on opinion leaders in the national media, the address's function as a transition from campaign to governance, and what the text portended for Reagan's rhetorical presidency.

Newspaper and television commentary attended to the inaugural address's substantive and stylistic features alike, rendering a mixed verdict on the speech's quality and potential impact. Frank Reynolds, George Will, and Sander Vanocur of ABC television were impressed with the tenor of Reagan's performance. Vanocur contended that as his presidency opened, Reagan "is like FDR: all things to all people." He urged caution, however, pointing out that Reagan would soon learn that "governing is not that simple." Despite his colleague's reservations, Will expressed high praise for Reagan's performance. Will termed the speech "pure Reaganism" for its uplifting tone and conservative message. Roger Mudd at NBC endorsed Will's positive assessment, describing the address as "uplifting" and masterful, despite John Chancellor's claim that the inaugural was "not a piece of art."[19] Print reporters were taken with the president's vigorous demeanor and optimistic spirit, frequently citing the speech's treatment of economic issues and America's role as world leader as evidence of his preparation for governing.[20] In the all-important task of effecting positive media coverage, Reagan acquitted himself admirably well in his first public performance as president.

Reagan's success may be attributed, at least in part, to the speech's role as a critical point of transition between his campaign for the presidency and the inception of his first term. Unsuccessful presidential campaigns in 1968 and 1976 prepared Reagan for 1980. Shifting from a strategy in the earlier campaigns that warned of the evils attendant on the election of an opponent, Reagan urged his audiences in 1980 to share with him a vision of America as a blessed land of unlimited opportunity. In contrast to Jimmy Carter's portrayal of an America victimized by "too many of us" who had become worshipers of "self-indulgence and consumption," for example, Reagan offered optimism. Whatever "else history may say about my candidacy," he declared in a televised address during the final two weeks of the campaign, "I hope it will be recorded that I appealed to our best hopes, not our worst fears, to our confidence rather than our doubts."[21] The uplifting themes and optimistic manner characteristic of his inaugural address extended the form and content of his campaign oratory.

From the adoption of his primary campaign slogan in 1979—"Together, a New Beginning"—through his defeat of Carter at the polls the following year, Reagan consistently pledged his candidacy to a coherent policy program. Once America achieved economic renewal, always at the core of the program, the nation's resurgence as a dominant global power would inevitably follow. An appealing litany of abstract, but politically potent American values accompanied virtually every policy proclamation. The litany evolved in increments, congealing in the refrain of his nomination acceptance speech at the Republican National Convention: "family, work, neighborhood, peace, and freedom." Thus, the prominence of "freedom" in the First Inaugural, both to promote domestic economic competitiveness and to announce an active foreign policy, at once extended familiar campaign themes and foreshadowed Reagan's rhetorical presidency.

Once in office, Reagan's persuasive practices on behalf of his policies, as much as the policies themselves, sustained his presidency. The president's skill, in fact, calls into question Sander Vanocur's admonition that while one may be all things to all people in a ceremonial address, "governing is not that simple." The more accurate observation in Reagan's case is Hart's claim that in a rhetorical presidency, "speaking *is* governing." Consider Reagan's promise to his more ideological supporters to pursue vigorously a conservative social agenda on such issues as school prayer and abortion.

Less than two years into his term, conservative voices were among the president's most ardent critics, demanding an explanation for his apparent desertion of the principles he alleged to share with them.

Pointing to the inaugural address, among other proclamations, Reagan asserted that both his principles and his policies remained in place. He urged his audiences to understand, though, that change would take time and that no progress of consequence could be achieved without first gaining implementation of his economic recovery program. At the core of Reagan's explanation was a hierarchy of values, the application of which warranted acceptance of economic renewal as the most important policy objective the administration might pursue. A social agenda without freedom, he reminded audiences, held little value. Reagan reiterated the importance of economic stability and a strong defense to the perpetuation of freedom, thereby assuaging doubters and redoubling the support of his adherents.[22]

Ronald Reagan's First Inaugural thus not only illumines the potential deliberative force of an ostensibly ceremonial speech but reveals the inaugural's multiple roles in presidential rhetoric as well. In Reagan's case, the inaugural address brought his first successful presidential campaign to closure, evidenced the extent to which medium and message merged in the president's public discourse, and foreshadowed a unique facility for meeting the demands of the modern rhetorical presidency.

NOTES

1. Theodore Otto Windt, Jr., and Kathleen Farrell, "Presidential Rhetoric and Presidential Power: The Reagan Initiatives," in *Essays in Presidential Rhetoric*, ed. Theodore Otto Windt, Jr., and Beth Ingold (Dubuque, Iowa: Kendall/Hunt, 1983), 310–22; Robert L. Ivie, "Reagan's First Inaugural Address: Emphasizing Contemplation and Action" (paper presented at the annual meeting of the Speech Communication Association, 1986); Gregg Phifer, "Two Inaugurals: A Second Look," *Southern Speech Communication Journal* 48 (1983): 378–85.

2. Three key analyses are from a collection edited by Herbert W. Simons and Aram A. Aghazarian, *Form, Genre, and the Study of Political Discourse* (Columbia: University of South Carolina Press, 1988): Roderick P. Hart, "Of Genre, Computers, and the Reagan Inaugural," 278–98; Bruce E. Gronbeck, "Ronald Reagan's Enactment of the Presidency in His 1981 Inaugural Address," 226–45; and Jane Blankenship, "Toward a Developmental Model of Form: ABC's Treatment of the Reagan Inaugural and the Iranian Hostage Release as an Oxymoron," 246–76. In addition, see Ernest G. Bormann, "A Fantasy Theme Analysis of the Television Coverage of the Hostage Release and the Reagan Inaugural," *Quarterly Journal of Speech* 68 (1982): 133–45.

3. James W. Ceaser, Glen E. Thurow, Jeffrey Tulis, and Joseph M. Bessette, "The Rise of the Rhetorical Presidency," *Presidential Studies Quarterly* 11 (1981): 158–71; Roderick P. Hart, *The Sound of Leadership: Presidential Communication in the Modern Age* (Chicago: University of Chicago Press, 1987), 14.

4. These characteristics are delineated in, among other works, Kurt Ritter and David Henry, *Ronald Reagan: The Great Communicator* (Westport, Conn.: Greenwood Press, 1992), chaps. 4–5; Kathleen Hall Jamieson, *Eloquence in an*

Electronic Age: The Transformation of Political Speechmaking (New York: Oxford University Press, 1988), 118–200; Hart, *The Sound of Leadership*; Walter R. Fisher, *Human Communication as Narration* (Columbia: University of South Carolina Press, 1987), chap. 7; Paul D. Erickson, *Reagan Speaks: The Making of an America Myth* (New York: New York University Press, 1985); Mary E. Stuckey, *Playing the Game: The Presidential Rhetoric of Ronald Reagan* (New York: Praeger Publishers, 1990); Robert Dallek, *Ronald Reagan: The Politics of Symbolism* (Cambridge: Harvard University Press, 1984); and Michael Rogin, *Ronald Reagan, The Movie* (Berkeley: University of California Press, 1987).

5. Jeffrey K. Tulis, *The Rhetorical Presidency* (Princeton: Princeton University Press, 1987), 189–202; David Henry, "Ronald Reagan and Aid to the Contras: An Analysis of the Rhetorical Presidency," *Rhetorical Dimensions in Media*, ed. Martin J. Medhurst and Thomas W. Benson, 2d ed. (Dubuque, Iowa: Kendall/ Hunt Publishing, 1991), 73–88.

6. Albert R. Hunt and James M. Perry, "Interviews Suggest Voters Don't Demand Miracles from Reagan," *Wall Street Journal*, January 20, 1981, 1, 15; "Waiting for Reagan," *Wall Street Journal*, January 20, 1981, 22; George Skelton, "Reagan, Advisers Prepare for Power," *Los Angeles Times*, January 20, 1981, I:15; Ronald Reagan, *Speaking My Mind* (New York: Simon and Schuster, 1989), 60.

7. Cited by James M. Perry and Albert R. Hunt, "Reaganites Have Much They Plan to Do Early, Few Staffers to Do It," *Wall Street Journal*, January 9, 1981, 1, 15; Skelton, "Reagan, Advisers Prepare for Power"; Ben J. Wattenberg ("Yes") and Erwin Knoll ("No"), "Are the Right Ideas Back in the Saddle Again?" *Los Angeles Times*, January 4, 1981, 4:1, 3.

8. Hart, "Of Genre, Computers and Reagan's First Inaugural," 289.

9. On Reagan's use of stories as argument, see William F. Lewis, "Telling America's Story: Narrative Form and the Reagan Presidency," *Quarterly Journal of Speech*, 73 (1987): 280–302; Erickson, *Reagan Speaks*; Fisher, *Human Communication as Narration*.

10. Ritter and Henry elaborate the substance of Reagan's First Inaugural in *Ronald Reagan: The Great Communicator*, 63–66.

11. Karlyn Kohrs Campbell and Kathleen Hall Jamieson, "Inaugurating the Presidency," *Presidential Studies Quarterly* 15 (1985): 394–411. The authors extend their analysis in *Deeds Done in Words: Presidential Rhetoric and the Genres of Governance* (Chicago: University of Chicago Press, 1990), chaps. 1–2. For an alternative treatment of the inaugural genre, see Kurt Ritter and James R. Andrews, *The America Ideology: Reflections of the Revolution in American Rhetoric* (Annandale, Va.: Speech Communication Association Bicentennial Monograph, 1978), 40–68.

12. Ronald Reagan, "First Inaugural Address," January 20, 1981, in Ritter and Henry, *Ronald Reagan: The Great Communicator*, 155. Based on the version published in the *Public Papers of the Presidents of the United States: Ronald Reagan, 1981* (Washington, D.C.: U.S. Government Printing Office, 1982), this text has been verified and corrected by comparison to a videotape at the Vanderbilt Television News Archive, Vanderbilt University.

Perhaps ironically, Reagan's homage to President Carter reflects an introductory tactic employed by his predecessor four years earlier. See, in this book, Craig A. Smith's analysis of Jimmy Carter's Inaugural Address (chapter 20).

13. Ivie lays open these functions from a somewhat different perspective in "Reagan's First Inaugural: Emphasizing Contemplation and Action."

14. The narrative here on the work by Khachigian and Reagan on the speech text is based on Lou Cannon, *President Reagan: The Role of a Lifetime* (New York: Simon and Schuster, 1991), 95–100.

15. Robert E. Denton, Jr., even argues that the entirety of Reagan's tenure is best understood in terms of his mastery of the medium: *The Primetime Presidency of Ronald Reagan* (New York: Praeger Publishers, 1988).

16. Jamieson, *Eloquence in an Electronic Age*, 165.

17. Ritter and Henry, *Ronald Reagan: The Great Communicator*, 103–5.

18. Blankenship, "Toward a Developmental Model of Form," 264.

19. The citations from the ABC News and NBC News discussions of Reagan's First Inaugural are based on my notes during the broadcasts, January 20, 1981.

20. George Skelton, "Speech Displays Enthusiasm for Nation's Future," *Los Angeles Times*, January 21, 1981, 1:1, 15; Timothy D. Schellhardt, "Reagan Takes Oath, Making Economy First Priority and Putting 'Strict Freeze' on Federal Civilian Hiring," *Wall Street Journal*, January 21, 1981, 3; "Hail to the New Chief," *Newsweek*, February 2, 1981, 47–51; George Will, "There's No Panic in the Oval Office," *Newsweek*, February 2, 1981, 50–51; and David Treadwell, "Doughboy Provides Theme," *Los Angeles Times*, January 21, 1981, 1:15.

21. Cited by Ritter and Henry, *Ronald Reagan: The Great Communicator*, 51. General comments about Reagan's campaign oratory in 1968, 1976, and 1980 are drawn from the same source, 42–53.

22. Martin J. Medhurst explains fully the controversy that engulfed Reagan, and the president's successful resolution of the discord, in "Postponing the Social Agenda: Reagan's Strategy and Tactics," *Western Journal of Speech Communication* 48 (1984): 262–76.

Chapter Twenty-Two

President Ronald Reagan's Second Inaugural Address, 1985

Kurt Ritter

Ronald Reagan's Second Inaugural address seemed destined for obscurity. The bitterly cold weather in Washington, D.C., on January 21, 1985, forced the inauguration managers to cancel the parade and to move Reagan's address inside the Capitol building. With these changes, the event was deprived of its most attractive television images. Instead of standing on the West Front of the Capitol facing 140,000 people framed by the national memorials to Washington, Jefferson, and Lincoln, Reagan found himself in the Rotunda, addressing a tightly packed audience of one thousand. Network television had to rely on a "pool feed," whose camera angles were limited by the confines of the room.[1] Hence, Reagan could not present a video oration as he did in his First Inaugural.[2]

Yet the problems with Reagan's Second Inaugural had begun long before the cold January weather. Quite aside from the limited visual potential of the event, Reagan's speech itself fell below his normal standard for major addresses. It lacked focus and coherence; its organization was repetitive, its style uneven. Most critical, it failed to set forth clearly the principles from which Reagan's second administration would draw its policies. Because of these deficiencies, the speech was quickly forgotten. It was not even included in Reagan's own anthology of speeches. Landon Parvin, a former presidential speech writer from the Reagan White House who was responsible for compiling the anthology, explained that he omitted the speech because "I didn't think [it] was very good."[3]

THE INAUGURAL ADDRESS

Reagan opened his address, just under twenty-one minutes long, with a brief but sweeping panorama of American history that carried the audience from George Washington's America of 1789 to Ronald Reagan's America of 1985. Contrasting the nation's continuity and change, Reagan noted that America had transformed itself from a young republic on the edge of "raw, untamed wilderness" into a powerful nation that had "journeyed to the moon and safely returned." Speaking with wonder in his voice, Reagan observed: "So much has changed, yet we stand together as we did two centuries ago."[4]

Reagan rapidly moved to contrast his view of America in 1985 with the America he had seen in 1980. First, he noted that America's leaders had forgotten the nation's original principles of limited government and free enterprise. Then he recounted the trials and tribulations that had befallen an America beset with government regulations and high taxes and pointed to America's recovery during his first term: "Tax rates have been reduced, inflation cut dramatically, and more people are employed than ever before in our history." Finally, he announced that America's restoration was not yet complete: "There are many mountains yet to climb"—social, moral, economic, and international objectives. Reagan pledged not to rest "until every American" enjoyed "the fullness of freedom, dignity and opportunity," until "our values of faith, family, work and neighborhood" took root again in contemporary America, until "our economy was finally freed from government's grip," and until America had "turned the tide of history away from totalitarian darkness and into the warm sunlight of human freedom."

The inaugural unfolded in a circular and repetitious manner rather than in a linear fashion. Reagan repeatedly covered the same rhetorical ground. Three times he returned to his pattern of past national sin, present national reform, and future national redemption. The first portion of the address applied the pattern in a global fashion, the middle of the address applied the pattern to domestic issues, and the last third of the speech applied it to foreign affairs.

Scattered throughout the address were appeals for national unity and offers of conciliation to Democrats whom Reagan had vanquished in his 1984 reelection campaign. America's complete restoration, Reagan predicted, could be achieved if the nation "came together not as Democrats or Republicans, but as Americans united in a common cause." In perhaps the most effective portion of the address, Reagan recounted the story of Thomas Jefferson and John Adams—old political enemies who had reconciled late in life and had corresponded on the meaning of America before both dying on the same day, July 4, 1826, the fiftieth anniversary of the Declaration of Independence. Having held up the example of the founding fathers, Reagan turned to his audience and remarked: "Well, with heart and hand let us stand as one today . . . determined that our future shall be worthy of our past." Later in the speech he repeated his unity appeal, praising those who had "worked and acted together, not as members of political parties but as Americans."

Reagan concluded with another panorama of American history as he recalled the "echoes of our past": Valley Forge, the Civil War, the Alamo, and the westward expansion. The speech's conclusion employed a self-consciously literary style that was out of character with the language of the rest of the speech and inconsistent with Reagan's typical style in formal speeches. The world was described as "lit by lightning." History was depicted as "a ribbon always unfurling"; it was "a journey." As settlers blazed their westward trail, they sang "a song, and the song echoes out forever and fills the unknowing air. It is the American sound. . . . We sing it still . . . [as] we raise our voices to the God who is the Author of this most tender music."

Reagan's chronological pattern of national sin, national reform, and national redemption was consistent with the pattern of the political jeremiad, which was employed in a number of important inaugural addresses, including Lincoln's Second Inaugural, Franklin D. Roosevelt's First Inaugural, and Reagan's own First Inaugural.[5] But in his Second Inaugural, Reagan used the political jeremiad poorly. Part of his problem was an uncertainty over whether national redemption had been accomplished. In celebrating the achievements of his first administration, Reagan at first seemed to be declaring the battle won, yet after each litany of conservative reform measures, the address lurched forward with the phrase, "but much remains to be done." In addition to its problems of repetitive organization and uneven style, Reagan's Second Inaugural lacked the focus required of a political jeremiad: It failed to announce clearly how Reagan's second administration would complete national reform and achieve national redemption.

Although the speech mentioned scores of specific policy issues, it did not unite them into a coherent whole. On several occasions Reagan seemed to be announcing a commitment to breaking down racial, ethnic, and economic barriers among Americans. He called economic opportunity "a birthright" for all groups in America. Later, he called for "a new American emancipation" and still later advocated "an American opportunity society." Sandwiched between those references to civil rights were calls for "meaningful arms reductions," for the reduction of "a bloated Federal Establishment," for a constitutional amendment mandating balanced budgets, for decentralized welfare and private charity, and for protection of "the unborn." Unlike Reagan's First Inaugural, which set forth the premises for Reagan's economic policy in his first administration,[6] his Second Inaugural failed to articulate a unified public philosophy to support his policies during his second administration.

The undistinguished quality of the address is striking in the light of Reagan's well-earned reputation as the "Great Communicator." Reagan was not only a skilled television performer; he was an excellent speech writer who valued a good speech text. Indeed, he appeared to devote more time and effort to his speeches than to other presidential duties. In addition, Reagan's White House speech-writing department was staffed with dedicated and skilled individuals.[7] What accounts for Reagan's Second Inaugural? His problems with the speech can be traced to two factors. First, his White House had not developed a clear policy agenda for the second term. Hence, it was difficult to present an inaugural that set forth the philosophical premises for a missing agenda. Second, the inaugural suffered from having too many speech writers. In order to consider those factors, one must examine the speech-writing process for the Second Inaugural.

THE INAUGURAL SPEECH WRITERS

The creation of Reagan's Second Inaugural stood in contrast to his First. As an address presented after four years in office, the Second Inaugural was created within the context of a fully staffed White House and a full-blown executive administration. One index of this more complex organizational setting was the circumstance that the Second Inaugural had four principal speech writers (Ronald Reagan, Bently Elliott, Peggy Noonan, and Tony Dolan), while the First Inaugural had only two (Reagan and Kenneth Khachigian).[8]

Of the three writers who assisted Reagan with his Second Inaugural, Noonan had the least experience as a Reagan speech writer. She had joined the White House speech-writing department in 1984 after a career writing radio copy, including a stint as a writer for Dan Rather's CBS radio commentaries. In contrast, Tony Dolan had first joined the Reagan speech-writing team during the 1980 presidential campaign and was one of the first speech writers to enter the White House in January 1981. Bently Elliott had joined the department in April 1981. Reagan advisers, such as Martin Anderson, regarded Elliott as "one of the most talented and ideologically consistent writers in the country."[9] By the time of the Second Inaugural he had assumed the position of director of the speech-writing department, which placed him in charge of five full-time presidential speech writers.

Reagan's speech writers generally viewed an inaugural address as a hybrid speech with important deliberative and epideictic dimensions, neither of which could be ignored. When asked whether he viewed an inaugural as a policy speech or a ceremonial speech, Tony Dolan looked astonished and replied: "Now, that seems like a false dichotomy." For Dolan, an inaugural address was "the liturgy of the national culture. . . . a moment of self definition." As such, Dolan explained, an inaugural needed to argue for public policy on a high level of abstraction. It would not do to "talk in an inaugural about medical care . . . or proposals for tax code changes." Instead, "the really important national policies are what you talk about in an inaugural"—the nation's historic mission, its role in the world, and its aspirations for the future.[10]

Peggy Noonan was less concerned with policy issues in inaugurals. In her view, an inaugural should be a "broad and thematic tone poem." It should "declare" rather than "defend." Anticipating the literary career that she would launch a year later when she departed from the White House, Noonan concentrated on imagery rather than deliberative rhetoric as she "attempted to evoke something of the national spirit, to lasso it for a moment, present it, bucking and kicking, and let it go again."[11]

Like Dolan, Bently Elliott appreciated the deliberative dimensions of an inaugural address: "We would never consider that [it] would be merely ceremonial. I mean, it was the greatest audience that the president would ever have. Therefore, he needed to marshall his best arguments, his best words, put out what he wanted to do and where he wanted to go. . . . We considered it highly political." Elliott conceded that the policy aspects of an inaugural might be less obvious than its ceremonial function, but he viewed the address as a situation where "the policy tail wags the ceremonial dog."[12]

CREATING AN INAUGURAL IN A POLICY VACUUM

Two circumstances made it difficult for the speech-writing department, and for Reagan, to produce an inaugural that could speak to the deliberative as well as the epideictic functions of the occasion: the 1984 reelection campaign had not created a policy mandate for Reagan, and the Reagan White House was between managers.

An inaugural address can be seen as the discourse that links the election campaign to the presidental administration that follows—as the last speech of the campaign and the first speech of the new administration. Certainly Reagan's First Inaugural had functioned in that manner. The difficulty with the Second Inaugural was the manner in which Reagan had achieved his decisive victory over Democratic nominee Walter Mondale. Looking back on the 1984 election, Reagan's campaign manager, Ed Rollins, ruefully remarked: "We'd run an issueless campaign. . . . There was no second-term plan"—a telling admission from a man who was the "Assistant to the President for Political and Governmental Affairs."[13]

Speech writer Tony Dolan has objected strenuously to the notion that the 1984 campaign lacked issues, for he had written campaign speeches that contrasted Walter Mondale's liberalism with Reagan's conservatism.[14] But those in charge of the campaign recalled it differently. Larry Speakes, Reagan's press spokesperson, has recounted: "We decided to run a pure image-based campaign. It was 'Morning in America,' the 'feel good' campaign. Our objectives were to offend no constituency, make no mistakes, create no controversy. And so, we returned to the White House with no new agenda. The overwhelming electoral mandate from the voters failed to translate into any kind of mandate to Congress."[15]

To make matters worse, the Second Inaugural was drafted in December 1984 and January 1985 while the Reagan White House was in a state of transition. James Baker and his key staff members were preparing to move to the Treasury Department; the new chief of staff, Donald Regan, had not yet completed his move from the Treasury Department to the White House. Indeed, he would not present Reagan with his plan for the second administration until seven months *after* the inaugural address.[16] As a result, the top-level supervision of speech writing was relaxed. This was a significant change, for during its first administration, the Reagan White House had instituted a thorough system for reviewing speeches. Presidential adviser Martin Anderson believed that speech writers had "enormous" power "to do good or bad" because they shaped national policy, in part through the process of drafting presidential speeches. Anderson has explained that "the rough drafts of every major statement or speech were systematically sent to a dozen or so senior advisers for criticism and review." In Anderson's view, "the net result was a very fine review sieve that usually strained out any factual errors or deviation from policy."[17]

The speech writers had long chafed under the "staffing process," which subjected their speech drafts to revision at the hands of policy experts whose own writing was often uninspired. As another Reagan speech writer complained after leaving the White House, "Anyone who can pick up a crayon thinks he can write a presidential speech."[18] The speech writers enjoyed the greater latitude they gained during the changing of the guard at the White House, yet it actually deprived them of assistance in shaping the deliberative dimensions of the Second Inaugural. For example, Baker's assistant Richard Darman had been a key figure in the process of reviewing and revising speech drafts during the first term, but now he was departing with his boss. Peggy Noonan, who respected Darman greatly, noticed in him an uncharacteristic detachment during these weeks. She has recounted a conversation during this period in which Darman "seemed as if he'd lost some of his investment in the place; some level of engagement had been blocked, some plug pulled from the wall. . . . [He appeared] aimless and unconnected."[19]

THE PERILS OF PRESIDENTIAL SPEECH WRITING

The Second Inaugural also suffered having too many contributors, a problem that resulted, in part, from the palace politics of the White House. As in a European court of old, the modern White House is full of people plotting to be close to the king.[20] This was true of the speech-writing department as much as other divisions of the administration. To draft an important speech was to rise in stature. To draft an inaugural address would be to have a place in American rhetorical history.

In this climate, Tony Dolan was concerned that Reagan's role in the speech writing would be limited. He recalled that for several weeks he had issued a series of memos to Richard Darman, urging that Reagan draft his own address. He believed that "the second Inaugural, like Lincoln's second Inaugural, had a chance at greatness, particularly if Reagan did his own." Dolan noted that "Reagan really was his own best speechwriter." Such a procedure, Dolan believed, would also "dispel this nonsense" that Reagan's staff was responsible for his successful speeches.[21] Apparently unconvinced by Dolan's arguments, Darman instructed Elliott, Noonan, and Dolan to write separate drafts. The three drafts were submitted to Reagan on December 26, 1984, so that he could work on the speech during his New Year's holiday in California.[22]

Reagan constructed his own draft of the inaugural, drawing in part from the material submitted by Dolan.[23] According to Noonan, his draft was found wanting by White House staff members. Noonan herself was disappointed with it, which she has characterized as insufficiently "thematic" and "chock-full of facts and statistics and percentages."[24] Elliott and Noonan set about to rewrite the speech. In effect, they reinserted material from their earlier drafts but did not consult with Tony Dolan.[25] The final version was not so much a unified speech as a series of passages that had originated from Reagan and the three writers. To the extent that a thesis could be found in the address, it was essentially epideictic rather than deliberative. Talking with journalists on Inauguration Day, Elliott reported that Reagan wanted to focus on the theme "that the future is rich in possibilities, that the American revolution is reborn."[26]

Without question, the speech writers wanted to create the best possible address, yet they had other concerns as well. Noonan has recalled that the decision to rewrite Reagan's draft was a matter of survival in the palace politics of the White House. At one point, Elliott explained to her: "If we let it go as it is and it's a flop, I'll be fired and you'll be fingered. Someone will have to take the fall."[27] When Elliott himself recalled the writing of the Second Inaugural, he did not mention a fear of retribution but stressed the need to capitalize on the excellent writers in his department. His rationale implied that as a manager, he was trying to reward his subordinates and boost morale by using their material in the address.[28]

CONCLUSION

By their manner of reporting and interpreting Reagan's speech, the news media reinforced its epideictic function. Unable to find a clear statement of principles that would guide Reagan's second administration, news commentators, such as Bob Schieffer of CBS-TV, observed that the address "promised more of the same." The *New York Times* announced: "familiar themes echoed"; the *Los Angeles Times* used the headline: "President Vows to Stay on Course in 2nd Term." CBS's congressional correspondent, Phil Jones, concurred. Reagan's supporters, he explained, heard the speech as a commitment to "stay the course," while his opponents heard it as "stay the curse."[29]

Democrats and Republicans joined news commentators in praising the conciliatory appeals in Reagan's address. On ABC-TV, David Brinkley noted that as a second inaugural, the speech was "gentler, kinder, softer"; on NBC-TV Roger Mudd commented that presenting the speech indoors had created an "intimate quality." Almost all commentators mentioned Reagan's "subdued tone." These sentiments were echoed by political figures as diverse as senators Robert Dole (R, Kan.) and Patrick Moynihan (D, N.Y.). By treating the speech as an exclusively ceremonial event, Democratic leaders could praise the speech while continuing to oppose Reagan's policies. Senator Joseph Biden (D, Del.) called it a "brilliant speech. It made people feel good about their country"; the Democratic party chairperson, Charles Manatt found it "a very impressive speech."[30] Using the same epideictic criteria, news commentators could promptly declare the speech a success—and just as promptly forget it. On ABC-TV, for example, George Will characterized the speech as "a conscious attempt to communicate enthusiasm . . . to set a mood of optimism in the country." On CBS-TV Bruce Morton noted: "There's a fair amount of flowery language in here. . . . The speechwriters worked hard."[31]

Reagan's Second Inaugural has receded from the national rhetorical memory with little attention. The address is not mentioned in the memoirs of Reagan's cabinet members;[32] it is ignored in books written for the popular press by Reagan's White House aides;[33] and it passes without comment in lengthy volumes written by both sympathetic and hostile political journalists.[34] Scholars have also found the Second Inaugural of insufficient value to merit much study. Although more than a dozen scholars have assessed Reagan's First Inaugural,[35] the Second Inaugural has been treated in only one work.[36] Indeed, the two most comprehensive studies of Reagan's presidential speeches do not mention it at all.[37] Yet the speech stands as an illustration of what can go wrong in writing an inaugural address.

Even those closest to the address were a bit disappointed. Peggy Noonan concluded that "it wasn't a great speech."[38] Although Tony Dolan regarded it as a success, he was disappointed that it had not reached its full potential. "The sad part," he explained, "was when I later read the draft that Reagan had done initially; it was shorter, and in my view it was much better. What the president came up with was a fine first draft that he needed to work on a little and expand. It really could have been great if someone had done a memo and said 'Mr. President, you might want to address one or two other issues and this paragraph you might want to move to the right or the left.' "[39] Dolan regretted that the final version of the speech simply became "an attempt to get everybody's draft in."[40]

Reagan himself had doubts about the speech. A week before Inauguration Day, he had given his draft of the speech to his chief of staff and reportedly commented: "Maybe I'm losing my touch."[41] At best, Reagan's Second Inaugural only half succeeded. It addressed the epideictic requirements of an inaugural but neglected the deliberative dimension. Even the "Great Communicator" had not been able to overcome the problems created by too little public policy and too many writers.

NOTES

1. Videotapes of the television coverage of Reagan's Second Inaugural by CBS, NBC and ABC were viewed courtesy of the Vanderbilt Television News Archive, Vanderbilt University, Nashville, Tennessee.

2. Kurt Ritter and David Henry, *Ronald Reagan: The Great Communicator* (Westport, Conn.: Greenwood Press, 1992), 63–66, 103–105.

3. Interview with C. Landon Parvin, August 3, 1990, Fredericksburg, Virginia. The anthology is Ronald Reagan, *Speaking My Mind: Selected Speeches* (New York: Simon & Schuster, 1989).

4. Ronald Reagan, "Inaugural Address," January 21, 1985, in *Public Papers of the Presidents of the United States: Ronald Reagan, 1985* (Washington, D.C.: U.S. Government Printing Office, 1988), 1, 55. Subsequent references to the address are from this text.

5. For a description of the American political jeremiad, see chapter 16 in this book. For an analysis of Lincoln's inaugural jeremiad, see Ernest G. Bormann, *The Force of Fantasy: Restoring the American Dream* (Carbondale: Southern Illinois University Press, 1985), 226–31. On the jeremiad in FDR's and Reagan's First Inaugural addresses, see Craig Allen Smith and Kathy B. Smith, "Paradoxical

Dimenions of Presidential Jeremiads: The Political Significance of a Rhetorical Form" (paper presented to the Southern States Communication Association, San Antonio, April 1992).

6. Speech writer Kenneth Khachigian drafted Reagan's First Inaugural, as well as Reagan's major economic policy speeches in February and March 1981. He has described the First Inaugural as the "blueprint" for Reagan's subsequent economic speeches. Interview with Khachigian, February 23, 1990, San Clemente, California.

7. See Kurt Ritter, "Ronald Reagan as Speechwriter: The Campaign Years, 1966–1980" (paper presented to the Western States Communication Association, Phoenix, 1991); Jeffrey K. Tulis, *The Rhetorical Presidency* (Princeton, N.J.: Princeton University Press, 1987), 190–91; and William Ker Muir, Jr., *The Bully Pulpit: The Presidential Leadership of Ronald Reagan* (San Francisco: Institute for Contemporary Studies, 1992), 19–42.

8. The file on Reagan's Second Inaugural at the Ronald Reagan Presidential Library was not available to scholars in 1992 when this chapter was written, and it will not become available in the near future. Hence, this analysis of the writing of the inaugural is based on the recollections of White House staff members. I interviewed Bently Elliott (January 8, 1992, Armonk, New York) and Tony Dolan (August 2, 1990, and January 10, 1992, Washington, D.C.) and also drew upon Peggy Noonan's White House memoir, *What I Saw at the Revolution: A Political Life in the Reagan Era* (New York: Random House, 1990), 187–192.

9. Martin Anderson, *Revolution* (San Diego: Harcourt Brace Jovanovich, 1988), 256.

10. Dolan interview, January 10, 1992.

11. Noonan, *What I Saw at the Revolution*, 189–90.

12. Elliott interview.

13. Rollins quoted in Jane Mayer and Doyle McManus, *Landslide: The Unmaking of the President, 1984–1988* (Boston: Houghton Mifflin, 1988), 19.

14. Dolan interview, January 10, 1992.

15. Larry Speakes, "TV as 'Opinion Maker': How Reagan Used It, and How It Could Improve," *Television/Radio Age*, June 22, 1987, 61.

16. Donald T. Regan, *For the Record: From Wall Street to Washington* (San Diego: Harcourt Brace Jovanovich, 1988), 265.

17. Anderson, *Revolution*, 256.

18. Landon Parvin speaking on "Preparing a Presidential Speech," C-SPAN, January 20, 1989. This program featured presidential speech writers Parvin (Reagan) and Hendrik Hertzberg (Carter) as they anticipated George Bush's inaugural address. For Noonan's objections to policy advisers revising her drafts of presidential speeches, see *What I Saw at the Revolution*, 75–91.

19. See Noonan, *What I Saw at the Revolution*, 186–87, 195.

20. The parallels between a modern White House and a monarchical court were called to my attention by Martin Anderson (interview, Stanford University, May 25, 1989). Also see Muir, *The Bully Pulpit*, 19–21.

21. Dolan interviews, August 2, 1990, January 10, 1992.

22. Noonan, *What I Saw at the Revolution*, 187.

23. Dolan interview, January 10, 1992.

24. Noonan, *What I Saw at the Revolution*, 189–90.

25. Dolan interview, January 10, 1992.

26. Elliott quoted in Lou Cannon, "Reagan's Speech Draws on Past Images of Golden Future," *Washington Post*, January 22, 1985, A26. Cannon noted that this idea was "restated in different ways throughout the speech."

27. Noonan, *What I Saw at the Revolution*, 191.

28. Elliott interview.

29. All quotations from television newscasters are from videotapes of news commentaries broadcast immediately following the inaugural address (Vanderbilt Television News Archive); Bernard Weinraub, "President Sees U.S. at 'Turning Point' as 2d Term Begins," *New York Times*, January 22, 1985, A1; and Jack Nelson, "President Vows to Stay on Course in 2nd Term," *Los Angeles Times*, January 22, 1985, I:1. Also see Hedrick Smith, "Muted Trumpet: Reagan Hails Gains But Sounds No Clear Future Theme," *New York Times*, January 22, 1985, A17; and Cannon, "Reagan's Speech Draws on Past Images," A21, 26.

30. David S. Broder, "President Sets Lofty Objectives," *Washington Post*, January 22, 1985, A1; and Cannon, "Reagan's Speech Draws on Past Images," A26. Biden is quoted in George Skelton, "Reagan Aims at 'Window of Opportunity' for Goals," *Los Angeles Times*, January 22, 1985, I:1. Manatt made his comment during ABC-TV's news coverage following the inaugural address (Vanderbilt Television News Archive).

31. Will's and Morton's comments were part of the postspeech news commentaries (Vanderbilt Television News Archive).

32. For example, see David A. Stockman, *The Triumph of Politics: How the Reagan Revolution Failed* (New York: Harper & Row, 1986); and Caspar Weinberger, *Fighting for Peace: Seven Critical Years in the Pentagon* (New York: Warner Books, 1990).

33. See Michael K. Deaver and Mickey Herskowitz, *Behind the Scenes* (New York: Morrow, 1987); and Larry Speakes and Robert Pack, *Speaking Out: Inside the Reagan White House* (New York: Scribner's Sons, 1988).

34. See Lou Cannon, *President Reagan: The Role of a Lifetime* (New York: Simon & Schuster, 1991); and Haynes Johnson, *Sleepwalking Through History: America in the Reagan Years* (New York: Norton, 1991).

35. See Ritter and Henry, *Ronald Reagan: The Great Communicator*, 86 n. 10.

36. Amos Kiewe and Davis W. Houck, *A Shining City on a Hill: Ronald Reagan's Economic Rhetoric, 1951–1989* (New York: Praeger, 1991), 180–81.

37. Muir, *The Bully Pulpit*; Mary E. Stuckey, *Playing the Game: The Presidential Rhetoric of Ronald Reagan* (New York: Praeger, 1990).

38. Noonan, *What I Saw at the Revolution*, 191.

39. Dolan interview, August 2, 1990.

40. Ibid., January 10, 1992.

41. Noonan, *What I Saw at the Revolution*, 190.

Chapter Twenty-Three

President George Bush's Inaugural Address, 1989

Bernard K. Duffy

An inaugural address may be read by later generations as ingenuous or disingenuous, eloquent or hackneyed, preternatural in its assessment of the status quo or mundanely uninsightful. In the wake of a disastrous presidency, historians and critics can read comments made in inaugural addresses as portents of national misfortune, while after an unusually successful or popular presidency, they may speak of an inaugural as a beacon that lit the path to progress. The course of history often determines whether an inaugural is well or ill considered, or even considered at all. Historians and rhetorical critics rightly perceive in inaugural rhetoric the seeds of tangible developments during a presidential administration, because inaugural addresses establish principles and propositions that ground later deliberative arguments and thus become the basis for action.

George Bush's address does not on first inspection appear to be deliberative. It is far less explicit in its policy objectives than, for example, Franklin Roosevelt's First Inaugural, which outlined the New Deal. Bush's inaugural made use of an extended narrative that preferred images, symbolism, and sentimentalism to concrete policy proposals. *Newsweek* encapsulated the view of the press when it said: "It wasn't so much that his Inaugural Address was vague; nearly every president's is. But rarely in recent history has a chief executive come to office revealing so little policy direction." The temptation, therefore, would be to regard the address as epideictic rather than deliberative, involved more in satisfying the demands of the ceremony and giving new voice to the beliefs undergirding the nation than in arguing on behalf of programs or policies to be pursued by the new administration. This judgment might lead one to discount some measure of its significance. Dante Germino's account of inaugural addresses as successive expressions and refinements of a public philosophy defining "the Nation" might erroneously be taken to imply that all inaugurals, including George Bush's, are epideictic in character. Without question inaugural addresses serve a ceremonial and ritualistic function and do so expressly and self-consciously. Bush's inaugural, like all others, articulated and identified him with the propositions that are constitutive of American democracy. The sources of his rhetorical invention were both illuminated and circumscribed by prior inaugurals. As a genre, inaugural addresses are overarchingly and essentially deliberative, although most are abstract, and some, like George Bush's, purposely avoid explicit discussions of policy. They are a genre because they respond to the expectations and constraints of an occasion, make use of traditional *topoi*, tend to be propositional, and are linked in content one to the other. Each, however, responds to a unique set of historical circumstances and each is a prelude to and an argument for political action. In this sense they are deliberative.[1]

BUSH'S INAUGURAL: GENERIC CONSIDERATIONS

The paucity of concrete policy proposals in Bush's address and their replacement with imagery and affirmations of national principles might lead one to argue that the address is epideictic. However, the inaugural identifies national and international problems, as well as goals for the future, while it leaves unstated the precise means that will be used to achieve them. The principles Bush articulated justified his ruminations regarding the role of government in addressing domestic social problems and pursuing its international role as democracy's standard-bearer. The reexpressions of "the Nation" Germino identifies in inaugurals, which are exemplified in Bush's inaugural, do not, however, make it epideictic; just as the paean of George Washington that Senator William Borah incorporated in a famous speech he delivered against the League of Nations does not alter its essentially deliberative character. In *The Invention of Athens*, Nicol Loraux argues that the classical funeral oration, which celebrated Athenian values by reviewing its history, is not precisely epideictic in the sense Aristotle defined it, because it does not address its audience as spectators or mere observers but as citizens. In the same sense, modern presidential inaugurals do not fit comfortably into the epideictic genre even when one focuses upon their most value-laden and philosophical passages. Even discounting the policy implications of inaugural addresses, they, like the ancient funeral oration, are civic. As the Greek funeral oration "invented" Athens, Bush's inaugural idealized the nation with the specific purpose of influencing civic beliefs. Additionally it called for action on several fronts, including helping the poor and homeless, battling against drugs, assisting in de-mocratization, and negotiating the release of American hostages.[2]

The address is strong in imagery and weak in intimations of policy. Several valid reasons explain this emphasis in rhetorical invention. First, Bush, the first vice president since Martin Van Buren to be elected pres-ident directly after his vice presidency, did not intend to repudiate the policies of his predecessor's largely popular administration. He did wish to indicate, however, that his administration would differ from Reagan's but this could best be accomplished through the imagery of the "new breeze," denunciations of materialism, and affirmations of concern for the poor and the problems that beset the poor, such as homelessness, unwanted pregnancy, and drug addiction. "It was," said the *San Francisco Chronicle* of the speech, "a vivid but unstated contrast to Reagan, a president who sometimes denied that there is a homelessness problem, was criticized for exalting an ethos of acquisitiveness and prided himself on confronting Congress." Second, Congress was Democratically con-trolled, and Bush found he could identify with Democrats by discussing domestic problems through pleasing images of volunteerism and prop-ositions concerning the importance of stewardship, whereas an explicit discussion of the Republican view of social welfare programs would have distanced him from Democrats in Congress and among the elec-torate. In his inaugural address, Bush needed to find a basis for bipar-tisanship, without which the administration could be mired in political struggles. At the same time, Bush's abstractions did not risk alienating Republican voters, and on some issues, such as abortion, drugs, and the return of American hostages, he took positions that courted his Republican constituency.[3]

A large portion of the inaugural called forth the traditional *topoi* of previous inaugural addresses, lending support to Germino's conclusion that inaugural addresses attempt to reconstitute "the Nation." It also confirmed Germino's observation that all inaugurals from Theodore Roo-sevelt's onward have been concerned with the active role of the nation in meeting change. Bush did not simply recite a public philosophy. Rather, speaking from "democracy's front porch," he invited "neigh-bors" and "friends" to participate in an idea of the nation that, as Bush said, "We know in our hearts." The central image of the address is first expressed in the narration, a lyrical, image-laden assessment of the con-dition of the world and of the country:

We live in a peaceful, prosperous time, but we can make it better. For a new breeze is blowing, and a world refreshed in freedom seems reborn. For in man's heart, if not in fact, the day of the dictator is over. The totalitarian era is passing, its old ideas blown away like leaves from an ancient lifeless tree. A new breeze is blowing, and a nation refreshed by freedom stands ready to push on. There

The joy and moral stimulation of work no longer must be forgotten in the mad chase of evanescent profits."[7] At the close of another decade of unparalleled prosperity and a raft of financial scandals, Bush made fresh use of this familiar *topos*: "Are we enthralled with material things, less appreciative of the nobility of work and sacrifice. My friends we are not the sum of our possessions. They are not the measure of our lives." Bush telescoped his argument with a melodramatic foreshadowing of how we might be remembered after our deaths: "That we were more driven to succeed than anyone around us? Or that we stopped to ask if a sick child had gotten better and stayed a moment there to trade a word of friendship?"

The political significance of Bush's antimaterialistic remarks did not go unnoticed by the press. *U.S. News and World Reports* said frankly: "He repudiated the ethos of the Reagan era." The *New Republic* maintained that it "was an interesting mix of political parricide and filial piety," in that it symbolically killed the image of Ronald Reagan while honoring Bush's father, Senator Prescott Bush, from whom the president apparently derived many of his commitments. Although Bush's antimaterialistic beliefs have their origins in patrician sensibilities remote from those of the working class and from most Democrats, their expression was, nevertheless, a potent declaration of his commitment to bipartisanship. The best way Bush could find to persuade Democrats of his sincerity was to give voice to the domestic concerns of the Democratic party.[8]

Bush's denunciation of materialism provided a bridge to his belief that, armed with a humanitarian spirit, individuals, rather than government, might be counted upon to assume more of the responsibility for social welfare. With resonances of Wilsonian idealism, Bush expressed a public philosophy that emphasized the stewardship shaped by his upper-class upbringing: "America is never wholly herself unless she is engaged in high moral principle. We as a people have such a purpose today. It is to make kinder the face of the Nation and gentler the face of the world. My friends, we have work to do." Abstract enough to encompass any brand of humanism, the thought of a "kinder," "gentler" America was a theme of Bush's campaign and provided in his inaugural a means of melding his ethos with certain practical aims of his presidency. No matter how abstract and moralistic, the thought anticipated and justified a policy of reducing welfare programs in favor of volunteerism. Because of their breadth and abstractness, the philosophical ideals of the nation have been used in previous inaugurals to encompass a wide range of political ideologies and to justify a panoply of policies.[9]

Commentators on Bush's inaugural found it to be conciliatory in its sensitivity toward the plight of the poor. Bush described a litany of social problems and acknowledged the enormity of national social problems.

However, his expression of faith in the moral rectitude of the people led him to a solution contrary to that of Lyndon Johnson, whose praise of the people provided passionate substantiation for the social programs of the Great Society. Bush's declaration, "For not only leadership is passed from generation to generation but so is stewardship. And the generation born after the Second World War has come of age," seems continuous with a passage from Johnson's inaugural, "In each generation—with toil and tears—we have had to earn our heritage again." Although the rhetoric is parallel, Bush and Johnson represent vastly different perspectives on the role of government is solving social problems. Undergirding their positions with a historic American idealism, Bush for his part was as secure in his denial that government money cannot save the people as Johnson was in his belief that it could. "The old solution, the old way," said Bush, "was to think that public money alone could end these problems. But we have learned that that is not so. And in any case our funds are low. We have a deficit to bring down." A Bush aide felt the need to explain a few days later that Bush was not proposing liberal solutions but rather suggesting that government should offer assistance through such programs as tax credits for day care.[10]

Despite the pessimistic tone of his argument against further spending programs, Bush's rhetoric, like Johnson's, was overwhelmingly affirming and positive. To some observers it undoubtedly appeared that Bush intended for government a greater, rather than a lesser, role in social welfare. He conceived his vision in an image used in his nomination acceptance speech and in his campaign: "I have spoken of a Thousand Points of Light, of all the community organizations that are spread like stars throughout the Nation, doing good. We will work hand in hand, encouraging, sometimes leading, sometimes being led, rewarding." In ultimate support of his policy, Bush associated it with the store of ideas identified with the national heritage: "The old ideas are new again because they're not old, they are timeless; duty, sacrifice, commitment, and a patriotism that finds its expression in taking part and pitching in." Another supplicant to American idealism, Jimmy Carter, had said much the same in 1976: "I have no new dream to set forth today, but rather urge a fresh faith in the old dream."[11]

Bush's rhetoric incorporated elements of populism without embracing the Democrat party's political ideology. His focus was on the people and what they might do individually and collectively to solve the problems that beset the nation. In an opening prayer he affirmed that "there is but one just use of power, and it is to serve the people," and in explaining his program to assist private social programs, he strongly declared, "I will go to the people." In speaking of the west front of the Capitol building as "democracy's front porch," and in thanking children "for watching democracy's big day," Bush attempted to demystify presidential leadership and to dissolve the barriers that stand between the public and government. These resonances of Jacksonian democracy were especially useful to Bush, whose privileged background make him as remote from the average citizen as any other president since Kennedy. They were also useful in distinguishing his style of leadership from that of Ronald Reagan, who despite his geniality was criticized for an aloof style of management. Although the veneer of populism in Bush's remarks and his description of social problems made him appear a Democrat in Republican cloth, an attentive reading of his rhetoric reveals that he remained faithful to his conservative ideology. When, for example, he discussed social problems, he listed welfare as a form of enslavement, in the same category as drugs; and when he discussed mothers of unwanted children, he identified himself with an antiabortion position. Moreover, Bush's solution to social ills, emphasizing private relief programs, bowed to a cherished conservative principle of limiting the responsibility of government in such activities.

Bush's appeal to the moral resolve and united effort on the part of the nation was matched or exceeded in importance by his appeal to the Congress for bipartisan cooperation. In his inaugural address, Bush was as concerned about congressional cooperation with the executive branch as Franklin Roosevelt was in his First Inaugural. Roosevelt's concern was that Congress would retard the enactment of the New Deal; Bush, who faced a fiscal crisis of a different sort, in the form of a $165 billion budget deficit, needed to solicit the cooperation of a Democratically controlled House and Senate. Democrats outnumbered Republicans by ten in the Senate and by eighty-five in the House. The numerical superiority of Democrats in the House was, according to one reporter, "the biggest such margin against a new President in the 200-year history of the Constitution."[12]

While Bush's rhetoric attempted to unify the public at the level of ideological abstractions, vague policy objectives, and sentimentalism, it also established the basis for congressional unity. In calling for a balanced budget, Bush transcended partisan division by appealing to the need for domestic strength: "And we must ensure that America stands before the world united, strong, at peace, and fiscally sound." In some minds, Bush's focus on domestic affairs grew out of a recognition that the Reagan administration had emphasized national security issues at the expense of domestic concerns. Not merely did Bush recognize the importance of domestic well-being to international prestige and power, the domestic thrust of his address revealed to observers such as the *Financial Times* that his would be a different presidency from Reagan's. It is through his identification with domestic issues that he wished to identify with congressional Democrats. Bush's explanation for congressional division indulged in what might be taken as an oversimplification,

particularly since it failed to take into account Ronald Reagan's difficulties with Congress: "And our great parties have too often been far
apart and untrusting of each other. It's been this way since Vietnam.
That war cleaves us still." Bush, who had supported the war, was the
first president to utter the word *Vietnam* in an inaugural address.[13] The
Vietnam War, as the *New York Times* suggested, "gave birth to years of
Congressional suspicions about Presidential power and executive hos-
tility to Congressional assertiveness in foreign policy." By word and
gesture, Bush offered his hand to both House Speaker Jim Wright and
Senate Majority Leader George Mitchell, in what the *Times* interpreted
to be "as much of a challenge as an invitation." He asked for a renewal
of post–World War II congressional bipartisanship, paraphrasing Senator Arthur Vandenberg to the effect that our differences once "ended
at the water's edge," a principle also articulated by Bush's father, who
had helped formulate postwar foreign policy.[14]

In content, the address is as interesting in what it did not discuss as
in what it did. It did not survey the international scene or speak explicitly
of the need to reach new accords on specific international issues, a silence
that would not be predicted from Bush's background as director of the
CIA and his experience in foreign affairs as vice president. Given the
celebrated difficulties that Ronald Reagan had with Congress on foreign
policy, culminating in the Iran-contra hearings, domestic affairs surely
appeared to Bush a more likely topic on which to find consensus, even
if the approach of conservatives to domestic matters has traditionally
separated them from Democrats. It is significant that Bush chose to
explain the cleavage of the political parties in terms of Vietnam, a foreign
policy fiasco for which neither political party was entirely responsible.

Apart from heralding the advances toward freedom abroad, Bush's
indications of his foreign policy consisted in little more than assuring
the Soviet Union that "the new closeness" would continue but carefully
punctuating his remark with the caveat, "consistent both with our security and with progress." His comments concerning the Soviet Union
represented the clichéd, guarded optimism of all recent presidents: "But
hope is good, and so is strength and vigilance." The only explicit foreign
policy objective Bush mentioned was the emotional issue of American
hostages, a Republican cause célèbre, given as a reason for the Reagan-
Bush administration's politically embarrassing arms sales to Iran. In his
inaugural Bush called for international assistance in securing the release
of hostages and promised in a simple maxim: "Good will begets good
will. Good faith can be a spiral that endlessly moves on."

ELOCUTIO ELOQUENTIA NON EST

The tenor of Bush's address is distinctive not only because of its studied avoidance of the confrontational rhetoric of the cold war but also

because of its reliance on imagery, appeals to patriotism and citizenship, simple language, sentimentalism, and explicit revelations of the speaker's character. Bush's diction is informal and in some sections particularly characteristic of his conversational style. William Safire commented that the inaugural might legitimize the use of *and* as the first word in a sentence. Long before the inaugural, commentators joked about "Bush-speak," which in its most colorful form incorporated terms such as *go ballistic*, for "serious response," and the *vision thing*, referring to criticisms that he had not provided any. One article parodied the president's language use by rephrasing the Gettysburg Address in Bush-speak.

The inaugural, although not colloquial, at times represents Bush's fragmentary conversational style. Phrases are assembled almost by association into loosely connected sentences. Two exemplary sentences should serve to illustrate this. "And he [Washington] would, I think, be gladdened by this day; for today is the concrete expression of a stunning fact; our continuity, these 200 years, since our government began." "And I am speaking of a new engagement in the lives of others, a new activism, hands-on and involved, that gets the job done." The rhetorical effect of such sentences is to create an informality that underscores the populism that the content of many of Bush's remarks conveys.[15]

The diction of Bush's inaugural is discontinuous, interlacing conversational passages with lyrical ones. The inaugural's metaphors and similes are sometimes heaped one upon the other in quick succession. No better example of this is the previously quoted passage that introduces the repeated image of the new breeze: "A new breeze is blowing. . . . This is a time when the future seems a door you can walk right through into a room called tomorrow. . . . The people of the world agitate for free expression and free thought through the door to the moral and intellectual satisfactions that only liberty allows." Evocative narration such as this is a vehicle to elicit an emotional response to images with multiple and ambiguous meanings. The image is linked to a reaffirmation of freedom and, in the next paragraph, to "free markets, free speech, free elections, and the exercise of free will unhampered by the state." Although the repository of such beliefs as these is arguably both intellect and emotion, Bush seeks to move his audience largely through an appeal to patriotism stimulated by imagination. Germino, whose book on inaugurals predates Bush's inauguration, quotes a lyrical passage from Wilson's First Inaugural that enlists an archetypal image that is close to yet quite different in tone from Bush's "new breeze": "The feelings with which we face this new age of right and opportunity sweep across our heartstrings like some air out of God's own presence, where justice and mercy are reconciled and judge and the brother are one." Germino concludes that "the lyrical tone of Wilson's address, which today would be too 'hot' to convey over the tube (as Marshall McCluhan would say), should be carefully attended to as one of the most important expressions of American public philosophy as expressed by presidents." Bush's rhetoric is no match for Wilson's in eloquence or in depth and complexity of thought. Its lyricism is in a different key from Wilson's. Both inaugurals appeal to sentiment, but Wilson's images encourage a literary transport to a sophisticated philosophical idealism, while Bush's more homely images, though far more available to the general public, do not take the audience further than simple conceptions of national ideals. They could be taken simply as pleasant pictures linked with a few affirmations of American freedoms and not requiring any particular intellectual acumen to apprehend. They offer something like the immediate gratifications of advertising slogans or the unabashedly sentimental lyrics of country music. By comparison, what is too "hot" for television in Wilson's lyricism is not, it would appear from Bush's address, its appeal to imagination but its "spaciousness," its "widths of sound and meaning," as the conservative rhetorician Richard Weaver glossed the term.[16]

Interestingly, Wilson, fearing perhaps that his spacious expression of idealism might be misread as sentimentalism, explicitly criticized sentimentalism as the wrong motivation for the duties of government, while Bush less convincingly denied that he wished to be sentimental directly after a passage when he waxed most sentimental: "But my thoughts have been turning the past few days to those who would be watching at home, to an older fellow who will throw a salute by himself when the flag goes by and the woman who will tell her sons the words of the battle hymns." One might argue that Bush's sentimentalism is, in terms of both literary and intellectual depth, a poor substitute for the eloquent idealism of Wilson but an inevitable accommodation to mass communication and its mass audience.[17]

Bush's expressed acknowledgment of the television viewership offers a key to explaining much of the sentimentalism of this address. One part of the Reagan legacy that the new president did not wish to discard was Reagan's successful handling of his television image. No president was more unabashedly sentimental before the television camera than he, although, unlike Bush, Reagan frequently achieved this effect through anecdotes. The overt sentimentalism of Bush's inaugural reminds one of the unembarrassed emotional pyrotechnics of television evangelists. Addressing "our children watching in schools throughout our great land" demonstrates that in a television era, even presidents must use what airs well, even if it means emulating the familiar, soothing didacticism of Mr. Roger's neighborhood. Bush exploited the decision to address children by recasting in yet simpler terms the "new breeze" image: "For democracy belongs to us all, and freedom is like a beautiful kite that can go higher and higher with the breeze."

THE INAUGURAL AS A VEHICLE TO REPAIR ETHOS

As Bush's informal linguistic choices and sentimentalism are adaptations to the electronic mass media, they are also designed to make him appear the common man he is not. His nomination address attempted to drive home the point that he was no different from other Americans in his commitments to family and country. Bush's inaugural, like his nomination speech, was characterized by a tendency to confide in the audience the speaker's personal traits and attributes. In the campaign, it was useful for Bush to differentiate himself as more caring and human than Michael Dukakis, whom Bush in his nomination address implied was a technocrat.[18] In Bush's inaugural, the tone of his administration and its broad policy objectives were portrayed as concomitant with and justified by George Bush's personality. The emphasis on Bush's character was occasioned in part by his election to the presidency directly after serving as the vice president of a popular president, whose policies he did not wish to repudiate but from whose personal character he wished to distinguish his own. *U.S. News and World Report* suggested that Bush's problem in the address was much the same as Herbert Hoover's, who took the helm from fellow Republican Calvin Coolidge. Another reason for Bush's self-revelations, no doubt, was to begin the process of improving Bush's image, which according to the *New York Times* had been damaged in a "mean-spirited campaign." Even when not addressing the issue of his personality directly, much of what Bush said in his inaugural revealed him indirectly, including his appeal for "kinder" America and a "gentler" world, his stated determination to be a model of these ideals, and his prayer to "use power to help people." More direct were Bush's declarations about himself and the office of the presidency:

A president is neither a prince nor pope, and I do not seek a window on men's souls. In fact I yearn for greater tolerance, and easygoingness about each other's attitudes and way of life. . . . I do not fear the future. I do not fear what is ahead. For our problems are large, but our heart is larger.

Bush's denial of fear evokes the famous fear-allaying exordium of Franklin Delano Roosevelt's First Inaugural, although it was expressed in the first-person plural.

Bush's ethos appeal is no less self-revelatory than John Kennedy's noting that in what he described as freedom's "hour of maximum danger

. . . I do not shrink from this responsibility, I welcome it." The difference lies in the character of the disclosure. Indeed, Bush surely had in mind a passage of Kennedy's inaugural, "Now the trumpet summons us again, not as a call to battle thought embattled we are," when in his peroration he averred,

Some see leadership as high drama and the sound of trumpets calling. But I see it as a book with many pages. . . . The new breeze blows, a page turns, the story unfolds. And so, today a chapter begins, a small and stately story of unity, diversity, and generosity—shared and written together.

Bush presents his administration as a projection of his sense of stewardship, self-sacrifice, and modesty. His personality became a focus of the campaign, both offensively in criticisms that Bush was "wimpish" and defensively in portrayals of his valor, family values, loyalty, and competence. Columnist Meg Greenfield suggested that Bush's tendency to self-disclosure during the presidential campaign might be explained by the media's interest in the personalities of political candidates. Bush, if as modest as his speeches profess him to be, may have been less inclined to self-portraiture without his speech writer, Peggy Noonan, who crafted both the inaugural and the Republican nomination address. The self-revelations in the address may in part result from Noonan's desire to create authenticity in the address by wedding the speaker with his speech. Whatever the cause, Bush's self-revelations were reminders of the importance of his personality as an issue in the campaign. To the extent that this issue was influential in his election, it is reasonable that the audience would want to be reminded of Bush's virtues in the inaugural address and that he would feel some need to oblige them.[19]

CONCLUSION

The Bush inaugural address responded to a powerful set of political constraints. Bush could neither offend the Republican coalition Ronald Reagan had created nor the Democratic Congress whose support he required. His greatest task in the address was to gather bipartisan support for his administration, which he could more easily do by speaking in abstractions than by adumbrating the accomplishments of the Reagan-Bush administration or by reviewing the controversial aspects of its foreign policy. Consequently, the address ventured little into international affairs, except symbolically to celebrate the democratization of communist countries, and it dealt most clearly with domestic problems without, however, attributing their causes or offering programs to solve them apart from the pledge to assist in altruistic efforts. In choosing to describe domestic problems rather than to decry liberal solutions to them, Bush put the best possible face on economic conservatism after a presidency criticized for its callous devotion to supply-side economics. Understandably, the strongest policy statement in the address concerned drug abuse, an issue that would not invite partisan division: "This scourge shall stop." The Bush inaugural was one characterized by its substitutions. In place of arguments, examples, and policy directions were vivid images and evocative narratives that revealed Bush's character while creating a tenor for his administration. The address relied for its validation on the audience's tacit acknowledgment that the principles Bush expressed were, indeed, what they knew in their hearts and on their willingness to share in the sentiments Bush expressed. The effectiveness of the address rested in its broad optimism, its studied avoidance of controversial issues, its resonances of Democratic themes, its appeal to bipartisanship, and its conviction that a skillfully chosen image offers greater rewards while posing fewer risks than the dry exposition of problems and solutions.

NOTES

1. Eleanor Clift et al., "Bush Reaches Out," *Newsweek* January 30, 1989, 25–26; Dante Germino, *The Inaugural Addresses of American Presidents: The Public Philosophy and Rhetoric* (Lanham, Md.: University Press of America, 1984), 6; George Bush, "Inaugural Address," *Public Papers of the Presidents of the United States: George Bush 1989* (Washington, D.C.: U.S. Government Printing Office, 1989), bk. 1, 1–4.

2. William Borah, *Congressional Record*, November 19, 1919, 8781–84; Nicol Loraux, *The Invention of Athens*, trans. Alan Sheridan (Cambridge: Harvard University Press, 1986), 225.

3. Larry Liebert "A Different Kind of Conservatism," *San Francisco Chronicle*, January 21, 1989, A1.

4. Germino, *Inaugural Addresses*, 8; Haynes Johnson, "Television and the Bush Inauguration: Made for Each Other," *Washington Post*, January 21, 1989, A7.

5. Kenneth Burke, *A Rhetoric of Motives* (Berkeley: University of California Press, 1969), 184; see also Germino *Inaugural Addresses*, 23.

6. Germino, *Inaugural Addresses*, 19; Woodrow Wilson, *The Papers of Woodrow Wilson*, ed. Arthur S. Link (Princeton, N.J.: Princeton University Press, 1980), 33:150; *Inaugural Addresses of the Presidents of the United States from George Washington 1789 to Richard Milhous Nixon 1969* (Washington, D.C.: Government Printing Office, 1969), 260; Kurt W. Ritter and James R. Andrews, *The American Ideology: Reflections of the Revolution in American Rhetoric* (Speech Communication Association, 1978), 58.

7. *Inaugural Addresses of the Presidents*, 200, 236.

8. Harrison Rainie, "His Moment Arrives," *U.S. News and World Report*, January 30, 1989, 19–20; Henrik Hertberg, "This Nice Age," *New Republic*, February 13, 1989, 4.

9. Concerning this last point, see Ritter and Andrews, *American Ideology*, 58.

10. *Inaugural Addresses of the Presidents*, 273. E. J. Dionne, Jr., "Which Way Does the New Breeze Blow?" *New York Times*, January 22, 1989, IV:1.

11. Jimmy Carter, "Inaugural Address," in *Public Papers of the Presidents of the United States: Jimmy Carter 1977* (Washington, D.C.: U.S. Government Printing Office, 1977), bk. 1.

12. Robert Shogan, "Bush Enters Office Amid Sharp Partisan Division," *Los Angeles Times*, January 22, 1989, I:1; "Mr. Bush's Hand," *New York Times*, January 22, 1989, IV:24.

13. Stewart Fleming, "Friends We Have Work to Do," *Financial Times*, January 21, 1989, 6; David S. Broder, "Speech Mixes a Pinch of Carter, Dash of FDR," *Washington Post*, January 21, 1989, A1, A11.

14. "Mr. Bush's Hand," IV:24; Broder, "Speech," A1.

15. William Safire, "Marking Bush's Inaugural," *New York Times*, February 5, 1989, VI:10; Charles Bremner, "Bushspeak Fires Laser Shots at Linguistic Custom," *London Times*, December 24, 1988, B6; Ross K. Baker, "The President Speaks at Gettysburg," *Los Angeles Times*, February 12, 1989, V:5; Paul Taylor, "Bush's Vivid Self Portrait," *Washington Post*, August 19, 1988, A1.

16. Germino, *Inaugural Addresses*, 9; Richard Weaver, *The Ethics of Rhetoric* (South Bend, Ind.: Henry Regnery, 1953), 169.

17. *Inaugural Addresses of the Presidents*, 201.

18. Taylor, "Bush's Vivid Self Portrait," A1.

19. Rainie, "His Moment Arrives," 19; Michael Greskes, "He's a New Man Now, Thanks to Press," *New York Times*, January 22, 1989, IV:1; *Inaugural Addresses of the Presidents*, 269; Meg Greenfield, "Self-Portraits Don't Work," *Washington Post*, August 15, 1988, A13.

Chapter Twenty-Four

President Bill Clinton's Inaugural Address, 1993

Halford Ryan

In 1913, 1933, and 1961, Americans heard inaugural addresses of exceptional eloquence. Woodrow Wilson's First, Franklin D. Roosevelt's First, and John F. Kennedy's Inaugural were all speeches of the first water. Thus, every twenty to thirty years or so, especially after a hiatus of Republican chief executives, Democratic presidents have persuasively charted new courses for the American people in their inaugural speeches: Wilson described his New Freedom, FDR his New Deal, and JFK his New Frontier. If this cyclical axiom was to hold true, then the auguries for another Democratic tour de force, on January 20, 1993, were particularly auspicious. Twelve years of Republicanism favored a politically propitious response. Yet, as the ancient Romans realized, the Olympians occasionally disappointed the mortals.

A thesis of this book has been that conventional twentieth-century inaugural addresses have been merely ceremonial, epideictic, and contemplation oriented, whereas the exceptional ones have been action oriented; of these, a few addresses have advanced to a preeminent position. Thus, Wilson's First inaugurated not only progressivism but also a lofty idealism that was lacking in early twentieth-century American politics; FDR's First charted the New Deal and also conquered the endemic fear that paralyzed the Depression-era United States; JFK's Inaugural summoned citizens to patriotic service while inspiring civic idealism that had faltered in the flaccid decade of the 1950s.

But the issue now is to explicate President Bill Clinton's Inaugural. This inquiry is framed by the motto of the United States of America: *E Pluribus Unum* (from many, one); or, can copious resonances of the inaugurals of Wilson and Kennedy make Clinton's speech many or one?

CONTEMPLATION- VERSUS ACTION-ORIENTED

Clinton's Inaugural was not an action-oriented, deliberative speech in the style of FDR's First Inaugural. One combs the address in vain for hints of political principles or for ways and means to right the wrongs that Clinton had excoriated in the 1992 campaign: the deficit, health care, unemployment, and so forth. Certainly, the speech's introduction, which was based on a felicitous seasonal trope, could have pointed the way: "Today, we celebrate the mystery of American renewal. This ceremony is held in the depth of winter. But, by the words we speak and the faces we show the world, we force the spring."[1] The rest of the speech, however, never quite addressed the figurative summer, when the work begins in earnest, or the fall, when one reaps the harvest.

Indeed, the speech's epideictic nature is foreshadowed in the third word of Clinton's speech: "Today we *celebrate* [author's emphasis]. . . ." To be sure, towards the end of the speech, where Clinton's transitional language seemed to move to an action-oriented position—"Today, we do more than celebrate America; we rededicate ourselves to the very idea of America"—he nevertheless halted. True, the "very idea of America" was parsed in anaphora, an elegant figure of sound used for parallel structure. Four times Clinton inculcated an "idea," but not any particular or general action:

An idea born in the revolution and renewed through two centuries of challenge.

An idea tempered by the knowledge that, but for fate, we—the fortunate and the unfortunate—might have been each other.

An idea ennobled by the faith that our nation can summon from its myriad diversities the deepest measure of unity.

An idea infused with the conviction that America's long heroic journey must go forever upward.

Although Clinton concluded with language that could be considered action oriented (he asked Americans to "work until our work is done"; quoted Galatians 6:9, "in due season we shall reap, if we faint not"; and, building on the metaphor of heeding the trumpets, he implored: "And now—each in our own way, and with God's help—we must answer the call"), the rhetorical effect was flat.

Those who know well John Kennedy's Inaugural will understand why this happened. Clinton's Inaugural ended with: "We have heard the trumpets." In persuasive parlance, the metaphor of the trumpet is a clarion call to action. Kennedy clearly understood that such a metaphor needs linguistic closure or completion. One will remember that after

Kennedy uttered "Now the trumpet summons us again" (and is not Kennedy's "summons" more energetic than Clinton's "have heard"?), he asked a rhetorical question—"Will you join in that historic effort?"— and he further displayed inaugural eloquence with his famous chiasmas—"And so, my fellow Americans: ask not what your country can do for you—ask what you can do for your country."[2]

The last untraveled rhetorical route, of an action-oriented bent, was Clinton's allusion to "what Franklin Roosevelt called 'bold, persistent experimentation.' " Surely this was an instance of Democratic name dropping. Had Clinton borrowed the rest of Roosevelt's rhetoric, his inaugural then would have veered toward action. FDR's "bold, persistent experimentation" phrase is serviceable, yet in the original speech the phrase marched to an inevitable, periodic climax. (FDR excelled in rhetorically using the periodic sentence, which suspends completion of the thought until the end, as in these examples from his First Inaugural Address: "[T]he only thing we have to fear is fear itself"; "This nation is asking for action, and action now"; and "There are many ways in which it can be helped, but it can never be helped by merely talking about it."[3]) Thus, at Ogelthorpe University in Atlanta, Georgia, on May 22, 1932, candidate Roosevelt declared:

The country needs and, unless I mistake its temper, the country demands, bold, persistent experimentation. It is common sense to take a method and try it: If it fails, admit it frankly and try another. But above all, try something.

It is unclear from his 1993 inaugural what President Clinton would try.

ELOCUTIO

Since the time of the ancient Greeks and Romans, theorists and practitioners alike have recognized that a polished style—the Greeks called it *lexis*; the Romans, *elocutio*—could make a pedestrian speech stand out. If President Clinton's speech excelled in, and will be remembered for, any of the classical canons of rhetoric, surely it will be style.

Metaphors were especially well chosen for the inaugural theme of renewal. The introduction contained such images as "[W]e force the spring" and "warmed by the sunshine of freedom," and the motif was reiterated thematically later when Clinton exhorted: "Now we must do the work the season demands" and "From this joyful mountain top of celebration, we hear a call to service in the valley." (Those familiar with the Reverend Dr. Martin Luther King's "I Have a Dream" speech will certainly compare King's imagery of the valley versus mountain with Clinton's employment of that trope. In 1963 King necessarily had to speak of "the dark and desolate valley of segregation" and implored people to "not wallow in the valley of despair," juxtaposing that with the freedom that would ring from an archetypal "Stone Mountain of Georgia" and "Lookout Mountain of Tennessee."[4] In 1993, however, Clinton reversed the polarity: Americans should return to the valley, after the inaugural celebration, so that the racial conditions of the United States in the 1960s would not revive.) And, in one finely constructed sentence, Clinton combined a military metaphor with an architectural metaphor to craft an enduring leitmotif of the American people:

From our revolution to the Civil War, to the Great Depression to the civil rights movement, our people have always mustered the determination to construct from these crises the pillars of our history.

Clinton employed the hortatory subjunctive. The speaker exhorts the faithful—"Let us"—to accomplish some object that is contrary to fact. "Let us embrace [change]"; "let us all take more responsibility, not only for ourselves and our families but for our communities and our country"; "let us resolve to reform our politics"; "let us put aside personal advantage"; "let us resolve to make our government"; and "let us give this capital back to the people to whom it belongs" were noteworthy instances in which Clinton described what was not the current situation but what he conceived the nation could be under his leadership.

Clinton's utilization of the hortatory subjunctive echoed Kennedy's Inaugural. JFK delivered four thoughts that addressed the United States and the communist world and that began with "Let both sides. . . . " The repetition of "Let both sides" was anaphora, or parallelism. Moreover, Kennedy delivered a famous chiasmas in the hortatory subjunctive: "Let us never negotiate out of fear. But let us never fear to negotiate." Clinton did not have any chiasmas in his address.

Alliteration, words with the same or similar sounds, added verbal interest to Clinton's Inaugural, although it was scattered sparingly throughout the speech. The following selections are illustrative: "Though we march to the music of our time, our mission is timeless"; "we pledge an end to the era of deadlock and drift"; "profound and powerful forces"; and "powerful people maneuver for position." The president artistically combined anaphora with alliteration in the phrase, "Our hopes, our hearts, our hands." Moreover, this passage featured asyndeton, or leaving out the connective, for normal diction would indicate the conjunction "and": "Our hopes, our hearts, *and* our hands." Asyndeton allows the orator to phrase the ideas equally and separately, an effect Clinton secured.

One will have to decide whether the following passage from Clinton's Inaugural reverberates the rhetoric and measured language of the Reverend Jesse Jackson. Clinton intoned: "Communications and commerce are global; investment is mobile; technology is almost magical; and ambition for a better life is now universal." In terms of rhythm and rhyme, the quotation is arguably evocative of Jackson's cadenced speaking.

Clinton's speech was permeated with maxims, the persuasive utility of which Aristotle well understood:

Maxims make one great contribution to speeches because of the uncultivated mind of the audience; for people are pleased if someone in a general observation hits upon opinions that they themselves have about a particular instance . . . so that if the maxims are morally good, they make the speaker seem to have a good character.[5]

Clinton connected with his audience by uttering self-evident truths to which few Americans would object:

There is nothing wrong with America that cannot be cured by what is right with America.
We must provide for our nation the way a family provides for its children.
Let us give this capital back to the people to whom it belongs.

These maxims satisfied the epideictic nature of the address. They invited the audience to contemplate verities but not to question in a deliberative sense how such platitudes could be attained.

By far the most intriguing stylistic device Clinton used was antithesis. Antithesis is a figure of thought that emphasizes contrast, opposition, and juxtaposition. Inherent in antithesis is a battle between dualistic thoughts that are irreconcilable; hence, the mind works to resolve the tension in favor of one thought over the other. For instance, the first sentence in Kennedy's Inaugural was antithetical: "We observe today not a victory of party but a celebration of freedom—symbolizing an end as well as a beginning—signifying renewal as well as change."[6] How can an "end" be a "beginning"; how can "renewal" be "change"? In short, how can Dwight D. Eisenhower be John F. Kennedy and how can Kennedy be Eisenhower? We know this is inconceivable, but antithesis coaxes us to consider the possibilities. After doing so, the astute observer concludes that the inaugural *was* a "victory of party" (the Democratic over the Republican), *was* a "beginning," and *was* a "change" (Kennedy's presidency).

President Clinton used antithesis in the second sentence of his Inaugural. This opening antithesis set the mood for much of the address: "This ceremony is held in the depth of winter," Clinton said, "But, by the words we speak and the faces we show the world, we force the spring." The audience knows that winter cannot be spring, but the antithesis entices listeners to conclude figuratively that winter—George Bush—has been shunted aside for spring—Bill Clinton.

Other antitheses were not so easily divined, however. Clinton did not communicate how he would confront the following contrary problems that plagued the United States:

Today, a generation raised in the shadows of the Cold War assumes new responsibilities in a world warmed by the sunshine of freedom—but threatened, still, by ancient hatreds and new plagues.

Raised in unrivaled prosperity, we inherit an economy that is still the world's strongest, but is weakened by business failures, stagnant wages, increasing inequality, and deep divisions among our own people.

We must invest more in our people, in their jobs and in their future—and at the same time cut our massive debt.

Let us put aside personal advantage so that we can feel the pain and see the promise of America.

Today, as an old order passes, the new world is more free but less stable.

Indeed, these antitheses sprang from the seedbed of contention in the 1992 campaign. Clinton campaigned against President Bush by arguing that the latter either ignored these issues or failed to propose workable solutions for these exigencies. Yet Clinton was vague in his Inaugural on how he would resolve the problems that he inherited from the Reagan–Bush team.

In fact, if Edward Kenny correctly opined that "antithesis is ideally suited to a problem–solution posture,"[7] which was a rhetorical role Kenny found in Kennedy's Inaugural, then it may be that the stylistic device of antithesis was inappropriate for Clinton's Inaugural. Three arguments warrant the claim. First, the speech was epideictic, not deliberative; hence, whereas Clinton alluded to problems in the body politic, he proffered no solutions.

Second, President Wilson's First Inaugural abounded in antithetical structure, which also characterized Clinton's Inaugural. Wilson's antitheses were situated in a deliberative matrix, however. Without belaboring the point,[8] consider the following example: Barely into his address, Wilson proclaimed: "We have been refreshed by a new insight into our own life." (Is this suggestive of Clinton's forcing the spring?) Wilson's insight was antithetical: "Our life contains every great thing, and contains it in rich abundance. But the evil has come with the good, and much fine gold has been corroded." "We have come now to the sober second thought," he told his 1913 audience. And, in resolving his antitheses, Wilson then itemized "with some degree of particularity the things that ought to be altered and here are some of the chief items."

Third, when Kennedy asserted that "Now the trumpet summons us again—not as a call to arms, though arms we need—not as a call to battle, though embattled we are," he sought acquiescence for an arms race, and he steeled citizens to battle communists around the globe. Thus, Wilson's New Freedom antitheses, centering around domestic issues, would be settled by forthcoming legislation; and Kennedy's New Frontier antitheses, pivoting on foreign issues, hinged on whether Americans, as Kennedy beseeched them, would "join in that historic effort?"

However, when Clinton promised to revitalize democracy, as Wilson did in 1913, Clinton offered hortatory subjunctives, not the concrete proposals that Wilson listed to ensure democratic government. When Clinton employed the antithesis of the winter of our discontent with the spring of his administration, he consumated his conclusion with a cliché that defies particularization: "Now we must do the work the season demands." And, when Clinton contrasted some Americans, who are "enriched," with other Americans, who "are working harder for less, when others cannot work at all," while concomitantly excoriating the costs of health care, fear of crime, and the poor's inability to "imagine the lives we are calling them to lead," he conceded that "We know we have to face hard truths and take strong steps." Yet Clinton detailed no solution, for he would not (or could not?) specify the "strong steps" to achieve "hard truths."

Thus, one can read Clinton's antitheses in at least two ways. From a purely stylistic perspective, the antitheses ornamented the speech admirably well. If one seeks resolution from the opposites, as one finds in Wilson's First Inaugural and Kennedy's Inaugural, however, then Clinton's antitheses were inapplicable. One may safely conclude that the antitheses were meant solely to adorn the speech in an epideictic, celebratory manner, rather than to actuate, in a deliberative mode, the nation's needed restorative policies—the lack of which arguably contributed to President Bush's defeat.

GENERIC ELEMENTS

The epideictic nature of Clinton's Inaugural has already been demonstrated. Therefore, it remains to delineate the degree to which the four generic elements are present in the speech.

President Clinton referred to communal values. By mentioning George Washington and Thomas Jefferson, whom Clinton used to warrant his assertion that the country needed "dramatic change from time to time," and by thanking George Bush and by alluding to Franklin Roosevelt, Clinton was able to anchor his speech in a broad bedrock of American political values. With the fall of the evil empire, however, one particular communal value was conspicuously absent. Gone were castigations against communism and attendant Manichaean dualities, which had figured more or less prominently in inaugural speeches since the time of Harry Truman's in 1949. Instead, communism barely merited one sentence: "Communism's collapse has called forth old animosities and new dangers." Old habits die hard, however, and the United States would still be a supernation and the world's policeman: "When our vital interests are challenged, or the will and conscience of the international community is defied, we will act—with peaceful diplomacy whenever possible, with force when necessary." Clinton strengthened the nation's resolve by mentioning troops "in the Persian Gulf, Somalia, and wherever else they stand."

President Clinton reconstituted the people. For all intents and purposes, divisive rhetoric is agreeably lacking. To be sure, the speech alluded twice to "powerful people" and to "power and privilege," but these references were so indeterminate that the we-versus-they polarities, which are sometimes found in inaugurals, are essentially missing in Clinton's. Instead, in a truly epideictic vein, Clinton praised the people for electing him (and implicitly subsumed those who did not), and then indicated that he would answer their united call:

The American people have summoned the change we celebrate today. You have raised your voices in an unmistakable chorus. You have cast your votes in historic numbers. And you have changed the face of the Congress, the presidency, and the political process itself. Yes, you, my fellow Americans, have forced the spring. Now we must do the work the season demands.

This passage may also serve as an exemplar for another observation. Throughout the speech, Clinton repeatedly reconstituted the people with personal, collective pronouns. As the *vox populi*, Clinton made it abundantly clear that he was, and presumably would continue to be, the voice *of the people*, and not the *voice* of the people.

With regard to powers and limitations, the best that can be said about President Clinton's Inaugural is that the speech fulfilled the letter, if not the spirit, of that generic element. Clinton did not mention the Constitution, but he did comment on Congress three times. In addition to noticing that the people "changed the face of Congress," Clinton promised the people that he would turn to the nation's business "with all the authority of my office. I ask the Congress to join me. But no president, no Congress, no governments, can undertake this mission alone. My fellow Americans, you, too, must play your part in our renewal." Perhaps Clinton reasoned that he did not have to pay particular attention to powers and limitations because he enjoyed a Democratic Senate and Congress. Presumably, the executive and the two houses of Congress read the election returns, and together they would quite naturally end the "deadlock and drift" that had characterized the previous administration, which the electorate had rejected.

As argued throughout this chapter, President Clinton's political principles were vague. Since this was not a deliberative speech, one might expect as much. Moreover, the stylistic device of antithesis entangled the speech in a paralysis of thought and action. Therefore, it is difficult to discern in his Inaugural what political principles Clinton would use to address the country's predicament, the existence of which had propelled him to the White House and the solution for which was still indefinite after the inaugural.

In addition, Clinton validated the aphorism that in American rhetoric the deity is mentioned in the last sentence of a political speech: "Thank you and God bless you all."

If recent inaugural addresses are a harbinger of genre building in process, then one element could be added to the list, although perhaps it should be eschewed. Although dormant since 1928 when President Hoover thanked Calvin Coolidge for his service to the country, President Carter revived the practice by obliquely recognizing Gerald Ford, President Reagan acknowledged Jimmy Carter, and President Bush expressed gratitude to Ronald Reagan.[9] President Clinton continued the tradition (is it now a generic element?) of thanking his predecessor. Yet, as Carl Burgchardt observed, there was a "minor dilemma" in Hoover's mentioning the outgoing Coolidge.[10] This difficulty was certainly present with Carter and Ford, Reagan and Carter, and Clinton and Bush, which can be appreciated in Clinton's Inaugural: "On behalf of our nation, I salute my predecessor, President Bush, for his half-century of service to America." Of course, the Machiavellian mind questions why, if the service were so salutary, did the challenger contest such a sitting president? Except in the case of George Bush, who declared fealty to Reagan's foreign policy but gently distanced himself from the former's domestic policies,[11] the rhetorical hypocrisy of thanking one's predecessor, especially one from another political party, is carrying reconstitution too far; therefore, its generic credo should be: *Requiescat in pacem.*

ACTIO

President Clinton's delivery was dynamic. Although this speech was delivered with the aid of a teleprompter, and hence he appeared to have good eye contact, he overcame the disadvantages inherent in using the device. (1) Clinton avoided the tiresome right-to-left and left-to-right head and eye movements that often plague teleprompter speakers. (2) He cadenced his speech effectively, for the phrasing of thought groups was varied for oratorical impact. (3) He effectively exploited variation in pitch and loudness when delivering his speech. For instance, he observed with some force that millions of Americans were able to compete, but appropriately softened his tone when he spoke of less fortunate citizens. (4) He cued potent rhetorical climaxes. With increasing vocal loudness and a faster speaking rate, coupled with hand-chop gestures, the president roused applause when he uttered one of his hortatory subjunctives, "Let us give this capital back to the people to whom it belongs."

Clinton's favorite gesture was the lightly clenched fist (with the index finger slightly extended but bent) that punctuated important thoughts. For instance, he used that gesture to emphasize "a new season of American renewal has begun." Occasionally he used the pointed-finger gesture, which parents periodically use to chide their children, in order to manifest more force—as when he admonished his audience: "Well, my fellow Americans, this is our time. Let us embrace it." A few times he used outstretched arms to signal exhortation, as when he extended his arms to summon all Americans: "From this joyful mountain top of celebration we hear a call to service in the valley."

CONCLUSION

In its immediate ceremonial context, President Clinton's Inaugural Address was an interlude between the prelude of pre-inaugural festivities and the postlude of Maya Angelou's poem, "On the Pulse of Morning,"[10] as well as inaugural balls and galas that contributed to the most expensive inaugural celebration in the nation's history. Yet, after the confetti and commercialism were relinquished to the dust bins of Washington, a speech delivered by the forty-second president of the United States on January 20, 1993, still remains as a record of Clinton's first state utterance. What, finally, can be said of his address?

With regard to previous presidents' inaugurals, the rhetorical scholar confronts a corpus of received opinion. Based on books and articles, and, where appropriate, buttressed by archival sources, the critic can situate, and perhaps adjust, his or her critical conclusions. Thus, a commentator does not ordinarily stray too far from the prudent path. For Clinton's Inaugural, however, there is no such pathway. Normally, in such instances, one could turn to reactions in the media in order to marshall evidence for one's findings. Although such a strategy has its strengths, I eschewed that gambit, for it smacks of *argumentum ad verecundiam* (an appeal to authority).

Rather, I attempted to start from scratch—to embody, to the degree possible, the critical stance of the *tabula rasa*—to make Clinton's Inaugural resonate with the genre of twentieth-century inaugurals that preceded it and of which it is now a part. When I did that, the speech assumed a position that is generically and rhetorically antithetical.

Generically, the address is clearly epideictic (so far, so good), but it nevertheless lacked political principles that will govern the new administration, and the element of powers and limitations was only marginally present. Although the speech was located in a celebration that reconstituted the people and their communal values, one waited fruitlessly to hear how the new president proposed to address the nation's problems. That Clinton's Inaugural conformed marginally to the generic theory is neither a weakness nor a strength; rather, the generic theory is not particularly valid in yet another instance of inaugural oratory.

Rhetorically, the speech is a paradox. On the one hand, the various stylistic figures are significant. Because they are faint echoes of more eloquent presidential inaugurals, however, they are not singular. On the other hand, Clinton's Inaugural, with its stylistic attainments and its oratorical delivery, is certainly a cut above pedestrian inaugurals. I venture, however, that it will not rank among those preeminent persuasions—such as Woodrow Wilson's First Inaugural, Franklin Roosevelt's First Inaugural, and John F. Kennedy's Inaugural—that charted Democratic, deliberative directions for the American people on Inauguration Day.

NOTES

1. Bill Clinton, "An 'American Renewal': Transcript of the Address by President Clinton," *New York Times*, January 21, 1993, A15. All subsequent citations are from this text.

2. John F. Kennedy, "Inaugural Address," in *Contemporary American Public Discourse*, edited by Halford Ross Ryan, 3rd. ed. (Prospect Heights, Ill., 1992), 196. All subsequent citations are from this text.

3. Franklin D. Roosevelt, "First Inaugural Address," in *Contemporary American Public Discourse*, 13, 14, 15. All subsequent citations are from this text.

4. Martin Luther King, Jr., "I Have a Dream," in *Contemporary American Public Discourse*, 215, 217.

5. Aristotle, *On Rhetoric*, trans. by George A. Kennedy (New York: Oxford University Press, 1991), 186.

6. Compare Kennedy's introduction with the conclusion of Woodrow Wilson's First: "This is not a day of triumph; it is a day of dedication. Here muster, not the forces of party, but the forces of humanity."

7. Edward J. Kenny, "Another Look at Kennedy's Inaugural Address," *Today's Speech* 13 (November, 1965), 18.

8. See, in this book, James Andrews's chapter on President Wilson's First Inaugural Address, especially page 32.

9. See, in this book, Craig Allen Smith's chapter on President Jimmy Carter's Inaugural Address, page 247, and David Henry's chapter on President Ronald Reagan's First Inaugural Address, page 261.

10. See, in this book, Carl Burgchardt's chapter on President Herbert Hoover's Inaugural Address, page 88.

11. See, in this book, Bernard Duffy's chapter on President George Bush's Inaugural Address, pages 288 and 290.

12. Maya Angelou, "On the Pulse of Morning," *New York Times*, January 21, 1993, A14.

Bibliography

For information on a given inaugural address of a twentieth-century American president, consult the Notes following the appropriate chapter. They contain references to historical and rhetorical resources, such as materials in an archive and/or a presidential library, books by or about a president, and scholarly essays and articles.

For critical and practical purposes, printed inaugural addresses are accurate and acceptable. Thus, the inaugural texts provided in the *Public Papers of the Presidents* are adequate, given that there have been no earth-shaking ad-lib remarks in presidential inaugurals. Still, for a voice recording and verbatim inaugural speech text, contact the appropriate presidential library.

For eighteenth- and nineteenth-century presidential inaugural addresses, several sources are useful. The following collections give inaugural texts and brief-to-extended commentaries on the inaugural's historical milieu:

Humes, James C. *My Fellow Americans: Presidential Addresses That Shaped History.* Foreword by Senator Sam Nunn. New York: Praeger, 1992.

Inaugural Addresses of the Presidents of the United States from George Washington 1789 to George Bush 1989. Washington, D.C.: U.S. Government Printing Office, 1989.

Speeches of the American Presidents. Edited by Janet Podell and Steven Anzovin. New York: H. Wilson, 1988.

For general treatments of the historical, generic, and rhetorical roles of inaugural addresses, see:

American Orators of the Twentieth Century: Critical Studies and Sources. Edited by Bernard K. Duffy and Halford R. Ryan. Westport, Conn.: Greenwood Press, 1987.

Ceaser, James W., Glen E. Thurow, Jeffrey Tulis, and Joseph Bessette. "The Rise of the Rhetorical Presidency." *Presidential Studies Quarterly* 11 (1981): 158–71.

Form, Genre, and the Study of Political Discourse. Edited by Herbert W. Simons and Aram A. Aghazarian. Columbia: University of South Carolina Press, 1986.

Germino, Dante. *The Inaugural Addresses of American Presidents: The Public Philosophy and Rhetoric.* Preface and foreword by Kenneth W. Thompson. Lanham, Md.: University Press of America, 1984.

The President and the Public: Rhetorical and National Leadership. Edited by Craig Allen Smith and Kathy B. Smith. Lanham, Md.: University Press of America, 1985.

Ritter, Kurt W., and James R. Andrews. *The American Ideology: Reflections of the Revolution in American Rhetoric.* Falls Church, Va.: Speech Communication Association, 1978.

Tulis, Jeffrey K. *The Rhetorical Presidency.* Princeton, N.J.: Princeton University Press, 1987.

Wolfarth, Donald L. "John F. Kennedy in the Tradition of Inaugural Speeches." *Quarterly Journal of Speech* 47 (1961): 124–32.

Index

About the Editor and Contributors

JAMES R. ANDREWS is Professor of Speech Communication at Indiana University. He teaches courses in rhetorical criticism and public address. He authored *A Choice of Worlds* and *The Practice of Rhetorical Criticism* and co-authored *American Voices*, *Contemporary American Voices*, and *The American Idealogy*. He received the Winans-Wichelns Award and twice received the American Forensic Association Award for outstanding research.

HAL W. BOCHIN is Professor of Speech Communication, California State University at Fresno. He teaches courses in rhetorical criticism, argumentation, and the history of American public address. He is author of *Richard Nixon: Rhetorical Strategist* (Greenwood, 1990) and co-author of *Hiram Johnson: A Bio-Bibliography*. He has contributed articles and chapters to books on political rhetoric and to history and communication journals.

BERNARD L. BROCK is Professor of Communication, Wayne State University, Detroit, Michigan. He teaches courses in rhetorical criticism, political communication, and contemporary public address. He co-authored *Methods of Rhetorical Criticism* and *Public Policy Decision Making*, and he contributed to *American Orators of the Twentieth Century* and *Oratorical Encounters*.

CARL R. BURGCHARDT is Associate Professor of Speech Communication, Colorado State University, Fort Collins. He teaches and publishes in the areas of critical methodology and the history and analysis of

American public address. He is the author of *Robert M. La Follette, Sr.: The Voice of Conscience* (Greenwood, 1992).

DANIEL ROSS CHANDLER, a minister of the United Methodist church, teaches communication at Loyola University of Chicago. He is the author of *The Reverend Dr. Preston Bradley* and *The Rhetorical Tradition*. His articles have appeared in *Religious Humanism, Journal of Communication and Religion, Religious Communication Today, Harvard Divinity Review,* and *The Quest*.

WARREN DECKER is Associate Professor of Communication, George Mason University, Fairfax, Virginia. He teaches courses in argumentation, argument and public policy, and communication theory and directs the debate team. He has authored a number of articles concerning presidential rhetoric, and he contributed to *Rhetorical Studies of National Political Debates: 1960–1988* (Praeger, 1990).

BERNARD K. DUFFY is Professor of Speech Communication, California Polytechnic State University, San Luis Obispo. He teaches courses in rhetorical theory and American public address. He is co-editor of *American Orators before 1900* (Greenwood, 1987) and *American Orators of the Twentieth Century* (Greenwood, 1987). He is also co-adviser of the Great American Orators series for Greenwood Press.

ROBERT FRIEDENBERG is Professor of Communication, Miami University, Hamilton, Ohio. He teaches courses in American public address and political communication. He has authored, co-authored, or edited four books, including the only book-length study of Theodore Roosevelt's speaking, *Theodore Roosevelt and the Rhetoric of Militant Decency* (Greenwood, 1990).

DAVID HENRY is Professor of Speech Communication, California Polytechnic University, San Luis Obispo. He teaches courses in rhetorical criticism and theory, persuasion, and argumentation. He co-authored *Ronald Reagan: The Great Communicator* (Greenwood, 1992) and has published in *Communication Studies, Communication Education, Southern Speech Communication Journal,* and the *Quarterly Journal of Speech,* for which he was also an associate author.

THOMAS A. HOLLIHAN is Associate Professor of Communication Arts, University of Southern California. He teaches courses in argumentation, rhetorical criticism, and political communication. He has published in *Quarterly Journal of Speech, Communication Quarterly, Western Journal of Speech Communication, Southern Communication Journal,* and *Argumentation and Advocacy*. His book, *Arguments and Arguing,* is forthcoming.

MARTIN J. MEDHURST is Professor of Speech Communication, Texas

A&M University, College Station. He teaches courses in rhetorical theory and criticism and is the author or editor of five books, including *Dwight D. Eisenhower: Strategic Communicator* (Greenwood, 1993), *Eisenhower's War of Words: Rhetoric and Leadership*, and *Cold War Rhetoric: Strategy, Metaphor, and Ideology* (Greenwood, 1990). His articles and reviews appear regularly in communication journals.

JOHN T. MORELLO is Associate Professor of Speech at Mary Washington College, Fredericksburg, Virginia. He teaches courses in public speaking, argumentation, political communication, and communication theory. His essays on argumentation and presidential campaign debates have appeared in *Communication Studies* and *Argumentation and Advocacy*.

KURT RITTER is Associate Professor of Speech Communication, Texas A&M University, College Station. He teaches courses in American political rhetoric. He has received the Aubrey Fisher Research Award, the Karl R. Wallace Memorial Award, and the Winans-Wichelns Memorial Award. He co-authored *Ronald Reagan: The Great Communicator* (Greenwood, 1992) and *The American Ideology: Reflection of the Revolution in American Rhetoric*.

HALFORD RYAN is Professor of Public Speaking, Washington and Lee University, Lexington, Virginia. He teaches courses in American public address and presidential rhetoric. He has co-edited, edited, or authored ten books, three of which are *Franklin D. Roosevelt's Rhetorical Presidency* (Greenwood, 1988), *Classical Communication for the Contemporary Communicator*, and *Harry S. Truman's Presidential Rhetoric* (Greenwood, 1993).

CRAIG ALLEN SMITH is Professor of Communication Studies, University of North Carolina at Greensboro. He teaches courses in political communication and the rhetorical presidency. He has published numerous journal articles and chapters in books, and he authored *Political Communication*, co-authored *Persuasion and Social Movements*, and co-edited *The President and the Public: Rhetoric and National Leadership*.

CRAIG R. SMITH is Professor of Speech Communication and Director of the Center for First Amendment Studies, California State University at Long Beach. He teaches courses in rhetorical theory, American public address, and freedom of expression. He has authored twenty-five articles and eight books, two of which are *The Road to the Bill of Rights* and *Defender of the Union: An Oratorical Biography of Daniel Webster* (Greenwood, 1989).

MICHAEL WEILER is Assistant Professor of Communication Studies at Emerson College, Boston. He teaches courses in rhetorical theory, argumentation, and political rhetoric. He is the author of several essays on rhetoric and contemporary political idealogy and is co-editor of *Reagan and Public Discourse in America*.

THEODORE OTTO WINDT, JR., is Professor of Political Rhetoric, University of Pittsburgh, where he is a Chancellor's Distinguished Teacher. He authored *Presidents and Protesters: Political Rhetoric in the 1960s*, co-authored *The Cold War as Rhetoric: The Beginnings, 1945–1950* (Praeger, 1991), co-edited *Essays in Presidential Rhetoric*, and edited *Presidential Rhetoric*.

GARY C. WOODWARD is Associate Professor of Communication Studies, Trenton State College, New Jersey, where he teaches courses in politics, mass media, and public discussion. He is the author of *Persuasive Encounters: Case Studies in Constructive Confrontation* (Praeger, 1990), and coauthor of *Political Communication in America* (Praeger, 1985) and *Persuasion and Influence in American Life*.